Administration

2nd edition

NVQ LEVEL 2

Carol Carysforth

Student handbook

Heinemann

OCR

D0419836

Heinemann Educational Publishers,
Halley Court, Jordan Hill, Oxford OX2 8EJ
a division of Reed Educational & Professional Publishing Ltd

Heinemann is a registered trademark of Reed Educational & Professional Publishing Ltd

OXFORD   MELBOURNE   AUCKLAND   JOHANNESBURG   BLANTYRE
GABORONE   IBADAN   PORTSMOUTH NH (USA)   CHICAGO

First published 2001

2005   2004   2003   2002   2001
10 9 8 7 6 5 4 3 2 1

A catalogue record for this book is available from the British Library on request.

ISBN 0 435 45148 0

Typeset by 🇫 Tek-Art, Croydon, Surrey

Printed and bound in Great Britain by Biddles Ltd, Guildford

Tel: 01865 888058 www.heinemann.co.uk

To Ant and Cath with love.
May you live the dream for ever!

Contents

GROUP B OPTION UNITS 355

Unit numbering

Unit numbers in this student book are the same as the unit numbers used by the Council for Administration. Please note, however, that some awarding bodies may choose to use a different numbering system of their own.

SPECIAL NOTE

Guidance on the following skills and finance option units is freely available on the Heinemann website at

www.heinemann.co.uk/vocational/NVQ:

Unit 210 Produce and distribute mail merge documents
Unit 215 Produce simple spreadsheet documents
Unit 216 Produce documents from own notes
Unit 217 Produce documents from recorded speech
Unit 219 Receive and make payments
Unit 220 Process financial information
Unit 221 Support the collection of debts.

Please see page 358 for further details of how to access these units.

Acknowledgements

As ever, I would like to thank all those friends and colleagues who have helped, supported and advised me over the content of this book. Especial thanks are due to Christine Blackham and Sue Willetts for their IT expertise and to Antony Carysforth and Vince Higham for their technical assistance. Thanks, too, are due to Roger Parker, who edited the book so expertly and Anna Fabrizio for her patience, tenacity and excellent organisational skills. I am also grateful to Paul and Caroline who helped to convert the final indexing into a relatively painless event and to Sue Bretherton for her expertise on debt collection and endless cups of coffee!

A final thanks must, as ever, go to Margaret Berriman who has overseen the whole project with me from its inception; advised, consoled and cajoled me as required and whose taste in wine still cannot be faulted.

Carol Neild
May 2001

Introduction to NVQ awards, the structure of this book, and choosing your option units

This section looks at the main features of the NVQ Administration award and gives information on how this book has been designed to help you – including the 'Key Skills signposts' you should find useful if you are also taking Key Skills units. It also summarises the option units available and explains how they are covered in this book. It gives advice and guidance on choosing appropriate options for your own job role.

Understanding NVQ awards

There is a considerable difference between an NVQ award and other qualifications you worked towards at school or college, such as GCSEs and GNVQs. If you are already familiar with NVQs, you can skip this section and turn to page xv. Otherwise, you are advised to read this section carefully.

The main differences between NVQs and other awards are listed below.

- NVQs are designed to be undertaken by people in the workplace. If you are seeking an NVQ as a full-time student then you will have to do work-related tasks in a working environment, such as on work experience or in a college office.
- The aim of an NVQ is to check whether you are **competent** at carrying out certain tasks that are relevant to the type of job you do. Administration NVQs are designed for people working in administrative jobs.
- NVQ awards are offered at certain levels. The level you take usually depends upon the amount of responsibility you have. Level 1 is the first level for administrators and level 5 the top level, for very senior administrators.
- An NVQ consists of a number of **units**, each one covering a specific area of work. Each unit is divided into two or more **elements**.
- To achieve the full Level 2 award, you must do **five** mandatory (compulsory) units, **one** option unit from a choice of two, and **two** further option units from a choice of fifteen (**eight** units in total). Choosing option units is covered on page xvi.
- You are assessed on tasks you can do competently. If you are competent it means you can do a task consistently to a high standard. You have to

demonstrate or provide evidence to show that you can do all the tasks specified for each unit. These are called **evidence requirements**.

- You also have to prove that you know and understand what you are doing and why you are doing it. This is called **knowledge and understanding**.

- Many NVQ candidates also undertake Key Skills units at the same time. Ideally you should link your evidence for both awards together (see page xv for more information).

Providing evidence

Most NVQ candidates provide evidence in a **portfolio**. This can be an A4 lever arch file containing documentary evidence relating to your work. You will start a portfolio almost as soon as you start the scheme. Your portfolio becomes very valuable and must always be kept in a safe place. Losing it will be disastrous unless you have kept copies of all your evidence.

You will be guided through the scheme by a **tutor**, **trainer**, **adviser** or **supervisor**. This depends upon where you work and where you are taking your NVQ award. Regardless of their title, this is the person who will help you at every stage to understand the scheme and provide the right kind of evidence.

As you complete each unit, an **assessor** will check all your evidence to make sure that it meets the requirements of the scheme. Your assessor may be your tutor or trainer or could be someone else. At certain intervals, an **internal verifier** will check particular units in certain portfolios. Don't be surprised if your assessors and your internal verifier want to talk to you about your evidence – they should do this so that they know who you are and how you have obtained your evidence. An **external verifier**, sent by the awarding body, will examine a number of portfolios as a final quality check. Your awarding body is the organisation that will issue your final certificate, such as OCR or Edexcel.

You will not know which units in your portfolio may be checked by a verifier. However, if your assessor has passed them, this usually means they are fine.

About your portfolio

You will need a set of dividers, to separate each unit. You will also need tracking sheets or other documentation provided by the awarding body. Your tutor or assessor will give you these and tell you how to complete them.

Starting out

It is always best if anyone assessing or verifying your portfolio knows who you are and what you are doing! It is therefore sensible to start with a **title page**, which states your name and the scheme title – NVQ Administration Level 2.

Then give **information about yourself**. *If you are working*, this should include:

- a CV
- your official job description
- your own version of the job description, expressing in your own words what you do
- a short description of your organisation, what it does and the people you work with
- an organisational chart (add this only if you believe it will help people who read your portfolio to understand your specific job role).

If you are a full-time student, provide:

- a CV
- details of any work experience you undertake
- details of any part-time job you undertake where you may be obtaining evidence towards your award (e.g. on working as a member of a team or dealing with customers)
- details of any work placements you have in your own organisation, such as in a college office or training office.

Your portfolio should also contain a list of all the people who have helped to provide evidence, such as witness testimony (see below), and the names of tutors or advisers or supervisors who have countersigned evidence. List these clearly using the following headings:

- Name of person
- Job title
- Sample signature.

Unit evidence

Each unit will probably start with a **tracking sheet**. This is because you need to link your evidence to specific parts of the scheme. Your tutor or adviser will show you how to do this.

You may then be asked to write a brief **storyboard**. This summarises what you have done in relation to the unit or element, to help to guide the assessor and verifiers through all your evidence. It is often a good opportunity for explaining what you know and understand about the topic – and this can save you time having to answer verbal questions. Again your tutor or adviser will tell you how to write a storyboard. If you are working, it is better if this is on letter-headed paper and signed by you *and* by your line manager at work. This confirms that what you are claiming really happens.

Then include your **evidence**. You do *not* have to fill the portfolio full of paper to gain the NVQ award – there are other ways to prove you can do a task! However, as administrators often deal with paper, it is likely you will include some documentary evidence, as it is called, so we will deal with this first.

Documentary evidence

Documentary (paper) evidence can be described as:

- **primary** (or personal) evidence – which is very valuable
- **secondary** evidence – which is less valuable.

Unfortunately, many candidates like to fill their portfolios with paper, regardless of its value!

Identifying primary evidence

The best evidence comes from **working documents** that *you personally* have produced, or written on, or somehow made your own. They could include:

- a typed list of jobs you were given, on which you made notes about what you were doing and ticked off each job as it was completed
- copies of notes you made over the telephone – then a copy of the message you wrote out or e-mail you sent as a result
- a diary or log you kept over a period of time, listing the jobs you did relating to a particular unit
- a typed document or prepared spreadsheet – with the draft or original manuscript or amended version attached, plus a note clearly showing the instructions you were given.

NEVER think that evidence is better if it is clean and pristine! A beautifully printed document may be the final result, but your evidence will be much more valuable if it shows the vital scribbles and notes you made on drafts beforehand. That is what really proves you had a personal involvement with the work.

Identifying secondary evidence

Secondary evidence comprises documents prepared by other people. These documents may have given you information, but that is all. Examples include:

- formal health and safety policies you have been given
- photocopies from books – such as this one
- photocopies of documents from files and office manuals.

None of these really counts for anything *on its own* and will not help you to achieve your award. The only time you should use this type of evidence is if you can 'convert it' into primary evidence by doing something positive with it. For instance, if you issued a brief safety sheet on operating the new fax machine *then* you could include a copy of pages in the fax machine instruction booklet that you used as a basis of your safety sheet. However, you would need to highlight or otherwise identify what you decided to use and what you decided to leave out.

Other types of evidence

It is not realistic to think that there will *always* be a piece of paper to prove you can do something. Sometimes this is not appropriate and there are much better ways of checking what you know and what you competent at doing. This can be called **activity evidence**.

Observation by your assessor

Some people find this a bit unnerving, especially if it takes place on a special occasion. It is better if your assessor can simply watch you working in a normal situation. You can then prove easily that you can put files away properly, photocopy, deliver mail and so on.

Normally your assessor will then provide you with an observation report to go in your portfolio.

Witness testimony

This is a signed document provided by a colleague, or your supervisor or line manager, confirming that you regularly do a particular job well, or that you have provided help on a certain occasion. Witness testimony must be specific, however! You cannot ask your boss to write five lines to say you are good at everything and just get your award! Again, your tutor or adviser will give you advice. Witness testimony should be written on headed paper and signed by the person who wrote it – not by you! The signature should be included on the list at the front of your portfolio. If you write a statement saying what you have done this must be countersigned to prove it is authentic. Normally, however, you will write your own version in your storyboard.

Oral questioning

Your assessor may find out what you know and understand by talking to you and asking questions. This should be more of a conversation than an oral 'test' and is done to check whether you understand *why* you have done something, or to find out what you would do in a particular situation that hasn't occurred whilst you have been undertaking the award. You may be given a list of the questions asked, to put in your portfolio, together with a summary of your answers – or you can even include an audio tape on which your conversation has been recorded.

Final notes on evidence

There are certain other points you should note about evidence.

a   All the evidence must be **recent** and **sufficient**. This means that you can't put in one piece of paper which is five years old to provide all your evidence for one unit!

b Your evidence must be **relevant** – that is, it must meet the requirements of the unit as specified in the NVQ scheme.

c All the evidence must be **authentic**. This means the evidence must belong to you and must relate to *your* work.

d You should not take confidential documents or sensitive information away from the workplace without permission. Often such documents can be used when certain information has been blanked out, or your supervisor may agree to provide witness testimony instead (see also page xiii).

e You can use the same evidence *in more than one unit*, if it clearly meets the requirements of both. This is called **cross-referencing**. It will save a lot of effort if you can identify opportunities where evidence can be used more than once. Again your tutor or adviser will give you help until you get used to this.

f The best type of evidence is that which is **naturally occurring**. This means that you produce it as a natural part of your job. It is a good idea, whilst you are undertaking the NVQ award, to start a box file and put into it copies of documents you produce and evidence of work you have undertaken – so that you can use this to find appropriate evidence when you get to later units in the scheme.

CHECK IT OUT!

You cannot start to identify what type of evidence is required until you have received – and read – a copy of the NVQ scheme. Obtain one now, if you have not already done so. Don't try to understand the whole scheme the moment you receive it. Instead look at unit 102 on health and safety which is the first mandatory unit covered in this book.

- The first page is a **summary** which identifies all the things you have to do.
- The next two pages explain the two **elements**. They explain what you must always do and the evidence you must provide in each case. Specific additional evidence is also listed that you need to provide in certain circumstances.
- Then, on another page, the **knowledge and understanding** requirements are listed.

All the knowledge and understanding requirements are covered in this book. In addition, the evidence collection sections in the units match the evidence listed in the scheme. By the time you have finished the units you should feel confident that you could answer questions to prove your understanding and know how to provide the evidence required.

The structure of this book

This structure of this book has been designed to help you in the following ways.

- Each of the mandatory (core) units is covered in detail in the Core Units section, pages 1–279.
- Both optional group A units are covered, in slightly less detail. *Remember you have to choose one only of these units.*
- Eight of the optional group B units are covered, but in less detail again. It is assumed you have some basic understanding of each area and the opportunities to obtain evidence or you would not be choosing that unit! However, full guidance is given on the evidence you need in each case. The remainder can be accessed free of charge on the Heinemann website at www.heinemann.co.uk/vocational/NVQ – full details are given on page 357.
- In each unit there are special features to help you. These are summarised below.

Key Skills signposts

There is a Key Skills signpost in each mandatory unit, which you may find useful if you are taking a Key Skills award. Discuss with your tutor or trainer which signposts are useful for you – as you may not be taking all six Key Skills units.

The signposts indicate the most logical Key Skills unit to link to that NVQ unit and tell you the tasks you would have to carry out to obtain most, if not all, of the evidence required for a Key Skills portfolio. In some cases the evidence links so well that you merely have to refine and extend your evidence a little to cover both the NVQ and the Key Skills unit. In other cases you will have to undertake additional work to obtain evidence.

You can, of course, use evidence from *any* NVQ unit to help achievement of some Key Skills units – such as Communications. Your tutor or trainer will give you further details if you are taking a Key Skills award.

The signposts have been written for candidates taking Key Skills units at level 2, but in every case the evidence can be extended relatively easily if you are studying a particular unit at level 3 (or simplified if you are taking level 1). Discuss the changes you would have to make with your tutor or trainer.

Check it out!

These sections give you the opportunity to find information for yourself – often linked to the tasks and facilities you are currently using at work or at college.

Information updates

Here you will find the latest information on a particular subject or area, linked to what is currently happening in business organisations.

Test your knowledge and understanding

These sections give you the opportunity to assess how well you have understood information already covered. Sometimes they are in the form of a quiz or self-assessment.

Evidence collection

These are possibly the most important sections of all! Here you will find guidance, hints and tips on obtaining evidence to cover a particular section of a unit.

Key notes (optional group B units only)

These boxes contain summaries of important facts you should know.

SPECIAL NOTE

You should note that:

1 The knowledge and understanding sections in this book have been written to help you to test that you have a clear understanding of the information which you have just read – and to enable you to check any topics about which you are uncertain with your tutor or trainer. These sections may be used to contribute to your knowledge and understanding evidence, but the extent to which you need to provide additional evidence will be up to your assessor. Sometimes you will be able to prove that you understand something by the way you carry out a task, or by talking to your assessor about it. Therefore, do not automatically expect that you will have nothing else to do to prove you understand something after you have read through a unit and done these exercises!

2 Similarly, the evidence collection sections are intended to *contribute* towards your evidence and to help you to identify opportunities for obtaining appropriate evidence *throughout* the unit. However, on many occasions your competency will be assessed in other ways, such as by specific performance or questioning. Therefore, simply collecting a number of relevant documents does not mean that you have necessarily completed a unit. Again you will be guided by your tutor, trainer or assessor on this.

Choosing your option units

- The core of the NVQ scheme at level 2 comprises **five** compulsory units – which you must do.
- You then have to choose **one** unit from optional group A. The units in this group relate to selecting *either* paper-based filing *or* using a database package. The units are covered on pages 281–354 of this book.
- You then need to select **two** units from optional group B, which contains a choice of 15 (see below).

For all your option units it is sensible to choose those which link most closely to your job role, so that you can obtain the evidence from your job as it 'naturally occurs'. If you are not working yet, and will be obtaining evidence largely through placements in a training office or college office – or on work experience – then it is sensible to discuss with your tutor which options would be best.

More about the group B options

Eight of the group B options are included in this book, and the remainder can easily be accessed on the Heinemann website (see page 357 for details). Read the scheme very carefully and look at one or two of these subsidiary units before you make your final choice.

Do note that you can choose *any* two options in group B.

Administrative support options

All the following options are concerned with providing an administrative support service in the following areas.

- Unit 218: **Photocopy, present and distribute complex documents.** Select this unit if you are *regularly* involved in photocopying and distributing a variety of documents.
- Unit 208: **Maintain and issue stock items.** This unit is appropriate if you are responsible for looking after stationery stock and issuing it to users.
- Unit 209: **Coordinate mail services.** If a key part of your job is receiving and distributing incoming mail, and despatching outgoing mail, then this unit may be a good choice.
- Unit 211: **Contribute to the arrangement of events.** If your organisation regularly holds or organises conferences, workshops and/or meetings, and arranges travel and accommodation – and if you help with these arrangements – then this unit could be interesting and appropriate.

People-based options

All administrators deal with people – their colleagues, customers and visitors. Dealing with your colleagues is covered in mandatory unit 201 (Support the work of your team), but some other options concentrate on people and may be appropriate if you deal with many people and enjoy this aspect of your work.

- Unit 207: **Provide effective customer service**. If you regularly deal with customers – who may be either internal or external people – and help them if they have a problem or complaint, then you may find this unit a good choice.
- Unit 212: **Receive and assist visitors**. If you work in reception and deal with visitors to your organisation, then you are likely to find this option very appropriate.

Computer skills options

Most administrators use a computer. If you use one for many tasks, and enjoy doing so, you may find one or two of these units particularly appropriate.

- Unit 213: **Support the use of information technology**. If you regularly use a computer for a variety of different tasks, and are interested in developing your knowledge and skills in this area, then you will find this unit interesting and appropriate.
- Unit 214: **Communicate information electronically**. If you regularly use e-mail and/or the Internet as a part of your job, then this unit could be useful.
- Unit 215: **Produce simple spreadsheet documents**. If you regularly use your computer to enter and process data on a spreadsheet and print out documents, then this would be a good choice.
- Unit 210: **Produce and distribute mail merge documents**. This unit will be appropriate if you produce letters or other documents by merging information from appropriate software and then make sure they are distributed properly.

Communications skills options

Communication is an essential skill for all administrators and some useful hints and tips to improve your communication skills are included in the Appendix on page 495.

- Unit 216: **Produce documents from own notes**. This unit is designed for administrators who regularly take notes and use them to produce finished documents.
- Unit 217: **Produce documents from recorded speech**. If audio typing is a key aspect of your work, you would be sensible to include this unit as one of your options.

Financial options

If you work in a finance, accounts or credit-control office then you might find these units give you some useful ideas.

- Unit 219: **Receive and make payments**. If you handle payments – by cash, cheque and credit or debit card – on a regular basis and record these, this unit may be appropriate for you.
- Unit 220: **Process financial information**. If you process financial information using a computer system, you are likely to find this unit would be suitable.
- Unit 221: **Support the collection of debts**. If you help to collect overdue debts, by asking people to pay and checking who has paid and who has not, this unit may be a good choice.

Making your choice

When making your choices you might find it useful to start by ignoring all those option units which are *not* related to your job or tasks you regularly do. Then see how many you have left.

a First check whether you have an obvious unit to select for option group A. Most people undertake some paper-based filing, so unit 205 will be the most likely choice for many people. If you also operate a database, read through each unit carefully before you make a decision, and check with your tutor or supervisor which one is likely to be the more appropriate.

b Now look through the group B units. If more than two units relate to your job, decide which ones you do the most often. You would also be well advised to read your scheme to see *exactly* what you have to do for each unit. This may help to narrow down your choice.

c If you have less than two, you need to see whether there is any other area of work you could request to do, so that you could broaden your skills.

It is always sensible to discuss the choices with your supervisor or tutor. Remember that at this stage you don't have to make a definite decision, but it is useful to have a good idea. This is especially valuable if you want to be able to make a note of evidence that could be cross-referenced (see above) from another area as you progress through the compulsory units.

Linking options to your own self-development – a useful tip!

When you reach the final element of mandatory unit 202 (Plan, organise and improve your work), you will have to identify what new responsibilities you could take on – and link these with your on-going learning or development plan. Use this requirement to identify any new areas of work you would like to do that would help with a particular option unit that attracts you. This may give you the opportunity to broaden your skills and your expertise over a wider area of work.

It is also worth remembering that you are likely to have several jobs in your career, and no two jobs will be exactly the same. An individual is more employable – and worthy of promotion – if he or she *has developed several skills and has a good knowledge of administrative work over a wide area*. For that reason, even if there are several options covered in this book or on the Heinemann website that you are not interested in at the moment, save them for the future. Then, when you are about to attend an interview for a new job which requires this skill, you could find that they come in very useful indeed!

Carol Carysforth-Neild
May 2001

CORE UNITS

Unit 102   Ensure your own actions reduce risks to health and safety

Health and safety is important for all employees, whether they work in a factory, a shop or an office. No one wants to work in a dangerous place. Neither do customers or contractors (such as plumbers or decorators) want to visit business premises which may be hazardous or where they may have an accident.

Various laws have been passed to ensure that employers and employees keep their workplace safe. This affects the way all businesses operate. It also affects how you do your job every day. You need to know the laws and regulations that relate to your own job and what you need to do to help to reduce risks for yourself, your colleagues and any visitors to your workplace.

This unit is divided into two elements. The first is concerned with being able to identify hazards and evaluate risks in your workplace, the second with actions you can take to reduce risks yourself. Before we examine each element in detail, we will first look at the knowledge and understanding you need for the unit as a whole.

KEY SKILLS SIGNPOST

If you are taking your Key Skills award, you can extend your knowledge of health and safety and use this as evidence in your portfolio for **Application of Number** Level 2 if you undertake the activities below. If you are studying **Application of Number** at Level 1, your tutor will show you how to simplify this list.

N2.1

You need to obtain current information on the following:

- the number of accidents and/or days of absence in the workplace today
- the number of working days lost in the UK because of accidents or illness
- the current cost to industry of absence from work

- similar information from your own employer and/or information on student absences from college
- current regulations on sick pay for employees.

Use this to supplement and update the figures given in this unit. You can find this information by visiting your library or by researching on the Internet. Useful websites include the TUC (www.tuc.org.uk), the Health and Safety Executive (www.hse.gov.uk), and newspaper sites such as www.newsunlimited.co.uk and www.telegraph.co.uk. Or, type your enquiry into a search engine such as Ask Jeeves on www.ask.co.uk to find relevant sites – but make sure these are English sites and not American ones!

Next find data on the space available for members of staff in your workplace or college in at least two different situations and the amount of space used for furniture and equipment. Note that at least one item of data you obtain must include a graph.

N2.2

Use your data on accidents and absences to calculate:

- the average number of days lost per person both nationally and in your own organisation or college – and the difference between the two
- the percentage number of days of absence for different groups of employees or students
- whether absences are increasing or declining and whether the trends are the same for different groups of employees (or students) or whether these vary
- what the figures would be if these trends continued over the next ten years, and the future cost to your industry
- an estimate of the cost of an accident to an employer, allowing for costs, such as first-aid materials, first-aider time, writing of the accident report and damage to property or equipment
- the cost to an employer of paying sick pay for two different grades or categories of employees.

Use your data on space to calculate:

- the average space per person in each location, and compare this with health and safety requirements.

Prepare a diagram showing how the furniture in one area could be rearranged to improve safety, and attach all your calculations.

N2.3

Present your findings by preparing a summary of all the information you found, the calculations you did and what you found out from these. To support your arguments, include:

- a graph of national and local accident or absence statistics identifying the trends
- a pie chart displaying the costs of one accident
- a chart showing the cost of different types of accidents or absences on different grades or categories of employees.

Your legal duties for health and safety in the workplace

Some people think that health and safety issues are less important for administrators. They know that workers on a farm or an oil rig or in a factory may run the risk of having an accident, but do not think this is likely to happen in an office. Yet offices have many hazards which can affect the health of people who work in them. Computers are a good example. If you spend hour after hour hunched up over your keyboard then you are likely to suffer a range of aches and pains very rapidly. If you stare at your screen most of the day this may affect your eyesight. Other factors which can affect your health and safety are: office equipment, office furniture and design; lighting; heating; and other people's working habits.

 INFORMATION UPDATE

In October 1999, the Health and Safety Commission announced that work-related injuries and illnesses cost Britain £18.1 billion a year. Although the total number of injuries had fallen, more than a million people were still injured at work and 1.3 million people affected by work-related ill-health. In the previous twelve months, 24.3 million working days had been lost and 27,000 people had been forced to give up work because of injury or illness. Although injuries are more likely to occur in industries such as construction and manufacturing, illnesses were being reported in many 'new jobs' in an office environment – such as telesales and computing.

Health and safety legislation

In the early 1970s, there were nearly 800 fatal accidents a year in British workplaces. By 1999 this number had fallen to 257. A major reason for this improvement has been the introduction of various laws which make it illegal

KEY ASPECTS OF THE HEALTH AND SAFETY AT WORK ACT 1974

This Act applies to *all* work premises, regardless of size. Anyone on the premises is covered by the Act (e.g. employees, managers, visitors and external contractors carrying out maintenance work). They also have personal responsibilities under the Act.

All employers must:

a   Ensure the health, safety and welfare at work of their employees 'as far as is reasonably practicable'. Specific aspects include:
   • safe entry and exit routes
   • a safe working environment and adequate welfare facilities
   • well-maintained, safe equipment
   • safe storage and transport of articles and substances
   • provision of protective clothing
   • information on health and safety, instruction, training and supervision.

b   Undertake the preparation and continual updating of a written statement on the health and safety policy of the company, where there are five or more employees. This must also be circulated to all employees.

c   Allow for the appointment of safety representatives selected by a recognised trade union. Safety representatives must be allowed to investigate accidents or potential hazards, follow up employee complaints and have paid time off to carry out their duties.

All employees must:

a   Take reasonable care of their own health and safety.

b   Take reasonable care for the health and safety of others who may be affected by their activities or actions.

c   Cooperate with their employer or anyone acting on his or her behalf to meet health and safety requirements.

CHECK IT OUT!

Your employer must display the main terms of the Health and Safety at Work Act in a notice for all employees to read. You should see this notice anywhere you work *and* in all colleges and training establishments. Find where this notice is situated and read it carefully. Then note what action you should take if you think there is a health and safety problem on the premises.

for employers or employees to endanger the health and safety of each other or visitors to the premises. Organisations or individuals who break the law can be fined and prosecuted.

The most important Act which governs health and safety requirements is the **Health and Safety at Work Act** 1974. This is an 'umbrella' or 'enabling' Act under which other *Regulations* can be passed to make sure that health and safety laws are kept up to date and improved across a wide range of areas relating to the workplace. The key aspects of this Act are shown in the table opposite.

EVIDENCE COLLECTION

Whether you are working or studying as a full-time student you should have been informed about health and safety during your induction. You may even have had specific training since then, such as fire drills. If you are on a Foundation or Advanced Modern Apprenticeship then your training adviser will have covered health and safety with you and completed a review form.

1   Collect all the information you have received so far on health and safety as a basis for some of the personalised evidence you will need to produce for your portfolio. However, remember that on its own, this evidence does not prove that you, personally, can do anything yet! (See also page xii.)
2   Find out and make a note of those people in your workplace or college who are responsible for health and safety. This may be your supervisor or line manager, or a safety officer or safety representative. Reading the Health and Safety notice displayed in your workplace will help. Check that you know where each person is located, and note down his or her telephone extension number.

TEST YOUR KNOWLEDGE AND UNDERSTANDING

1   The following incidents take place in an office. Under which part(s) of the Health and Safety at Work Act would each be categorised as an offence?
    a   A receptionist, searching for a file, leaves the bottom drawer of her filing cabinet open when a visitor appears.
    b   Her colleague breaks a glass and throws it, unwrapped, into the waste paper bin.
    c   A delivery driver leaves a large stack of boxes behind the rear door leading to the car park.

d A supervisor removes a 'What to do in the case of fire' notice from the office because she says it is looking tatty.

e A new employee in a central photocopying room is told to clean some equipment but not provided with an overall or gloves. After he has finished he leaves the chemicals on a bench with the tops loose.

f Four people slip on a newly polished floor and one sprains her ankle badly, but no one does anything about it.

g An administrator decides the portable fax machine would be better on the opposite side of the office, despite the fact that the cable is stretched to its limit when plugged in.

2 The Health and Safety at Work Act uses the phrase 'as far as is reasonably practicable'.

a What do you think this means? Discuss your ideas with your tutor, trainer or supervisor.

b An office building has a tiled reception area which becomes very slippery in wet weather.

i What actions do you think the company should take, that are 'reasonably practicable', to ensure no one is injured?

ii What ideas might some people suggest which would not be considered 'reasonably practicable'?

Legislation covering your job role

The Health and Safety at Work Act applies to all employees. Other Regulations may, or may not, apply to you. It depends upon your job and the tasks you carry out. You must, however, know which Regulations relate to your job and how they affect what you do. Remember that if your job changes, some Regulations may then affect you which are not applicable now.

Those which apply to every office employee are:

- **Workplace (Health, Safety and Welfare) Regulations 1992.** These give more specific details of your employer's responsibilities under the Health and Safety at Work Act. For that reason, they are usually of considerable interest to employees (see page 10).

- **Fire Precautions Act 1971**, the **Fire Precautions (Factories, Offices, Shops and Railway Premises) Order 1989**, the **Fire Precautions (Workplace) Regulations 1997**, and the **Fire Precautions (Workplace) (Amendment) Regulations 1999.** You do not have to remember the names of all these Acts and Regulations – but they are very important because they state the minimum precautions employers must take to protect employees and other people on the premises from being injured in the case of fire.

Unless you work in a very small firm, it is likely your company has to have a fire certificate which gives a plan of the building and shows the position of fire-resistant doors, fire extinguishers and break-glass alarms. There must be a proper fire alarm system and protected means of escape.

- **Employers' Liability (Compulsory Insurance) Regulations 1969.** These compel all employers to take out insurance against accidents and ill-health to their employees. This means if you were injured whilst you were doing your job, you could claim compensation and this would be met by your employer's insurance company. Otherwise, some firms may say they could not afford to pay compensation to an employee – even if the injury had been caused by the company's negligence.

- **Health and Safety (First Aid) Regulations 1981.** These require all organisations to provide adequate and appropriate first-aid equipment and facilities and sufficient first-aiders who are suitably trained and qualified. The actual number of first-aiders depends upon whether the environment is classed as 'high-risk' or 'low-risk'. A low-risk environment, such as a small office, may nominate an appointed person to be responsible if the first-aider is absent or, in some cases where the risk is minimal, the appointed person can be responsible *instead* of a first-aider.

- **Health and Safety (Safety Signs and Signals) Regulations 1996.** These require all organisations to display specific safety signs to identify risks and hazards. There must also be written instructions on the use of fire-fighting equipment. All signs must be to a specified design and in the correct colour. Red is used for an action which is prohibited; blue for an action which is mandatory (must be done), and green for a safe condition.

- **Reporting of Injuries, Diseases and Dangerous Occurrences Regulations 1992** (RIDDOR for short). Under these Regulations all organisations must notify the Health and Safety Executive of any serious or fatal injuries, and keep records of certain specific injuries, dangerous occurrences and diseases.

CHECK IT OUT!

1 First-aid boxes should be regularly refilled but should contain only items that first-aiders are trained to use. They should also not contain drugs of any kind. Discuss with your tutor or supervisor why this is the case.

2 Either at work or at college or on premises where you are undertaking off-the-job training, locate the first-aid box and check whether it has the correct items. Ideally it should contain individually wrapped sterile adhesive dressings, sterile eye pads, triangular bandages, safety pins, sterile wound dressings in various sizes, cleaning wipes and disposable gloves. Could you recommend improvements, or is the box complete?

The Workplace (Health, Safety and Welfare) Regulations 1992

These complement the Health and Safety at Work Act, and provide more detail for employees. It is therefore important that you know what they contain.

KEY ASPECTS OF THE WORKPLACE (HEALTH, SAFETY AND WELFARE) REGULATIONS 1992

The main requirements of these regulations are listed below.

- **Work environment:**
  - effective ventilation
  - reasonable temperature
  - adequate and emergency lighting
  - sufficient space
  - suitable workstations
  - protection from adverse weather conditions for workstations outside a building

- **Safety:**
  - traffic routes so that pedestrians and vehicles can circulate in a safe manner
  - properly constructed and maintained floors
  - safe windows and skylights
  - safely constructed doors, gates and escalators
  - safeguards to prevent people or objects falling from a height

- **Facilities:**
  - sufficient toilets and washing facilities
  - an adequate supply of wholesome water
  - adequate seating
  - suitable accommodation for clothing
  - rest areas, including provision for pregnant women or nursing mothers
  - provision for non-smokers in rest areas
  - adequate facilities for people who eat at work

- **Housekeeping:**
  - proper maintenance of all workplaces, equipment and facilities
  - cleanliness of workplaces.

Under these Regulations employers and other people in control of workplaces must comply with several requirements which cover the work environment, safety, workplace facilities and 'housekeeping' – i.e. maintenance and cleanliness. The key aspects are shown in the table opposite.

TEST YOUR KNOWLEDGE AND UNDERSTANDING

On your own, read the following extract from Rachel's diary and decide how many offences her employer might be committing under the Workplace (Health, Safety and Welfare) Regulations. Then compare your answer with those of other members of your group.

Arrived at 8.50 but had to wait 10 mins, in the rain, whilst a large lorry backed through the gates. The security men must be cold – as their checkpoint is open at one side. Office very cold, too, the heating must be faulty again – kept my coat on all morning. Started by clearing the rubbish from yesterday – wish Mr Blake would replace the cleaner who left. Saima off with tummy ache – again. Mrs Jenkins says she's workshy but my Dad thinks it's because she drinks the water here and the pipes are old. I bring bottled water now. Anyway, it's better when one of us is off as we have more room – the office is so cramped with desks and filing cabinets – and the new girl still hasn't got a desk or chair of her own. Worked hard this morning – we were busy, but had to eat lunch at my wobbly old desk as the little storeroom we sometimes use was full of boxes. The window in there is still broken – we must have reported it four times now. It won't close so the rain was pouring in. What a miserable day!

Other important regulations

In addition to the Workplace (Health, Safety and Welfare) Regulations, there are several other regulations which are likely to apply to you. The table on page 12 lists the main Regulations but divides these into those which are more likely to apply to all administrators and those which would apply under certain circumstances.

However, one regulation is more likely to apply to you as an administrator than any of the others. This is the **Display Screen Equipment Regulations 1992**. The reason for this is simple. These Regulations relate to the use of computers – although they are termed as VDUs (visual display units) and workstations. Most administrators use computers for much of their working day. Therefore, the main requirements of these Regulations are likely to relate to the job you do. For that reason, the key aspects of the Regulations are summarised in the table on page 13.

HEALTH AND SAFETY REGULATIONS

Group 1 – applicable to most administrators

- **The Control of Substances Hazardous to Health 1999 (COSHH)**
  All hazardous substances (such as toxic cleaning substances) must be stored in a special environment and users provided with protective clothing.

- **Provision and Use of Work Equipment Regulations 1998 (PUWER)**
  Employers must ensure that all equipment (such as photocopiers and fax machines) is well maintained and provide appropriate training and instructions for users.

- **Manual Handling Operations Regulations 1992**
  These relate to lifting and handling items, such as heavy boxes of paper. Where possible an automated or mechanised process should be used but employees who have to move items should be trained properly to minimise injury.

Group 2 – may be applicable to administrators under certain circumstances

- **The Electricity at Work Regulations 1989**
  These Regulations relate to the design, construction, use and maintenance of electrical systems.

- **The Noise at Work Regulations 1989**
  Employers must check noise hazards and reduce these where possible and provide ear-protectors to employees where necessary.

- **Personal Protective Equipment at Work Regulations 1992**
  Protective clothing and equipment must be provided when risks cannot be eliminated. This must be free of charge, fit properly and be maintained in good condition.

KEY ASPECTS OF THE DISPLAY SCREEN EQUIPMENT REGULATIONS

These Regulations introduced minimum standards for the use of VDUs and the design of workstations. A workstation is not just your desk, but your complete working environment including your screen, keyboard, printer, chair and work surface – as well as the space around you, the lighting, temperature and noise levels.

a   **All employers must:**

- Ensure that all workstations, related furniture, computer software and the working environment of VDU users meet the minimum requirements of the Regulations.
- Ensure that all users have regular breaks or changes in activity – it is illegal to work continuously at a computer all day.
- Offer eye examinations, on request, to employees who use a VDU for more than one hour a day and provide special spectacles if the test shows these are needed.
- Provide users with relevant health and safety training.

b   **All equipment must conform to the following standards:**

- **Display screens** must have clear characters of adequate size, a stable image, adjustable brightness and contrast, be tiltable and able to swivel easily. There must be no reflective glare.
- **Keyboards** must be tiltable and separate from the screen. There should be space in front of the keyboard to provide a 'rest' space. The surface should be matt, the keyboard easy to use and the symbols clear on the keys.
- **Work surfaces** must be large enough for the work being done and must have a low reflective finish. The equipment must be flexible so that it can be arranged to suit the needs of the user.
- **Work chairs** must be stable and allow easy movement and a comfortable position. The user must be able to adjust the height of the seat and the seat back – which must provide good back support. A footrest must be provided if requested.
- **Working environments** for VDU users should provide satisfactory lighting but minimise glare. Windows should have blinds or workstations be positioned to avoid reflections. Noise and heat levels should be comfortable. Radiation levels must be negligible and humidity controlled so that it is constantly at a satisfactory level.
- **Software and systems** must be appropriate for the task, user-friendly and appropriate to the level of knowledge of the user.

1 The Health and Safety Executive has prepared several booklets on VDUs, including *VDUs: An Easy Guide to the Regulations* and *Health and Safety (Display Screen Equipment) Regulations 1992*. Guidance on the regulations should be available from your local or college library. Alternatively you can ask your library to obtain it through the inter-library loans service.

2 Surf the net to find out more. The HSE site (www.open.gov.uk/hsehome.htm) includes a useful booklet you can download to read free of charge – *Working with VDUs*. You will need Acrobat Reader installed on your computer to do this. If you are not sure what this means, check with your IT tutor or your workplace supervisor.

3 Check your own workstation – or one that you use – and your own working habits to see how you fare. As a start, check how you sit and the position of your chair. You can adjust it – but do you? Where is the back rest – supporting you or miles away? Are you hunched up or sitting straight? What about the position of your screen? And the contrast/brightness? How often do you adjust it? Can you be bothered to adjust the blinds if the sun shines – or to turn the lights on when it doesn't? Bear all these factors in mind when you reach page 16. Remember, all the legislation in the world won't help you if you don't help yourself!

Enforcing the law

Health and safety is monitored and enforced by the **Health and Safety Executive (HSE)** which has its own inspectors. It also operates an advisory service, providing guidance to employers and other people responsible for implementing health and safety legislation. It issues Approved Codes of Practice (called AcoPs) which give advice on how companies can comply with the law.

An HSE inspector can visit any industrial premises without warning to investigate an accident or complaint or to inspect the premises. Offices and shops are visited by an environmental health officer (EHO) who is employed by the local authority.

If a visit by an inspector shows that there are unsatisfactory working practices, then the employer is issued with an **improvement notice**. This gives a specific time by which all problems must be rectified. If working practices are so poor that the safety of workers or the public would be a risk if work continues, then a **prohibition notice** can be issued. In this case the employer must stop operations immediately. Employers can appeal if they feel the decision is unfair; but if the company loses the appeal and still fails to put the matter right, then the organisation can be fined or the owner imprisoned.

Hazards and risks in the workplace

What is meant by a 'hazard' or a 'risk' in the workplace? Knowing some important terms and their meanings is necessary to understanding this part of the unit.

*   A **hazard** is anything which has the potential to cause you harm or injury (such as a slippery floor).

- A **risk** is the chance that you will be harmed or injured. In some cases the risk may be high, in other cases medium or low.
- **Evaluating risks** means looking at the *degree* of risk (high, medium or low) and deciding whether there are sufficient precautions or whether more could be done.
- **Risk control** means reducing the possibility of risk by taking action to reduce any danger from the hazard (e.g. by instructing cleaners to put up a sign to warn people when they are approaching a wet floor).

Under the Management of Health and Safety at Work Regulations 1999, your employer has a legal responsibility to undertake regular **risk assessments** – by checking that risks are either eliminated or controlled as much as possible. If necessary, a specialist consultant may be asked to do the job if no one in the organisation can do it. However, all staff – including you – also have a responsibility to inform your employer if a new hazard is identified or if you think the degree of risk has changed in some way.

Risks relating to your own job role – and taking precautions

Offices are relatively safe places in which to work. However, according to TUC statistics, more than 5000 *serious* injuries occur in offices every year and many more are never reported. Why? Because there are a variety of *potential* hazards in an office. These include:

- machinery and equipment (including plugs and sockets)
- materials and substances
- unsafe working practices
- unsafe behaviour
- accidental breakages and spillages
- environmental factors.

Remember that these *may* or *may not* constitute a risk – but don't get too enthusiastic and label everything a potential risk. Otherwise you would never ride in a car, use a knife or sit next to a fire! Identifying hazards and risk levels means looking sensibly at the situation and the precautions that are taken. In many cases you will find there are specific workplace policies which say what you must do in relation to certain identified hazards – such as cleaners having to put up warning notices when floors have been washed.

If you are trying to identifying hazards it is important to ask yourself:

1 Is the hazard something trivial or is it significant because it may harm several people?
2 Is the hazard covered by a manufacturer's manual so that you know how to reduce the risks?
3 Who could be injured? Just the operator or various people including staff, visitors or members of the public in general?

4   What precautions are taken at present? To what extent will they protect people?
5   Could you get rid of the hazard or, if not, could the risk be better controlled? If so, how?

CHECK IT OUT!

Each of the following situations may occur in any office. In each case, decide:

a   whether a hazard exists at all

b   if so, whether the risk of an accident or injury occurring is high, medium or low

c   how you would reduce the degree of risk.

Discuss your suggestions with your tutor or supervisor.

1   A member of staff is asked to return some files to a high shelf where they are stored.

2   The administrator in charge of stationery stock has to unload a trolley full of heavy boxes of paper.

3   A member of staff takes three parcels to the Post Office in the pouring rain.

4   During a cold spell, several members of staff want to bring in fan heaters from home to improve the heating. There are not enough sockets so the supervisor provides adaptors so the appliances can be plugged in.

5   The newest member of staff is asked to use a powerful electric stapler on her first day.

6   The receptionist spills hot coffee on her hand and on the floor as she leaves the coffee machine

7   A member of staff runs down the stairs and slips, spraining his ankle.

8   A paper jam occurs in the photocopier. The sheet of paper inside starts to get hot and smoulder.

9   An overflow from a sink on the first floor causes a flood which seeps through the floor. On the ground floor several ceiling tiles are dislodged, the wiring in the ceiling is wet and the carpet on the floor is soaked and shrinks away from the walls.

10 An assistant administrator traps her finger in her desk drawer when she is hurrying to find something.

You may find it useful to keep your suggestions to one side until you have read more of this unit.

Remaining alert to hazards and dealing with risks

Even if you work in an office where there are regular risk assessments and health and safety is excellent, other people's actions can contribute to creating a hazard. This is particularly true if they are careless, untidy or simply try to do something without knowing how to do the job properly. Before you can identify hazards properly, you therefore need to know something about the equipment you are using and the environment in which you work. You also need to be aware that hazards and risks can occur *at any time* and that is why you need to be constantly alert to them – not identify them once and then forget all about it!

You will find more information on the types of risks you have to know how to deal with in the Evidence Collection box on page 22.

Dealing promptly with risks

Remember that a risk is the chance that someone will be injured. If you identify a hazard and consider there is a risk, then the action to take will depend upon the *degree* of risk. If it is very high, then you may have to take drastic action. For instance, if you suddenly detected a strong smell of gas in the room there is a high degree of risk – and you would need to evacuate the area and notify someone in charge immediately. If the risk is small – for instance, a carpet tile in the corner of the room has become dislodged – then you would still have to notify someone in authority (or your maintenance people), but you could not reasonably expect them to treat the situation as a full-scale emergency!

However, there is no situation in which you should ignore a risk altogether. You need to know your organisation's procedures for reporting risks, and who to report them to (see page 21).

Requirements and guidance on precautions

Always bear in mind that 'prevention is better than cure.' Health and safety training, guidance manuals and manufacturer's handbooks *all* provide a considerable amount of detail on good working practices and precautions to take when using equipment or handling specific products. If you ignore these, then you constitute a risk yourself – both to yourself and others.

All workplaces have policies and practices which include guidance on precautions and methods of working, which should be known by all staff – as you will see in Element 102.1.

Element 102.1 Identify the hazards and evaluate the risks in your workplace

You have already learned about hazards and risks and the difference between these. However, theoretical knowledge is not much use if you don't know how to identify a hazard, evaluate a risk – or what action to take if you do. This element is concerned with the way in which organisations try to reduce risks for employees and the action you should take if you notice a risk.

Workplace policies and working practices

By law, all organisations must have a **safety policy**. This must state, clearly and simply, the aims of the company in relation to the health and safety of employees. It should also name key members of staff and state the arrangements for carrying out the policy. The policy is likely to include:

- arrangements covering training and instruction
- company rules
- emergency arrangements
- the system for reporting accidents
- the identification of risk areas.

The policy is usually signed by a senior manager and must be revised regularly, to make sure it stays up to date.

The organisation will then decide its own **codes of practice** which state the procedures all employees must follow in the event of an emergency, such as a fire, gas leak or bomb scare, or if an accident occurs. This will include how to contact a first-aider, where the medical room is situated, how to contact a doctor or send for an ambulance, and when an accident report must be completed.

In many organisations there is a **safety committee**, made up of representatives from management and employees. This group will check that legal requirements are being followed and also inform management if any working conditions breach safety regulations or company policy. If there is no safety committee then you are likely to find these duties are undertaken by the **safety officer**. Safety committees, or the safety officer, will also monitor local accident trends and study accident reports and then suggest preventative action to prevent a recurrence. They regularly report on a wide range of safety matters and make recommendations to managers.

Many businesses also have **safety representatives** who attend meetings of the safety committee. These representatives are appointed by recognised trade unions and elected by the union members, *not* the employer. They are involved in accident and hazard investigations, follow up employee complaints about health and safety, carry out inspections, and are involved with any consultations involving HSE inspectors. They must also be consulted by the employer about any proposed changes in the workplace which may affect health and safety, or about any information or training planned for the staff.

Accidents

All accidents must be recorded and companies with more than 10 employees must keep an accident book and accident records for at least three years. Many organisations also record 'near misses' as well as actual accidents, as these often indicate where improvements are required.

If you witness an accident, or are involved in one, then you will have to complete an accident report form. You must provide all relevant information relating to the accident and the names of any witnesses. Serious accidents are investigated and, until the safety officer or safety representative arrives, nothing must be moved or changed. Accidents are monitored to check that accident rates are not increasing and are not above the national average. The safety officer or safety committee can recommend improvements, when these are required, and then check that appropriate action has been taken.

CHECK IT OUT!

1 Find out more about the HSE and its work by visiting your local or College library or, if you have Internet access, linking to the HSE site at www.open.gov.uk/hsehome.htm. Reading some of the latest press releases will enable you to see current issues with which the HSE is involved.

2 Write down the procedure in your own workplace which you must follow if you witness an accident. Discuss with your supervisor or tutor why nothing must be moved or changed until the safety officer or representative arrives.

Your own responsibilities related to your job description

All employees have a legal responsibility to cooperate with their employer over health and safety matters under the HSW Act. In some cases, individuals have specific responsibilities related to health and safety in their job description.

Even if health and safety isn't specifically mentioned in your job description, you should be aware that all workplaces should have workplace policies giving clear health and safety guidance to staff – for instance, on how to use particular items of equipment or certain materials or substances. These policies therefore govern the *working practices* of individuals, i.e. the way in which you must do a certain task or use certain materials or a particular item of equipment. However, all the policies in the world won't help if you don't read them, or ignore them when it suits you – as you will see on page 26!

Reporting health and safety matters

At induction you should have been informed of the persons to whom you should report health and safety matters in your organisation. In a large company, you may have safety representatives and a safety officer. However, they will not usually expect you to contact them over minor maintenance issues (such as a frayed carpet or a spilled liquid). Instead you would notify the person responsible for putting this right, such as maintenance or cleaning staff. It usually becomes a matter for a safety representative or safety officer only if nothing is done about the matter – or if a hazard is identified which cannot be solved through routine operations.

In a small organisation, you should inform your supervisor or manager if you identify a hazard. You should also check, in a larger organisation, whether you should consult your supervisor out of courtesy if you are concerned about a hazard, before contacting anyone else.

EVIDENCE COLLECTION

1 As part of your induction you should have been informed:
    a what to do in the case of fire
    b what to do if you have an accident
    c how to find a first-aider or appointed person in an emergency
    d where the first-aid box is located.
    Check that you have received all this information and prepare a short emergency checklist for yourself.
2 Obtain a copy of the safety policy for your own workplace and keep it safely – you will find it useful when you analyse how health and safety policy affects your own job role later in this unit. Find out whether your company has a safety officer, a safety committee and safety representatives, or the name of the person to whom you would report a health and safety matter. If you work on more than one site, or in more than one area (e.g. in different branch offices), check whether the person would be the same or different at each location.
3 Check your job description, if you have one, and highlight any part of it which is concerned specifically with health and safety. If you work only part-time and study during the remainder of the week, then it is still worth checking your job description as your responsibilities in any job are appropriate to this unit.

INFORMATION UPDATE

The Trades Union Congress (TUC) is concerned that many young workers aged 15–24 are injured at work. According to statistics, ten young British workers are seriously injured at work every week, and one in three receive no health and safety training at all at work – even though that is against the law. The TUC wants more young workers to know their rights and to realise they can refuse to do something at work that is dangerous or which might 'put them in serious and imminent danger'.

As part of the TUC's Play it Safe campaign, they have issued a free leaflet *Play it Safe at Work* which you can obtain from careers advisers, from the National Union of Students, or direct from the TUC. Their 'know your rights' number is 0870 600 4882 or you can obtain and download information from their website at www.tuc.org.uk.

Regulations have existed for some time to protect young people who are undertaking training or work experience in a workplace – **the Health and Safety (Training for Employment) Regulations 1990**. This is because lack of experience and training can mean young people – such as school pupils on work experience – are at greater risk. These regulations were strengthened by **the Health and Safety (Young Persons) Regulations 1997** which require employers to carry out special risk assessments to cover young people in the workplace.

EVIDENCE COLLECTION

For your evidence of this element, you have to prove you can deal with at least two risks from the following list. You will also have to explain how you would deal with the remainder:

a   the use and maintenance of machinery or equipment
b   the use of materials or substances
c   working practices that do not conform to laid-down policies
d   unsafe behaviour
e   accidental breakages or spillage
f   environmental factors.

Read the following section which covers all these risks. Then keep a record of any risks you actually deal with over the next few weeks or months. In each case, identify the risk and clearly state what action you took. Then ask your supervisor to countersign your evidence to verify it as accurate and true.

The use and maintenance of machinery and equipment

Typical machinery and equipment in an office may include a photocopier, computer, laser or ink jet printer, fax machine, shredder and stapler. They need to be assessed in terms of:

* how they should be used
* how they should be maintained
* what staff training is required.

All staff should be trained before they use office machinery and equipment. Their training should include clear instructions on:

* normal usage
* faults they can rectify themselves
* faults they must report to a supervisor.

Trying to mend faults you have been told to leave alone is not clever no matter what the outcome. In many cases, staff can leave themselves open to an unacceptable degree of risk by taking this action.

Possibly the piece of equipment with the greatest *potential* for being hazardous is the photocopier – particularly if it is old:

* There are a number of fumes emitted by a photocopier, particularly if it is used a lot. Ozone is the worst – it has a very distinctive, almost sweet smell, but can be highly irritating. Other chemicals may include carbon monoxide and carbon black from the toner. The toner is the black ink substance which is required to make copies. Modern copiers have sealed toner units but old ones often need refilling with powder toner. Use rubber gloves if you ever have to do this job; and if you do get any on your hands or clothes, wash it off *immediately* using *cold* water.

* Additional hazards include noise (particularly when collating or making multiple copies), the bright ultraviolet light seen when the copier 'scans' the original, and hazards from rectifying paper jams, when the operator is in contact with hot and sharp surfaces.

These dangers are lessened when the photocopier is an up-to-date model and is sited in a separate room, the area is well ventilated and the filters are cleaned regularly by a mechanic. Some modern copiers will not work when the lid is open so that the ultraviolet light can be seen. However, although this can be unpleasant to view, it will not cause eye damage unless you stand and stare at it deliberately over a long period. All operators who are expected to remedy minor problems, such as paper jams, *must* receive proper training.

Computers are not particularly hazardous provided they are properly connected, the wires are not left trailing and you confine your activities to operating it and don't attempt to repair it or move it! You should also know how to clean it properly and use one of the standard products – *never* water or a wet cloth. Ideally your workstation will have channels for the wires (called 'wire management') so that they are out of sight and out of the way. All liquids, including cups of coffee and cans of drink, should be kept *well* away from your computer and keyboard.

Dust can affect the way your keyboard and mouse function. Tiny battery-powered vacuum cleaners can be used to suck up dust from keyboards. Your mouse will last longer and work better if you use a mouse mat and regularly clean the 'ball' inside. Your workstation should be designed to conform to the Display Screen Equipment Regulations and you should have received instruction about your posture and the importance of taking regular breaks or doing different work to vary your routine (see also page 13).

Laser printers can present a hazard, particularly if they are sited on a desk-top next to you. This is because, like photocopiers, they produce ozone and the filters need changing regularly. If ever your printer 'smells odd' then switch it off and report it to your supervisor immediately. Noise can be reduced by fitting an acoustic hood.

All other machines are relatively safe *provided you know what you are doing* and never try to tamper with them. If you are allowed to try to remedy a minor fault, unplug any electrical equipment first.

Interestingly, items which are portable normally pose a greater risk than those which are not. This is because they are regularly moved, may be sited in inappropriate places and may be plugged into a socket which is too far away. Strange though it may seem, an electric fan which is shared around the office during a heat wave, and may have just been stored at the back of a cupboard all winter, may therefore pose a greater *potential* hazard than a large photocopier or fax machine which is a permanent fixture. The best way of assessing any appliance is to look at it closely:

a   Does it look relatively new or old and scruffy?
b   Is there any obvious damage?
c   Is the plug damaged or loose or new and firmly attached?
d   Is the wire or cable smooth and undamaged?
e   Is the equipment dry and safe to plug in?
f   Is there any evidence of previous overheating – such as burn marks or discoloration on the plastic?
g   Is the fuse in the plug the correct one to use? If you know nothing about plugs and fuses, ask for advice. Basically, if there is an electrical fault the fuse should 'blow' first, before the equipment has chance to overheat and catch fire.

In each of the following situations, what action would you take – and why?

1   Your printer jams and won't work in the middle of an urgent report.
2   You are told to shake the toner container before putting it into the photocopier and some toner puffs out on to your hands and clothes.
3   The fax machine next to you starts to make a funny smell.
4   Your friend likes to go out straight from work. On an evening where she has a special date she brings her hairdryer to work with her. You notice the plastic is cracked, it is scorched around the nozzle and it makes a funny noise when she plugs it in.
5   You return from lunch one day and find someone has jammed a plastic ruler in the shredder.
6   You see your colleague banging her keyboard, upside down, to remove the dust as two keys keep sticking.
7   A new member of staff starts work a week after the rest of the staff have had comprehensive training on how to use the new photocopier.

The use of materials and substances

Probably the most potentially hazardous material in any office is paper. Why? Because it is sharp and can give you a very tiny but painful cut. Thankfully, self-seal envelopes have reduced the danger of people cutting their tongues by licking envelopes, but handle a piece of paper wrongly and you can soon give your finger or hand a nasty nick. The golden rule – keep your fingers and hand well away from the edges of paper when you are refilling your printer or paper tray or folding a letter. Paper on the floor is also a hazard – particularly on carpet – and is the office equivalent of a banana skin!

Staples can also be nasty if you get one stuck in your finger instead of in the paper for which it was intended. This happens if you don't watch what you are doing. Trust me – you will do this only once in your career! The force with which the stapler drives it into your finger will stay in your mind for a very long time.

One potentially dangerous substance – toner – was dealt with above. Others which are used in an office can include correcting fluids, cleaning materials and certain glues – for two reasons: firstly because the fumes given off can be dangerous if you breathe them; and secondly because they can cause skin rashes, particularly if you have sensitive skin. For these reasons:

- Keep the tops securely fastened on all bottles unless you are actually using the product.
- Don't lean over the bottles or breathe in the fumes.
- Use protective gloves if you are cleaning equipment.
- Wash your hands or arms (or face!) promptly if you are a rather messy worker and get the stuff everywhere.

Workplace practices that do not conform to laid-down policies

Sometimes rules or policies in the workplace may seem over-fussy and, particularly if you are in a hurry or the policy would inconvenience you, it is tempting to take a short-cut by ignoring it. *Don't!* In each case you are not only putting yourself – and possibly others – in danger but you are also flouting the law. You are ignoring your responsibilities under the Health and Safety at Work Act to cooperate with your employer over health and safety matters.

Think of a few examples:

1 You are particularly busy when the fire alarm sounds. It is raining outside, it is likely to be 'just another drill' and the temptation to ignore it is tremendous. You therefore ignore the workplace policy on 'what to do when the fire alarm sounds'.

2 You need to move some files from one office to another. You decide it would be easier to wedge open one of the fire doors whilst you finish the job, and are distracted afterwards when the phone rings – so you forget to close it.

3 Your chair is relatively easy to adjust but you have never really got to grips with all the levers. You know it doesn't support your back properly but think if you sit up straight you will be fine.

4 You have a jug kettle in your office for making drinks but yesterday you dropped the plug and it cracked. You know you should report it but it's winter and you're desperate for a hot drink *now.*

5 Your new printer has been delivered and you are so keen to use it you try to connect it without reading the instructions.

6 You have asked to leave early and your supervisor has agreed provided you finish a long document you are producing on your computer. You decide to work solidly without taking any breaks.

In each of these cases you are ignoring your workplace policies.

- In the first two you are disregarding policies designed to protect employees in the case of fire.
- In the next you are ignoring the fact that special equipment has been provided to help you.
- In the remainder you are disregarding specific instructions or required ways of working.

Unsafe behaviour

Many types of unsafe behaviour are covered in workplace policies. However, because human beings can be quite ingenious – and because certain aspects of health and safety may seem to be common sense – it is doubtful you will find a workplace policy to cover absolutely every silly thing that someone might do in an office!

For instance, you are unlikely to find there is a policy to cover how many files you should carry at once – common sense should tell you that if you carry so many you can't see where you are going then you are in danger of walking into something and hurting yourself.

Other examples of unsafe behaviour include:

- practical jokes that get out of hand, such as letting off a fire extinguisher or throwing water around
- using a new piece of equipment without reading the instructions
- running along a corridor, up or down stairs or around a corner
- leaving a drawer open so someone falls over it
- stacking dozens of lever arch files on a high shelf so they overbalance and fall on people working below
- deciding to use a backpack to carry books and papers to work and completely ignoring the fact that people behind you are in danger of being hit as you turn round suddenly or squeeze into the lift
- handing over the office scissors (or paper knife) with the point(s) facing forwards
- using a wet cloth to clean electrical equipment.

In each of these cases you may be endangering yourself but may also be endangering other people as well. The answer is to think first, act later.

CHECK IT OUT!

Discuss with your tutor, trainer or supervisor what you would do if a colleague or fellow student was indulging in unsafe behaviour. Would you say nothing, talk to them or report them to your boss or tutor? Under which circumstances would each be best – and why?

Accidental breakages or spillages

Anyone can damage or break something – it's what you do immediately afterwards that matters. Workers in supermarkets, for instance, are instructed that if something falls and breaks, the area must be cordoned off immediately and the spillage cleaned. This is to prevent anyone slipping or cutting themselves on broken glass.

The same rules apply in an office. Anything spilt makes a floor wet and therefore hazardous – although the risk is higher on a tiled floor. No matter how busy you are, or how tempting it may be to leave the mess for someone else to clean up, if you drop or spill anything it is up to you to do something about it – immediately.

Anything broken can present a hazard to the person who has to move it, particularly if it has sharp edges. A broken plastic box, a coffee cup or glass all present a potential hazard. Anything broken should be wrapped in strong paper before being put in the waste bin. Otherwise you are putting the person who empties the bin at risk.

Environmental factors

The word 'environment' here relates to the space and area in which you work. It refers to factors such as:

- ventilation and temperatures
- clean air
- noise
- maintenance and cleanliness
- lighting
- space
- floor areas
- rest rooms and welfare facilities.

The main requirements are covered by **the Workplace (Health, Safety and Welfare) Regulations 1992.** Turn back to page 10 and refresh your memory about these.

Ventilation and temperatures

The recommended temperature in an office is 20°C – but this is not a legal requirement. Legally, the temperature has to be 'reasonable'. If everyone is frozen, because the heating has broken down, or sweltering, because there are no blinds at the windows, then something is wrong and you should report the matter.

Ideally you should have access to fresh air, but if you work in a building with air conditioning you may find that the windows are sealed. If the system is working properly you should be fine, but if the air becomes too dry you may find you get a headache or feel ill. This is why air-conditioning systems have to be regularly monitored and maintained.

Clean air

All workers have the right to breathe unpolluted air – though there is little your employer can do if you work in an office block in a city centre with traffic fumes everywhere. Good ventilation will reduce the problem but you can help by not polluting the air yourself – for instance by leaving the top off a smelly cleaning liquid, or smoking in a no-smoking area.

Today, most employers have a no-smoking policy to protect their workers from the dangers of passive smoking in the workplace. Legally, non-smokers can claim that smoke is a substance hazardous to health and should therefore be controlled. Any designated smoking room should have good ventilation, and separate rest areas should be provided for non-smokers.

Noise

The **Noise at Work Regulations 1989** state that all workers should be protected from loud noise. You may think that this is only likely to apply if you are a construction worker or in a noisy factory – but you would be wrong. A recent survey showed that staff in many restaurants, pubs and clubs are in danger, because the combined noise levels of music, people talking, eating and drinking are more than the legal limits! The worst danger for office staff is the combined noise of equipment, telephones, people speaking and the noise from outside – many offices are situated next to busy main roads where the traffic noise is considerable.

Basically, if you have to raise your voice for someone to hear you, the noise level is too loud.

 INFORMATION UPDATE

Silence, believe it or not, has been identified as being stressful! Accountants at the BBC claimed that their office was too quiet – and insisted that soft, taped background music be introduced. The new condition was termed 'pin-drop syndrome' by the press. The accountants had claimed that if they did try to have a conversation with someone else, everyone else could 'listen in' and this made their job too stressful.

Maintenance and cleanliness

All organisations have maintenance policies – but you can reasonably expect them to give a higher level of priority to problems which could cause a hazard than to other breakdowns. For instance, if there is an electrical fault so that the emergency lighting won't work, or a rail on a steep staircase breaks, these would be given higher priority than your desk drawer jamming. In addition to repairing faults, 'maintenance' also means checking and inspecting equipment regularly. You must cooperate with your employer – no matter how inconvenient it is that you temporarily close down your computer or do without your photocopier whilst it is checked.

Dust is not only unsightly but can also lead to air pollution. Obviously the degree of cleanliness should be appropriate to the situation. In an organisation which undertakes food handling or preparation, the levels of cleanliness required by law are far greater than in an office. Equally, if you work as a medical administrator and are employed in a hospital or health centre, then the levels of cleanliness should be higher than in, say, the office of a building contractor.

Basically, the area should be cleaned so that it is not a health hazard. This also means that rubbish should be cleared away regularly. A related point here is that you shouldn't throw away uneaten food (such as the remains of an apple) with paper rubbish if it won't be cleared away quickly.

Lighting

Poor light in an office environment can be caused by a variety of factors:

- insufficient natural light; insufficient or dirty windows – or positioning your desk too far away from the window to benefit
- dark colours on the walls or dark furnishings and carpets which make the office appear drab and dull
- dirty or poorly maintained lights, such as fluorescent tubes that flicker or light bulbs that have dimmed with age
- insufficient 'local' lighting (such as desk lamps)
- badly designed central lights – which are not positioned over workstations or desks.

According to the law, every workplace must have 'suitable' and 'sufficient' lighting. Therefore, if you are employed to mend watches the light must be much better than if you are mending shoes. Ironically, if you use a computer, *too much* light can also be hazardous – particularly if this results in glare which means you can't read your screen properly. Glare is defined as 'light in the wrong place' – so if you are dazzled through bright light, let someone know. Glare can be reduced by:

- fitting blinds to windows and *adjusting these,* as necessary, when the sun shines
- fitting special attachments (called diffusers) to lights
- reducing the number of reflective (glossy) surfaces in an office
- moving workstations to a more suitable position
- relocating the lights in an office so that they are positioned better for the people working there
- redecorating the office so that it is light and bright but with non-reflective walls and floors.

Space

Everyone needs enough space in which to work safely. You are not expected to be crowded into a tiny office with several other people. The recommended space is 11 cubic metres as a minimum, but the number of people who can be safely accommodated in an office will also depend upon the amount of furniture and equipment which is taking up space. Your employer cannot argue that you have no space around you but plenty above you because the room has a high ceiling!

Obviously you cannot take a tape measure to work with you every day to check that you have enough space. However, if you work in a small office and there is a proposal to install a large piece of equipment or to move in three more people, you should ask your safety representative or supervisor for advice.

Windows, doors and floors

Glass in windows and doors must be specially laminated or strengthened to make it safe, or be protected against breakage or marked (for instance, by black criss-cross wires) so that its presence is obvious. The aim is to prevent you accidentally walking through an unmarked glass door or cutting yourself on broken glass. All windows and skylights which are meant to open must be safe, so that you are not in danger by opening or closing them, or sitting near them.

Doors which slide must have special devices so they cannot be dislodged from their tracks, and doors which open upwards must be specially secure to prevent them falling down on anyone. You will also find that doors which open in either direction are fitted with a viewing panel so that you can see someone approaching from either side.

As you will see on page 32, many people are hurt because they slip, trip or fall. For that reason the type of floor covering must be appropriate. Floors should not be uneven or slippery, stairs and steep slopes should have a handrail, areas which get wet regularly should have good drainage. Damaged floor surfaces should be repaired promptly and, in winter, outdoor routes used by staff should be salted or sanded.

Floors are also hazardous when something is placed on them which causes an obstruction, if a pile of boxes is badly stacked, if rubbish is left lying around, or if trailing wires could trip someone. As you already know, they also need to be kept clean and spillages mopped up quickly.

What you wear on your feet can also affect your safety as you will see in the next element.

Rest rooms and welfare facilities

Your employer must provide sufficient toilets and washing facilities and these must be kept clean. Firms which require staff to change into uniforms or overalls must provide appropriate space for staff to leave their outdoor or normal clothing and, if necessary, changing rooms.

Large companies often have a restaurant or canteen which provides a full meal or a snack. If you work in a small office you should still have the means to prepare or obtain a hot drink and the facility to heat up your own food.

However, you cannot always argue that you should have a separate place in which to sit and relax and eat it. Your employer can argue that your office can be classed as a 'rest room' provided you are not continually disturbed during your break.

ⓘ INFORMATION UPDATE

According to government statistics, 3709 non-fatal injuries occurred in offices in the five years to 1997/98. Of these, 614 were major injuries and 3095 were less serious but resulted in an absence of over three days. Do remember that these are not the only injuries – as many went unreported.

Most of the serious, reported injuries occurring in offices were as a result of falling from a height. These included four fatalities. Other injuries and their main causes are given in the table below ('less serious' injuries in this table still required more than three days off work).

Cause of injury	Major	Less serious
Slipping or tripping (often over an obstruction)	49%	26%
Falls from a ladder, chair or racking	22%	12%
Struck by moving, flying or falling object (including a moving door)	9%	12%
Striking a fixed object (e.g. walking into a desk)	–	7%
Handling, lifting or carrying an awkward or heavy object	6%	29%

TEST YOUR KNOWLEDGE AND UNDERSTANDING

A group of staff in an office have given their boss a list of complaints about their working environment. How many do you think she must take action on?

a   no appropriate materials available for cleaning VDU screens
b   windows which don't open because the office has air conditioning
c   excessive noise from a large photocopier in the corner of the office – plus a 'funny smell'
d   a missing carpet tile near the door which was first reported a month ago

➡

e no blinds at the window so that VDU screens can't be seen when the sun shines in

f no space in the small kitchen for people to sit and eat their sandwiches

g no protective gloves provided for the member of staff who cleans the reprographic equipment

h waste bins are emptied nightly but cleaners polish desks and vacuum the floor only twice a week

i safety stool broken, so no safe means of obtaining stationery on high shelves in stockroom

j it's annoying when maintenance people insist on disrupting work to check equipment.

EVIDENCE COLLECTION

Look carefully around your own working environment.

1 Decide which aspects of your workplace or college are *potentially* hazardous, i.e. they could harm you, your colleagues or customers.

2 Now decide which pose a high risk, either to you or to other people, and which pose a low risk. You may find this easier if you consider risks under the headings given in this section, i.e.

   a the use and maintenance of machinery or equipment

   b the use of materials or substances

   c working practices that do not conform to laid-down policies

   d unsafe behaviour

   e accidental breakages or spillages

   f environmental spillages.

3 In addition to keeping a record about how you dealt with any risks in any of the areas above, also note any hazards you see and state how you have dealt with them and to whom you reported the matter. Remember that if a hazard has a high risk it must be reported immediately, if it has a low risk you should deal with it according to your workplace policies – or you should ask your tutor or supervisor for advice.

Element 102.2 Reduce the risks to health and safety in your workplace

You already know that workplace policies give you guidance on what to do and how to carry out tasks where health and safety is important. In addition, you will also be expected to refer to suppliers' or manufacturers' instructions which relate to equipment, materials and products. In this element you have to show that you can follow workplace policies or specific instructions, that you can be vigilant to new hazards or risks occurring and take action to reduce these, and that your own personal conduct and presentation helps to maintain health and safety in your workplace.

Workplace policies

By now you should know why workplace policies exist and which are likely to relate specifically to an administrator's job role. It is worth noting that these often change as they must be kept up to date. Good policies have a date on the front or in the heading. Always make sure you have the latest version to refer to.

Suppliers' and manufacturers' instructions

Every time a piece of equipment or a special product is bought, you will find an instruction leaflet inside. This applies in your private life as well as at work – as you will know if you have ever bought a mobile phone, a box of paracetamol, a bottle of hair dye or a vast number of other products. People tend to fall into three different types:

- Type A always read the leaflet or instructions very carefully before using the product.
- Type B scan it quickly, because they are impatient.
- Type C try out the product first. Then, if it doesn't work properly, they refer to the instructions – if they can still find them.

Which are you? And why does it matter? With some products it may not be very important, but with others it can be critical. You would be very brave indeed to use hair dye or artificial tanning lotion without referring to the instructions beforehand!

Tempting though it may be, it is always far safer to read the instructions first; then you are less likely to make silly, even dangerous, mistakes. Apart from anything else, most manufacturers and suppliers include a 'help sheet' which you can use as a guide if anything does go wrong or if the equipment develops a fault. This saves you looking ridiculous by calling out the repair person when you haven't even checked whether something is switched on!

TEST YOUR KNOWLEDGE AND UNDERSTANDING

Each of the following instructions relates to one of the office products or items listed below. Can you match them up correctly?

Items: (1) CD-ROM; (2) fax machine; (3) photocopier; (4) telephone; (5) packet of paper; (6) computer printer; (7) VDU (monitor); (8) printer cartridge; (9) telephone answering machine; (10) cleaning solution.

Instructions:

A Use this way up.

B Clean the handset with a damp (not wet) cloth or antistatic wipe. Never use a dry cloth as this may cause a static shock. Never spray cleaning fluid directly on to the equipment.

C No picture? Check the power cord is connected and the power switch is on.

D May be harmful if swallowed. Avoid contact with eyes.

E Keep sealed until ready for use.

F Hold by the inner and outer edges only with the label facing up.

G Avoid using envelopes which are shiny, embossed or have windows – use labels instead.

H Avoid using during an lightning storm as there is a slight risk of electric shock.

I Never use stapled paper, aluminium foil or other conductive paper. Otherwise a fire might occur.

J Do not place on or near a radiator or where the machine may be affected by high temperature or exposed to direct sunlight, dust or fibres from carpets.

(If you are stuck, the answers are given at the end of this unit!)

Safe working practices

To prove your competency for this element, you have to show that you can follow workplace policies covering at least four of the following areas. Bear in mind that this also means following manufacturers' or suppliers' instructions where they are relevant:

1 the use of safe working methods and equipment

2 the safe use of hazardous substances

3 smoking, eating, drinking and drugs

4 what to do in an emergency

5 personal presentation.

However, there are two points to note.

Firstly, what should you do if your workplace policy does not say the same thing as the manufacturers' instructions? The golden rule is to STOP – and ask for guidance. If no one can help, then you should follow the workplace policies *first* – on the basis that you may have misunderstood the manufacturers' instructions in some way. Then make sure you report the matter to someone as soon as you can.

Secondly, what should you do if there is no workplace policy for one or more of the areas listed? In this case you are sensible if you talk to your supervisor who should be able to give you guidance. You may find it useful to read the section which follows, which deals with each of these in turn, before you ask for help.

EVIDENCE COLLECTION

Start by checking through the workplace policies you obtained for the previous element to ensure that at least four of the five areas above are covered. If not, and you talk to your tutor or supervisor about any missing area, then make a record of the conversation and type up a summary for your portfolio. Ask your tutor or supervisor to sign it.

It is also worth making copies of relevant pages of instruction manuals for equipment you use regularly. The relevant pages are mainly those relating to safety, not general operating instructions. You will make this evidence more valuable if you add your own comments to relevant places – such as instructions you need to refer to regularly.

Safe working methods and equipment

If you are *not* using safe working methods, you are exposing yourself to a higher level of risk than you should. Examples of unsafe working practices relating to an administrative job role are likely to include:

- not switching off equipment when you should do so
- not using appropriate equipment such as a safety stool
- not reading instructions – or not following them
- using liquids near electrical equipment
- using equipment you have been told you are not trained to operate or which you have been told not to use because it is faulty

- being untidy and slipshod so that you make a mess which can create a hazard for yourself and others
- not using protective clothing when instructed to do so
- not taking a break when you are told to do so
- ignoring specific instructions you have been given.

You are working safely when you:

- comply with instructions (whether or not you agree with them!)
- walk, not run, around the building
- lift only acceptable weights and ask someone to help you if anything is heavy or cumbersome
- carry only a small number of items so that your view isn't obscured
- close drawers of cupboards, desks and filing cabinets *immediately* after use
- keep your working area clean and tidy and put your personal belongings away
- put rubbish in the correct container
- stack items safely
- use the correct equipment for the job
- only do what you have been trained to do, and ask for help on other occasions.

INFORMATION UPDATE

A musculoskeletal disorder doesn't sound like something you might expect to develop in an office! However, these problems account for more cases of work-related ill-health in Great Britain than any other health hazard and often include office workers.

Musculoskeletal disorders cover a variety of problems affecting the body's muscles and joints – with the back, neck, shoulders and upper limbs being particularly at risk. They include a stiff neck, tenosynovitis and slipped disc. Tenosynovitis is normally known as RSI (repetitive strain injury). It is caused by repetitive movements (such as constant keyboarding) which cause pain and swelling or constant 'pins and needles' in the hands and wrists. Additional problems are caused by trying to wedge a telephone between the shoulder and neck so that you can continue typing at the same time or take written notes. This can lead to tendon and joint problems, muscle stiffening and disc troubles, recently named 'phone neck'. Even having your 'copy' in an awkward position for long periods so your head is tilted awkwardly whilst you are keyboarding can quickly lead to neck aches and pains.

The safe use of hazardous substances

Fortunately, in most offices, there are not a great number of hazardous substances. A hazardous substance is anything that could cause you harm, either by irritating your skin or eyes, or by being dangerous to swallow. You might find these listed in your workplace policies under 'COSHH Regulations' (Control of Substances Hazardous to Health).

All hazardous substances should be clearly labelled and properly stored. Under COSHH Regulations, they may need to be kept in a special location. Even substances which are just irritants can prove very harmful to people with sensitive skin (ask any hairdresser or beautician!). If you are instructed to wear protective gloves, then do so.

It is absolutely imperative that you read the instructions on hazardous substances *very carefully* before you use them. You must know what to do immediately if an accident occurs.

Finally, treat all inflammable substances as potentially hazardous. These must be stored in a cool place and well away from naked lights or fires.

Smoking, eating, drinking and drugs

If you are a non-smoker you will probably be pleased that your workplace restricts smoking. If you are a smoker, you may have a very different view. It is obviously more satisfactory, in that case, if your employer provides a smoking room so that you do not have to stand outside during your break time. However, don't be tempted to see whether you can 'get away with' smoking in forbidden areas, or even in the toilets. Non-smokers can tell immediately as tobacco smoke has a very distinct odour. You are likely to be formally disciplined if you ignore your employer's policies on smoking.

Eating may be permitted at your desk – in moderation. This is less likely if your company has a separate eating area or a restaurant or canteen. However, do have some consideration for your colleagues if you bring food to work – anything which is very strongly spiced or has a distinctive odour might annoy everyone else if they have to work in the same space as you, and breathe the same air.

Drinking (soft drinks only!) at your desk is more likely to be acceptable, but do keep liquids away from any equipment or machinery – preferably well out of the way, so that you are less likely to knock them over. Alcohol is likely to be banned on the premises, unless there is a special celebration, and today lunchtime drinking is normally discouraged or even forbidden. This is particularly the case for employees who operate machinery or equipment or undertake potentially dangerous operations. Check what your company's views are on alcohol. Under normal circumstances it is better to restrict it to special occasions, such as leaving parties, and to schedule these, if possible, for after working hours.

There is normally a clear policy on the use of drugs on the premises, apart from those prescribed by a doctor. Your organisation, of course, has a legal duty to comply with the law on harmful or illegal substances and will take disciplinary action against anyone who contravenes these instructions.

ℹ️ INFORMATION UPDATE

One reason why people may be tempted to smoke, drink alcohol or take drugs, such as tranquillisers or sleeping pills, is because they are under stress. Stress occurs when someone feels they cannot cope because of work or personal pressures. However, people's stress levels vary – whereas one person may thrive on tight deadlines, another may become quite ill.

The first symptoms of stress may be irritability, no sense of humour, loss of concentration, tearfulness, constant tiredness, not being able to make a decision, or even explosive anger.

Workplace stress can be caused by various problems, such as:

- too much work to do – or even too little
- insufficient or inappropriate equipment for the job
- long hours with few breaks
- boring or repetitive work
- no one to talk to and a feeling of isolation
- not getting on with your colleagues
- too much supervision – or too little
- an unreasonable or bad-tempered boss
- no control over one's own work
- conflicting instructions or demands.

According to the Health and Safety Executive, stress should be considered a health hazard and it is in the interests of employers to try to reduce stress. According to the Institute of Management, 270,000 people take time off work every day because of work-related stress, at a total cost of £7 billion through sick pay, lost production and healthcare costs.

If you feel you cannot cope, that the work is too much for you or that your boss is making your life a misery, then it is important to talk to someone. If you have a fair and reasonable supervisor, then ask to speak to him or her in confidence. However, if your supervisor is the main problem, life may seem more difficult. In this case, if you are an FMA or an AMA you should talk to your adviser or assessor – or personnel manager. If you are a full-time student, talk to your tutor or to someone in Student Services. Remember that wherever you are undertaking your off-the-job training there should be someone you can talk to – in confidence. Whatever you do, don't assume that things will automatically put themselves right. Even talking through your worries with someone, confidentially, can often help.

What to do in an emergency

Your workplace policies will give you clear instructions on what to do in the case of most emergencies, but no one can think of everything that might occur. Policies should also cover what to do about other people on the premises, such as visitors, customers or outside contractors. This is one of the reasons why organisations have a visitor book, so that it is known how many people are on the premises. It is also useful if visitors are informed, on arrival, what to do if the fire alarm sounds, and where to assemble.

You are likely to find a difference between the exact procedure laid down if there is a bomb threat or a fire alarm. In there is a bomb alert you may be told to take your belongings with you, because this reduces the number of items that have to be searched. If there is a fire alert you should leave everything behind except any personal belongings that are near at hand.

You should think what you would do in the case of other, unforeseen, emergencies. Here are some examples:

- smoke is seen pouring out from under the stockroom door
- there is a smell of gas
- water starts coming through the ceiling near an electric light fitting
- a suspicious package is received in the mail
- a bomb threat is received over the telephone
- a colleague suffers an electric shock
- someone chokes in the canteen.
- a visitor faints in reception
- you witness a serious accident.

CHECK IT OUT!

1 Research what you should do in each of the situations suggested above. Start by checking which are covered by your workplace policies.

2 Discuss with your tutor or supervisor how you should react in each of the remaining situations.

3 Try to think of any other emergencies. Ask your colleagues or tutor for ideas. Then write a summary for your portfolio.

EVIDENCE COLLECTION

If you are involved in an emergency, keep a record by writing up an account of what happened and what you did. Identify the workplace policy relating to this type of situation and confirm that you followed this. Your evidence will be better if you use letter-headed paper and ask your supervisor to sign and date your account to confirm it.

INFORMATION UPDATE

Another type of emergency may threaten some kinds of workers. This is violence at work caused by threats, verbal or physical abuse. Obviously the type of work you do is likely to affect your vulnerability. According to statistics, the people most at risk are those who are involved with:

- handling money
- providing care, advice and information to the general public
- working with violent people
- dealing with complaints.

Safety representatives should check that risk assessments include the possibility of violence at work. Risks can be reduced, for instance by installing personal alarms or doubling up staff in certain situations, and by training workers on what to do if an emergency occurs. Staff should also be trained to recognise the warning signs, should be taught techniques to diffuse the tension, and should never be encouraged to handle a potentially serious problem alone.

If you ever feel threatened or intimidated by a caller, stay calm and say nothing that would make the situation worse. You can get help quickly simply by saying that you need to refer the matter to your supervisor as you do not know the answer to your caller's request. If you work in a potentially difficult environment – such as a debt collection agency – security equipment such as panic buttons may be installed, so make sure you know how these operate. Finally, never feel silly or a nuisance if you press a panic button or ask for help. Far better to be safe than to take a chance.

Personal presentation

Administrators are fortunate that their personal presentation is less regulated than in many other jobs. For instance, if your job involved handling food you would almost certainly have to wear special clothes, tie back your hair and wear a hat or cap. In a factory you might have to wear safety shoes. If you were on a building site, a helmet (hard hat) would be compulsory. However, if you have to wear personal protective clothing for any reason (such as rubber gloves to clean a machine) *always* comply with the requirement gracefully. Making a fuss is childish; and a downright refusal could result in disciplinary action being taken against you.

Sensibly, however, you should bear in mind that some items of personal clothing and jewellery can be more hazardous than others, particularly if you operate equipment. Leaning over a shredder while wearing a dangling tie is not the wisest thing you can do! Remember:

- dangling bracelets can be hazardous as they can get trapped in machinery
- long hair should be kept back from your face if you are leaning over moving equipment
- high-heeled or 'clumpy' shoes can make you unsteady on your feet, particularly when you try to move quickly.

Very tight or short skirts are not practicable as they allow little freedom of movement without becoming positively indecent. Equally, low-cut, tight or skimpy tops are inappropriate in an office. Generally it is best to avoid over-casual clothes such as jeans, T-shirts and trainers, unless you are certain that such clothes are completely acceptable in your organisation.

You also need to be vigilant about personal grooming and freshness so that you are not unpleasant to be near. Try to avoid eating garlic and other highly flavoured foods during the working week – unless you are prepared to buy a good breath freshener and use it regularly.

The importance of personal conduct

'Personal conduct' relates to your behaviour, your working habits and your general attitude towards other people.

Behaving sensibly and responsibly doesn't mean that you have to be a humourless person. It means being aware that *all* your actions have *consequences* – and these may be good or bad for other people and the organisation. It also means that you are prepared to take responsibility for your own actions. Ensure that you can be trusted to act in the same way when you are unsupervised as when someone is watching what you do.

You can avoid making mistakes and causing problems if you are prepared to ask when you are not sure about something. If you dislike doing this, remember that everyone needs to ask for help at times; no one knows everything!

Being a neat and tidy worker will generally lead to the least number of problems, for yourself and everyone else.

Finally, you have to accept that, at work, other people will have some authority over you. Obviously, if your boss and colleagues are wonderful to work with, that makes things much easier. It also helps if you understand *why* you are being asked to do something.

TEST YOUR OWN ATTITUDES AND BEHAVIOUR

As a quick check, see how you fare with the quiz below. How to score it is given at the end.

1 On an average day:
   a your desk drawers are wonderfully tidy
   b you can usually find something if you rummage a bit
   c you have no idea what is in them, but they were a tip the last time you looked.

2 Your 'in', 'out' and 'filing' trays are:
   a checked daily to ensure urgent jobs are done and papers are filed promptly
   b checked daily for urgent jobs – with filing done when you can
   c overflowing with papers.

3 Your boss has left early for an appointment. You are supposed to stay until 5.15 pm but no one is around to check. Do you:
   a stay until at least 5.15 and tidy up before you leave
   b stay until 5.15 and then leave on the dot
   c disappear as quickly as you can?

4 Last night you were out with some friends until late. This morning you feel rather the worse for wear. Do you:
   a drink as much water as you can stand, have a shower and get in on time (just)
   b stagger in looking weary and hope you'll feel better by lunchtime
   c ring in sick?

5 The front door of the photocopier won't close properly. Do you:
   a report the fault immediately and check the manual to see if the machine can still be used
   b report the fault, but carry on using the photocopier
   c push a box of paper in front of the door to keep it closed?

6 The last time you checked that your chair was in the best position to support your back, and at the right height for your desk, was:
   a within the last week
   b within the last month
   c can't remember.

7 Your friend offers you a bottle of cleaning solution which she says is wonderful for computers. You can't understand a word on the

➡

label as it is written in Japanese. Do you:

a   thank her but refuse the offer

b   accept it and take it to work, in the hope someone might be able to understand the label

c   try it out on your office computer?

8   Your office has a high window which you can open either with a long pole or using a safety stool. Both of these have gone missing at the moment. Do you:

a   look around until you find one of the items and then open the window

b   look around for a short while, and complain about the heat when you can't find them

c   ask a friend to hold your swivel chair still whilst you stand on it?

9   The electrical items in your office are checked every year. After the electricians have left this year you suddenly remember you have a fan heater in a cupboard which you forgot to give them. Do you:

a   ring them up and tell them, and put a note on the heater so it won't be used until it has been checked

b   ring them up and tell them, then put the heater back in the cupboard

c   ignore it – the tests are a waste of time, anyway?

10 You drop some paper when you are walking into the office and about three or four sheets fall on to the carpet. The phone is ringing as you enter. Do you:

a   pick them up immediately

b   answer the phone and then pick them up

c   leave them for someone else to pick up?

For each 'a' answer give yourself 2 marks; for each 'b' answer award yourself 1 mark. No marks for any 'c' answers!

How did you score? 18–20: You are so virtuous it takes some believing! Well done if you told the truth *every* time! 13–17: You are generally a responsible and sensible person to work with, but occasionally make the odd mistake so people know you are human. 10–13: Some room for improvement, but generally not too bad. 6–9: Not very impressive! You are an accident waiting to happen! 0–5: You are a walking disaster for yourself and everyone around you.

Taking action to reduce risks

There are two types of risks you may encounter:

- those you can put right yourself
- those you need to report to someone else.

Risks you can put right yourself

These are risks which fall within the scope of your own job role, such as:

- your own workstation
- your own working area
- your own working methods
- your own behaviour and personal conduct
- your own personal presentation.

CHECK IT OUT!

If you use a computer, carry out a risk assessment for yourself to make sure you don't suffer from RSI or phone neck – or other painful problems. Then list your findings.

Seating – are you sitting pretty?

a   Is your chair comfortable, with well-padded upholstery?

b   Is your lower back supported?

c   Can you change your seat height and backrest position?

d   Do your feet touch the ground? If not, do you have a footrest?

e   Do you have a swivel chair so you can move around easily?

f   Do you have armrests? If so, do these help you or restrict you?

Workstation – a place for everything?

a   Is all your work and equipment within easy reach?

b   Is there enough space for everything you have to use?

c   Have you enough space between the keyboard and edge of the desk to rest your hands in front of the keyboard?

d   Are you positioned so your hands are parallel with your elbows?

e   Is there enough room for your legs under your desk?

f   Can you see any information you are inputting without straining your eyes or your neck?

g   If you are left-handed, has your workstation been arranged with this in mind?

h   Is your screen clean and at the correct angle?   ➡

Environment – restful or stressful?

a   Is there sufficient light, even on a dull or dark day?

b   Are there blinds at the window – or can you adjust your screen on a bright day to avoid reflections?

c   Have you enough space around you to move safely?

d   Are all wires safely out of the way?

e   Have you received training so you are confident using the equipment?

f   Do you have regular breaks or changes of activity?

g   Do you know the procedure for obtaining an eyesight test if you are a regular computer user?

HELPING YOURSELF!

You can reduce risks to yourself by taking appropriate action:

* Adjust your chair and sit up straight – as a guide, your arms should be horizontal when keyboarding.

* Place your feet in front of your knees and flat on the floor.

* Adjust your keyboard and screen so both are best for you.

* Clean the screen regularly to remove dirt and dust.

* Pull down blinds on a sunny day.

* Adjust your brightness and contrast settings as required.

* Refocus your eyes from time to time and change your activities so that you move around.

Risks you should report to someone else

Many risks will be outside your own scope and responsibility. It is not likely to be your job to mend a carpet, repair a plug, buy a safety stool or arrange training for someone – even if these actions are required. However, if you identify a hazard which presents a risk then you should report it. If the risk factor is high – i.e. many people could be quite seriously hurt – then this should be reported promptly and preventative measures taken immediately.

There will usually be workplace policies for handling risks. You need to know what these are and who to contact if help is needed in an emergency.

Each of the following situations constitutes a risk. In each case state:

a whether you could correct the problem yourself or should report it, because it is outside your own area of responsibility

b whether the risk factor is high or low

c what you would do in your own organisation to comply with workplace policies

d what suggestions you would make to reduce the risk immediately.

1 Black smoke starts pouring out from the back of the fax machine during transmission.

2 You slip on the steps up to the building one winter morning because it's very icy.

3 You knock some paperclips inside your printer by accident when you open the lid to replace the printer cartridge.

4 You spill coffee over your computer keyboard.

5 The door to your office has a large glass panel which cracks in two when the door slams shut.

6 You are using methylated spirits – as instructed – to clean the fax machine. When you have finished you can't find the top of the bottle.

7 Your colleague asks for help to push the photocopier against the wall to make more room in the office.

8 The fluorescent light in your office starts to flicker.

9 You see a colleague having a secret cigarette in the stationery cupboard.

10 When you return from lunch, a new delivery of stationery has been 'dumped' just inside your office.

EVIDENCE COLLECTION

Start a health and safety diary, or work log. Suggested headings are given below:

Date	Hazard	Risk level	Action taken	Relevant workplace policy/instructions

Now keep your eyes open! It will be very unusual if you work in an office where hazards and risks *never* occur. Some of the situations described in the exercise above may have suggested some ideas. Remember that your own working area and work habits may sometimes create a risk – and you can list these, too.

When you have several items on your list, identify which of the headings they belong under:

1 the use of safe working methods and equipment;
2 the safe use of hazardous substances;
3 smoking, eating, drinking and drugs;
4 what to do in an emergency;
5 personal presentation.

Remember that you have to follow workplace policies for four of these headings. If one of these has not been covered by your list, you will have to explain how you would follow the policy.

TEST YOUR KNOWLEDGE AND UNDERSTANDING

1　Look back at the previous Check it out exercise. Classify all the risks there according to the categories you have to use. Is any one missing?

2　How well do you know manufacturer's instructions and workplace policies? Check by saying (or finding out) how you would advise a colleague who asked you:

　a　how to safely dispose of used toner containers from the photocopier

　b　how to help disabled visitors to your multistorey building when the fire alarm sounds

　c　whether or not your fax machine must be disconnected from the mains before cleaning

　d　whether it is safe to throw used batteries from the answering machine in a fire

　e　where the assembly point is for your office in case of a fire ➡

f   what action to take – immediately – if the fax machine develops a paper jam during transmission

g   who to contact in your organisation in the case of a serious emergency.

EVIDENCE COLLECTION

As your final piece of evidence for this unit, obtain *witness testimony* from your supervisor which confirms that you abide by health and safety policies at work (or college) and that your personal presentation helps to ensure your own health and safety and meets any legal duties or workplace requirements. If you have been involved in any specific health and safety duties, then ask your supervisor to confirm this also.

Answers to quiz on page 35

A = 5, B = 4, C = 7, D = 10, E = 8, F = 1, G = 6, H = 2*, I = 3, J = 9.

* However, if you suggested that the answering machine should also be disconnected from the mains or not used during an electrical storm, you would also have been right. Faxes, answering machines, and land-line phones that use an earpiece connected to the base unit, should all be avoided if there is a lightning storm. It is also wise not to log on to the Internet if your computer is directly linked through its own telephone line.

Unit 201   Support the work of your team

A young administrator started her first job working in a small business that had three other people. They were all out of the office regularly, leaving her completely alone. After a few weeks, even though she liked the work, she left and moved to a larger firm. Why? Because she was lonely.

Some people enjoy going to work because they can mix with others. These may be members of their team or colleagues in other areas of the organisation. For you, some of these will be senior or older, some may be remote or distracted, or simply not the kind of people you would normally choose to be your friends. However, there will be others you will like and some with whom you may become close friends. In an office with a friendly atmosphere, there will be an exchange of opinions, people to talk to and obtain advice from, people to laugh with and work alongside. This is a very important part of your working life – an office where the staff work well together is usually both more productive *and* more enjoyable to be in.

This unit concerns your relationships with other members of your team, as well as your own contribution to the team. You may think that a 'team' is more suited to a sports field than an office, but you would be wrong. Teams are found in many places and the term is used to describe a group of people who *collectively* work together to achieve a common objective. This can be beating a rival team on a football field, or getting an urgent and complex job done quickly and efficiently in an office. The idea is the same – members of the team 'pull together' for the good of the team as a whole.

Therefore, before studying the two elements in detail, we will firstly focus on teams and how they function in business.

 KEY SKILLS SIGNPOST

If you are taking your Key Skills award, you can link the evidence you produce for this unit to your evidence for **Working with Others**. In that case you need two examples for each of the following areas, one to show you can work in a one-to-one situation and the other to show you can work in group or team situations. Remember, the following list equates to Level 2. See your tutor or supervisor if you are doing a different level.

WO2.1

Identify your own job role and the objectives you have to achieve each day. In addition, identify the objectives of working together as a team.

Explain the tasks you need to carry out to achieve these objectives and the resources and time needed.

Explain how you exchange information to check each person's responsibilities, including:

- how you can help
- how you find out what other people want to do
- how you check you know exactly what is required
- how your confirm your working arrangements.

WO2.2

Give examples of how you have organised tasks to make sure you have the correct resources and can complete the tasks on time.

Include in your examples evidence to show that you work safely and accurately and produce good-quality work.

State how you support cooperative ways of working – for instance, by anticipating the needs of other people, by avoiding behaviour which causes offence, and by acting assertively when necessary.

Give examples of occasions when you have asked a colleague, your tutor, supervisor or other appropriate person for advice about a difficulty you cannot solve on your own.

WO2.3

Keep a log of your work with others and use this to provide information on occasions when things have gone well and times when things have gone less well. Include examples of occasions when your quality of work has not been of the required standard.

Identify occasions when you have been given progress reports from others and how you have responded to these and asked questions where necessary.

Give examples of times when you have made suggestions to improve working with others to help achieve objectives.

The importance of teams

Teams are not a new invention – you have probably been part of one at school. How effective it was may be debatable. In fact, if you were a member of a sporting team which was regularly beaten by every other team it ever met, you could probably identify that the problem was for one of two reasons:

- the skills of the team were poor
- the team didn't work together very well.

In Euro 2000, for example, the English football team did poorly – yet many of the players were very talented. Instead it was their poor teamwork that was criticised.

To function as an effective member of a team in the workplace you need to possess the skills required to undertake your part of the work. Assuming you have these, you also need to know two things:

a   what teams are – and what they are supposed to do – particularly in a business context

b   what other factors also operate to make a team effective – or disastrous (in other words, what exactly *is* teamwork?).

Definition of a team

A team is different from a group. You may go out at the weekend with a group of friends, but that does not make you a team. You could all have different interests, for one thing. There may be a half-hour debate each week on where you should go and what you should do. But even if you and your best friend have the same interests, this doesn't make the two of you a team. You only become a team when you work together in a complementary way.

A simple example should make this clearer. If you ever see two nurses make a bed you will witness teamwork. Each knows his/her own role. They work together to do the job in less than half the time it would take each of them to do it individually. They may then split up to do different, complementary jobs in different places. They don't get in each other's way, they don't argue about 'who does what', they don't 'check up on each other'. They are both equally responsible for doing the work properly and by the required deadline.

Our definition of a team, therefore, is

> A small number of people who possess complementary skills and who are working together to accomplish common goals.

Teams in business

You may wonder why teams are considered important in business organisations. The reason is that effective teams have several benefits – both for the organisation and for the individuals who are in them. These include:

- a variety of skills and abilities
- higher standards of work – as jobs can be allocated to maximise the strengths of individuals
- work done more quickly (this is often called **synergy**)
- more flexibility – members can be multi-skilled to cover for absences or to meet particular challenges
- less duplication of work or effort – especially if communications are good and the team is used to working together
- better cooperation between people – who see the 'team achievement' as important
- a happier and more motivated workforce – because team members support and help one another
- improved communications – because the team consult each other
- a higher level of commitment from staff – people are usually more motivated if they work with other people, can share problems and ideas, especially if this is done in a friendly atmosphere.

The organisation benefits because work is of a higher standard and productivity is better. Individuals benefit because they get support from other team members, they can exchange information and obtain advice, and they obtain greater job satisfaction by working cooperatively with other people.

Effective teams

Not all teams are effective. A team will be useless if its members criticise or distrust each other, if one person is forever taking the credit, if the team members are always disagreeing, or if no one knows what they are supposed to do – or why! It is the difference between five untrained amateurs trying to create a meal in an unknown kitchen and a well-practised team of trainee chefs doing the same thing. One is chaos, the other is a slick operation.

There are several common characteristics of effective teams:

- Each person knows what the team is trying to achieve – and is committed to this. The team's aim should be more important than an individual's personal aims.
- Each person knows what his or her role is as a member of the team – and the roles of other members.
- Everyone takes collective responsibility for the quality and quantity of the work produced.

- Each member feels that his own efforts are appreciated by the others.
- Each member knows the other members can be relied upon for support when necessary, for instance if they are very busy or having difficulty with something.
- No one feels 'put down' or ignored – all have an equal status or contribution to make.
- Each member respects the others and listens to what they have to say.
- The team knows how to relax and how to have fun together!

A good team is not formed overnight. This was the major reason put forward for England's disastrous performance in Euro 2000. A team needs time to 'grow' – for the members to get to know each other and to learn about each other, to develop trust and to find out about the others' strengths and weaknesses – and how to respond to or compensate for these. A team put together quickly, for a particular purpose, is unlikely to be successful immediately – as Kevin Keegan found out at Euro 2000!

The team can also be strengthened or weakened by the choice of team leader. A good team leader, who is respected by all the members and who is the 'natural' leader, can do wonders for team morale and performance. A poor leader does the opposite. You will learn more about the qualities required of team leaders as you progress yourself and study at level 3 or beyond. Being a good team leader can be a difficult job – as can being a good team member! People often have to make a positive effort to function well in a team as it isn't easy to put the aims of a group of people higher than the things you personally want to achieve.

Your contribution to your team

People who are very self-centred or interested only in themselves rarely make good team members. However, there is nothing to stop you being good both in a team and on your own as well. You will find it easier to work in a team if you possess most, if not all, of the following qualities:

- You find it easy to be loyal, supportive and cooperative with other people.
- You like communicating with people and are happy to listen to other people's ideas and help to build on these.
- Your natural tendency is to roll up your sleeves and 'muck in' to help if there is a crisis.
- You want to support other people, particularly when they are having difficulties.
- You are flexible and are happy to learn new skills.
- You honour your commitments and don't let people down.
- You don't expect other people to be perfect.
- You prefer to do things with other people and are quite happy to 'share the glory' if things go well.

- You think before you speak – and don't needlessly upset people by making tactless remarks.

INFORMATION UPDATE

The vogue for teams in Britain came from America, but it arrived there from Japan! Teams had their origins in the 1950s and 1960s when organisations such as Volvo in Sweden used teams for car production. However, in the 1970s and 1980s, Western producers also associated the success of Japanese businesses – especially their car manufacturers – with the use of teams. To many people teams then became a possible magic solution to improving quality and productivity so there was a huge surge in the idea that anywhere a group of people undertook work, a team could do it better.

Today people are more aware of the limitations of teams. They are not suitable in every situation or for every person. High-flying entrepreneurs like Richard Branson, for instance, may not be good team players but are still very successful. Teams are also no good if you work in a cut-throat business where it is 'each person for him/herself' – such as competing sales reps who each has his or her own territory. Where teams are ideal, however, is when a group of people have a variety of skills, all of which are needed to do a job well (e.g. teachers who have a joint responsiblity for the success of students taking a particular course). If people work cooperatively together *on those particular types of task* this can still bring many benefits – even though they are not fully operational as a team all the time. Moreover, if they see the work they do together as being important, and work towards this as a collective goal, everyone will benefit.

TEST YOUR KNOWLEDGE AND UNDERSTANDING

1 State which of the following you consider (or hope) are teams and which are not, and justify your decision in each case:
   a an emergency crew of paramedics
   b hairdressers who work in the same shop
   c the pilot and co-pilot in an aircraft
   d the cabin crew on the same flight
   e the teachers in a school
   f a pit crew which changes tyres and refuels Formula One cars during a race
   g a band of musicians.

2   Each of the following people belongs to a **dysfunctional** (not
    working very well) team. Read their descriptions of a recent event
    and say what essential team factor(s) are missing in each case:

    a   Mandy: 'Sharon never trusts us to do anything. She's constantly
        checking up on us and this wastes time.'
    b   John: 'It's hopeless working alongside Brian. He's so slow
        I could do the job myself in half the time.'
    c   Karen: 'Emily is a pest. She never tells anyone anything – unless
        you're psychic it's best to leave her to do her own thing.'
    d   Phil: 'Rob'll promise you anything, just to get rid of you. I've
        tried everything from pleading to screaming but nothing
        changes.'
    e   Keith: 'I don't care what anyone says, collecting the post is
        Carla's job. I don't see why I should have to learn to do it.'

Identifying your team

In a small business, your 'team' may comprise three individuals in a tiny
office. In a large organisation, it may be more difficult to identify exactly
who belongs to your team – especially if you work somewhere where the
word 'team' is rarely used or seldom used in its correct sense. Generally a
good test for identifying your team is to recognise:

* who you work with regularly on the same type of job(s)
* who you collaborate with over certain jobs
* which people have a shared responsibility, with you, for certain goals or
  certain areas of work.

In some organisations, teams are formed for certain purposes and then disbanded.
Such a team might have to prepare everything required for an exhibition or to
develop a website, or even to think up the name of a new product. In that case
individuals might be members of more than one team – for a short time anyway.
If you work somewhere where there are official teams then you may be
responsible to a team leader, rather than a supervisor or manager.

In any team, however, you should find that people have different roles or tasks
to do. The team leader's role is fairly obvious, but what about the others?

Each person in the team will have his or her own job description and job
role. Ideally, if you put them all together, these should cover all the work
which needs to be done by that particular team. There should also be some
overlaps – so that if one member of the team is absent the work can be done
by another member.

In many large organisations there are **functional teams**, which operate in
different departments. There is a sales team, a customer service team, a finance
team, and so on. In those circumstances you are likely to identify your team as

being the members of your department. A word of warning, however. If you work in a large department there are likely to be various teams and, if you are one administrator among many, you are probably better identifying with this team than with a larger group of people.

Ideally, of course, if you take all the different teams you can see how each fits into and contributes to the whole work of the organisation. It's rather like a large jigsaw – only instead of viewing your organisation as a set of departments, you are thinking of it as groups of teams instead.

CHECK IT OUT!

In addition to different job roles, a specialist who did a lot of research on teams, Dr Meredith Belbin, also identified that different members have different **behavioural roles**. Belbin is famous for saying that an individual can never be perfect but a team can be – by this he meant that with the right mix of abilities a team can have more strengths than any one individual.

Therefore, an ideal team has people with different personalities and attributes. One person is keen on rapid action (to 'push' the team forward), another is a 'people-person' (who takes on a caring role), another is the 'detail' person who sees that tasks are finished properly, another is the creative genius who comes up with the bright ideas, another is the coordinator who brings things together. Obviously in a team of two or three this means that people have to take on two or more behavioural roles. Equally, if you and your co-workers are all 'action' types you may have a problem with co-ordination or checking details unless one of you takes over these roles.

Look around your own team and try to identify the behavioural styles of the people in it. Equally importantly, think about your own. Finally, do you think there are any key behavioural roles your team is missing? Note down your ideas. You may like to note that this type of thinking will come in useful when you start to assemble your evidence for the second element in this unit.

Team responsibilities

If each team is responsible for part of the organisation's work, removing one would be rather like taking a piece out of the jigsaw – the picture would then be incomplete. For that reason, the contribution of every single team is important to the organisation as a whole. However, on certain occasions some teams are more important than others, particularly if they have been formed for a particular purpose. A team of salespeople visiting a prospective major customer will be considered more vital to the organisation's goals, at that moment, than a team of painters redecorating an office – for fairly obvious reasons. However, the situation may be different if the boss is expecting a visit from a VIP the following day!

Administrators often undervalue their roles – both individually and as members of a team. Yet if a team of administrators ceased to function or fulfil its responsibilities the effects would be quite dramatic and would soon have repercussions throughout the organisation. For instance:

- on reception, visitors would stand around not knowing where to go or who to see
- in sales, orders wouldn't be processed, customer queries would receive no response, the organisation would rapidly lose money
- in finance, invoices wouldn't be sent, payments wouldn't be banked, debtors wouldn't be chased for money
- in purchasing, goods wouldn't be ordered, stocks would run low and eventually run out.

However, teams can divide their responsibilities into those that are critical to the organisation and those that are less critical. Processing orders, for instance, is more important than clearing out some old leaflets if you are a member of the sales team. The easy way to identify the major responsibilities of your team is to think of the critical jobs which it does – jobs which one of you would have to take on fairly promptly if another member of the team were absent. The other test is to think what would happen, and what is the worst that could happen, if the job wasn't done at all.

Your organisation – its business, aims and objectives

In many businesses, the most critical parts of any job are those which affect the customers – either directly or indirectly. Anything that could cost the organisation money is considered a 'critical area'. The reason is quite simple. If organisations don't remain profitable they go out of business and there will be no teams or individuals working there at all.

If you work as a hospital administrator or in your local town hall you may think you are exempt from this kind of thinking. However, even these types of service organisations have to be aware of their customers these days (think of the Patients' Charter) and have to keep costs as low as possible.

The best way of finding out how you, as an individual, and the work done by your team fits into the business as a whole is to find out more about the aims and objectives of your organisation.

The aims may be formally written in a **mission** or **vision statement**. For instance, if you work for McDonald's the mission statement tells you that you are working in the food industry because it says 'To provide great-tasting food backed up by excellent operations and friendly service in a relaxed, safe and consistent restaurant' and you could easily deduce that friendly (and speedy) service was fairly important to their operation. Equally, if you were working for Shelter (the charity) you would find its mission statement was 'To pursue the aim of the right to a stable and affordable home for every member of the community' so you should realise you would be involved in housing issues relating to the homeless.

Your organisation may publish specific aims each year – together with a list of objectives. The aims say *what* the business intends to achieve over the next few years, while the objectives state *how* the aims are going to be achieved. This will often affect your own work in the future, so it is useful to have some idea what they are! You can also usefully use this information to identify areas where you would like to develop personally in the future. Finding out that your organisation intends to develop or expand sales over the Internet, for instance, should prompt you to develop your IT knowledge and skills, particularly if you work in an area such as sales which is likely to be directly affected.

EVIDENCE COLLECTION

Prove to your assessor that you have the knowledge and understanding required for this part of the unit – and set the scene for the rest of your evidence – by preparing a brief summary about your own team and its work. You may be asked to put this into your portfolio or, alternatively, you can use it as a basis for a discussion with your assessor.

1 Think about the teams you work with – that is, the areas where you have to cooperate with other people. You may belong to more than one team (for instance, if you are an administrator in a finance department).

2 Make a list of the people in your team(s) apart from yourself.

3 State each person's name and their official job title.

4 Provide a brief description of the work carried out by your team(s). State, too, how this contributes to the aims and objectives of your organisation and helps the business as a whole.

5 Identify the main responsibilities of your team(s) – particularly the critical areas of work which must be done, no matter what.

If you feel you work far more as an individual than as a member of a team, and are having difficulties identifying your 'team', then do ask your adviser or your assessor for help. Even the administrator described at the start of this unit could classify herself as a member of a team if she also included the three people who ran the business as well!

Element 201.1 Work effectively with other team members

Who are your team members at work? It will help if you look back at the definition of teams on page 52. Your team may consist of those people:

- who work on the same type of jobs as you
- who work in your office
- who work in the same section or branch as yourself.

In addition to the team members there will also be a team leader. This may be your line manager (the person most directly senior to you), your supervisor or someone else.

For this element, you also have to provide evidence that you can communicate with the members of your team in *all* of the following ways:

- face to face
- by telephone
- in writing.

For this unit, your written communications can be brief reports or relatively informal documents, such as telephone messages and short progress reports.

Communicating with other team members

Unless you have a very unusual job, you are likely to communicate with most of the members of your team every single day you are at work. They will rely on you to pass on information, both formally and informally, in a variety of ways.

Your communications may range from very informal verbal exchanges across the office, to more formal events, such as attending a team meeting or having a discussion with a manager. Much will depend upon the type of organisation you work for and its 'culture' or 'style' as to the general style of internal communications.

Organisations operating on more formal lines, such as most solicitors' or accountants' offices, are likely to be relatively quiet and the atmosphere is more subdued. In this situation you may have little contact with senior partners or anyone outside your own team. This contrasts sharply with organisations which operate on more informal lines or which deal in rapid information as part of their trade. If you work for a newspaper or radio station, for instance, you are likely to find that the style is much more frenetic and informal with everyone on first-name terms. In this case you may make regular contact with a much wider range of people.

Generally, in all businesses, internal communications are more informal than those sent externally. However, that doesn't mean that you can use the same style or 'tone' as you would with your friends and relatives! You may be able to do this if you are communicating with people of your own age who you work alongside every day and know very well. However, you would be wise to remember that your supervisor and manager – and anyone much older to you – will usually expect a slightly different approach.

Face-to-face communications

There are a variety of methods of communicating face to face. The most basic, and informal, is when you simply talk to someone at the next desk. A more formal method is when you have an appraisal interview or a discussion with your boss about your work. These are both examples of 'one-to-one' communication, because only two people are involved. However, face-to-face communication also occurs at meetings – large and small, informal and formal. The difference is, of course, that you are one person among a number of people on those occasions – all of whom are communicating different information and opinions.

When you are communicating with someone face to face, the meaning of your verbal (spoken) 'message' or information is affected by your **body language**. This is the non-verbal (unspoken) signals you send out by your posture, your facial expressions, your gestures and your eye contact (or lack of it). All these give a message to the other person or other people present about your general manner and attitude.

With our friends, there is a normally a straightforward match between body language and words. If you or your best friend are approached by someone you both don't like very much, your body language will show this. You may turn away from them, refuse to make eye contact and speak dismissively or sharply to get rid of them. At work, this is normally not advisable. Scowling at your supervisor as you approach her desk is hardly likely to do much for your future prospects, so there are times when you have to be more aware of the non-verbal signals you are sending out. You also have to be careful that your body language matches the words you are saying. Claiming you don't mind re-doing a job and sighing deeply immediately afterwards is an obvious example of your attitude and manner 'cancelling out' the words you are saying!

This is usually more important when you are dealing with your managers and supervisors than when you are talking to a colleague of your own age across the office, and the following 'golden rules' are most relevant when you are communicating more formally face-to-face. However, some of the points are simply good manners – so they are worth noting for all occasions.

Golden rules for face-to-face communications

1   Look pleasant (it costs nothing to smile).

2   Pick your time – don't try to give someone important information when he or she is distracted, on the telephone, or trying to do something else.

3   If the information is at all confidential or sensitive, pass it on only when you are alone with the recipient.

4   Think about what you are going to say before you say it.

5   Use an appropriate tone of voice and choice of words for the person you are talking to. The same phrases you would use to a colleague of your own age may be less appropriate for an older manager.

6   Speak clearly and concisely – don't take ten minutes to say something which could be condensed into two.

7   Keep to the point – don't wander off the subject.

8   *Listen* to the reply – don't be in such a hurry to speak again that afterwards you can't remember what was said.

9   Watch the other person's body language for clues as to how he or she is reacting to what you are saying – and adjust your style if necessary.

10   Don't interrupt someone mid-way through his or her reply.

11   If you are naturally shy, especially in a group or when speaking to a senior manager, try to forget yourself and concentrate on what you want to say. If you are providing relevant or important information, people will want to hear it.

12   If you are in a meeting, and can't get a word in edgeways, use body language to try get the attention of the person leading the meeting by leaning forward and making eye contact.

13   If you are in a long meeting and are bored, try to avoid 'switching off' and leaning back or staring out of the window! Firstly, you might miss something important. Secondly, your body language will give you away immediately.

TEST YOUR KNOWLEDGE AND UNDERSTANDING

1   In the team meeting illustrated opposite on page 63, which of the members are bored and which are interested in what is being said?

Maria is new in your office and is rather scared of the manager, John Temple, who is apt to be rather short with people, especially when he's busy. As a result, when Maria has information to give him she either asks someone else to do it or, if they are too busy, she gabbles the message to him so quickly he can't understand it. This makes him cross and even more sharp with her – which makes her even worse. What advice would you give to Maria to help?

Communicating by telephone

Telephone technique and telephone systems are covered in detail in Unit 203. However, some points you may wish to bear in mind relate *only* to internal calls and communicating with members of your team

- On most systems you can differentiate between internal and external incoming calls by the type of ring. Knowing the difference is useful, but note that you should answer internal calls just as quickly as external ones. It could be your boss or a senior manager on the other end, getting more irritated with every ring!
- Always identify yourself to the person at the other end. If you work in a large organisation, give your extension or your section/department as well.
- Don't ignore a ringing telephone if another member of your team is away from his or her desk for a short time – or in the middle of a job which would be difficult to leave.
- If you are going to be away from your desk, either warn people if you are expecting a call *or* divert your calls to another extension so they won't go unanswered.
- If you share an extension, find out who is calling before you pass the handset over – and tell your colleague who it is.
- If you take a message for someone, make sure you find out all the information likely to be needed. Don't make double the work for them trying to work out what was requested.
- If you are making the call on behalf of a member of your team (or your supervisor or manager) then say so. Simply say, 'Paul Webster asked me to ring you about ... .'

- Don't make jokes or banter unless you are speaking to someone who knows you *very* well. Remember that on a telephone your body language cannot be seen, so the listener cannot tell whether you are serious or not. The listener might also not share your sense of humour.
- Don't divulge confidential or sensitive information – even to another department – without checking with your supervisor first.
- Be as courteous, clear and concise on the telephone to your colleagues as you would to outside callers.

Communicating in writing

In this unit we will concentrate on brief messages and reports – and general hints and tips in relation to written communications. More information on written communications is given in the Appendix, page 495.

A first tip. Over the telephone you may say something tactless or insensitive that you later regret – but at least the moment has gone and you can hope no one else will remember it. If you do the same thing in writing, the proof is there for ever more – and for everyone to see. Therefore, even though you should 'think before you speak' on the phone, it's doubly important that you think before you write – even when the message is going to be passed on only internally.

The following are examples of the many types of occasion on which you have to produce written information:

- your boss wants a brief update on something you have been doing
- you have to send an e-mail or a memo to a member of your team
- you are asked to put a suggestion or an idea in writing
- you take a message for someone in your team.

Because the communication is internal, this does not mean that you can hurriedly scrawl anything you want on a piece of paper. Even your closest colleagues will expect messages they can read and understand. Your team leader may expect rather more.

Golden rules for written communications

1 Watch your tone! The wording should be different if you are communicating with a senior member of staff rather than with your closest friend in the office.
2 Bear in mind the reason for the communication – who will see it and why it will be used. Don't add remarks that you wouldn't like other people to see.
3 Think about the type of communication. A brief report should be more formal than a handwritten note or e-mail.
4 Keep to the point and don't add any personal remarks or observations – unless you have been specifically asked to give your opinions.

5   Make sure all the key items are included: the recipient's name, the date, all the main points you must include, your name as the sender.

6   Check it carefully for punctuation, spelling and grammar (see also the Appendix, page 495).

EVIDENCE COLLECTION

Label a folder 'Unit 203 – Communications evidence'. Put into this copies of any documentary evidence you have which proves how you have communicated in writing with your manager, supervisor or other staff in your team. These may be copies of messages you have passed on, copies of brief reports or summaries you have prepared. Remember you will need evidence to cover communicating with *both* your line manager (or supervisor or team leader) *and* other people in your team.

Start a log on which you can enter information about times you communicated with them on a face-to-face basis or over the telephone. Useful headings would be the date, method of communicating, person you communicated with and the reason for the call or chat.

Supporting and helping team members

On page 73–74 you will learn about the attributes people value in other members of their team. One of the most important of these, without doubt, is a willingness to be both supportive and helpful. This may seem straightforward – we all like to think of ourselves as supportive and helpful! However, can you honestly answer 'yes' to the following:

- Do you understand 'supportive' to mean totally loyal? That is, you would never let down a colleague, unfairly put the blame on anyone, talk about someone behind their back (no matter what you really thought of them), never spread gossip about them, and do your best to 'cover' for them if they had a problem (even if you advised them they should really talk about it with their supervisor).

- Do you understand 'helpful' to mean being prepared to help in a crisis (even with a really boring job you hate doing) and *volunteering* to help without having to be asked, if you have the time to spare?

Additionally, different types of team members may have slightly different expectations about you:

- Your **supervisor**, **line manager** or **team leader** depends on you to do the work they have given you, as agreed, unless there is a particular problem which means you cannot. In this case, they depend on you to tell them in good time for them to take remedial action! They also depend on you to do the work to the standard required by your organisation. They also expect you to be loyal to the company and to be interested and committed to its success. After all, if it is *not* successful you would be directly affected by its closure.

- Your **other team members** depend upon you to work with them cooperatively, to be pleasant and friendly, not to be pleasant one day and unpleasant the next, and not to let them down in a crisis. Presumably, you depend upon them in much the same way.

The limits of your job role

There are, of course, limits to what you should be asked to do as part of your job. As an administrator, for instance, you should not be asked to sweep the floor or clean the windows. Your job description is the first basis which indicates the sort of work you will be asked to do. However, this does not mean you will be expected to check every request against it to see if it fits! To prevent this, most job descriptions have a 'catch-all' phrase in them anyway, which is worded something like 'and any other duties commensurate with the post'.

The phrase 'commensurate with the post' is important. It means you should not be asked to take on responsibility which is too much to expect for the level of your job. If your supervisor is off ill, for instance, you shouldn't be asked to take sole responsibility for the office.

It can be difficult to know, however, what you are allowed to do and not allowed to do if you are just asked to help someone. Legally, you shouldn't be asked to do anything which is unlawful (such as writing the wrong figure in an expense claim) or which is dangerous (such as walking across a building site without being issued with a protective helmet or rectifying a paper jam on a photocopier if you haven't been shown how to do this). However, this still allows people a fair amount of scope on the type of jobs they may ask you to do!

Broadly, if you are *capable* of doing the job *and* can do it without endangering your own deadlines and responsibilities, then it is churlish to refuse. If you are nervous about doing something new and are worried about making a mistake, then say so. If you are shown, you may learn something and enjoy the experience. If you feel that what you are being asked to do is unethical or wrong in any way, then have a quiet word with your supervisor *before* you agree. As you work longer for an organisation and get to know it better, you will get used to the type of 'extra' jobs people are asked to do – and those which are allowable and those which are not. You may, for instance, work for a firm where your boss asks you to do the odd personal errand during your lunch hour. You have the right to say 'no' – but how wise this will be if you want your boss to think well of you is another matter.

Finally, if you do get on in the organisation and move to a more responsible position, never be 'too important' to help out your previous team members who are now 'below you' – if you have the time – especially if there is a crisis. Otherwise you are likely to destroy many of the good relationships you have worked so hard to develop.

EVIDENCE COLLECTION

Identify the people you consider to be your team members at work (i.e. your supervisor or manager and other staff in your team). In each case identify:

a the person

b their job role (e.g. supervisor, manager or team leader)

c over what aspects of your job you relate to each person

d how you think each person depends upon you – and how you depend upon them.

This information will help your assessor to put into context the evidence you produce for this unit as he or she will have a better understanding of the people you classify as your team members at work.

How to say 'no' – nicely

There are times when, even though you would like to help someone and even though it would be quite acceptable for you to do so, you are too busy yourself to even think about it. On these occasions you have no alternative but to refuse.

Saying 'no' is something many people find very difficult – particularly if the person making the request is very persistent, important or likely to take offence easily. The best way is to give a clear explanation followed by, if you can, a positive suggestion, along the lines of: 'I'm really sorry I can't help at the moment but I have to finish sending the post. Have you asked Louise if she can spare a minute? – I think she's just finished what she's doing.'

Some people are expert are saying 'no' without causing offence. In this case you are likely to find that they have learned the difference between passivity, assertion and aggression!

If you are **passive**, meekly agreeing to everything and objecting to nothing, then – unless you are very fortunate – you will find that you are often overloaded, stressed and feeling miserable. You may also fall behind with your own work and then get the blame. In this case you may feel you are a victim, or the office martyr, and can do nothing about the circumstances in which you find yourself. If, however, you are **aggressive** and regularly challenge and confront other people then you are unlikely to be very happy either – and neither will anyone else! People will very soon avoid you as they will not want to provoke a strong, negative reaction.

Being **assertive** means stating your case, but in such a way that you do not upset other people. This isn't always easy. Try the following steps as a guide:

a Listen while a request is being made, or while a statement is being made about which you disagree.
b Use the word 'I' when you respond, not the word 'you' (which can sound accusatory).
c Don't *start* your response with the word 'no'.
d Acknowledge the other person's point of view or reason for asking.
e Then state, clearly and pleasantly, why you can't comply or why you disagree.

TEST YOUR KNOWLEDGE AND UNDERSTANDING

1 Jenny's boss wants her to rearrange her holidays, if possible, because another member of her team will be away at the same time. Which are the assertive, aggressive and passive responses in the situations below?　　➡

a 'Why me? You must be joking. Ask Mary instead.'

b 'I suppose I'll have to, won't I?'

c 'I understand the problem and I'd like to be able to help but unfortunately it's impossible for me to change at this stage without losing my deposit.'

2 A member of Sam's team, Ben, is always leaving a mess around the office. This morning, to Sam's annoyance, there are a number of papers and files spread around his desk – which Ben had 'taken over' after Sam had left yesterday. Which are the assertive, aggressive and passive responses in the situations below?

a 'Please can you clear up the mess on my desk if you've a minute. Or if you're too busy, I suppose I'll have to do it.'

b 'Ben, I'm really unhappy about having my desk cluttered with your papers. I've stacked them up on your desk as I needed to work here myself. In future, please can you find somewhere else to work in this situation?'

c 'I'm sick and tired of the mess you make around here. If you clutter my desk again with anything I'll put the whole lot in the shredder.'

3 Identify two difficult situations when it would help you to be assertive. Then suggest an appropriate assertive response in each case.

INFORMATION UPDATE

In a survey by the recruitment consultancy Office Angels, bad habits which irritate people at work included: deserting the photocopier as soon as there is a paper jam – without trying to fix it or warning everyone else; people who let their mobiles ring in meetings; gossips; 'borrowers' who don't return items they have taken; and those who make a coffee for themselves without offering to make one for anyone else!

Other surveys have identified the following as 'irritating workers': those who moan and grumble all the time, those who are obsequious (will say anything to flatter the boss), those who tell tales, and those who 'disappear' when there's an emergency or a lot of work to be done.

The most valued, in many cases, are those people who *offer* to help, without being asked, when they see there is a problem.

Essential information

At work you will handle many different types of information every day. Some of this will be routine, other types will be more critical. Information is critical or *essential* if it must be passed to other members of your team promptly. You will learn more about this in Unit 203, but it is important for this unit, too.

Information is essential if it would have an effect on:

- a decision which is being made
- a job someone else is doing
- the actions of someone else.

If you fail to pass on essential information (or pass it on incorrectly), you could very well create serious problems for someone else at worst, or considerable annoyance at best. There is nothing more infuriating than to be given a critical piece of information some time after you needed it – such as someone saying, just after you have missed lunch and worked furiously to finish an urgent report for your boss, 'Oh, sorry, didn't I tell you? Brian had to leave to see a client so he said it would do in the morning.'

There is a *slight* excuse if your colleague could have argued that she didn't know you were working on the report – although it is only slight, because if you are members of the same team and communicate properly she should have been aware of what you were doing. However, as an administrator it is your responsibility to learn, as quickly as possible, what types of information are likely to be essential and which are not. With experience you will develop a sixth sense for this in your own workplace (although you will have to relearn this if you change jobs). The golden rule is: if in any doubt whatsoever, err on the side of caution and pass it on quickly. Any reasonable person would far rather be given the odd piece of information promptly which wasn't essential than be in danger of not receiving information which is.

The importance of passing on messages and how to do this – even if the recipient is unavailable – is covered in Unit 203 on page 166.

TEST YOUR KNOWLEDGE AND UNDERSTANDING

1 Jack likes to give the impression he's fairly laid back and little bothers him. However, recently he has created a few problems by his inability to pass on information properly. On Monday he told the supervisor that a visitor called in during the lunchtime to see her, but he'd forgotten the man's name. On Tuesday, he gave her a telephone number which was incorrect so when she dialled it she got the 'unobtainable' signal. Yesterday, he gave the manager

information about the times of trains, but inaccurately – with the result that his manager is now stranded for an hour on a railway station 200 miles away. Despite Jack's attitude, he is not looking forward to tomorrow!

a   Give three serious consequences which could result from Jack's errors on Monday, Tuesday and yesterday.

b   Think of one example yourself (preferably from your own workplace) for which inaccurate or incomplete information could have serious consequences.

c   Jack's other major fault is to forget to pass on information altogether. If Jack had forgotten to tell the supervisor about Monday's visitor, would this have been better or worse? Give a reason for your answer.

d   If you were to advise Jack, as his friend, on how to improve his communications skills, what would you say?

2   Your boss is preparing for an important meeting tomorrow and has put the sign 'Do not disturb' on his door. You receive a phone call from a customer who says he must speak to your boss that afternoon. What will you do – and why?

3   Your supervisor, who is also your team leader, will be away from the office tomorrow to attend a meeting at the head office about the current level of sales. You have the following items on your desk to pass on to her:

(i)   three non-urgent orders to be signed;
(ii)   confirmation of a hire car booked for next week;
(iii)   last month's sales figures for your branch;
(iv)   a serious complaint from a customer;
(v)   a query about an invoice;
(vi)   a fax from head office saying the meeting will start an hour later than planned.

a   Which will you ensure she receives before she goes, and which could you safely hold back until she returns?

b   If you could give her only two items, which two would you choose?

c   What would you do with any other items you consider are essential or important?

Types of working relationships

A common aim for people at work – and their organisations – is overall harmony and cooperation between staff. You may hear of exceptions or read about them in the press, such as bosses who think they can rule by fear or will get more out of people by bullying them. Fortunately, these are in the minority for one simple reason. Unhappy staff do *not* work harder or better. They are normally so distracted by their problems they cannot even concentrate, let alone produce good work. Therefore, the vast majority of organisations and managers want their staff to be 'free' from personal anxiety, as much as possible, to focus on the job in hand. Your colleagues, too, will normally prefer a quiet life where they get on well with each other, can enjoy a joke, can rely on each other for support and reassurance. After all, everyone spends many hours working each week – so it is sensible to make this time as pleasant as possible.

However, this does not mean that you will always, in all circumstances, get on well *automatically* with everyone. Productive working relationships, like all other types, need some effort. In addition, given the fact that you cannot choose who you work with, there will be some people you like more than others – that is natural. How to cope when you find yourself continually at loggerheads with someone else is covered on page 77. In this section we look at the type of behaviour that will help you to develop and maintain good working relationships with the vast majority of people you work with, including other staff in your team.

Productive working relationships

These exist when:

- people are cooperative and consider each other's feelings
- there is a basic atmosphere of courtesy – people say 'please' and 'thank you' and don't find it difficult to apologise if they have done something wrong
- people are respected and supported when they try something new, and are not blamed or criticised even if it has not been as successful as was hoped
- there is loyalty and team camaraderie
- people are praised for doing well and feel valued by their managers and other members of the team
- decisions are fair and made for good reason, and these reasons are explained to people
- all team members make an effort to listen to and understand each other's views (if they disagree they debate the *issue* and don't attack the person).

Unproductive working relationships

These are created or made worse by:

- an atmosphere of blame and distrust
- poor or indecisive management – or a boss who obviously has favourites
- self-opiniated or dictatorial team members who don't listen to other people but insist they are always right
- open conflict and infighting between individual team members which affects everyone else
- some team members working less hard than others, and being allowed to, so the others feel they are 'mugs' for putting up with it – and promptly work less hard themselves.

Developing interpersonal skills

Some people find it much easier than others to get on with people. If you are naturally quiet and reticent you may find a large and noisy office quite overwhelming until you get used to your colleagues. Normally, however, if you watch how people behave at work you can notice certain attributes which are common amongst those who have good interpersonal skills. You can easily apply these yourself, no matter where you work.

With your team leader, supervisor or manager

- Appreciate the pressures these people are working under, and how these may affect them.
- Make your priorities the same as theirs.
- Don't make a drama out of a crisis. If you have a problem state the facts clearly and unemotionally, and in plenty of time for something to be done to put matters right.
- Give due respect for seniority and status.

With other staff in your team

- Treat them all fairly. Don't be nice to some and not to others.
- Make allowances for individual personalities. *Expect* people to have views different from your own (that's part of what makes life interesting!) and to have different ways of working.
- Don't expect people to drop everything if you have a last-minute crisis.
- Repay favours whenever you can.
- Give people 'space' if they are having a bad day or are out of sorts.
- Don't deliberately cause problems in the team, for instance by challenging the views of the team leader behind his/her back. If you have a problem with a decision, ask to speak to the team leader yourself in private.

With everyone else

- Be courteous and polite – it costs nothing! Remembering to say 'please' and 'thank you' may not seem like much, but it will influence how people respond to you.
- Be loyal – don't talk about people behind their back, don't spread gossip, don't point out their mistakes to other people. This is a key aspect of being supportive.
- Learn to admit your mistakes. It isn't easy to say you were wrong or made an error, but you will be respected for doing so. Don't grovel, simply apologise. *Never* blame someone else for something you have done wrong.
- Don't rush relationships. Accept that you will get on better with some people than others, especially at the start. Try not to form hasty judgements about anyone – you could be very wrong!
- Be generous – give praise when praise is due, give help when you can without jeopardising your own responsibilities. *Never* take the credit for someone else's good idea.
- Learn to think before you speak, so that you don't upset people by being tactless or thoughtless.
- Learn to listen when other people are putting their point of view – and try to see what they mean or where they might be making a valid point. Remember, no one is ever *completely* wrong!
- Keep secrets you are told and promises you make.
- Learn to be a prompt, accurate and reliable communicator (see pages 61–65).
- Be prepared to help out when there is a problem or if you see that someone needs a hand.

Finally, bear in mind that, like friendships, positive working relationships with other people and in teams take time to develop and cannot be rushed. We are all wary of strangers until we get to know them. With all the people you work with there will be times when you have to bite your tongue and show tolerance – but this is well worth while.

TEST YOUR POTENTIAL AS A VALUABLE COLLEAGUE AND TEAM MEMBER

We are all critical of other people in some way – but equally we are all apt to think that we are the perfect person to work with! See how well this applies to you by selecting one answer from each of the options to the questions below.

1   On your second day in a new job, another member of your team shows you how to send faxes on the office fax machine. It is identical to one you have used before. Do you:

  a   say that you think you know how to use it and offer to demonstrate whilst she watches you send the first one

  b   immediately say that you don't need to be shown – you've used the machine before

  c   wait until after the demonstration – then tell your colleague she needn't have bothered showing you?

2   Your new boss is annoyed because he can't find a file you had yesterday. You think one of the other administrators, Sarah, had it this morning. Do you:

  a   apologise furiously and then try to find it

  b   say you'll find it as quickly as you can – and go and find Sarah

  c   tell him Sarah must have taken it when you weren't looking?

3   You take an urgent and complicated telephone message for a colleague who is at a meeting. Do you:

  a   carefully check all the details, write the message out neatly and make sure your colleague receives it the moment the meeting has ended

  b   write out the message on a piece of paper and put it on your colleague's desk

  c   pass it on verbally in the corridor when you next see your colleague?

4   You are in the middle of an urgent job and realise you won't get it finished in time. You ask a member of your team for help but she says that she is too busy herself at the moment to spare you any time. Do you:

  a   say nothing but wait until she needs your help – then refuse, just to get your own back

  b   stomp off in a rage to see your supervisor, and be icy cold with your colleague for weeks?

➡

c withhold judgement until you can assess whether she really is too busy to help you – but warn your supervisor there is likely to be a problem finishing the work?

5 An older team member is moody and critical and you find it difficult to get on with her. Do you:
a ignore her as much as you can
b have a word with someone who knows her better and try to find out the best way of handling her
c have it out with her, face to face, and ask her why she is so awkward with you?

6 You are trying to do a difficult job which needs concentration when a colleague interrupts you for the third time. Do you:
a visibly show your annoyance and respond snappily
b simply accept it as part of the job
c answer, but then ask if you can be left in peace for a while until you have finished what you are doing?

7 You find out through a mutual acquaintance that a male member of your team is having marital problems. Do you:
a say nothing
b tell the rest of your team, but only when he's not around to find out if they know any more
c just tell your best friend at work, and swear her to secrecy?

8 You hear a member of your team give a caller some incorrect information. Do you:
a say nothing – you don't want to make him look silly in front of a visitor
b immediately put your colleague straight – in front of the caller
c point out to your colleague that the situation has now changed and give the correct information to the caller?

9 The year-end accounts are due and everyone in your office is working hard to get them done in time. You want a day off for personal reasons, but think your request may be refused. Do you:
a stay off anyway, and say you are ill
b say nothing – there's no point in asking
c ask your supervisor if it's possible, and offer to work late for the next two nights to help?

➡

10 One evening you get home and realise in horror that you forgot to give some important and urgent information to a senior manager, who will be travelling to see a customer tomorrow. You don't have his home number. Do you:

a ring your team leader at home and tell her about the problem

b put it out of your mind overnight, but tell your team leader in the morning

c keep quiet and hope no one will find out?

Check your answers with the key on page 92.

When things go wrong: coping with difficult working relationships

If you asked a hundred people what makes a good team member or colleague it is very likely that the attributes they chose would be very similar – someone who is pleasant and friendly, helpful and patient, has a sense of humour, is a good listener, is neat and tidy, arrives on time and will stay to help in an emergency. This question is often asked by interviewers who want to bring new people into the organisation who will 'fit in' with the rest of the staff. Yet wherever you work you will find that you are with a mixture of people who have a variety of different characteristics – some more pleasing than others. How can this happen, given that each one of them will have all claimed to be friendly and helpful people when they were asked?

The reason is, of course, that all the members of your team are human beings – not angels or robots. They have good days and bad days. They may be stressed because they have too much work to do, a serious problem to solve or problems in their personal lives. In addition, they will have individual personalities so that they are each likely to react differently in a given situation. In a crisis one person may be superb, another may panic, a third may become irritable or short-tempered. If the third one is the boss, then this will affect how *other* people react – and so on.

For that reason, working effectively with the other members of your team means that you need to be aware of:

• how they individually, and collectively, react to situations

• how *you* respond to situations – and how this affects them.

Fundamentally, the best measure you can use to assess your own behaviour is to ask yourself if you are treating other people as you would like to be treated yourself – and if you are following the main guidelines you have already read. If you are, and you are still having problems with someone else in your team, what should you do?

Types of conflict

Broadly, there are two main types of conflict one can have with other people:

- conflicts over issues or ways of working
- conflicts over personal characteristics – often called a 'personality clash'.

Conflicts over issues

Conflicts over issues are normally easier to resolve than conflicts over personal characteristics, because they have a focus – something in particular is causing the problem. If a new filing cabinet is being delivered and staff are arguing about where it should go, this is a conflict over an issue. If you are trying to do a job with someone who wants to do it in a different way, this is a conflict over ways of working. Again it has a focus – and a decision will have to be made quickly unless you are both going to miss the deadline!

If you are involved in this type of conflict, ask yourself how important the issue is to you. People often get very het up over very minor matters – particularly if they are busy or stressed. Try not to do this. Does it *really* matter where the filing cabinet goes? Does it *really* matter if you have to do a job in a slightly different way for once – so long as it is done properly? Often, if you are prepared to compromise on unimportant issues, then the odd time you really feel strongly about something people may be more happy to do things your way. In this case, state your reasons calmly and logically. Stick to the facts – don't make it an argument against a particular individual.

Conflicts over personal characteristics

Personality clashes between two people can cause more problems, because there is not a clear focus and it is often difficult for other people to see why there is a problem. Yet this will not help you if you have to work alongside someone you really do not like.

A key factor in how we react to other people is whether they make us feel good about ourselves, or bad. It is human nature, if we meet someone who makes us feel bad, to want to retaliate (to make them feel as bad as we do) or to avoid them completely. Whilst you may be able to stop seeing someone in your private life, this is often impossible at work.

What type of behaviour makes you feel bad about yourself? Most people would respond by saying they have this reaction when:

- they are criticised in front of other people
- they are 'put down' if they suggest something
- they feel strongly that another person or group doesn't like them or is deliberately trying to exclude them
- they are subject to hurtful or tactless remarks
- they think someone else is deliberately trying to make life difficult for them (e.g. by being moody, sulking, being temperamental)

- someone else's way of working is so alien to them they almost feel that they are being deliberately difficult.

You may be able to add several more items to this list – and it is worth stopping for a moment to think what type of behaviour really annoys or upsets *you* – given we are all individuals and you may not agree with everything in the list above. You should also note that the word 'deliberately' occurs often in the list above. We are all more irritated (or hurt) if we feel someone has been *intentionally* awkward or nasty, rather than accidentally acted like this. Yet this isn't always the case!

Positive action over personality clashes

Once you have identified what it is in the other person's behaviour which is troubling you, the next part is very important. No matter how unreasonable they are, or how you think they should change, there is *absolutely nothing* you can do to make them change. The only behaviour you can change is *your own*.

This may come as a shock, particularly if you feel you are already doing everything you can to be a normal and pleasant human being.

The good news is that normally this has a positive effect. We all react to situations and individuals – so much so that we tend to do this in a 'pre-programmed' way, based on our previous experiences with them. Because we think we know what they will do and how they think and respond, we act accordingly. Think about this for a moment. If you work with two other team members and one is always fun and the other is often a bit of a moaner, you would normally react more positively with the first one and less so with the second. You are reacting to how you *think* they will behave – which is why you will get a slight jolt if the first happens to be upset on one occasion and the second is having a 'happy day'! And you would have to change your own responses to match.

If you don't get on with someone at work, then you need to change the way you respond to them. How you do this obviously depends upon how you were reacting originally, but some examples might help:

a If you were always trying to please them, stop for a while and give them more space. For a change wait until they want something from you.

b If you were being sharp or aggressive, or overly passive, re-read the section on assertiveness on page 68. For instance, if someone criticises you in public, say simply, 'I really wish you would speak to me alone if you want to make a criticism. I find it upsetting to be spoken to like that in front of everyone else.' However, *you* set the good example and say this when the two of you are alone. The other person then has to react to you on a one-to-one basis – without the benefit of an audience.

c Try to think of any other factors which might be influencing that person to behave towards you as he does – which may be out of your control. One person was particularly unpleasant to another in an office when she found out that the new administrator was better qualified – because this made her feel inadequate and insecure. It didn't help that before the new administrator started, the boss went on and on about how much better qualified she was than everyone else in the office. Her colleague reacted by trying to make life as difficult as possible in the hope that the new recruit would leave – and it took several months before they could work together cooperatively. So patience is sometimes the key.

d   Do think long and hard about whether you are over-reacting to the situation by taking remarks personally which weren't meant that way. Is the person really being deliberately difficult – or is this just your own perception? Is there anyone you can talk to who may have a more objective view of the situation?

e   Talk it over with a trusted friend or your mentor (see page 99). Talking about a problem often helps to get it into perspective. Try to choose someone else who also knows the person you are having problems with – but *not* someone who is having the same problems you are having, otherwise you'll probably just moan about it together.

f   Watch other people deal with this person. Are there any fundamental differences in the way they act or behave which will give you any clues?

g   If you are still having no success, and the situation is getting you down, discuss your problem with your mentor or with your supervisor – again in confidence. You may be given one or two suggestions you hadn't thought of, or one or two ideas to try, some of which you may not like the sound of very much. However, if you want to resolve the issue it is important to be as cooperative as possible – and this may become vital if the situation becomes serious.

h   If you get desperate, or the person causing the problem is senior to you, then you basically have three choices. If you work in a large organisation you could talk to personnel or to your supervisor and find out if there is any possibility of a sideways move to another section or department. You can look for a new job, or you can investigate the procedures in your organisation to deal with conflict – which is the topic of the next section.

Organisational procedures for dealing with conflict

In most organisations, the first stage for dealing with conflict which cannot be resolved between the people involved is normally informal. Your manager or supervisor will try to find out what the fundamental cause of the problem is. If the dispute is between two people, the manager would probably talk to them both individually first. If a group of people or a team have a grievance, the manager may want to speak to one or two as representatives of the others.

If you are involved in this type of discussion it is important to keep an open mind and to be as reasonable as possible. Keep to the facts. Don't bring in irrelevant arguments or pre-empt the meeting by lobbying everyone in the office for support. Don't assume people will be against you from the start, otherwise you'll behave defensively and aggressively.

Your supervisor, manager or team leader will be searching for some 'middle ground' on which agreement can be reached. This may mean instigating a new way of working or a reallocation of duties. This may be done over a trial period, after which the situation will be reviewed to see if it has improved.

Even if you are not totally happy with all the suggestions put forward, be as positive as you can. Your boss will be aiming for what is called a 'win, win' situation – where neither of you lose face. This is not easy, and can mean that there has to be some adjustment on both sides. It is useful if you have already thought about the situation so you know what your 'bottom line' is. This is the best you can reasonably hope for in the circumstances, which is probably rather less than your ideal solution.

Getting serious: grievance procedures

There are some issues which can occur at work which have to be dealt with more formally. Two examples are victimisation and harassment, whether sexual or racial. You have certain legal rights at work and, whilst these are beyond the scope of this scheme, it is sensible to find out what these are (see page 82). Most people are aware, however, that it is against the law to harass another person sexually or racially.

If you have a serious complaint against another member of staff then you need to find out about your organisation's grievance and appeals procedures. You should have been given details of these when you received your contract of employment. Normally there are three stages:

1　There will first be an interview with your line manager, in confidence, at which you can have a third person (a 'friend') present. This could be your mentor, your supervisor, another colleague or your union representative – it is your choice.
2　If the problem isn't resolved at stage 1, then an interview is held with a more senior manager, usually outside the department. Often this is the human resources or personnel manager. If you are a member of a union, they would be involved at this stage, too.
3　If the problem is still not resolved, an outside third party will be asked to make a recommendation. An official body which often undertakes this role is called ACAS – which stands for the Advisory, Conciliation and Arbitration Service.

However, using the formal grievance procedure is relatively rare. In most organisations, where there is good management and communications and hard-working employees, problems and conflict are usually solved informally at a very early stage.

TOP TWENTY EMPLOYEE RIGHTS IN THE WORKPLACE

1 To work in a safe environment.
2 To receive written details of your employment within two months of starting work, normally in a contract of employment.
3 To receive an itemised pay-slip, which shows your gross and net pay and details of any deductions.
4 To be paid a fair wage or salary – at or above the minimum wage level for your age.
5 To be provided with information about your rights at work.
6 To have any grievances properly dealt with.
7 To be accompanied by a union official when attending a disciplinary or serious grievance hearing.
8 Not to be discriminated against or harassed on grounds of race, sex or disability.
9 To be allowed to chose whether or not to join a trade union.
10 A working week limited to 48 hours over a 17-week reference period unless you have freely agreed to work longer hours or work in an 'excepted' occupation.
11 Freedom to choose whether to work on a Sunday, if you are requested to do so.
12 A minimum of four working weeks' paid holiday a year.
13 Payment for up to 26 weeks if you are suspended from work on medical grounds.
14 A minimum notice period of between one and 12 weeks, depending upon the length of time you have been continuously employed.
15 To be consulted over matters which significantly affect your terms and conditions of employment.
16 To be treated reasonably.
17 Time off for antenatal care and the right to paid maternity leave and the right to return to the job afterwards.
18 Up to 3 months' unpaid 'family' leave if you have children under 8.
19 Reasonable unpaid leave if you have a family emergency or domestic incident.
20 The right to claim unfair dismissal if you are sacked for no good reason, provided you have worked for the organisation for more than one year.

The law gives every employee certain rights at work. The top twenty rights are summarised in the chart opposite and you should have a broad appreciation of these for your own protection.

However, your employer also has certain rights. You have to arrive at work in person (you cannot send someone else to do your job); you have to be reasonably competent; you have to take care of your employer's property; and you have to carry out reasonable and legal instructions. You must also be honest and not give away trade secrets to your employer's competitors.

In addition, your employer's requirements in relation to your hours of work, holiday entitlement, place of work and the duties you have to carry out are detailed in your **contract of employment**. This is a legal document and both parties have to abide by the terms and conditions in it – so if you've never read it properly, now's the time to start! Finally, you must also comply with the health and safety procedures at your workplace, work towards the objectives of the organisation, and behave responsibly towards other employees.

Employees who do not comply with these requirements can be disciplined. You should have been informed where you can find details of your employer's disciplinary rules and procedures when you received your contract of employment. These are, in effect, the opposite of the grievance procedure and are instigated when your employer has a complaint about *you*, rather than the other way round. There are usually three stages – a verbal warning, a written (or final) warning, and instant suspension or dismissal for a very serious offence.

Check that you know both the grievance and disciplinary procedures at your workplace – for your own benefit, not just because you are studying for your NVQ award.

TEST YOUR KNOWLEDGE AND UNDERSTANDING

Each of the following situations has recently occurred in Mark's office. Identify which concern issues or ways of working and which relate to 'personality clashes'. In each case suggest how the problem might be resolved.

1 The aged fax machine is failing rapidly and Mark's supervisor has told the staff to choose a new model. Mark and Jenny cannot agree. Mark wants the larger model but appreciates the only space for it is alongside Jenny's desk. Jenny prefers the small one as this could be put midway between them.

2 Jenny, Mark and Karen all work in the sales office. The sales manager frequently visits customers and doesn't arrive back in the office until 4 pm – and always has several urgent jobs which must be done. Even with all three of them working hard they can rarely finish everything by the time they should normally leave at 5.15. Jenny lives some distance away and likes to leave promptly. Mark, too, likes to get away on time – so Karen is often the one who has to stay late. She feels very resentful about this and starts being uncooperative with Mark and Jenny as a result. Her supervisor sees what is happening and calls Karen in for a chat.

3 To help to cope with the increasing workload in the office, a new member of staff is appointed. Justine Parker is older than the other three and has had a considerable amount of previous experience in another organisation. By the end of the second week, Jenny, Mark and Karen are tired of hearing about how much better things were done where Justine previously worked. Jenny, in particular, gets very annoyed. She thinks Justine is patronising and difficult. A row erupted yesterday when it was Jenny's turn to make coffee for everyone and she became engrossed in typing a report. Justine angrily swept past her, saying 'If you want a job doing round here, do it yourself' and put the kettle on herself.

EVIDENCE COLLECTION

1   You will need to provide evidence to your assessor that you are capable of working effectively with your manager, supervisor or team leader and other staff in your team. You can do this in the following way.

   Write a description of how you interact with all these people and provide examples of when you have cooperated with them. Ask your supervisor to sign this for authenticity.

   Ask other members of your team for witness testimony. This is when they write about you. Do note that each one should provide specific examples – not just give you a general glowing report!

   Talk to your assessor about your working relationships and introduce him/her to your team.

2   You should also be prepared to talk to your assessor about problems with working relationships and what you would do if you were involved in a conflict you couldn't solve directly with your team members. This does not mean you need to instigate a conflict with someone just to provide evidence! If you have not been involved in this sort of situation, or if you have but would prefer to keep the issue confidential, then it is quite acceptable simply to answer questions to prove that you have considered this seriously and know what type of action would be appropriate to take – and what would not.

Element 201.2 Help to improve the work of your team

At the beginning of this unit you learned about teams. Recall that it was mentioned that teams need time to 'bond' and to get to know each other and that teams are not 'high performing' the first day they get together. You have also seen that the introduction of a new member to a team can cause problems.

This element is concerned with the *development* of the team and your contribution to that process – firstly in terms of the way in which the team carries out its work, and then in the way the team members relate to each other.

CHECK IT OUT!

Some organisations arrange team-building activities to help teams to develop. Often the team will be given a problem to solve and feedback will be given not just on their solution but, more importantly, on how they worked together. Some of these activities are held in specialist centres, so that teams can be involved in outdoor activities such as abseiling, canoeing or orienteering. More wacky alternatives include laser fights and paintball throwing!

Find out what opportunities exist in your organisation for this type of event and whether you and other staff in your team could be involved in one. You may be able to persuade your boss, if you can provide some tangible benefits for the organisation – and you will be better able to do that when you have finished this unit!

Continuous improvement

The phrase 'continuous improvement' can be applied to both organisations and teams. The theory is simple and is based on the fact that the environment in which everyone works is constantly changing, so that ways of working which were appropriate yesterday are not necessarily the best today. If organisations and teams are open, and willing to look at what they do, how they do it and what improvements can be made on a regular basis, then they will continually adapt and improve. They will learn from their previous experiences and move on. They will keep getting better. However, because things still change they will have to undertake this review process continually.

With a team this can be very important as, in addition to outside changes which affect the team, the membership of the team is also fluid. People leave and new people arrive. Teams may be adjusted or altered for specific reasons. Therefore a new group of people has to learn how to operate as a team. A new team is less likely to take advantage of all the opportunities it faces. It may not be too sure of its responsibilities. The team members may struggle to relate to each other. A well-established team, however, may become complacent and not realise that new priorities have become important. They may be poor at assessing their own performance and seeing how this could be improved. In this case, even though they were functioning well originally, today they will be less effective.

For teams to be continually effective, both the individual team members and the team as a whole must continue to develop.

Individuals must be aware of their personal development – both in terms of the skills they bring to the team and their ability to relate to other team members.

The *team* must be willing to:

* learn from past experience
* listen to each other
* be 'open' with each other (and not harbour grievances or resentment)
* consider new ideas and be prepared to change opinions
* work hard to foster good relations with each other.

This is a tall order and calls for a fair amount of maturity. The most difficult task, for most people, is being 'open' and being prepared to change one's mind. This is where your assertiveness skill becomes essential.

INFORMATION UPDATE

Much has been written about how teams develop, which you will learn about if you continue to higher levels of study. At this point it is useful to think of it as a four-stage process, as described below. As an example, think of any class you have belonged to at school or college, or even a group of friends you have been away with. Although these are not 'teams', as such, their development process is very similar.

1 Team members are at first strangers who have no knowledge of what is required. They are wary and both unwilling and unable to relate to all the others.

2 Team members settle down. They become more receptive but still do not know enough about each other to work together productively.

3   Team members now understand the work that is required. They start to focus more on the tasks they have to do. They start to work together better, though there may still be some misunderstandings and conflict between individual members.

4   Team members understand the task and understand each other. They have learned to respect each other's point of view and to allow issues which worry or concern them to be discussed openly. At this point the team is working together at its best.

Teams which are then disbanded often enter a fifth stage, where they can become quite emotional about parting. Think of situations in which you have had to leave a group of people you knew well – whether it was your last day at school or your last day on holiday with friends. At this point all disputes tend to be forgotten and everyone vows undying allegiance over a farewell meal!

Identifying improvements

A major contribution that effective team members can make is to suggest improvements or put forward good ideas about how the team could work better. You should never just do a job mechanically, without thinking about why it is done in that particular way, and whether it could be done any better. Normally, the person doing a task is the first one to see that improvements can be made. These may be very basic, such as:

*   suggesting that telephone message pads be used, so that there is an automatic copy made each time in case it is needed

*   recommending that a form be redesigned so it matches the type of information required by the computer database.

If you are recommending an improvement which will affect your own area of work, then you might have just your team leader or supervisor to convince. If you are recommending an improvement which will affect other people, this can be more difficult – as they may not see things quite the way you do.

Often this type of improvement can be identified from *external feedback*. If your customers regularly complain that they don't get a response to the messages they leave on the answering machine, it would be sensible to devise a new method of dealing with these. If your reprographics department says that it could deal more quickly with your section's work if you sent the work in batches, rather than individually, then their suggestions should be taken on board.

Equally, changes – such as new machines or equipment or even additional staff – can mean that you may be able to suggest new ways of doing things which would be a distinct improvement on what you do now. You may, for instance, be able to suggest how the team could function better and working relationships could be improved, by for instance:

- suggesting that a coffee rota be made out to prevent arguments about whose turn it is

- suggesting the best people to work on a particular task
- offering to help if someone is overloaded with work.

Suggesting improvements and dealing with the response

Most people would define an improvement as something which means they:

- can do a job more easily
- can do a job faster
- don't have to replicate work
- don't have to do an unnecessary job.

From your manager's point of view, improvements which don't cost anything are normally preferable to those which do!

Bear in mind that if you are suggesting an improvement which would bring benefits for you – but may involve other people in doing more – then they are unlikely to view this idea quite as positively as you will.

They may also have reservations about improvements which affect *only* them – unless they were the ones who thought about it in the first place! For a moment, think how you would react if someone else suggested you should be doing something differently.

Therefore, if you are making a suggestion which is going to affect anyone else, in any way, this is a clear test of your communication skills. How can you make the suggestion so that it considered openly and objectively by everyone?

Golden rules for making suggestions and dealing with responses

1   First, think through your idea. Identify the benefits, not just for yourself *but* for the team as a whole. Then think about possible objections and how valid these would be. It is always better if you can think of any drawbacks yourself, and how these can be overcome.

2   Pick your time and place. If the improvement concerns only you, then see your supervisor or team leader at a time convenient for them. If the improvement involves other people, then generally it is better when the whole team is together. However, this will depend upon whether you have regular team review meetings or not. If you don't, you could have a word with your supervisor or team leader first – but the rest of the team should be told together, not individually. Lobbying for support from those people who will benefit and isolating those who will not is *never* a good idea.

3   Make your suggestion clearly and focus on the benefits. *Don't* criticise the existing method of doing things – it may be your supervisor or team leader who thought of it! If you are asked *why* you think a change should be made, give concrete reasons linked to the feedback you have received from other people or the changes that have occurred since the original method was devised.

4   Be prepared for some people to disagree with you – and *don't* take this personally. Often an original idea is improved upon when several people discuss it as they can see other angles and implications. It is very rare for someone's idea to be accepted immediately by the whole team without any comments at all.

5   Be ready to defend your idea. Recall that you will have previously thought about the likely objections and how these can be overcome. Remember that you are defending your idea, not your honour! Don't personally attack any of the other members of your team in defence – stick to being positive and assertive.

6   Try to be open-minded. The idea could well be good but be rejected on grounds of cost, because of the effect on other parts of the organisation you don't know about, or because there are other changes planned which would make it unworkable.

7   If the idea is rejected it is natural to feel downhearted. It is to be hoped that your supervisor or team leader will be sensitive and wise enough to thank you for your initiative. Even if he/she does not, try not to let this put you off thinking of other ideas. The worst type of team member is the one who never contributes or thinks of anything – and the worst type of team is the one which can never consider new ideas. Even if you are in a team which doesn't develop and improve, remember that *you* can still continue to develop as a person, and move on to work in a more appreciative team.

High-performing teams will also want to assess their own performance – and how this can be improved – and not just suggest how to do jobs differently. This can be a difficult area because it involves making suggestions that are concerned with how *individual* team members react to situations and relate to each other. This is tantamount to public feedback about how people work together. On page 130 you will learn how to respond positively if you hear comments you don't particularly like during a feedback session!

TEST YOUR KNOWLEDGE AND UNDERSTANDING

Saleema is well known for her 'good ideas'. She has had three this weekend! They are:

a an additional telephone extension in the office so that customer calls can be dealt with more quickly

b purchase of a scanner so that documents can be entered into the computers without the work of re-keying them

c a different method of booking staff holidays, so that everyone can tell when people are going away (this will also mean that everyone can see what leave is owing to people, as Saleema is convinced some people take more than their due).

1 Which of these do you think will be the easiest to suggest to her supervisor or team and which the most tricky? Give a reason for your answer in each case.

2 Identify the drawbacks people may put forward against her ideas.

3 Adam is against the telephone idea as the obvious place for putting it is on his desk. If you were Saleema, how would you counter his objections?

4 Jackie is very against the idea of a visible holiday rota as she says her holidays are dictated by her husband's job and she doesn't always know when she is going away. Jackie is the very person Saleema considers takes more leave than her due. What are the dangers of this situation and how can they be avoided?

EVIDENCE COLLECTION

For this element, you have to prove to your assessor that:

a you have used your own experience and feedback from other people to identify where improvements can be made

b you have made suggestions in a clear and constructive way and at an appropriate time and place

c you are capable of dealing positively with your team members' responses.

You can provide evidence in any of the following ways.

1 Invite your assessor to attend a team meeting at which you are making suggestions (but clear this with your supervisor or team leader first).

2 Write an account of improvements you have suggested, why you made them and how you dealt with the responses. Ask your supervisor to sign this for authenticity.

3 Keep a log of improvements you have identified and suggested and whether they have been implemented. To this you will need to add witness testimony from your team leader that you made your suggestions and dealt with the responses appropriately.

4 Keep copies of the minutes of team meetings at which suggestions were made by you. However, the minutes must be detailed enough for your involvement to be obvious to the assessor and you will probably need witness testimony as well.

5 Obtain witness testimony from other staff in your team.

Finally, do try to ensure your evidence covers more than one suggestion – otherwise it will look very much as if you rarely think of anything!

Answers to quiz on pages 75–77

1a; 2b; 3a; 4c; 5b; 6c; 7a; 8c; 9c; 10a

Unit 202 Plan, organise and improve your work

Three different surveys, carried out in 1999 and 2000, identified that the most important skills and abilities needed by administrators and secretaries have changed. Instead of proficiency in shorthand or audio typing, employers now prefer their administrative staff to be excellent organisers, very good at coordinating and prioritising, able to work with the minimum of supervision, adept at 'self-management' and able to show initiative. They also, needless to say, expect all administrators to possess excellent IT skills – but these are covered in a different section of this book.

This unit focuses on what are sometimes known as 'soft' skills – your personal attributes – as opposed to the 'hard' or technical abilities such as using your computer for word-processing or creating spreadsheets. However, whilst you can learn word-processing and IT skills on a course, and obtain a certificate to prove what you can do, there are fewer opportunities to learn how to plan and be well organised. This unit gives you the opportunity to develop a variety of skills related to this area which will be extremely useful in any job.

The unit is divided into three elements. The first is concerned with learning how to plan your work and the second concentrates on your organisational skills. The last element helps you to learn how to improve yourself continually so that you can progress both in your present job and in your future career.

 KEY SKILLS SIGNPOST

If you are taking your Key Skills award then you can extend your own knowledge and abilities from this unit and use this as evidence in your portfolio for **Improving own Learning and Performance.** You can also use your progress file, learning plan or any other action plans you complete. You need to produce *two* examples of evidence which shows that you can undertake all the following activities, to achieve Level 2.

LP2.1

Set short-term targets for yourself with the help of either your supervisor or tutor and plan how these will be met. Make sure that you:

- identify the targets you will set as part of this unit and include examples of what you have done previously and what you now want to achieve in your own learning, your personal life and at work
- identify anything which may prevent you from achieving success, such as illness, other commitments, personal difficulties
- set action points for each target, a realistic deadline for achievement and also identify the support you will need and how you will obtain this
- finally, say when you will review your targets to check if you have met them.

LP2.2

Review your plan regularly and use it to help to plan your time and decide how to achieve your goals.

Revise your plan to take account of new developments, unexpected problems, areas you want to pursue or skills you have learned faster than you expected.

Record your progress as you are learning:

- one particular subject, and
- undertaking a practical activity.

Make a note of when you needed additional support and say how this was helpful.

Try different methods of learning (see page 142) and identify how successful each of these is and how much it suited your own learning style.

Work on one activity, for a short period, with the minimum supervision and then describe how you coped.

LP2.3

With your tutor or supervisor, review your progress at regular intervals. After each review, prepare a record which states:

- what and how you learned during this period
- what you found easier, and what you found harder than expected
- the targets you have met and the evidence you have to prove this
- examples of ways in which you have applied your new knowledge to cope with new tasks
- ideas you have to further improve your performance between now and your next review.

Element 202.1 Plan your work to meet other people's requirements

Most people enjoy being busy and dealing with a variety of tasks. Work, today, is becoming more varied and administrators are often responsible for undertaking a wide range of different jobs – most of which are driven by a **deadline**. A deadline signifies the very last date by which a task must be completed. Whether you thrive on the challenge of meeting a deadline, or are terrified by the very thought, is important. Your ability to cope with deadlines is likely to determine the level of responsibility you can handle both now and in the future – and the type of organisations you can work for. Many senior administrative and PA jobs involve organising important events which occur on a specific date. Media companies – such as television and radio companies, newspapers and magazines – are focused on very tight deadlines. If you want to keep your options open in the future, learning how to plan is therefore very important indeed.

The benefits of good planning

If you become skilled at planning, you will:

- make fewer mistakes
- save time
- complete all your jobs by the deadline date
- very rarely have to 'start all over again'
- become a more valued employee
- enjoy your work more
- do your job better
- be able to take on more interesting and challenging jobs.

All these benefits occur because you develop a way of working which makes the most of your time and enables you to identify accurately when different jobs and tasks must be done – and how they must be done. Because you do the job 'right first time' you will have more pride in your work and be trusted with more difficult jobs and more responsibility.

TEST YOUR POTENTIAL FOR PLANNING!

Some people are natural planners. They don't even go for a walk without checking the weather forecast or for a drive without studying a road map. Other people are just the opposite – they haven't a clue what they might be doing tomorrow, let alone next week or next month. In some cases they may even think that planning ahead can spoil the fun and spontaneity. For them life is one long voyage of ➡

discovery! Whilst this may add spice to some aspects of your private life, it is not a method to use at work.

How good are you at 'thinking ahead'? Test yourself and find out.

1 You are due to meet a friend for a night out in half an hour. Do you:
   a take your time getting ready
   b get ready in something of a rush, but in time
   c leave it too late and go much as you are?

2 Are you:
   a always punctual
   b usually punctual
   c always late?

3 When you were doing assignments at school or college, you:
   a always handed them in before the deadline
   b always handed them in *on* the deadline
   c always tried to negotiate an extension.

4 If you promise to complete something for a particular date, and the work is not going to plan, you:
   a fret, worry and have sleepless nights
   b do your best, but warn the person concerned
   c shrug and think life's too short to worry.

5 You have promised a friend you will make supper one night. Do you:
   a check you have everything you need beforehand
   b make do with what you can find on the night
   c send out for a take-away?

6 Your friend asks you to collect some information about a language course for her whilst you are at college. Do you:
   a write down carefully what she wants
   b try to remember what she wants
   c guess what she wants and hope it will do?

Give yourself 2 points for each 'a' answer, 1 point for each 'b' answer and 0 points for each 'c' answer. Eleven or 12 points means you are a 'natural' planner – but you are also a worrier and struggle to cope if your plans are suddenly changed at the last minute. Learning how to respond in this situation is your most important need. 9–10: You get your planning right most of the time but have a well-adjusted approach when things go a little wrong. 7–8 points: You can cope quite well provided the situation isn't very important – but when it is you can sometimes come unstuck. 6 points and under: Your friends may tolerate you – because they are used to you – but in a work situation you are likely to have serious problems!

Planning, and the link to obtaining information

Planning means *thinking ahead*. Someone who is good at planning is always one step in front – and uses past experience and knowledge to anticipate potential problems and possible developments or changes.

There are six steps to effective planning. You can apply these when you are dealing with a variety of everyday jobs or if you have to cope with an important job with a fixed or tight deadline. They are illustrated below and each step is described in detail in this unit.

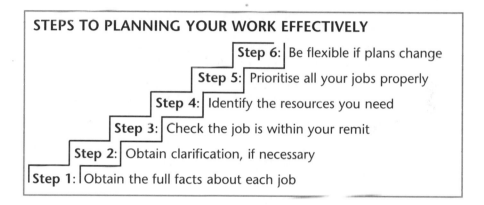

STEPS TO PLANNING YOUR WORK EFFECTIVELY

Step 6:	Be flexible if plans change
Step 5:	Prioritise all your jobs properly
Step 4:	Identify the resources you need
Step 3:	Check the job is within your remit
Step 2:	Obtain clarification, if necessary
Step 1:	Obtain the full facts about each job

Step 1: Obtain the facts

Everyone is apprehensive about their first day at work in a new job, no matter how experienced they are. Why? Because they have no background knowledge to help them to do the jobs they are given. The longer you work for an organisation, the more background knowledge and specialist knowledge you gain. So routine jobs become easy, because you know what to do, where to find information, who to contact. A new job is more difficult because you have less knowledge, so you have to find out as much as you can. The best person to ask, of course, is the person who asked you to do the work in the first place.

You need to find out:

a   what, *exactly,* they want you to do

b   when they want you to do it

c   how they want you to do it

d   who else you need to contact, or refer to

e   where/when you can find the person concerned if you need further clarification.

How to ask – and the people who may ask you

You may be asked to do a job by

- a colleague who is another member of your office or team
- your supervisor
- someone else – such as your supervisor's boss or a customer, supplier or other business you contact regularly.

Who asks you is likely to determine how you respond and how you ask for the information you need.

- If a colleague who is the same level as yourself asks you, then you are likely to have an informal discussion about the job. You can easily ask for further information – especially if you are doing someone a favour or helping them out.
- If your supervisor asks you, the conversation is likely to be slightly more formal. Even if you are asked to do a difficult job quite quickly, you can hardly respond '*You must be joking!*' Asking clearly for all the facts is likely to impress your supervisor and show you are taking the work seriously.

CHECK IT OUT!

1   Your boss has asked you for each of the following. For each task identify *all* the facts you need before you can start:

    a   a cheap day-return ticket to Edinburgh
    b   five photocopies of an important report
    c   a fax message to be sent to a customer
    d   sandwiches ordered for a lunchtime meeting
    e   a five-page document typing
    f   to arrange for her laptop computer to be repaired.

2   The following are the outcomes of your first attempt to do each of the above jobs. Identify those where you would need to ask *your boss* for further clarification and those where you could solve the problem yourself. In the latter case, state what you would do.

    a   the only available ticket is £175 return
    b   the photocopier is being serviced for the next hour, and so is out of action
    c   the customer's fax is out of order
    d   the canteen manager wants to know how many people are vegetarians
    e   you don't know how to integrate the table that needs to go in the middle from another package
    f   the supplier wants to know if it is still under warranty.

- If someone very senior asks you, then you are sensible to ask for the information but ask *someone else* (such as your supervisor) for help and guidance before you start – particularly if you are worried about anything.
- If a customer, supplier or other person external to your department asks you for something, make sure you are allowed to do the job or provide the information before you make any promises (see below).

Always write down carefully the facts you are given. Never rely on your memory.

Step 2: Obtain clarification

There is a difference between asking questions because you need further information, and pestering people because you never think of things in advance or expect other people to solve your problems!

Asking *legitimate* questions is quite acceptable – and don't let anyone tell you otherwise. It can be difficult to pluck up courage to ask someone for additional information if they are in a bad mood or very busy. But this is much better than carrying on and making the wrong decision.

In the exercise above, for instance, your boss should expect you to find out whether he approves the expensive train fare, is prepared to wait an hour for the photocopied report and can tell you when he bought the laptop. However, he can also expect you to solve all the remaining problems yourself!

A sensible way of coping with making these types of decisions is to ask someone else for advice or help. This is especially important if you have to make a decision quickly and the person who gave you the job is nowhere to be found. An experienced colleague, who is willing to help you when necessary, is often called a **mentor**. Mentors are very valuable people, as they can stop you from making silly mistakes or wrong decisions that you wouldn't want your supervisor or anyone else to know about!

 INFORMATION UPDATE

Everyone who is given something new to do has to learn a certain amount by experience. This is called your **learning curve**. When you start work in a new job the learning curve is very steep indeed – it may be as high as 90 degrees. It starts to flatten out as you become used to your job and the way the organisation operates as many tasks become familiar.

Good administrators learn from experience. If they have to do a new task, or deal with a different group of people, they either make notes or commit to memory what has happened. This reduces the steepness of their learning curve if a repeat performance is required.

Poor administrators rarely learn from experience. If their supervisor wants a monthly report presented in a certain way, then the following month they have to be told all over again how to set it out. If a contributor to the report was hard to find, they don't learn by experience and allow additional time for this the second time round. They have to re-experience their original learning curve over and over again.

This not only slows them down but is frustrating for everyone who works with them. Make a vow today – your learning curve should only be steep the very *first* time you do something.

EVIDENCE COLLECTION

Design a log sheet on which you can record specific tasks you are asked to do. A suggested format is shown opposite, but you can alter this to suit your own needs. The next time you are given a task to do complete the first part of the sheet. Information relating to completing the priority, resource and evaluation sections is given later in this unit. Note that you will need to complete task sheets for work you are given by *at least* two types of people including your line manager, another person requesting work or other staff in your team.

Step 3: Is the job within your remit?

Occasionally you will be asked to do a job which is not part of your responsibilities. Sometimes you will be absolutely certain that this is not your job or your responsibility, on other occasions the situation may be less clear.

For instance, if someone asks you to rectify a paper jam in the photocopier, when you have never been trained to do this, you have the right to refuse – although you should say why. Equally, if you are asked to do a job which you know someone else is already half-way through you should say so. Otherwise you are duplicating work and this is unfair on your colleague.

However, do bear in mind that today most employers value *flexibility*. There is a big difference between pointing out that someone else is doing a task and refusing to help out if that person is off sick and the job must be completed quickly. It is interesting to become involved in new jobs and it can help you to become multi-skilled and, therefore, a more valuable member of your organisation.

TASK LOG SHEET

Full description of task:

Task given by:

Questions asked to clarify uncertainties and responses:

Guidance given by:

Estimated time required:

Deadline date: PRIORITY LEVEL:

RESOURCES REQUIRED

Equipment:

Materials:

Information:

Resource difficulties (if any) and description of how problem was solved

EVALUATION OF TASK

(Explain any problems or difficulties you experienced in completing the task, whether the task was 'right first time' or had to be amended, whether the deadline changed at any point, and what you did to cope.)

Date task completed .... Quality of work ....

Signature of candidate .... Date ....

Signature of person giving task ....

Designation ....

If you work as part of a team, you will be expected to help out if there is a sudden crisis or an urgent deadline to meet. Your colleagues may also ask you to help them, from time to time, if they are particularly busy. Generally, you will be a more valued colleague (and can expect more cooperation in return) if you are usually willing to lend a hand. However, if you are already involved in an urgent or critical job, you should explain the situation to your supervisor – as it may be more important that you finish the work you are currently doing.

TEST YOUR KNOWLEDGE AND UNDERSTANDING

Which of the following requests would you consider acceptable and which not? Then say *why* and *how* you would refuse each one you decide is not your responsibility.

1   You are asked by a customer to give the home address of a colleague.

2   A member of your team asks you to help her with some urgent filing.

3   The manager of the department asks you to find out when everyone is taking their holidays. You know your supervisor is currently drawing up a rota.

4   You are asked to tidy up reception by your supervisor as some important visitors are due.

5   A 'flu bug has struck down half the office staff. Your supervisor asks you to update a spreadsheet, even though you have never done this before.

6   Someone from the bank telephones with a query about this month's payroll figures.

7   A supplier asks if a specific stationery item can be substituted with another product because they are out of stock.

8   Your supervisor asks you to find out who would be interested in becoming a first-aider.

 INFORMATION UPDATE

According to many supervisors and managers, negativity is the *worst* trait in an administrator. In other words, never say 'I can't do that' or 'It can't be done' or 'They won't do it'. Even if you genuinely think a job is almost 'mission impossible' there are better ways of phrasing your response than being so negative.

If a job you have been given fills you with dread, it is better if you say 'Of course I'll do it, but I'm worried that I don't have the skills you need' or 'I might struggle on my own to complete it by then'. This way you are sounding positive but being honest that you need more assistance on this occasion.

Step 4: Check the resources you need

It is virtually impossible to do a job if you don't have the right resources. You can't write down a message if you don't have a pen, or e-mail a customer if you don't have a computer. Many jobs will require only the routine resources that are available in virtually every office, but in other cases you may need additional items. You also, of course, want the resources you use to be in working order!

Resources can be divided into three types:

- **equipment** – such as computers, fax machines, photocopiers, answering machines, shredders, stapler, punch, calculator, scissors
- **materials** – such as paper, pens, filing folders, presentation wallets, floppy disks, sticky tape, envelopes
- **information** – paper-based, such as company files, brochures, catalogues, reference books; and electronic, such as company database, CD-ROMs, the Internet.

Identifying which resources are best for different types of jobs not only saves time and money, but also helps you to do the job better.

Access to equipment

A problem with equipment is often the most difficult to solve. Problems can occur if you simply don't possess the equipment you need – particularly if it is expensive – or if your equipment breaks down. Some offices are better resourced than others. However, if you work in an organisation which wants you to send out 5000 mailshots and put each letter into an envelope by hand, this is obviously a much bigger job than if you have an automatic filling and sealing machine you can use. If the mailshot is a 'one-off' then you may have to cope. If you are asked to do the task regularly it is worth having a word with your supervisor to see whether a good argument can be put forward for buying the equipment you need. An obvious point to make is how much time you would save with the right tools.

Small items of equipment should be more readily available – unless you work in an office where people routinely share one pair of scissors and your colleagues regularly help themselves to your ruler or calculator! You should aim to have your own 'key' items, such as a stapler, hole punch, ruler, calculator, desk tidy, roll of sticky tape, correction fluid and scissors. Another useful small item you are likely to find invaluable is a staple remover, which saves your fingernails *and* any document you are handling from damage. If you find people often borrow things from your desk without asking then you may need to take drastic action – such as locking them in your top drawer at night and removing the key.

Access to materials

Most organisations have a stationery store which holds routine items. However, if you are asked to do a big or unusual job you cannot just assume that you can obtain 10,000 envelopes or 50 presentation folders at a moment's notice. Usually such bulk items need to be ordered.

It is worth checking the procedure in your own organisation for obtaining such items, and finding out who the supplier is. Looking through catalogues *in advance* shows you what is available and can often give you good ideas about the best materials to use in different circumstances. Organisations are usually prepared to pay more for materials for an important job – for instance, if you are preparing information for a potential customer and want to make a good impression. In this case, useful suggestions to improve the finished result will be welcomed.

Access to information

This item is more under your direct control than is access to equipment and materials. You can use your initiative to obtain information but you can't obtain a better photocopier using the same method! In any office you are surrounded by a wealth of information, so the trick lies in obtaining a realistic amount of relevant information for the task in hand. If you obtain too much, you will simply not know where to start using it. This is rather like having 500 holiday brochures from which to choose your next break! If you have too little, you will have to trust to luck that you have enough to work with. If you include irrelevant, unnecessary or out-of date information you will confuse or mislead everyone, including yourself.

Key sources of information are:

- the office files and records – whether these are held in filing cabinets or on computer
- the people around you – who often know more than you think
- other people in the organisation, especially on specific matters, such as personnel issues or safety
- your home area or hard disk drive on your computer – if you can't find a document you created in the files you may be able to find it on disk
- reference books and materials – including standard reference books (such as *Yellow Pages*, timetables and travel guides, dictionaries and directories, brochures and catalogues)
- outside reference sources – such as your local town hall, library, travel agent, bank
- the Internet – provided you know how to find the type of information you need (see Option Unit 214)
- your own files and notes (if you are frequently asked for the same type of information, or need the same information to do similar jobs, you are sensible to file it carefully and refer to it regularly).

The words 'paper and envelopes' are often used with little thought about the *type* of paper or *type* of envelopes that are required.

Paper is sold in various colours and weights. The heaviest is the thickest and the most expensive. The lightest is the cheapest, but is unsuitable for important or prestigious jobs. Many printers and photocopiers specify the weight required, and if you use the wrong type you are likely to find the paper jams frequently.

Envelopes are sold in various colours (especially brown and white), in various sizes, and in a range of strengths and styles (e.g. self-seal, window, cardboard-backed).

Look through a stationery catalogue and identify all the different variations available. Then attempt the exercise below.

TEST YOUR KNOWLEDGE AND UNDERSTANDING

1 Which type of envelope would you choose to:
   a send out a mailshot to 5000 customers without printing labels?
   b send a 50-page A4 document to an important customer?
   c send a photograph to a newspaper?
   d send routine letters to customers?

2 Which type of paper would you choose:
   a to print a top-quality report on a laser printer?
   b to generate routine computer printouts?
   c to print a jazzy notice?
   d for your photocopier?

3 Samira has asked her boss for the following items. Identify what type of job she might be doing *in each case* to need the item.
   a a long-arm stapler
   b a heavy-duty stapler
   c a roll of bubble filmwrap
   d a trimmer
   e a laminator
   f a thermal binder.

Step 5: Learn to prioritise

All administrative jobs consist of several different kinds of tasks:

- **routine** tasks you do every day or week, such as filing, delivering the mail, reading your e-mails, answering the telephone, photocopying, sending faxes
- **larger tasks which are your responsibility**, such as checking and ordering stationery, word-processing a large document, and keeping financial records up to date
- **non-routine tasks which occur infrequently**, such as helping to prepare for the annual sales conference, preparing materials for a presentation to a customer, helping to clear out old files to create more space, or helping to prepare a large mailshot to customers
- **small, non-specific jobs** which usually occur on a day-to-day basis, often in response to a request from your supervisor or a colleague (e.g. for a file, a copy of a document or some specific information).

An administrator has the problem of 'juggling' these tasks and deciding when to do each one. This is always a more difficult problem on a busy day. How do you decide which jobs to do, and which ones to leave until tomorrow – or even until next week?

Good planners often prepare a **daily priority list** using the chart below to help them. The list identifies jobs in terms of their *urgency* and their *importance*. Remember:

- **Urgency** relates to to how quickly a task must be done – i.e. tasks which must be completed by a specific deadline. The task becomes more and more urgent the nearer you are to the deadline.
- **Importance** relates to those jobs for which you have personal responsibility as part of your job role or those jobs where there will be serious consequences for the organisation if they are not done. You are normally judged by how well and how reliably you complete the important jobs.

CLASSIFYING JOBS AND DECIDING PRIORITIES

Class A	Class B
urgent and important	urgent but not important
Class C	**Class D**
important but not urgent	not urgent and not important

Class A jobs are tasks that are *both* urgent and important. They may be small tasks, such as sending a fax, or large ones, such as preparing all presentation and advertising materials for an important meeting tomorrow morning. You need to decide how long it will take you to do each of your class A jobs *properly* and, even within this group, decide which are the most urgent. You can label these A1, A2, A3 if you wish. If you are overwhelmed with class A jobs it is very important that you consult your supervisor rather than simply miss the deadline without telling anyone.

Class B jobs are tasks that are urgent but *not* important. They include all the jobs you really should do today but for which there would be no serious consequences if you did not. If you have several class B jobs it is tempting to do them to 'get them out of the way' and perhaps put off a larger class B job.

Class C jobs are the danger jobs! They are important but – today – they are not urgent. If you put them off because the deadline is still some way off there is the danger that they can rapidly become class A jobs. Ideally, class C jobs are those which you *plan* to do at a specific time in the future and you schedule enough time to do them properly. This means entering them on a planner or in your diary (see page 115).

Class D jobs are, technically, the last ones you should do. However, if some of your class D jobs are easy, or involve an activity you really enjoy, then the danger is that you will indulge yourself with these jobs! This is fine if you have a quiet, routine day but can be disastrous on a crisis day.

Classifying your jobs

Most jobs will be relatively easy to classify. However, if you are dubious about a task, ask yourself the following questions:

a   How serious would be the consequences of not doing the job by the deadline – both in terms of your organisation and your own reputation?

b   Who gave you the task and how important or senior is that person?

c   How long will the task take to complete?

d   Is the deadline completely unalterable, or could it be extended if a serious problem arises?

This should tell you, for instance, that a job given to you by a colleague, with a suggested deadline of mid-afternoon, is not the same type of class A job as an urgent letter to a customer that your boss insists must catch tonight's mail.

CHECK IT OUT!

1   Identify how many 'crises' you normally have each week. How many of these are self-inflicted – because you had forgotten to do something and it became urgent or because you were doing a job you preferred to do rather than one you had to do. Try to pick a busy week as well as a quiet week when you are judging yourself.

2   List down all the jobs you do this week. Then categorise them. Decide which are class A, B, C and D jobs. Then assess yourself on how good you are at classifying and prioritising jobs correctly.

3   Could you accurately identify *your boss's* (or tutor's) priorities and link these to the jobs you do? Which jobs do you think he or she considers the most important and which ones the least? How well does this match your own priority list? Can you think of reasons why there may be some differences?

Step 6: Be flexible in planning

Flexibility is a highly prized attribute for administrators. No matter how good you are at planning and prioritising the work to be done, in every office there are days when crises occur and new class A jobs have to be fitted in to the schedule. This can happen because a completely new job has arisen or because a class C job suddenly has its deadline brought forward, which makes it more urgent.

It is on these occasions that your ability to 'think on your feet' and re-prioritise your work is crucial. It is also worth saying that you will also be well regarded if you treat such situations as an opportunity to show your abilities and good humour – and don't treat each change to your schedule as both inconvenient and a personal insult.

The problem, of course, occurs when so many 'urgent' or 'important' jobs hit you at once that you honestly can't cope. At this point, trying to pretend that you are superwoman or superman is useless. The earlier you admit to having a problem in meeting a deadline, the quicker someone else can try to help you. See your supervisor or team leader promptly, explain the difficulty calmly, have all the facts at your fingertips and ask for guidance. If possible, suggest a solution which would work.

Finally, never go away on holiday or even on a day's leave without checking your 'to do' list for tomorrow and making sure someone else is covering anything urgent. Otherwise, you are likely to find yourself rather unpopular on your return!

1 You have all the following jobs on your 'to do' list for today. Classify each one into class A, B, C or D. Then decide the order in which you would do each class A job:

   a water the plants in your supervisor's office

   b deliver this morning's mail

   c help out on reception from 11 am to 12 noon

   d send out three catalogues in response to requests from customers

   e type a letter from your supervisor's written notes in response to a complaint by an important customer

   f contact three colleagues to obtain information for a report your supervisor has to take to an important meeting in three days' time

   g get your filing up to date

   h read your e-mail for today

   i book a taxi to take your supervisor to the station tomorrow

   j prepare and send six letters to customers requesting immediate payment of unpaid bills

   k photocopy a long document your supervisor wants to take on his one-day trip tomorrow

   l check the staff noticeboards and remove out-of-date notices.

2 What measures could you take to prevent a task in class C suddenly becoming a class A task without your realising?

3 If you find a job you have categorised as class B is regarded as class A by your boss, would you change its category? Give a reason for your answer.

4 At 10 am your supervisor tells you that the important meeting he was attending in three days' time has been moved forward to the day after tomorrow. He must finish all the paperwork today as he won't be in the office tomorrow. He has asked you to help by:

   a creating two complex tables and inputting all the information he has hand-written on two pages

   b finding out the sales figures for each region for last month from the sales department

   c letting him have the files on two important customers immediately

   d sending an e-mail to three colleagues to inform them of the changed meeting date.

   Re-prioritise your day to allow for these developments.

EVIDENCE COLLECTION

You can now complete your task sheets – firstly by correctly inserting the priority class for each job; and secondly, when you have completed the task, by completing the evaluation section. This is particularly important as it will show your assessor how you respond when plans change and you have to be flexible.

If you have prepared documentary material, it will enhance your evidence if you can include *some* examples of the work you have done. Don't simply put in a finished, perfect document. Put in the drafts you created as well, to illustrate the stages it went through. One or two examples should be sufficient.

For your other tasks, be prepared to talk to your assessor about your task sheets and provide further details of the work you carried out or the problems you had to resolve. Be prepared to answer questions on any areas not covered by your evidence. For instance, how you would ask another person for guidance.

Finally, do make sure you ask the person who gave you the task to countersign the form so that your assessor knows it is authentic.

Element 202.2 Organise your work to meet other people's requirements

Some people are incredibly well organised. They are neat and tidy, they automatically make lists for everything they need to do and tick things off as they do them. They are very self-disciplined and don't just do the jobs they like to do but the jobs they need to do – in the correct order! They pay attention to details and check, and double-check, important jobs to make sure everything is right. They don't skimp and cut corners when they are bored, they don't spend ten minutes chatting to other people on a busy day and they very rarely seem to get flustered or stressed.

Such paragons of virtue are relatively rare! Most of us have some weak areas in relation to organisation skills which we would prefer no one to know about. However, the problem is that unless you are relatively well organised in an administrative job, your weaknesses are likely to be very well known before too long. It is therefore sensible to see where these lie and to try to take action to improve them.

The benefits of being well organised

There are several benefits to becoming more organised. You will:

* always to be able to make the best use of your time
* be able to find things quickly
* reduce the number of things you need to remember
* be less stressed and less likely to lose your temper
* have more time for things you want to do
* be able to complete jobs more quickly and more easily
* be more confident of your own ability
* be a much more efficient person to work with!

Most of these benefits occur because of the absence of all the negative aspects of work that disorganised people have to live with, such as needlessly spending time searching for things. As a start, do the quiz below and assess how 'naturally' well organised you are at the moment.

TEST YOUR ORGANISATIONAL ABILITIES

Respond to each of the following issues as truthfully as you dare.

1 If the most important person in your life saw the state of your bedroom this morning, you would be:
   a delighted
   b indifferent
   c horrified.

2 If your boss opened your desk drawer to look for something you would be:
   a unconcerned
   b annoyed
   c horrified.

3 The last time you forgot to do something important was:
   a years ago
   b weeks ago
   c days ago.

4 You rate your own proof-reading abilities as:
   a excellent
   b fairly good
   c atrocious.

5 When you need to do shopping you normally:
   a make a list beforehand and take it with you
   b make a list beforehand but forget to take it with you
   c try to remember what you want when you get there.

6 On an average day, you:
   a always know what you want to achieve
   b usually know what you want to achieve
   c rarely know what you want to achieve.

7 At the end of an average day, you:
   a have a very good idea how you spent your time
   b have a fair idea how you spent your time
   c wonder where the time went.

8 If you have to give someone a straightforward message, you prefer to:
   a send an e-mail later, when you are sending several others
   b telephone immediately
   c visit for a chat.

9 You last lost something important:

   a so long ago you can't remember

   b within the last few months

   c within the last week.

10 You have promised to ring an elderly relative at 7 pm next Wednesday. So you:

   a note it on a calendar, and in your diary, and make the call as agreed

   b make a note of it and ask someone to remind you – then remember when you are reminded

   c forget all about it, as usual.

Give yourself 2 points for each 'a' answer, 1 point for each 'b' answer and 0 points for each 'c' answer. 16–20 points: You are exceptionally well organised. Do be aware that other people may not have your high standards and you may find this annoying – especially if it causes your own plans to go awry. Try to be patient with those who have to work at being well organised! 12–15 points. You have the potential to be very well organised if you identify your weaknesses and work at improving them. 8–11 points: There is considerable room for improvement. Remember that colleagues at work are unlikely to be as forgiving or as tolerant as your friends and family. 0–7 points: More than half of your day is probably spent redoing previous jobs or finding what you've lost. Ask yourself one key question: Would *you* employ yourself?

Using time efficiently

Everyone's week consists of 168 hours, and about 40 of these are spent at work. Yet some people seem to do far more in this time than others. There is also normally a link between being able to use time efficiently at work and in your private life. People who are well organised and use time efficiently often seem to pack far more into their lives than those who are not – and therefore manage to 'find' the time to do things other people simply dream about.

However, time is not an object. You cannot therefore *really* find it, or make it – or spend it. Learning to use time efficiently does not relate to being able to manipulate time itself, but to improving the way you manage your own time in order to complete tasks and participate in a variety of activities.

Time boosters

You can 'make' time by following a few simple guidelines:

- know exactly what you want to achieve each day
- do important and urgent jobs when you are at your best

- do jobs you dread early in the day to get them out of the way
- save some 'nice' jobs as a reward for later
- have a 'place for everything, and everything in its place' – so you don't have to hunt for things
- 'batch' jobs – so you send a batch of faxes, a batch of e-mails or photocopy a batch of documents, to prevent repeat journeys
- use your head to save your legs – check you have everything you need before you go anywhere or start any job
- avoid time wasters (see below).

Time wasters

You will wonder where the time went if you:
- allow people to interrupt you constantly
- get distracted easily with things which aren't directly connected to the job you are doing
- chat and gossip whenever you can
- 'play' with paper without doing anything useful with it
- leave jobs partially completed because you are bored with them
- do jobs poorly or sloppily so you have to start all over again
- put off doing things when you have the time, so you are constantly trying to do things in a rush, when they must be done.

Golden rules for using time efficiently

1   Make a vow to use your time more efficiently from now on.
2   Start by looking at how you use your time *now*. Keep a diary or a calendar which records what you do, when, how long it took and what went wrong if it took too long.
3   Make a plan to prioritise properly and to stick to your priority list. Don't be distracted by anything or anyone (except by your own boss!).
4   Be brave! Learn to say 'no' if you are asked to do an unimportant task to help someone else on a busy day.
5   Do each job *once* (unless it needs to be redone through no fault of your own). Accomplish this by making sure you are doing the job 'right first time' and checking your work carefully.
6   Schedule jobs using a disciplined approach. Stick with a job until it is finished whenever you can.
7   Reduce interruptions as much as possible. If you have a very important and urgent job to do then *tell* people. Arrange to have conversations with people after you have finished.
8   Make sure that you don't waste other people's time. Don't be late so that you keep them waiting. Don't interrupt or distract people when they are busy. Don't ask unnecessary questions or expect them to remember to remind *you* about things!

Aids to planning

There are various aids you can buy to help you to plan. The traditional paper-based systems may seem old-fashioned but they are easily transportable and simple to use.

A diary can range from a large, page-a-day type to a smaller version with, say, a week on view on each two pages. Diaries are often useful for the *additional* information they contain, such as holiday dates and a tube map.

Planners are pinned on the wall. Some are designed for special purposes, others are more general. A 'perpetual' planner has no fixed dates so can be used every year. You can also choose between those which you can write on with a 'wipe-off' pen and those which are magnetic. A glance through any stationery catalogue will show you the variations available.

'To do' lists can be written in a notepad, typed out and clipped to the front of a file or even scribbled on a jotter. The system you use is less important than the fact that you regularly look at your list, check off the items as you do them and carry outstanding items forward *every day*.

These are not the only methods of planning, of course. Some people prefer to write their jobs on Post-it notes and fasten these to their noticeboard (or monitor!) until they have been completed. If you are more fashion-conscious you may prefer to carry a personal organiser, such as a Filofax which includes special pages for addresses, notes, 'to do' lists, and 'don't forget' pages.

 INFORMATION UPDATE

Technophiles may prefer to ask Santa Claus for a PDA next Christmas! PDA is short for personal digital assistant or 'electronic organiser', and for an outlay of between £15 and £400 you should find something to suit you.

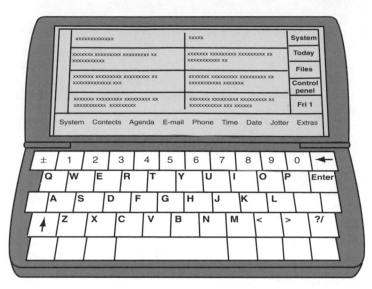

A PDA (personal digital assistant)

Most people want a PDA which will link to their computer. This means they can download information they have entered, such as important contact names and addresses, on their office system. However, be warned. Although these systems may look good and are certainly small enough to fit in your handbag or pocket, their value is minimal if you are never out of the office and don't need to send e-mail or contact your team from a distance. Unless you are good at keyboarding, it can also take an age to enter the information and, if you forget to renew your batteries regularly, you may lose everything. Sometimes a piece of paper is far more useful!

The importance of organising key items

There are three very good reasons why important items must be kept organised. First, serious problems can ensue if they go missing. Second, they last longer and are less likely to be damaged. Third, you will be able to find them more quickly.

Avoiding the horrors of losing key items

The personal item most people would least like to lose is probably their wallet or purse, especially if it also contains bank and credit cards. The reason is because of the worry and inconvenience experienced if these items are missing. It is quite possible to identify the key items you need in order to do your job properly by asking the same question. Which items would you least like to lose – or mislay?

The majority of administrators would refer to items such as:

- important original documents (e.g. a legal agreement)
- important files
- floppy disks containing back-up copies of documents
- their work diary
- their notebook or notepad.

Again, the reason is the same. A pair of scissors or a train timetable can be replaced quickly. If you lose an original document or file then there is no way you can simply replace it. You have either to spend hours hunting for the item you've lost, or spend roughly the same amount of time worrying about your boss's reaction when you admit the problem.

From now on, instead of thinking of every item you handle as having the same status, decide *how important* each item is by thinking about the consequences of losing it. If, for any item, these are too dreadful to contemplate, you need to make sure that the item is kept *precisely* where you would first think to look for it. This is better than a 'safe place' which you forget about later!

If you ever find yourself in the unenviable position of not being able to find something critical, tackle the problem by:

- thinking back over where you last saw it or handled it
- finding out whether anyone else has used or borrowed it
- finding out if anyone has a copy of a document you need
- keeping calm as long as you can
- not blaming anyone else
- admitting the problem and asking for assistance in solving it
- apologising
- remembering that everyone can be forgiven *one* mistake!

The benefits of keeping key items organised

People who are sloppy with their possessions find they have to replace them more frequently than those who are careful. This can become expensive. Children are warned about this all the time – dropping coloured pencils on the floor breaks the leads, leaving a bike out in the rain makes it rust – and so on. As we get older we learn to value our possessions more, especially those we particularly treasure or which have cost us a lot of money.

If you are naturally careful with your own possessions then it is likely you will be just as careful with the things you need to do your job. If you are less fussy, then you may find that you are constantly pleading for a new pencil or pen to replace the one you've been chewing, or asking for more paper to replace the crumpled pile at the bottom of your desk drawer.

Part of looking after your possessions is having a 'place for everything and everything in its place'. This is dealt with in the next section.

Keeping working areas clean and tidy

Your working area is *any area* in which you are doing a job – not just your desk. It should not be possible for your colleagues to identify exactly where you were last working because they 'recognise' you by the mess you left behind! If you are a naturally neat and tidy person then good working habits will not be difficult to achieve. If you are *not*, then think what it must be like to work somewhere after you have been there.

Good working habits mean:

- using the area allocated to you – not spreading work around everywhere and invading other people's territory
- doing each part of a job before you start the next – rather than attempting to do several things simultaneously
- clearing up after yourself
- putting things away (in the right place) when you have finished with them
- returning anything you have borrowed *promptly* and without having to be reminded.

If you *have* to leave papers, files or anything else in a communal area for some reason, put a clear note on it identifying yourself as the 'owner' and indicating when the items will be removed.

You will find it easier to keep your desk clear if you have the right 'tools' to help you. These are likely to include:

- trays in which you can put papers (e.g. 'in', 'out', 'pending' and 'filing' trays)
- a desk tidy for miscellaneous items such as paperclips, eraser, staple remover, elastic bands
- a pen tidy for pens and pencils
- file folders for specific groups of papers.

You should also use your desk drawers for storing items you need less frequently. The top drawer is usually lockable, so anything confidential can be kept in here. Stationery items and file folders you use regularly can be stored lower down. Wherever possible, try to keep the working surface of your desk clear of miscellaneous papers so that the only item on it at any one time relates to the job you are doing at the moment. When you have finished that job, put everything away before you get out the next. It really is that simple!

If you use a communal area regularly, such as the photocopying room or mailroom, keep your work to a specific area and make sure you tidy up *before* you leave. This also means leaving any equipment in the state you found it.

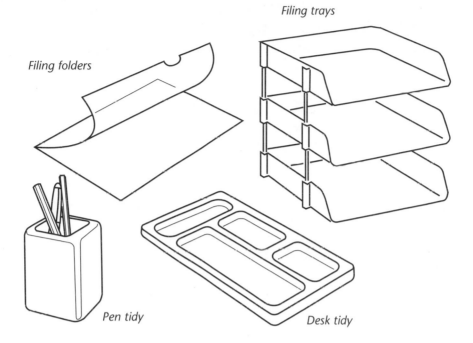

Filing trays

Filing folders

Pen tidy

Desk tidy

INFORMATION UPDATE

Believe it or not, but if you worked in the United States you could pay a professional organiser to come to your office and sort out your desk! Whilst this may seem a drastic (and expensive) solution it is quite possible to adopt some of their techniques yourself. They would improve your working area by following a few simple steps.

a Assess all the paper and files on and in your desk. How many are absolutely necessary? How many should be thrown away? How many need storing but could easily be kept somewhere else? The aim here is to reduce clutter.

b Place all essential items within *reach* – so you don't need to keep bobbing up and down to get items you use repeatedly. The exact location would depend upon whether you are right- or left-handed.

c Group items in sensible positions in relation to each other. If you are right-handed your telephone should be at the left and your pen holder to your right – so that you can pick up the receiver with your left hand and reach for a pen and write a message with your right hand.

d *Only* the task on which you are currently working should currently clutter your desk. Everything else should be in labelled files or folders.

One danger with this approach is, of course, that you will be so neat and tidy that everyone will think you've nothing to do! Alternatively your colleagues may be so envious they will tidy their desks as well!

CHECK IT OUT!

1 Check the top of your desk. Identify any inessential items causing clutter and find somewhere else for them.

2 Check the drawers of your desk. When did you last clear them out? Throw away the rubbish and check that items stored there are in the best place. Resolve to have another clear-out in three months' time.

3 Honestly assess yourself on your tidiness. If you work in a photocopying room, mail room or stationery store, how easy (or difficult) do you find it to keep your working area tidy?

Minimising waste

It is amazing how many people have serious concerns about the future of the environment and yet throw reams of paper into their waste bins every day without any thought at all. At the end of every year this probably results in the destruction of a small forest.

In any office there is bound to be some waste paper. Hopefully, this will be collected in a recycling bin. However, it is *unnecessary* waste that should be avoided – of any kind. This is because it adds to the overall costs of running the organisation as well as being environmentally unfriendly.

Examples of unnecessary waste include:

• printer paper used for repeated drafts of a document or for documents which haven't been proof-read properly

• photocopying paper spoiled because the original was poor quality or crooked, the size of paper or ratio was incorrectly selected or too many copies were made

• liquid paper which is useless because the top wasn't replaced tightly

- envelopes or paper which have become crumpled at the bottom of a desk drawer or discoloured because they have been left near a window or radiator.

Hints and tips to save waste and help the environment

You can save your own efforts, the environment and your company's money by habitually adopting the following techniques when you are working:

- Save paper by photocopying on both sides.
- Re-use manilla folders by turning them inside out.
- Re-use out-of-date headed paper by turning it into scrap pads.
- Store paper correctly and according to instructions – away from heat and direct sunlight, in a flat pack or box, so that it can't be creased or torn.
- Carefully proof-read all documents you produce and take one copy for a final check before printing out multiple copies.
- Take a 'test' copy of a multiple photocopy before setting the machine for a large print run.
- Resist making spare copies of a document 'just in case'.
- Re-use envelopes for internal mail items.
- *Think* carefully before you write on a folder, card or form, so you don't have to throw it away and start again.
- Lobby your company to have printer cartridges refilled where possible.
- Shred waste paper and use it for packaging. Put any remaining 'clean' paper in a recycling bin.
- Use a notebook or notepad properly so you don't waste pages.

CHECK IT OUT!

1 At work, identify and write down the areas where you are most likely to produce a lot of waste. Then think of *two* ways in which you could minimise this.

2 If you are studying for your NVQ at college, as a group identify *two* further ways in which you could help to avoid waste in general and help the environment, and add these to your list.

3 Check your waste bin at work (and at college) at the end of a day. Decide how many items *had* to be destroyed and how many were thrown away unnecessarily because you weren't concentrating. Make a positive effort to minimise the waste you create over the next few weeks. As a simple test, if you were fined every time you wasted a piece of paper, would this make a big difference to your life or very little?

Asking for assistance

You may think that being well organised is such a personal skill and attribute that you will never need to ask for help or advice in this area. Generally, this is true, but there are occasions when you may need to refer a problem to someone else, such as:

- when you are dealing with confidential information and are not sure how to handle it

- when you are asked to do a new task and don't know the correct way to do it in your organisation

- when you have a problem you have no idea how to solve.

One of the first things you need to be sure of is that you know *who* to ask for what type of help. Your supervisor is an obvious choice, so is your mentor – if you have one (see page 99). A very experienced colleague may also be a good choice. Try to avoid asking someone who is new or inexperienced as they are unlikely to be much help – and it isn't fair to expect them to guide you on a difficult matter. Whilst you are undertaking your NVQ scheme, your tutor, trainer or adviser may also be a useful source of assistance.

Dealing with confidential information

The problem with confidential information is that, if you need help, you have to be careful who you ask, otherwise the information may no longer be confidential. It is therefore usually wise to refer any queries to the person who gave you the information in the first place.

The type of information which is classed as confidential usually includes:

- personal details about staff (e.g. home address, age, etc.)
- appraisal or performance review information about staff
- payroll information
- product information which would be of value to competitors
- documents relating to internal plans and changes which have not yet been announced to the staff.

Much will depend upon the type of organisation you work for and the office in which you are employed. If you work in personnel or human resources, for instance, you will handle confidential information relating to staff. If you work in finance, you will know how much money your organisation spends on certain items and roughly how much profit it makes. If you work in sales you will know who your customers are and how much they spend.

Be aware that information such as this is 'sensitive' – even if it is not all labelled 'confidential'. If you are working with this type of information it is normal to:

- take special precautions (e.g. if you are photocopying, double-check to make sure you haven't left a copy on the glass when you leave the machine)
- keep files away from public areas, such as reception, and lock them away at night
- distribute documents in a sealed envelope
- shred draft documents, rather than simply put them in a waste paper bin.

If you are ever asked for information you even *think* may be confidential, it is always wise to check with your supervisor. The tactful way of doing this is to tell the person who asks you that you do not know the answer but you will try to find out. That is better than saying you know, but you don't think you can tell them! Then take advice.

Following organisational procedures

Generally, the larger the organisation the more likely it is that there will be specific procedures which will determine the way some jobs must be done. As a health and safety example, in a large company you would have to follow a specific accident reporting system if you hurt yourself at work. If you worked in a very small office with just two other people, then the system would be less formal. In other cases, procedures you have to follow relate to security in the workplace, such as having to take a document to a visitor in reception because he/she is not allowed access to your part of the building.

Other examples of procedures are:

- a requirement for all visitors to be instructed to report at a gatehouse or reception area on arrival
- a system for booking spaces for visitors in the company car park
- forms to complete if you want a large document printed by a central reprographics section
- a centralised filing unit from which you have to request certain types of files in a particular way
- a centralised mailroom where mail must be collected and delivered at specific times each day
- forms to complete if you want items from a stationery store.

If you ignore these procedures, and try to do 'your own thing', you are likely to find yourself being given a relatively mild rebuke on the first occasion and a much stronger warning if you do it again. In many cases, however, the end result will be that you don't get what you want because you *haven't* followed the correct procedure, and this is likely to throw all your well-made plans into chaos.

1 Find out what procedures in your own organisation affect the way you must carry out your work. The list above may give you some ideas of areas to investigate. If you had a formal induction at work, then you can refer back to information you were given at that time, or to any Staff Handbook you received. If you are at college, ask your tutor or trainer for examples of procedures which operate there. In particular, try to write down *at least* one procedure specifically related to security.

2 Identify the areas of your work where organisational procedures may not exist but where there is a specific way of doing things in your office which new people need to know, and add these to your list. For instance, in some offices all letters are signed by a supervisor or manager. Or you may have a supervisor who likes to be informed if you are leaving your desk for any length of time.

If you are at college and studying in a group, you may find it quite enlightening to compare your notes. Don't, however, be tempted to give away any confidential information whilst you are doing so.

TEST YOUR KNOWLEDGE AND UNDERSTANDING

You have just started work at Barlow's Insurance Services. You are surprised to find how disorganised the staff seem to be. In each of the following situations, identify what could have gone wrong, and what should be done to prevent the situations recurring.

1 At ten minutes to five Phil Barlow, the manager, is annoyed because a three-page document he wanted prepared this morning has still not been completed. The administrator doing the work is in a panic and her waste bin is overflowing with paper.

2 A second administrator is sitting on the floor surrounded by files. She has been like that most of the day, frantically trying to find a customer's file which is urgently required. She has already turned out her own desk and the carpet is covered in pencil shavings and bent paperclips.

3 Two customers ring to complain that they have each received the wrong quotations for life insurance which have obviously been put in the wrong envelopes. More than anything they are annoyed that someone else has received their personal details.

4 You receive a telephone call from the Royal Mail to say that yesterday's post was franked and yet it was posted in the letter box as ordinary mail. In future such mail will not be delivered. You realise the new junior administrator did this job on her own yesterday.

5 You decide to help your colleague to find the file she has lost, but in your rush knock a can of drink over all the papers on your desk.

Changing work plans and consulting others

You have already learned about the importance of flexibility. It is very rare (and would be very boring) to work in an office where life is so predictable that plans never need changing. There are several points you need to consider when work plans need to be changed because of new priorities:

* What will be the effect of the changes?
* Who else will be affected?
* Will there be any deadlines you cannot meet?
* Will there by any other requirements you cannot meet?

Possible effects

These can range from 'very few' to 'considerable'. It depends how busy you are and which other jobs have to be rescheduled. If the other jobs are *also* class A jobs (see page 107) the ramifications of the changes can be quite serious. You need to spend ten minutes thinking these through before you take any action, to make sure you have 'covered all the angles'.

Other people affected

If you work for several people, you will have to notify them if their work will be delayed for any reason. You should communicate with them if you think they will be affected in any other way.

If your supervisor will be affected it is sensible to ask for guidance as to the best way to cope with the problem. Even if the only person affected will be your closest friend in the office, it is courteous to keep that person informed.

Not meeting requirements

There may be several reasons why you cannot meet the requirements of the person who gave you the work:

* a vital resource you need is delayed or out of action
* the task is too complex to be completed by the deadline
* you are too busy to meet the deadline
* the task cannot be done in the way they wished because you do not have the equipment or resources available

- you have had several queries which have not been answered promptly enough for you to finish the job in time – or which are still outstanding.

If you find yourself in this position, there are two golden rules to remember.

1 Notify the person concerned *as soon as you are aware there may be a problem*. This enables them to take action before it is too late. In an emergency, this may mean drafting other people in to help you.
2 Notify the person concerned politely and give the reason for the problem. Apologise that you won't be able to meet their requirements (it won't cost you anything!). *Don't* be aggressive or defensive. If the reason for the problem is outside your control you can hardly be held to blame. If it is your fault, be prepared to apologise. If you are particularly worried about notifying a certain member of staff, ask your own supervisor for assistance.

Generally people are very reasonable if they get sufficient notification. What no one likes is to be presented with a serious problem when all other options have gone. You will also find you have fewer problems if you are renowned for trying to solve most difficulties yourself, are good at using your initiative, and are usually very reliable and efficient. The administrator who is *always* having problems meeting requirements is the one who needs to worry!

 INFORMATION UPDATE

One boss used to say 'Don't bring me a problem, bring me a solution'. Managers are used to solving problems – it is something they are paid to do. However, it is a refreshing change when an employee makes a useful suggestion as to how to get around a problem at the time.

If you have to notify a colleague, or your supervisor, that you are having a problem meeting their requirements about a particular job, you will enhance your reputation if you can suggest some practical measures that can be taken to rescue the situation. This also proves that you still have 'ownership' of the task – and are not simply trying to dump it back on someone else's lap.

TEST YOUR KNOWLEDGE AND UNDERSTANDING

In each of the following cases, something has gone wrong. What action would you take, if any, to try to solve the problem yourself? If this action were unsuccessful and you had to discuss the difficulty with your supervisor or colleague, what suggestions would you make to overcome the problem?

1 Your supervisor wants you to prepare some induction packs for ➡️

six new staff. When you go to the stationery cupboard you find there are only four presentation folders left.

2 You are half way through creating a complex spreadsheet when you realise that you did not ask your supervisor for the information you need for the third line. She has just left early to go to the dentist and wanted the spreadsheet completed by tomorrow morning.

3 You were relying on the help of a colleague to complete an important task for your supervisor. Today that colleague has rung in sick.

4 Your boss wants some important debtor letters sent out tonight. When you go to the franking machine you find there are insufficient units left and you don't know how to replenish them.

5 A 10-page report needs to be photocopied today and sent to a customer. At 2 pm – when you are half way through – the photocopier breaks down. You are told it can't be repaired until tomorrow morning.

6 You have promised a colleague all day that you will go to the local art shop and obtain some Velcro tape she needs for a display this evening. You have put off going because it has been raining, and when you arrive the shop has closed.

EVIDENCE COLLECTION

Your evidence for this element must show that you liaise with three types of colleagues:

a   your line manager

b   another person who has requested you to do work

c   another member of your team.

You have already seen that there are many issues on which you might consult them – for instance, about extending a deadline, about the way you should do a task, about organisational procedures, about changes to your work plans and problems meeting their requirements.

In many cases you may talk to them. If so, you will need to obtain witness evidence from each person. It is a good idea, therefore, to confirm many of your conversations in writing. A brief informal note, a message, a short memo or an e-mail are all perfectly acceptable. Sensibly you could link these to the task sheets you created for Element 202.1. In this case, whenever your evaluation section shows there was a problem, you can attach evidence that you kept the person concerned fully informed at every stage. If they respond to you in writing, attach their reply to your other documentary evidence.

Element 202.3 Help to improve your own work

Most of us like to move forwards in life. We have our own plans and dreams and want to take action to make some of them come true. There are two aspects to this. The first is to have some idea of what you want to achieve. The second is to improve your work so that you acquire more skills, have the opportunity to do more responsible jobs and gain enough experience to move upwards and onwards in your chosen career.

The importance of continuous development

Unless you are very unusual (or have a very hectic social life!), after you have mastered a job for some time you start to become restless or bored if you have no new challenges or nothing else to attract your attention and interest. However, it can be quite one thing to know that you are restless and in need of a change and quite another to decide what to do about it.

The tendency, if you are not careful, is to either stick in a rut or to 'job hop' without first thinking through the implications. You could end up worse off than you are now!

A sensible process of continuous development means that you seriously consider the benefits and weaknesses of your current situation and look at how you can improve yourself to take advantage of new opportunities which will be to your benefit. These may mean staying with your current employer and devising a method of learning new skills to develop your potential or, if this is not possible, taking time to consider suitable alternatives.

The value of *continuous* development is that this process never stops. As you grow older and gain more skills and experience your needs and wants will change again – and then again. If you continue to update your skills and abilities and move forwards, you will continue to progress throughout your whole career.

Part of this process, however, is developing self-awareness and self-knowledge – and this can be a painful experience! In other words, you need to know what people think of your skills and abilities now and your strengths and weaknesses. But beware! It is marvellous when people praise and flatter, but it is a different thing entirely when someone tells you that improvement is necessary. In this element you will learn about the type of feedback you can expect at work, and a few strategies for coping and dealing with it positively and constructively.

Feedback: what it is and how to react

Feedback is the response you receive from other people to your work and performance. Feedback is often informal, but there will be specific occasions when you receive formal feedback.

Informal feedback

Examples of informal feedback are: 'Great, just what I needed, thanks a lot' or 'We knew we could rely on you'. These are all examples of **positive feedback** – which makes you feel good. In fact, we often want praise to be said very loudly, so that everyone around can hear!

Other examples of feedback are comments such as 'Oh, no, what have you done?', or even simply a frown or shake of the head from side to side. Each of these is an example of **negative feedback** – you know the person isn't pleased and hope no one else has witnessed the event.

Formal feedback

Formal feedback is often written down so that there is a permanent record. A typical example is the school reports you used to receive. You will be involved with formal feedback sessions if you are on a Modern Apprenticeship scheme and have regular reviews about your progress. You will also receive formal feedback if you work in an organisation which operates an **appraisal** system.

Appraisals are regular reviews of your progress and abilities in relation to the aims and objectives of the organisation. Ideally they should be positive sessions where you talk about how you are finding your job, what you wish to do in the future and what additional training or experience you need. Your appraiser (usually your immediate supervisor or manager) should ensure that you have time to prepare for the interview, there is a review of your past performance and new targets are set which not only help the organisation but also help you to develop your career aims. The interview is confidential but ideally should end with the identification of your future training and development needs.

If the appraisal system is well organised and the interview done properly, this experience should be extremely positive. You will have had the opportunity to sit down with someone senior and talk about *yourself*. You will have had the chance to talk through your worries and concerns, hopes and fears, aims and ambitions. Your supervisor will have had the chance to give you feedback on your current performance and help you to identify new opportunities and areas for development.

However, appraisals should not be used as the only opportunity to give feedback. They may be the only chance you have to sit down, uninterrupted, for about an hour with your immediate superior, but this should not mean that everyone's moans and groans about you are kept until this time and then repeated one by one! Feedback is most effective when it is given promptly and when it is done in such a way that the overall experience is good – even if some of the specific feedback was not. However, this takes a level of skill which not all your supervisors and managers will possess.

The skills required to give feedback

You can quietly assess the skills of anyone who gives you feedback against the following checklist. A person who is good at giving feedback, especially that which includes a few criticisms, will always:

- talk to you on your own, in private
- get to the point quickly – you won't be left guessing what they think
- focus on the issue and not you as a person
- avoid sarcasm or hurtful remarks
- give you good, clear, specific examples to show what they mean
- give you the opportunity to reply, in full, and give your side of the story if there are any important issues to discuss
- try to agree mutually a way in which future problems can be overcome
- end by focusing on your positive aspects, not any negative points.

Dealing with positive feedback

If you are told how wonderful you are, that the organisation could not operate without you, that you are the most lively, intelligent and productive employee to join the company for years, then your first temptation might be to run from the room and tell everyone else. *Don't*. Not everyone may have had such a positive experience and you are likely to be extremely unpopular with your colleagues if you gloat about your glory. Someone may be tempted to bring you down to earth with a bump! If anyone asks, simply say the session went well.

The big danger in receiving very positive feedback is that you think there is nothing to learn. This is never true, no matter how old or experienced you are. The danger of letting good feedback go to your head is that, if you do, it may be the last time you receive it! Keep your head down and continue as you have been doing. It's your past performance that has gained you so much praise, so don't change your overall way of working.

Dealing with negative feedback

If you are criticised during a feedback session, the danger is that this is the part you focus upon. You forget any positive points and the criticism keeps going around and around in your head. Depending upon your temperament you may get angry or very upset. There are various strategies for dealing with criticism, both during the feedback session itself and immediately afterwards.

- If you are criticised, don't respond by being over-defensive and giving a twenty-minute explanation of what happened. Simply ask for an example.
- Never blame someone else – keep to the facts of the matter.
- If you think the accusation is unfair, ask the person talking to you for his/her suggestions about what you should have done.
- If you think the accusation is fair then try to swallow your pride. Try not to be too touchy or over-sensitive.
- If you find yourself getting angry, ask if the interview can be deferred until another time. Between times try to see the situation from your supervisor's point of view.
- If you find your boss is *very* critical and rarely gives praise, pluck up your courage and try to state how you feel, as unemotionally as possible. Simply say that you feel very upset, you feel that you rarely receive any praise and would find it easier to improve any weak areas if the session was more balanced.
- Remember that *no one* – no matter how old or experienced – likes being criticised. Yet if everyone gave us only good feedback we would never develop as individuals. Finding out that we could improve in an area is always painful to a greater or lesser degree – depending upon how sensitive we are and who tells us!
- If it helps, try to think that the session probably wasn't easy for your supervisor, either!

Contributing to feedback sessions

The best feedback sessions are those which end in an action-planning activity where both you and your supervisor identify areas where you are doing well, areas where you could improve and how this could be done. If you both agree on all these issues, then the session is likely to run very smoothly. If you disagree this tests the negotiation skills of *both* of you.

You will help yourself if you plan in advance.

1 Think carefully about all the areas of work you do. What do you *know* you are good at? What evidence (examples) do you have to support your opinion?
2 Which areas give you concern? What do you struggle with? Is this because you have never been shown properly or because you really feel this type of work is not your strength? What assistance would you need to get better at these tasks? How long do you think you will need to reach a consistently high standard?

3   What areas would you like to develop in the future? What additional skills would you need? How would this help the work that is done in your department and the overall work that is done by your organisation?

The only danger with planning out the session in advance is that you do not allow for your supervisor's input. The next stage is therefore to think about areas your supervisor may wish to discuss. If you work in an organisation where you are given regular feedback on your daily performance there should be few or no surprises during any formal sessions. This is always a healthier atmosphere than one where things are kept secret. Any surprises during a feedback session should always be positive ones, rather than negative.

If your supervisor surprises you by making a few suggestions you had never thought about, you are quite within your rights to ask for some thinking time. This is especially true if you are given the opportunity to take on more responsibility – the topic of the next section.

Agreeing new responsibilities

Many feedback and appraisal sessions have distinct sections – the last one being a discussion about the future. This is likely to focus on new responsibilities you could take on in the future. At one extreme, you may have identified one or two areas of work you would really like to develop and expand – jobs or tasks that you would like to learn how to do. This is an opportunity to be persuasive about your abilities, if your supervisor appears to have some misgivings.

At the other extreme, your supervisor may have one or two surprises for you and may offer you the opportunity of taking on additional responsibilities you had never thought about. This is a *compliment*. It indicates that you are doing well so far and your supervisor thinks you would cope with, and enjoy, new challenges. Depending upon how this is put to you, what the work entails, and your own temperament; this may seem the best news in years, and the most exciting development in your career – or the most terrifying idea you have ever heard.

If the idea of doing new or more challenging work alarms you, you are sensible to think carefully before conveying your misgivings to your supervisor. Think about it for a moment if you don't understand why. Staff who never want to move forwards or learn anything new are a handicap in today's fast-moving business world. And if your supervisor has previously thought that you were positive and forward-thinking, do you really want to destroy this impression? So if you are apprehensive, take some time to think things through before you voice your feelings. Otherwise it may be a long time before you are offered another chance.

There are, however, certain aspects relating to additional responsibilities that you would be sensible to discuss with your supervisor. These include:

- In what aspects of your work are you being asked to take on more responsibility?
- What, exactly, will your new responsibilities entail?
- How good at you at these jobs now?
- What additional skills and abilities will you need?
- Over what period of time will you have to learn new tasks?
- What help or assistance will you receive?
- Who will support you whilst you become more experienced?

Discussing these issues will impress your supervisor as it will be obvious you have thought through your concerns and are keen to be successful. It will also indicate a positive response – which will enhance your reputation both now and in the long term.

It is obviously much better if support and guidance has been planned into the process so that you will progress smoothly. However, this idea cannot always be realised in business. Very often, people have to take on new tasks and new responsibilities at a moment's notice because there is urgent work to be done. This is particularly the case if you work for a small, dynamic organisation which is growing rapidly. In this case, ask for a mentor who will give you help and advice when you need it.

Generally speaking, you are well advised to make the most of new opportunities – even if they may be rather scary at first. These are all 'learning opportunities' which provide you with more skills and abilities – and make you more eligible for higher-grade and better-paid jobs in the future.

CHECK IT OUT!

Carry out your own, personal feedback session on yourself. You can afford to be very honest when you do this exercise, as you don't have to share the results with anyone unless you want to. The aim is to come up with a list of your own strengths and weaknesses and link these to your overall aims and goals. A model form you can copy out and complete is shown on page 136.

1 Start by focusing upon yourself. What is your immediate aim in your current job? What would you like to be doing in two or three years' time? Think about the steps you would need to take to bridge the gap.

2 What are your current strengths? Think about things you are good at doing and enjoy. What evidence do you have to prove this – such as positive feedback from others or particular qualifications or achievements? What areas would you like to develop in the future?

3   What are your current weaknesses? Think about the occasions when you perhaps feel incompetent at something or worry about doing a particular task. Again, consider what evidence there is to support this – such as negative feedback from others or occasions when you have failed to do something properly. What suggestions can you make to overcome your weaknesses?

4   Extend your list by considering whether you are strong or weak in each of the following areas – which apply to every administrative job:

  • quality of work

  • output (i.e. quantity of work produced)

  • knowledge and skills

  • personal skills, such as punctuality, overall attitude to work, flexibility, organisational abilities, creativity, ability to use your own initiative, ability to solve problems

  • interpersonal skills (i.e. your ability to relate to other people – see Unit 201).

5   Use this information about yourself to generate some ideas about your future development. First try the easy part. Identify areas you really would like to develop in future. Now the harder one! Identify those you really should develop – even if you don't think at the moment that these will all be as enjoyable.

Keep your personal feedback form safely. You will need to refer to it again, later in this element.

Targets for improvement

Targets are important because they help you to achieve a specific goal. Setting precise, personal targets means that you can focus your energies on areas you want to develop and use your time more productively. Targets also help to improve your own self-confidence as you can see your progress clearly.

The benefits of setting targets include:

• giving you a clear plan of action, instead of drifting around aimlessly
• improving your performance in key areas you need or want to develop
• helping you to aim higher so that you achieve more
• giving you personal satisfaction when you achieve them
• improving your self-confidence in your own abilities
• reducing stress and worry as your future is more self-determined.

EVIDENCE COLLECTION

For this element, you have to ask for feedback from two of the following types of people, and say how you would obtain feedback from the third.

a   your line manager (who may be your supervisor or team leader)

b   a person for whom you undertake work

c   other staff in your team.

You also have to obtain *all* the following types of feedback:

a   what you do well

b   what you could improve

c   what new responsibilities you could take on.

You should therefore keep records of all feedback sessions you have, so that you can include them in your portfolio. Your line manager may undertake regular reviews or appraisals with you which will be documented and include any agreed new responsibilities. In the case of other people, you may have to ask for witness testimony. However, this is more likely to be positive than negative. If you have no evidence of what you could improve from anyone but your line manager, discuss your *own* evaluation of your performance to date with your assessor and suggest areas you could develop as part of your own continuous development plan.

Remember, however, that deciding your goals and targets is often the easy part. It needs self-discipline to carry them through – particularly in your 'least-favourite' areas.

Golden rules when setting targets

Many people fail to achieve their targets not because they are poor at self-discipline, but because the targets themselves were 'flawed' in some way. You can avoid this by observing the following rules. All your targets must:

- *Be specific.* Your target should be precise and clearly state what you intend to do.

- *Be realistic.* All your targets should be a natural progression from where you are now and achievable in a relatively short space of time – otherwise you will become disheartened. If you have a longer-term goal your targets should be 'small steps along the way'.

- *Be achievable.* Don't set a target which is too ambitious or which would require resources you haven't got.

PERSONAL FEEDBACK FORM

Name .... Current job role ....

Career aim (1 year) ....

Career aim (3 years) ....

Current strengths/areas of work I enjoy and would like to develop:

Current weaknesses/areas of work I don't enjoy but need to develop

Work area strengths and weaknesses

Quality of work		
Quantity of work		
Knowledge and skills		
Personal skills		
Interpersonal skills		

Ideas for future development

Things I want to do:

Things I should do:

- *Be positive*. Focus on what you would like to learn and improve, not on things would you like to get rid of or stop doing!

- *Be precise*. Set a date when you will review and measure your achievements on each target.

- *Be written down* – so that you have your own working plan (see page 141).

- *Be limited to your top-priority goals*. Otherwise you will have too many targets and be overwhelmed.

- *Be under your own control*. Don't set targets over which you will have no influence. For instance, it might be tempting to write a target of receiving a 10 per cent salary increase within the next twelve months, but no matter how hard you work the final decision on this will be subject to many factors over which you have no control.

- *Be 'owned' by you*. If you write down targets which other people want you to achieve – but you have no interest in – then you will be less committed to these than to achieving targets you have set for yourself. However, do note that you can realistically expect your supervisor to want you to set targets which help to turn your weaknesses into strengths and to develop in areas which are important to your own employer.

 INFORMATION UPDATE

Lifetime goals and lifelong learning are 'buzz' phrases of the twenty-first century. The aim is that people decide what they want to achieve all their life and take ownership of their own self-development and their own learning. This is sensible because it is based on three important truths:

- Work is only one area of your life – so what about the rest?
- Your employer is likely to be interested only in areas connected to your current job.
- Self-development is not 'age-related' – people can learn and develop throughout their lives.

For that reason, the importance of setting personal goals is often emphasised. If you want to do this, it simply means considering other areas of your life you want to include in the process, and not just your career. For instance, what personal interests would you like to develop or learn? What about your social life and pleasure activities – what goals do you have, such as places you want to see? What about health and fitness? What are your financial goals and aspirations? What about your friends and family? It is quite possible to think about goals and targets in far more areas of your life than your job or career.

1   Your friend, Selwyn, set several targets with his boss during his annual review. One of these was to learn how to use Powerpoint so that he could help to produce materials for the next sales conference. The date by which this was to be achieved was yesterday – but Selwyn has not achieved the target. From the list below, identify those reasons you think his boss would consider are *valid* or *acceptable* for non-achievement. In each case, what would you suggest if you were Selwyn's boss?

    a   Selwyn was too busy doing his normal work.

    b   He was ill and off work all last month.

    c   He was drafted in to help everyone with a major project with an urgent deadline so hadn't time to learn.

    d   He set himself so many targets that no one could have achieved them all.

    e   He tried Powerpoint but didn't like it. He now claims it is too hard for him to learn.

    f   He tried Powerpoint for a week and made so many mistakes all the work for the sales conference was given to his colleague, Jessica. She is resentful as she thinks Selwyn did it deliberately.

    g   He agreed the targets just to please his boss – and hoped they would be forgotten afterwards.

    h   The person who was going to instruct Selwyn has been too busy to show him.

2   Maxine is useless at taking messages and is not good at dealing with customers. She dislikes using the telephone and can be very abrupt when people ring. When she writes down a message the name is usually spelled wrongly, the telephone number may be written incorrectly and she never asks why people are calling. Often this results in other staff not being able to make contact with the person who left the message. Maxine's supervisor has asked her to write targets to help to remedy these weaknesses. As Maxine's friend and mentor, what targets would you suggest to her – and over what time scale?

Learning plans

Your learning plan is a personal, customised plan which links your overall goals and targets over a certain period. If the word 'learning' puts you off, because it reminds you of school, then please think again – for several reasons. Firstly, when you were at school you may have had limited choices about what you had to learn – whereas now you are (presumably) involved in an area of work you find interesting. Secondly, even then, you would have found some things more enjoyable than others. Often your interest will have been affected by *who* taught you and *how* you were taught. We all like some teachers more than others! Thirdly, your learning plan now should be directly related to your own future plans. It is designed to help *you* – and you alone. Finally, the amount you learn – what you know and how skilled you are – will directly affect the amount you are likely to earn in the future. So there are many benefits to devising a learning plan.

If you have already completed a National Record of Achievement or a Progress File you will be used to devising action plans linked to your progress to date. Your learning plan is no different. Usefully, it can include specific activities which will help you to achieve your targets. In other words, it can be used to translate your targets into a specific and manageable plan of action for the future. It identifies the knowledge and skills you need to learn to achieve your goals and helps you to identify a level of performance by which you can measure your achievements.

Before you start to construct a learning plan, it is helpful if you think a little bit more about yourself and your own preferences. This is because we all learn in different ways (see page 142) and certain *types* of learning suit some people more than others. If you can devise a learning plan which is the best one for you, you obviously have a better chance of succeeding.

CHECK IT OUT!

If you are doing your Key Skills award in Improving own Learning and Performance, turn back to the Key Skills signpost on page 93 to see how your learning plan can help you to achieve this goal, too.

Learning preferences

People are learning all the time. Every time you go somewhere new or find yourself in a different situation you undergo a 'learning experience'. In terms of your personal self-development almost any new activity will broaden your mind – whether this is visiting a foreign country, learning how to download music from the Internet, or joining a fitness centre. However, you are very fortunate if you work for an organisation that will help you to build such activities into a learning plan which is primarily concerned with helping you to improve your abilities in your current job role. If your organisation is more forward-thinking and will help you to develop in a variety of areas which will help you to improve your overall career and life prospects, then you are fortunate indeed.

Usually the best method is to start by thinking about yourself from the following aspects:

a   What skills do you currently possess?

b   What skills do you need to learn?

c   How do these link to your eventual career aims?

d   How do you see your future working life?

e   What career options are open to you in the future?

f   Could you pursue your ambitions with your current employer?

g   What can you learn which will help you in your present job?

h   What can you learn which would help you in the future?

i   What can you plan to learn over the next 12 months?

j   How up to date are you?

k   What methods do you use to keep up to date?

l   How best do you learn (see page 142)?

m   What opportunities are open to you for learning at work?

n   What opportunities are open to you for learning away from work?

If you link the information above, with the self-evaluation form you completed on page 134, you will find it easy to draw up a draft learning plan.

CHECK IT OUT!

Do you know your own learning style? A very famous questionnaire was designed by Honey and Mumford which identifies each person's own preferred learning style. If you are interested you can obtain a copy from your local college library. Even without doing the questionnaire you may be able to recognise yourself from the four main types:

- You are an **activist** if you prefer to learn by doing and dislike too much preparation and planning – or a lot of theory.

- You are a **reflector** if you enjoy listening and watching other people before trying out something yourself.

- You are a **theorist** if you like to be given plenty of information before you start something new. You will enjoy reading and finding out about new topics.

- You are a **pragmatist** if you are good at putting ideas and information you receive into practice and applying new things you have learned to your own job.

Knowing your own learning style can be useful, particularly if you have some say in what activities you can take part in to learn new skills and new knowledge – as you will see below.

EVIDENCE COLLECTION

You are now ready to start to devise your own learning plan. There isn't one correct way to draft out this document. You can use the format suggested in this book or agree a different one with your supervisor or trainer. However, once you have the basic information in place it is important to agree it with your supervisor, or someone else in your team. For that reason, it can be useful to discuss its development from the outset, rather than complete it and then have to start again.

It is sensible to divide your learning plan into specific areas, for instance:

a work skills and knowledge you want to learn or develop

b personal skills you would like to improve or acquire.

This is the model used in the suggested format overleaf.

1 Start by looking back at your Personal Feedback Form and write down your key areas of development under each section. If you have too many in one area, prioritise them so that you carry forward the most important and urgent to your learning plan. Remember to check that these link to any feedback you have received from your supervisor about your current strengths and weaknesses.

2 Think about any additional responsibilities you have agreed to take on, or would like to take on in the future. Consider the attributes you would need to be able to do this. Check that your learning plan includes any essential skills, knowledge or personal abilities you would need.

3 Now consider any targets you, or your supervisor, have suggested you should achieve. Check that your learning plan incorporates the skills, knowledge and attributes you would need to do so.

4 Finally, talk through your draft so far with your supervisor, tutor or mentor.

You will complete the final sections when you have learned more about the type of activities which might suit you best to achieve your plans.

PERSONAL LEARNING PLAN

Name .... Organisation ....

Job title ....

Date created .... Review date ....

Work skills and knowledge

Skills/knowledge identified	Learning method	Target achievement date	Progress made on review date

Personal development

Area of development	Learning method	Target achievement date	Progress made on review date

Additional comments. Use this section to record additional or unexpected learning opportunities since the last review date and their result; reasons for good or poor progress in particular areas; additional goals you wish to incorporate into any revised learning plans.

Selecting learning activities

There are two basic types of learning activity – those in which you participate when you are at work (generally known as 'on-the-job') and those where you leave work for a short time (known as 'off-the-job'). Both have benefits and drawbacks. Much depends upon what you are trying to learn.

You will benefit from learning at work if you are using equipment or methods of work that are specific to your own workplace – for instance, if someone shows you how to use a new fax machine or how to log and check invoices in your organisation. However, there are occasions when it can be very useful to get away from work to learn. You can concentrate because you are not distracted by the pressures of work, you can exchange your ideas with other people and make friends, and you can learn topics of general interest and from a wider viewpoint than just your current employer.

Learning activities at work

The most common of these are as follows.

- Learning by 'watching and doing', where you work with a more experienced person who shows you how to do a job.

- Coaching is a slightly more formal version of 'watching and doing'. In this case someone acts as your coach and mentor and guides you through a new task.

- Work shadowing can be used if you need to learn how another department operates, because you can literally 'watch and observe' to see how a job is done.

- Job rotation enables you to learn different skills because you exchange work roles with someone else for a short time. This can also help to give you more variety and is useful in a small office where everyone needs to be able to cover for everyone else in an emergency.

- 'In-house' courses for employees are more likely to be set up by large organisations which put on specific learning activities for their staff.

- Skills centres or interactive computer learning packages are, again, more likely to be made available if you work for a large organisation.

Learning activities 'off-the-job'

Here options can include the following.

- Short courses run by training organisations and colleges, such as those to learn specific computer skills.

- Longer courses which tend to focus on national qualifications.

- Evening classes where you can learn specific skills (such as shorthand or a foreign language).

- Self-study requires you to be very self-disciplined but can be useful if you are very interested in developing your skills in one area. For instance, several people who have taught themselves Web page design have done so with the help of a computer manual.

Finally, don't forget that you will have several other opportunities to learn, such as when another member of staff is away and you are asked to do something new to help out.

TEST YOUR KNOWLEDGE AND UNDERSTANDING

Sanjay is an activist. He doesn't much like books and prefers to get on with the job. Gemma, on the other hand, is a reflector, who hates to be asked to do something before she is ready. Meera is a theorist, who would prefer to read than get her hands dirty. Ishmail is a pragmatist who likes to link what he learns to his own job.

They all attended a short fire-training course. This entailed a one-hour talk by a fire officer on the dangers of fire, a half-hour demonstration of fire-fighting, a further half-hour during which they were expected to use fire-fighting equipment themselves, and a question and answer session at the end.

1 Try to identify which of them:
   a was bored during the one-hour talk and became interested only once the demonstration started
   b was the last in line to use the equipment
   c asked very good questions linked to fire assessment at work
   d carefully read all the leaflets afterwards.

2 Ideally, a good participant would have been interested in *every* part of the course!
   a From what you know about each person, what would you think their individual strengths and weaknesses would be if a fire *did* occur at work?
   b What positive action do you think each one should take to adjust and improve his or her learning style?

3 Which part of the course would you have enjoyed the most? What does this tell you about your own learning style – and your own strengths and possible weaknesses when learning?

Reviewing your achievements and learning plan

Regular reviews of your targets and learning plan are essential, for two reasons. Firstly, you must identify which targets have been achieved, which have not, and why not. Secondly, the learning plan must be kept up to date so that it reflects what you want to do *now* – not what you intended to do six months ago.

Targets and achievement

Some targets may not be achieved, for a variety of reasons. If you have failed to reach a target this is likely to be because:

- the target was unrealistic in the time allocated
- you had to give other targets greater priority
- you were not able to obtain the skills or knowledge you needed
- you didn't try hard enough, lost interest or forgot about it.

If you have failed to achieve *all* your targets then the time has come for some serious thought. If it is because you have no interest in any of them then a visit to a careers counsellor should probably be your next target!

Failing to meet a target is often disappointing, but can be turned into a positive experience. Learning to overcome difficulties and solve problems is a learning experience in itself. Your supervisor is likely to be less concerned with the target itself than with your *attitude* and how you intend to overcome the problem in the future.

Achieving targets, on the other hand, is always a positive experience. You have evidence that when setting out to do something, you can achieve it. However, still take time to consider how this achievement can influence you in future:

a   If you achieved it more quickly than you thought, do you set your targets too low, to 'play safe'? Should you give yourself a greater challenge next time?

b   If you achieved it, but only with great difficulty over a longer period, then make your next targets a little easier. Perhaps you are too hard on yourself (or not very good at planning).

c   How much did you *enjoy* achieving it? Do you want to pursue additional targets in the same area? Or has this made you decide that a particular area of work is not what you want?

d   Did your achievement highlight any other related areas of development that you would like to pursue?

Reviewing your learning plan

All the information obtained from your target achievements should influence your revised learning plan. You can expect your aims and goals to change as you gain in experience. That is natural. As you learn new skills and knowledge you are also learning to know yourself better. There will be new areas you want to develop. If you find that this is pointing you in a different direction, you owe it to yourself to investigate this more deeply. Treat it as an opportunity, rather than a problem!

Administrators can often choose to *specialise* as they move upwards from NVQ level 2. Some like financial work and decide to move towards accounting. Others prefer to develop their IT skills. Another group decide to further their administrative skills and abilities or move into secretarial or PA work. Opportunities exist to work in different sectors, such as legal work or in the health service.

Making these choices is very dependent upon knowing about yourself, about the type of work which interests you – and proving to employers that you have the skills and abilities to progress. This is an additional benefit of an ongoing learning plan. It provides evidence that you can set your own goals and achieve them. It enables you to update your CV regularly. It gives you the opportunity to prove to your current employer that you can handle additional responsibility and work towards promotion, and to any new employer that you have a positive attitude towards self-development.

If it turns out, during review of your learning plan, that there are some goals or targets you no longer wish to acquire, discuss this with your supervisor. State your reasons unemotionally and objectively. Unless the target or learning activity is fundamental to your job, it is preferable to drop it rather than having it sitting there for months as a threat! Deciding your own goals, setting targets and working towards them should be a pleasurable and positive experience and one over which you have control. It should not make your life a misery.

Ideally, your learning plan will be constantly evolving from your own improved self-knowledge, skills and abilities and the feedback you receive from your boss and your colleagues as you progress. It will constantly reflect your own aims and goals and will be focused upon helping you to achieve them.

EVIDENCE COLLECTION

Finalise your learning plan by negotiating the next progress review date with your supervisor or trainer, and deciding on the dates by which you hope to achieve your specific aims. This will complete all your columns.

Keep an ongoing record of progress towards your goals, particularly if your next review date is six months in the future. As you learned in the first section of this unit, if you are planning for some time in the future you should check your progress *regularly*. It is no use realising three days before your review interview that everything has gone wrong!

Keep *all* your learning plans and *all* your notes and records of progress. They are excellent evidence to prove that you have learned the basic skill of how to improve yourself.

Unit 203 Communicate information using telephone and fax

The growth in communications over the last ten years has been incredible, in terms of both the different methods and systems of communications *and* the amount of information communicated.

Today, a great many people have mobile telephones. Once people were restricted to being in a building when they made or received calls, but now those calls can be made from virtually anywhere. In addition, telephones are more sophisticated, with a variety of features. Mobile phones can even be used for Internet access. Office systems can be controlled by computer to enable callers to be greeted by a digitised voice and guided through their choice of operations. In some cases no contact with a human being is required for the caller's request to be fulfilled.

Other communication systems abound – including e-mail and fax – both of which are now commonplace in nearly all businesses. Fax machines are used routinely to send documents rapidly anywhere in the world, and these too contain a variety of features to make life easier for both sender and receiver.

Using a telephone and being able to send and receive fax messages are fundamental skills for anyone working in business today. You may be familiar with using a telephone yourself – both your home phone and your mobile. You probably don't own your own fax machine. However, to achieve this unit you have to prove that you can use both phone and fax machine efficiently in a business context.

The first element of this unit concentrates on developing your *telephone technique*, the second on sending and receiving faxes. However, as the importance of effective communications and a knowledge of 'who does what' in your organisation is essential to both elements, we will cover these first.

 KEY SKILLS SIGNPOST

If you are taking your Key Skills award, you can extend your knowledge of this area by undertaking several activities towards your **Communications** unit. These are listed below for Level 2.

C2.1a

Discuss – *either* with your tutor or supervisor *or* in a small group – one of the following topics:

- the importance of good communications to team working (see Unit 201)
- the advantages and disadvantages of mobile telephones
- the difference between social and business communications.

Make sure that you take part in the discussion positively by making clear and relevant contributions, by listening and responding appropriately to other people, and by helping to move the discussion forwards.

C2.1b

Prepare a short talk of approximately five minutes on one of the following subjects, using at least one image to help you:

- the importance of health and safety in the workplace
- modern communications systems in the workplace
- the role of computers in the workplace.

C2.2

From the information given in this book *and* another source of your own choice, write a brief summary on one of the following subjects:

- how to remedy problems on a fax machine
- how to prepare an original document for fax transmission
- how to take telephone messages for other people
- the importance of correct posture when using a computer.

C2.3

a You have just telephoned the Clifton Hotel, Bristol BR2 3MD, to book a single room for your boss for next Wednesday and Thursday. He (or she) won't be arriving until 6 pm and will be settling his bill by credit card. The hotel have asked you to write and confirm the reservation. Prepare an appropriate letter.

b Imagine you are working in an office in the year 2020. How do you think communications might have changed by then? Use the information in this unit, and that on e-mail and the Internet on Option Unit 214, to give you some ideas. Then write an essay of between 600 and 1000 words to describe your views and include at least one image (either a chart, graph or diagram) to illustrate your work. Use suitable headings and paragraphs and make certain that your spelling, grammar and punctuation are accurate (see below and Appendix, page 495).

The importance of effective communications

It is impossible to overstate the importance of communications in business in general and in an office in particular. The reason for this is simple. To survive, most businesses have to react and respond quickly to changes. They have to work hard to win customers and keep them. They have to provide competitively priced goods or a high-quality service consistently – in the right place and at the right time. All these demands put a tremendous strain on staff to work rapidly and yet make the right decisions, time after time. Added to all this, technological developments have meant that the amount of information flowing in and out of businesses has never been greater. Every day information arrives by post, by fax, by e-mail, by telephone from suppliers, customers and other organisations such as government departments, banks and insurance companies.

Every single item of information can affect a decision that is made or an action that is taken. For the decision or action to be the right one under the circumstances, all information must be communicated promptly, accurately and clearly. This, therefore, is a major responsibility of everyone who works in every office in every organisation.

Effective communications are those which:

* are technically accurate in every detail (nothing is missing or incorrect)
* are easy to understand
* have been prepared with the receiver's needs in mind
* have been sent using the most appropriate method
* are timely (they are sent in good time for the required response to be made).

These factors are so important that it is worth examining each of them in more detail.

Technical accuracy

It may seem obvious to say that inaccurate or misleading information can create problems – but you would be amazed at how many people are very casual about this, for one of a variety of reasons.

- They receive a telephone call when they are busy doing something else, so they don't concentrate on what is being said.
- They receive a call but have no pen or paper on which to write the information, and mistakenly think they will be able to remember it.
- Finding out information will take an effort, so they hazard a guess rather than look up the details.
- The information is complex or technical and they don't understand it properly – but don't like to admit this.
- They don't check they have noted down the details correctly before passing on the information.
- They have poor communication skills so don't express themselves clearly or concisely.
- They are thoughtless or casual and miss out important points without worrying about the problems this will create for the recipient.
- They are acting on incorrect information they themselves have been given.

You have a responsibility to other people to make life easier for them, not harder! It is therefore critical that you check all your communications carefully for accuracy before you send them. If you have any doubts about something it is always better to ask for advice rather than pass on information which is incorrect or inaccurate.

Clarity

Many people think that to communicate properly you need to be an expert at written English. Whilst good communication skills are obviously important, don't confuse this with knowing 'long words' or being able to write complex sentences. People have to read so much today that what they want are the facts – clearly and simply. It is often better in these circumstances to give key facts as a list of bullet points than to write an essay. Rather more skills are required for writing some types of business letters, but for most of your communications the ability to state clearly, and unambiguously, what you mean – and keep it brief – will endear you to everyone.

Do bear in mind that you cannot express yourself clearly if you don't know what you are talking about! If your information is difficult to understand, ask someone for help. Don't guess what it means or you are in danger of being both unclear *and* inaccurate.

You can check your own ability by referring to the Appendix, page 495.

The receiver's needs

When you are communicating with someone your mind should be on the needs of the receiver – rather than on yourself. This means thinking about the content, timing and method of your communication.

a   Will the content be clear to that person? Or have you used jargon, technical terms, slang or expressions they may not understand?

b   Are you timing your communication to suit yourself or them? How might this affect their response?

c   How do you intend to communicate with them – is this the best method under the circumstances? Whereas you obviously can't send a fax to someone without a fax machine, neither should you ring someone with complex information which would be better sent in writing (see below).

Method of communication

Although this unit concentrates on telephones and fax machines, you may have several other choices. You could send something through the post, transmit an e-mail, or go and see the person. All communication methods can be divided into two types – verbal and written. The table opposite shows the strengths and weaknesses of both types.

Timeliness

Realising just after midnight that you forgot to give your boss an important message from the travel agent about his trip today is not normally guaranteed to give you a good night's sleep! Quite obviously you then have to solve several problems to try to get the information to her or him in time for it to be of any use. There is also nothing more annoying than to receive information which, if you had seen it half an hour ago, would have saved you a lot of effort.

Some fundamental errors to avoid are:

*   leaving critical messages on voicemail and answering machines, without checking that they have been 'picked up'
*   leaving written messages on empty desks, without checking whether the person is away
*   leaving a written message in the middle of a stack of papers on a desk, because it will probably not be seen
*   forgetting to check the fax machine on a regular basis for incoming messages
*   delaying passing on messages promptly.

Under no circumstances put an urgent message into a mail tray when you suspect that it won't be collected until much later that day or even the next morning. Think of a very urgent and important message as a time bomb in your hands – which will go off if you don't pass it on. Until you have told someone else, that information is *your responsibility*, and if anything goes wrong you will get the blame. If you can't find the person you are looking for, tell your supervisor.

ADVANTAGES AND DISADVANTAGES OF DIFFERENT METHODS OF COMMUNICATION

	Verbal	Written
Advantages	Rapid Relatively cheap Can use voice for emphasis or to show feelings Immediate feedback possible from listener Can check listener(s) paying attention Body language (gestures, facial expressions) emphasise meaning and attitude if communication face to face	Is more formal Provides a permanent record if proof is needed Can be filed for future reference Can be read and studied at leisure Can be copied for other people Creates a 'distance' between sender and recipient, so useful for difficult communications (e.g. bad news) Can include visual information and colour to help understanding and add emphasis
Disadvantages	Clear speech essential Message must be clear and unambiguous to be understood Person must be able to hear the message properly Long or complex messages easily forgotten External factors may distract speaker or listener Can be difficult to handle hostility or disagreement shown by listener	Takes time to produce – particularly if long or complex Keyed-in documents need skill to be produced quickly and accurately Will be spoiled by use of inappropriate language or poor spelling or punctuation Must be legible – may depend upon handwriting ability of writer Permanency may prove a disadvantage if contents are inaccurate, out of date or writer later regrets sending message

INFORMATION UPDATE

Answering machines are now so commonplace they probably need little explanation. Many people have an answering machine at home to record calls received when they are out or otherwise occupied. For people who do not want to purchase a machine, answering services are available, such as BT's Call Minder. This also operates if the telephone is engaged, which is useful. All calls are recorded digitally by BT in the subscriber's personal mailbox and can be accessed by dialling 1571 and following the prompts. Virtually all other telephone service providers offer a similar service.

A variation on this operates on many organisational systems. This is called 'voicemail'. It can be set up from an extension by the user, and callers will hear a message which is similar to 'You are through to the voicemail box of (name). To record your message please speak clearly after the tone.' The messages are accessed by the extension holder by keying in his or her user identity code.

CHECK IT OUT!

On most automated answering systems there is a limit to the amount of time you can talk when leaving a message. This is quite generous and you would be warned, by an electronic voice, if you were running out of time. However, it is worth bearing in mind that messages you leave should be relatively concise and *clear*. You can help by speaking slightly more slowly than usual. It is also often a good idea to state the time and date you are calling, particularly if you need a response by a specific time. Although most systems give this information to the listener when the message is played, they only do this at the *end* of the call. Sometimes it is useful to have this information earlier.

Check how understandable you are when you leave a message by leaving a recorded message for someone and then arranging to hear it played back. You may get rather a shock, because no one sounds the same as they think they do! Try to ignore this aspect and simply concentrate on whether your message is clear and whether all your words can be easily heard.

In each of the following situations a communication was ineffective. First identify why this was so, and in each case state what the likely outcome would be and what, if anything, could be done to rectify the problem.

a An urgent order for stationery was faxed to the supplier but the essential catalogue reference numbers were missing.

b Amit rang his computer help-desk when his machine developed a fault, but did not understand what the technician was saying.

c A telephone message for your supervisor says 'ring Mr Jones' but doesn't give his extension number. There are three 'Mr Jones' in your organisation.

d A fax to a hotel confirming accommodation has the wrong date of arrival.

e An urgent message to a rep, who travels extensively for her company, is left on her answering machine at home.

f You can't understand clearly what a caller is saying when he gives his telephone number.

g A message on your desk says 'Paula told Noreen she could go with you to the meeting. Can you confirm the time with her.'

Your team – and their responsibilities

In Unit 201 you identified your team. This is relevant here, too, because it is important for you to know the best person to contact over different items of information. People who have worked in an organisation for some time find it easier to deal with queries and general items of information than do new or temporary staff. On the main switchboard of a large company, for example, it is vital that the operator knows to whom calls should be passed. Such an operator will, ideally, have a broad knowledge of all the sections and departments, as well as some knowledge about the best people to contact regarding specific issues.

In your own team, it is helpful to know:

- what areas of work each person does
- current issues with which they are involved
- who they deal with regularly, both internally and externally
- whether they are expecting any calls or messages
- if they are out, when they will be back

- if they are going out, whether there is anything important likely to happen and, if so, what action should be taken in their absence.

This helps you to communicate with people on their behalf far more effectively as you have some background knowledge to help. It also means you are perceived as being more professional – you will have more confidence and will be able to handle a wide variety of situations both knowledgeably and correctly.

It also means you are fulfilling your obligations as a team member far more effectively!

 INFORMATION UPDATE

Brevity of communications is becoming more and more important because of the increased number of items of information being received by office staff every day. It is estimated that today people receive up to 100 e-mails a day, dozens of phone calls on their office telephones and mobiles, faxes *and* a mixture of internal and external documents in their in-tray!

Some experts have classed this as 'information overload'. **Information overload syndrome** is the term given to people who are becoming stressed trying to cope with all the information they receive.

One way in which you can make other people's lives easier is not to add to this information overload yourself. Keep your messages short and to the point, so that people can take in the main points quickly. In that way, no one is going to have to waste time before they can establish what you really mean.

Element 203.1 Make and receive telephone calls

Whenever you use a telephone at work, either to make or to receive a call, *you become your organisation to the person at the other end.* Your company will therefore be judged on how you speak, on what you say and – if you are taking a message – on your ability to note down the important facts and pass these on promptly.

At work you will, of course, be expected to deal with external callers as well as your colleagues over the telephone. Your colleagues, in this sense, are likely to be internal contacts from various sections or departments in the organisation. If you develop a professional approach to using the telephone and communicating clearly, then it obviously doesn't matter whether the person ringing you is an important customer, a senior manager or Brian in accounts as you will be equally effective with all of them.

Organisational procedures for making and receiving telephone calls

All organisations have recommended procedures – or 'ways of doing things'. Large organisations may have these written down and ensure that all new, inexperienced staff receive some basic training before they are allowed to make external telephone calls in particular, or deal with customers. A small firm can be just as pernickity – but the instructions may not be given in writing, nor may there be any formal training – you might be expected to watch other people and copy their ways. It helps, however, if you have some idea of the type of procedures you can expect to find in operation.

Receiving external calls

You will either receive these for your organisation as a whole (e.g. if you are on a small switchboard, or operate a feature phone on a system whereby calls are received on behalf of all the others in a small office) or have a telephone extension which also 'doubles up' as a direct line – so that people can ring your extension and bypass the switchboard. There are various standard company greetings, and you need to check which one is used *wherever* you work – as these can range from very formal to much less so.

- An example of a formal greeting is: 'Good morning (or afternoon), Tilcot Financial Services. How may I help you?'
- Less formal could be: 'Hello, Parcels Express. Can I help you?'
- Even less formal would be: 'Hi, Software 2000, Paul speaking. What can I do for you today?'

You therefore need to establish how formal the organisation's standard greeting is, and whether you have to identify yourself by name. Doing this is very helpful for the caller, but more hazardous for you if you make a mess of the call!

Receiving internal calls

On many telephone systems you can tell whether the call is external or internal by the type of ring – although until you are certain of this you may wish to play safe and always give the standard greeting. If you work in a specific department where calls will have been routed to you from a central switchboard, you would *not* answer your internal extension with the standard greeting. Instead it is normal to confirm to the caller the section or department he/she has contacted and, usually, to identify yourself:

* 'Hello. Sales Department, Kavita speaking.'
* 'Customer Services, Jim Baxter. Can I help you?'

It is *not* standard practice to answer internal extensions with a simple 'Hello', nor to give the extension number as a greeting as this means nothing to most people.

Other organisational procedures

You can expect organisational procedures to cover other issues relating to telephone usage. In many cases these exist to try to control the overall cost of telephone usage by introducing certain measures. For example:

a If someone is not available, should you arrange for that person to ring back or is it standard practice for the *caller* to be asked to ring back later? Organisations that are keen to keep their customers happy will want you to promise that someone will call back later. However, if you work somewhere which receives a lot of general enquiries – such as a leisure complex – you will be told to ask the caller to ring back later as this reduces the overall telephone bill.

b Even if you normally arrange for someone from your company to call back, can you still do this if someone is calling long distance or from abroad – given this will be more expensive?

c Can you access directory enquiries on your extension or is this facility restricted because of the cost?

d Are there any other restrictions on your extension that you should know about or for telephone users generally?

e What is the company policy about personal calls? Many organisations allow staff to *receive* personal calls – given that anyone can have a family emergency – and will have no specific restrictions on this provided the privilege is not abused. Chatting to friends each day will be frowned upon in any organisation. If you need to *make* a personal call, this is usually allowed if the matter is important. However, if your organisation has provided pay phones for staff use, it is likely that personal calls from your desk will be prohibited.

Many people now take their mobiles to work, so issues about personal calls have changed, as friends and family can ring the mobile number. However, do not expect your organisation to be happy about you regularly taking or making calls on it during working hours. Save such chats until lunchtime and keep your mobile on 'message' mode whilst you are at your workplace.

Finally, even if your employer is fairly liberal about you receiving personal calls or using your mobile, don't take advantage. Keep personal calls short and to the point during office hours. Otherwise you will soon find your employer starting to put in place new procedures to cover this!

EVIDENCE COLLECTION

Start your evidence collection for this unit by proving that you know your organisation's procedures for making and receiving telephone calls.

Make a short list of the procedures that apply to your situation, and then try to note alongside each one at least one instance when you have applied the procedure. Before you include the list as evidence, check you have given it an appropriate heading and signed and dated it. Then ask your supervisor to sign it, too, for authenticity.

Establishing the key facts

When you are making or answering a call on behalf of your employer it is in everyone's interest for you to have the confidence to deal with the call effectively. This means knowing a few basic techniques and methods of working *in addition* to knowing how to deal with the caller.

Golden rules for answering calls

1 Answer promptly and identify yourself immediately.
2 Even if you were busy with an important or complex task when the phone rang, don't let the irritation of being interrupted show in your voice. If no one ever rang then you'd be lucky to still have a job!
3 Don't ignore a ringing telephone on someone else's desk – unless you have been told to or you are on the telephone yourself. Answer it and offer to take a message for the person who is absent.
4 Speak with a 'smile in your voice'. Surveys have shown this actually helps people to sound more helpful and pleasant.

5 If you are right-handed, pick up the receiver with your left hand and with a pen in your right hand (or next to you on the desk). If you are left-handed reverse this.

6 Always have a notebook or a telephone message pad within easy reach.

7 Don't answer when you are eating or drinking, even if you *know* the call is internal. Swallow first!

Golden rules for making calls

1 Prepare first. No one wants to deal with someone who doesn't seem to know what they are ringing about or forgets two or three important questions and has to keep ringing back.

2 If the call is complex, note down all the facts you must mention in a logical order.

3 Have space alongside (or below) on which to write the responses.

4 Always identify yourself when you get through.

5 Allow 'thinking time' for the other person – especially if you have a lot to say or the information is complex. You may have prepared well so you know it backwards, but it will be new to the other person who might have been heavily involved and distracted by another job when the phone rang. Speak relatively slowly and clearly.

6 Note the person's responses to your queries. If you don't understand what is being said ask for an explanation. If you can't keep up, ask for the information to be repeated. This is better than concluding the call and finding you have a page of incomprehensible information you cannot possibly pass on to anyone.

7 At the end, especially if the call has been a long one, it is useful to summarise the main points to make sure you haven't missed anything out or misunderstood something.

8 If the person on the other hand has been helpful or done you a favour providing the information, remember to say 'thank you'.

The professional touch

Once you become confident using a telephone in business it becomes an essential part of your life. However, no matter how confident you become you should always have a slightly different – and professional – manner when you are at work from the one when you are answering your mobile or your telephone at home.

All the techniques you have just read about are equally applicable whether you are dealing with other people on internal calls or external calls. However, if you really want to create an impression, particularly with the latter, you may like to note the following techniques which are often used by professionals.

• Using a person's name during a conversation has two benefits. It helps you to remember who you were speaking to, and it makes the person feel important. It is therefore useful when you are speaking to external callers – or to a senior manager – but don't overdo it.

- Don't use slang or colloquial expressions (e.g. 'that's cool' or 'hang on').
- *Never* say 'What?' – or even worse 'You what?' – if you don't hear something. The phrase you need is 'I'm sorry, could you repeat that please?'
- Try to avoid using the word 'OK'.
- Say figures in *pairs* rather than in threes. They are much easier to understand.
- Use the word 'zero' for '0' and *not* 'nought' – it's clearer.
- If you make the call, then technically you should be the one to end it. Equally, if someone is ringing you, then ideally they should conclude it. However, use your discretion. If the caller is very talkative it is quite acceptable to find a good reason for concluding the call yourself – 'I'm sorry, Amelia, I'd love to hear more about your shopping trip but I really have to finish this report urgently' or 'I really would like to talk to you for longer, Mrs Barnes, but someone is waiting to see me so I'll have to go' should suffice. It is not normally recommended, however, to use this approach if it is your manager who is on the other end of the phone!
- Ending a call from a customer with 'Thank you for calling' gives that person a good feeling from having spoken to you. Even if you receive a complaint you can still end the call in a similar way by saying 'Thank you for letting us know.'

Receiving calls and establishing the caller's identity

The first critical piece of information you need when receiving a call is the caller's name and, if the caller represents a business organisation, the name of that as well. This may seem very straightforward but various things can go wrong! Consider the following.

- The caller has a common name (e.g. Smith or Patel) so you need to find out the first name too, but don't.
- The name is foreign and you struggle to write it correctly as you cannot make out what the caller is saying. The same thing can happen if the caller has a very strong or unusual accent or dialect.
- The name is unusual or has an unusual spelling but you don't like (or remember) to check.
- There are several branches of the organisation and the caller forgets to say which one he/she is calling from.
- The caller doesn't state his/her name and you forget to ask. This is more likely to happen if you receive a call from a private individual – particularly someone who is unused to making calls, such as an elderly person.

Regardless of all these possible difficulties, it is essential that you establish accurately the caller's identity if you, or anyone else, is to deal with the call properly.

- If the person is a customer, you (or someone else) may need to access the customer file or other details.
- If the person has already made an enquiry you will probably need to refer to that record.
- If the person is making an enquiry, you need to log the details correctly for anyone else to call back with information or to send information through the post.
- If your organisation deals with several people with the same name, you do not want the wrong person being called back.

CHECK IT OUT!

Try always to establish the caller's identity at the *start* of the call. This may mean waiting until they have made their initial enquiry – or even mean stopping them in mid-sentence in some cases. Simply say, 'I'm sorry, but could you just give me your name first, please.' If you have difficulty understanding what is said, ask the caller to repeat it – and then repeat it back to check. It can be difficult to admit you still don't understand what is being said – the best way is to ask the caller to spell the name. And *then* check you are writing (and pronouncing) it correctly.

Traditionally, switchboard operators learned the 'telephone alphabet' so they could check that they had distinguished certain letters correctly – particularly 'T' from 'D', and 'B' from 'P'. Today this is less commonly known, but you can still use the same technique. 'Is that P for Peter or B for butter?' will still get you the right answer.

Finding out what the caller wants

It is important to find out why the caller is ringing your organisation. You may think this is unnecessary if you are simply going to transfer the call to someone else, but that is a misconception. Unless you handle dozens of calls, and you have strict instructions just to put a caller through as quickly as possible, then you should *always* try to establish what the caller wants. There are various reasons for this.

- You need to know the reason for the call before deciding whether you can handle the call yourself or need to pass it on to someone else.
- If you are passing it on to someone else, knowing what the caller wants means you can connect them to the best person to provide help or information.
- If you are putting the call through to your supervisor or manager, it helps them to decide whether they want to deal with it or would prefer someone else to handle it. Even if they are going to speak to the

caller, you are providing them with valuable 'thinking time' before connecting them.

- If you are going to take a message for someone, you will need to find out what the call is about, anyway.

If you receive a general enquiry, where the caller is not sure who to ask for, the caller is obviously going to tell you the reason for calling as part of the conversation. However, if the caller specifically wants to speak to someone else, and you want to know why, he or she is calling, you will have to ask tactfully (for example): 'Could I tell Mr Evans why you are calling, please?' Even then, the caller may not wish to tell you, which is perfectly acceptable. Callers tend to be more reticent about giving information when wishing to discuss sensitive issues, such as with a solicitor or an accountant.

EVIDENCE COLLECTION

For this element you have to provide evidence that you can deal with calls from people both inside and outside your organisation.

A sensible way of proving that you make and receive calls regularly as part of your job is to keep a log sheet which gives information on the type of calls you have dealt with. You can start to prepare one now. You may find it easier to complete if you set it out on A4 landscape paper. Head it with the title of this element and your name and your employer's name. Then divide it into columns with the following headings: Date, Name of caller, Internal/external caller, Reason for call, Action taken.

You can start to complete this at any time, but if you make and receive many calls it would be sensible to concentrate mainly on the types of call you need to have dealt with as part of this scheme (see pages 164–165). However, you *must* include both internal and external callers on your log sheet. If you respond to calls only infrequently, you may want to record every one, to be on the safe side – or ask your supervisor if you can do this more often.

Finally, if you regularly take messages for other people, it is a good idea *now* to put a copy of each one in a special folder.

Rachel Armstrong works for a car hire company and Bob Jenkins is her boss. In the office with her are Susan Knowles and Rizwan Bashir. This morning Bob is out of the office for an hour. Susan is busy with a client and Rizwan is outside on the forecourt trying to sort out repairs to a car that was involved in a collision yesterday. Rachel takes three calls. Read carefully what she says below. In each case identify what she did right, what she did wrong, and the probable outcome.

'Good morning, Acme Car Hire.'

'Good morning. Can I speak to Bob Jenkins, please?'

'No, sorry, you can't. He's out at the moment. He'll be back in an hour if you want to ring him then.'

'Will do. Bye.'

'Good morning, Acme Car Hire.'

'Good morning, it's Sally Dalgleish here from Swallow Insurance. Can I speak to Rizwan Bashir, please?'

'Well, er, Rizwan isn't available right now. He's a bit busy. Can anyone else help you. What is it about?'

'It's about the accident one of your cars was involved in yesterday.'

'Oh, well, I'll tell him you rang.'

'Please do, and get him to ring me urgently will you on 445028. Bye.'

'Good morning, Acme Car Hire.'

'Good morning. I'm ringing to enquire about your cars.'

'Right, well, I'd put you through to one of our sales staff, Susan, if I could but she's busy with a client at the moment.'

'In that case, could you give me some information? I really want to know if you've a car available for tomorrow – a large one like a Mondeo or something similar.'

'Look, can I get Susan to ring you back when she's free. I'm sure we can help you.'

'No thanks, I need to know immediately. I might ring you back if I've no luck with anyone else. Bye.'

Responding to requests

One of Rachel's major faults, in the exercise above, was that she effectively 'blocked' all callers, rather than helped them. Not one of them benefited from making their call! If you are answering a telephone it is your job to be a **facilitator** – in other words you are helping your callers to have a positive experience as they will have gained something from speaking to you. This is quite possible to achieve, even if you haven't the technical knowledge, skills or experience to deal with all the calls yourself and even if the office is half-empty one day.

There are three main types of requests you must prove you are competent at dealing with for your NVQ award:

- a request to be put through to a person
- a request for information
- a request to pass a message on to a relevant person.

To respond to these requests efficiently you need to:

- know the names of your colleagues
- know their extension numbers (or have a list on hand at all times)
- be able to use your telephone equipment properly
- know the information you are allowed to give out over the telephone and how to deal with requests for information which is sensitive or confidential
- know your office systems and 'who does what' in your office so you can find out information you need
- know how to take messages properly
- know how to communicate properly with the caller.

Routing calls to other extension users

If the call is internal and is for someone who is available, then on most systems you can redirect it to their desk (see page 171), or give the caller the correct extension number if they dialled yours in error.

If the call is external, there is usually a standard dialogue as you put someone through, such as:

'Good morning, Acme Car Hire.'
'Good morning. Is Bob Jenkins available now?'
'I'll just check. Can you tell me who's calling please?'
'Yes, it's Bill Bradbury from Jackson Brothers.'
'Thanks Mr Bradbury, could you tell me what the call is concerning?
'It's a personal matter – I'd rather not.'
'That's fine. Can you just hold the line a moment please.'
Rachel rings Bob Jenkins' phone
'Bob, there's a Bill Bradbury on the phone for you from Jackson Brothers.
   He's ringing about a personal matter. Are you free to speak to him?'
'Yes, fine. Put him through.'
Rachel speaks to Bill Bradbury again
'Putting you through now Mr Bradbury.'
Makes the connection
'Go ahead please.'
Disconnects own phone

This sequence may be varied at the end, depending upon your telephone system. On many internal systems, making the connection simply means transferring the call to the other internal phone, so Rachel would end her part of the call after she had told Mr Bradbury she was putting him through. See also page 171.

Do note that it is courteous to keep the caller informed about what you are doing. If you are transferring a call to a different person, section or department tell the caller what you are doing and why. Then, if anything goes wrong or the caller is cut off, he or she can resume contact without having to start all over again!

Requests for information

These may be internal or external requests, and more details about the type of information you should provide and how you should do this are given on page 175. An important point to note is that unless you have a virtual library on your desk, the likelihood of being able to supply everything you are asked for immediately is very slim.

You have two choices. You can either ask the caller to stay on the line whilst you find what you need, or you can arrange to call the person back when you have it to hand. Ask the caller to hold on only if your search will take under a minute. And remember that telephone equipment is very sensitive – so if the receiver is left lying on your desk the caller will hear all your groans and mutters as you hunt through your papers! It is therefore often wiser to arrange to call back and this should *always* be your response if you have any doubt whatsoever about whether you should be divulging this information anyway (see page 176). Having made the promise to call, you must do so, even if you have to say the information is not available.

Passing on messages to other people

If the call is for someone who is not available, and you cannot help the caller, then it is courteous to *offer* to take a message – even if the caller declines. Don't take this as a personal rebuke. The matter may be confidential or complex, or an instant answer may be needed. In all these cases a message wouldn't be appropriate.

It is best to have printed forms on which to write messages (and even better if these are printed in duplicate in small pads). There are two benefits:

• you are unlikely to forget to ask for any key items of information as the headings on the form will prompt you
• you have an automatic copy of the message in case this is needed.

However, even with the benefit of forms there are 'good' and 'bad' message-takers! Good message-takers are wonderful people. They can be relied upon to obtain all the details required so that the call can be actioned promptly and properly. Bad message-takers are a nightmare. They cause endless problems (and embarrassment) for everyone by missing out important information, transposing numbers (so 603849 becomes 603489), misspelling names, and writing illegibly and unclearly (so the message is often ambiguous). Therefore, although message-taking sounds a simple skill and one which you should be able to take for granted, it isn't. You will gain immediate friends and influence people if you become renowned as a conscientious and efficient message-taker in your organisation.

CHECK IT OUT!

If you had to design a telephone message form from scratch, what headings would you include to ensure that all the key information was included? If you use a message form at work, try to put down your ideas from memory, without referring to the actual form. You never know, you may improve on it!

Check your ideas against the printed form shown on page 170. Note, however, that these forms do vary quite considerably from one organisation to another – so you may have to get used to recording the details in a different order if you change employer.

Golden rules of message-taking

1   Even if you have had a preliminary discussion with the caller, once it is established that you will need to write down a message it is useful to almost 'restart' the conversation to ensure you record all the details correctly. You can see how this is done in the first conversation in the exercise below.

2   Make sure you include all the key facts you are given. These are likely to be:

   a   the caller's name and either his/her organisation or private address
   b   the caller's telephone number and local dialling code, plus an extension number if appropriate
   c   the name of the person to receive the message – if the caller knows this
   d   the main facts relating to the message, including:
       • the reason for the call
       • details of any information requested
       • details of any information given to you
       • an accurate record of dates, times, place names, product names, prices, quantities or other numerical data, given you can't guess any of these afterwards!

3   Although it is useful if you can distinguish key facts from supplementary information, if you are in any doubt, write *more* rather than less. For

instance, if a caller is asking for details of your products then the more information you give, the more you will be guiding the person who is calling back to discuss the caller's specific requirements. However, try to identify completely irrelevant information and leave this out.

4   Dates, days and times need to be particularly specific. 'Yesterday' and 'tomorrow' should not appear in your message, given that the reader will understand this information only if he/she knows exactly when you took the call. If any dates are given to you as part of the message, write both the day and date as a double check.

5   Before you conclude the call, check through the information you have received with the caller – particularly if it is detailed or about something you don't readily understand. Think, too, if there is any other information you could ask for that might be helpful.

6   Write simple, straightforward sentences and vary their length so your message reads better.

7   Write the information in a logical order so that it makes sense to the reader.

8   Check the tone of your message carefully – particularly if it is for someone senior. It should be phrased as a request, not as a command!

9   Check you have included your own name, the date the message was taken *and* the time. This could be important, especially if the caller has spoken to your colleague on other occasions on the same day.

10   Mark urgent messages clearly and do something with them! *Never* just leave them in a mail tray or on an empty desk or 'guess' which desk belongs to someone you don't know very well. Remember, your task isn't finished until the message has been passed on to someone who can take action on it by the deadline.

EVIDENCE COLLECTION

Check that your log sheet (see page 163), on which you are recording your calls, includes at least two or three where you have:

a   put through a caller to another person

b   had to provide information

c   had to pass a message to another person.

You can support your claims by witness testimony from other people to whom you have transferred calls, and by including copies of the information you have provided or the messages you have taken in each case. You will also strengthen your evidence considerably if you can obtain witness testimony from one or two internal *callers* who can confirm that you have responded correctly to their requests, kept them informed as to what you are doing and, if required, transferred them to another extension.

1 Rachel is improving a little at Acme Car Hire. She has just taken a
   calls for Bob Jenkins whilst he was out. Read the conversation
   below and compare this with her message on page 170:

   'Good morning, Acme Car Hire.'
   'Good morning, Bob Jenkins please.'
      'I'm sorry, Bob Jenkins is out of the office at the moment, can
   anyone else help you?'
      'I doubt it. It's concerning a Demonstration Evening we're
   having two weeks on Wednesday and I wanted to see if Bob would
   be free to be there.'
      'I can't confirm that in his absence, I'm afraid. If you'd like to
   give me the details, I'll take a message for him and ask him to ring
   you as soon as he gets back.'
   'That's fine.'
      'Could I just check all the details with you, please. Could you
   give me your name?'
   'Yes, it's Sam Sorrenson from White's Garage.'
   'Sorry, Mr Sorrenson, could you just spell your name for me?'
   'Yes, it's S-O-double R-E-N-S-0-N.'
      'And you wanted to know if Bob could attend a Demonstration
   Evening at your garage?'
      'Yes, we've a promotion for the new Ford range and I thought
   he may be interested. It's at our Wood Lane showroom.'
      'Fine. And that's two weeks on Wednesday, the (*Rachel checks
   her calendar*) 25th. Could you give me your telephone number,
   please, so that Bob can ring you back?'
      'Yes, he probably has it, give him my direct line number will
   you, it's 02839-496171.'
      Thanks Mr Sorrenson. I'll make sure Bob Jenkins gets the message.'
   'Thanks. Goodbye.'

   a Can you identify one key item of information Rachel has
      forgotten to include in her message?
   b Can you think of one additional item of information Rachel
      should have obtained for Bob Jenkins?

2 Rachel has gone to lunch and switched on the answering machine.
   When you return from lunch a message has been left:

      'Hello, it's Alana Bishop here, Kelvin Chemicals. Two things.
      We've booked four hire cars for next week from Monday to
      Thursday. Could we make this five cars please and extend the ➡

hire period to Friday. If possible we'd like them all to be Group 4 cars.

'Also, I've a problem with the invoice you sent last week – number 20398. It doesn't include our normal discount. Can you look into this?

'Can you get back to me about the additional hire car this afternoon, please? I'm on 01702- 305829, extension 2910.'

a From the information given, identify the key facts and then write it out clearly for Susan Knowles and check your wording and tone with your tutor or supervisor.

b If Rachel informed you, on her return, that Susan Knowles wasn't in for the rest of the day, what would you do?

MESSAGE FORM

TO *Bob Jenkins*   **DEPT.** —

DATE *22.01.01*   **TIME** *12.30 pm*

CALLER'S NAME *Sam Sorrenson*

ORGANISATION *White's Garage*

TEL NO. *02839–496171 (direct line)*   **EXT NO.** —

Telephoned	☑
Returned your call	☐
Called to see you	☐
Left a message	☐
Please return call	☑
Please arrange appointment	☐

Message:

White's Garage are having a demonstration evening on Wednesday, 25th of this month. It's a promotion for the new Ford range. Sam Sorrenson would like to know if you are free to attend.

Taken by: *Rachel Armstrong*   **Dept.** *Reception*

Operating telephone equipment correctly

There is a theory that, as equipment becomes more complex and offers more features, most people ignore the majority of them! For example, many people who own a video recorder never get beyond basic recording and playback.

Modern telephones are, unfortunately, rather similar. The user may plough through the manufacturer's handbook when the equipment is first installed, very impressed with all the features, and after that forget 80 per cent of them. However, even if you can dispense with some of the more fancy features, there are some essential ones you need to know about if you are to deal with calls efficiently.

The features on offer will depend, very largely, on your system and whether you work in a large organisation with a switchboard or a smaller one which has a key phone system installed. To find out what you have, you need to read the handbook.

1   Features on your central system are outside your control, but affect the way calls are answered and dealt with by your organisation. Examples include:

   • **Call sequencing** – where all callers are greeted with a pre-recorded message and then queued automatically. A further message is given every few minutes after that if the caller is still in the queue.

   • **Music on hold** – where callers are played pre-recorded music whilst they hold, whether they like it or not! On some systems, **user-defined music on hold** allows the operator to choose which music to play.

   • **Automatic attendant service** – which automatically answers incoming calls and directs the caller to the required extension. A similar facility is **digital voice announcement** which does much the same thing and can provide a useful support to the switchboard operator during busy periods.

   • **Bulletin board** – gives pre-recorded information to callers about the company's products or services. Many multiplex cinemas use them to give details of programmes to callers.

   • **Call logging** – which tracks and records calls from extensions. If you've just rung your friend in New York for a chat when the office was quiet it will show on your boss's next printout!

   Additional advanced and sophisticated features of the digital age are discussed in the Information update below.

2   Some features on your own phone will be designed to help you deal with callers more efficiently. It is essential that you know these and can use them without difficulty or without having to refer constantly to your handbook.

3   Other available features may be used by other members of staff, particularly your boss.

The types of features you can normally expect to find in use are listed in the chart on page 172. The list is divided into those which are *essential* for you personally, and those which may be used by other people in your office.

TELEPHONE FEATURES

Essential

Callback.   Automatically recalls an engaged extension when it is free, to save you keeping trying. You may find this described as **camp on busy** in your handbook.

Call forwarding.   Enables you to redirect your own calls to another extension if you will be away from your desk for some time. In some handbooks may be called **call diversion**.

Interrupt.   If your system has this feature, a 'bleep' on the your line will notify you whenever another call is waiting. The aim is that you will speed up your current call (or arrange to ring them back) to deal with the next.

Last number redial.   Automatically redials the last number you called.

On hold.   Allows incoming calls to be held whilst the correct person is found to deal with the call. On many modern systems, **reminder call holding** will prompt you that the caller is still waiting to be connected.

Redirect.   Enables you to reroute a call from one extension to another. This is essential if you put through a call to someone who is not available and then have to redirect the call to someone else, and you should be able to do this easily and quickly from your own extension.

Useful

Abbreviated dialling.   Saves time if you regularly call many long numbers or the same people on many occasions. On many systems you can set up your own **personal abbreviated dialling** numbers as codes from your own handset.

Caller display.   Shows the number of the person calling you.

Call barring.   If your system has this feature in operation it will be out of your control. It is used to prevent certain extensions making particular types of calls, e.g. to find out the weather or ring an International number. Only 999 can never be barred.

Conference calls.   Allows you to speak to more than one extension simultaneously – or to one outside caller and several extensions at the same time.

Direct dialling in. Your system will have this feature if you can give a direct line number to people. It enables outside calls to be connected immediately to the extension without going through the switchboard.

Distinctive ringing. If you work in an office with several telephones it is often possible to program different ringing tones so that you know which handset to pick up! This is different from **discriminating ringing** which is the difference in tones between internal and external calls. On some systems, a feature called **external/internal line distinction** enables certain buttons to be programmed instead to show whether an incoming call is external or internal.

Do not disturb. Temporarily blocks calls to a particular extension.

Hands-free speech. This enables you to listen to a call without lifting the handset. It is ideal if more than one person needs to listen to the call simultaneously, but less ideal if you work in an open-plan office! Never use it if confidential or sensitive information is being discussed.

Listen on hold. Linked to the above, this enables you to replace the receiver if you have been asked to 'hold' yourself, and continue with your work. You can then pick up the receiver and continue with the call when the other person comes back on the line.

Manager/secretary operation. Links two extensions so that the manager's calls are received by the secretary's extension and can then be announced properly.

Message waiting. Usually used in conjunction with voicemail. A special light (or bleep) indicates that a message has been taken in your absence.

Secrecy button. Invaluable if you want to speak to a colleague whilst a caller is on the line. Depressing this means that the caller cannot hear your conversation.

Trunk-to-trunk transfer. Enables incoming calls to a particular extension to be diverted to another phone, including a mobile. If your boss uses this feature you will have to take fewer messages as all calls will be diverted to a different phone.

In addition, of course, you must also operate the telephone equipment in relation to your organisation's procedures, as discussed on page 157. This also includes using any standard greeting you have been instructed to say.

ℹ️ INFORMATION UPDATE

The newest features of modern telephone systems are affecting the way calls and callers are handled. Today it is quite common to be able to dial extension users direct, without going through a switchboard. If you have a very modern system you may even find your telephone has a display screen which identifies the caller of all your internal calls, or has a cordless handset so you are not tied to your desk when you answer a call.

Outside callers are familiar with sophisticated queuing systems and **interactive voice response** (IVR) systems which ask for appropriate numbers to be depressed on the handset in response to recorded messages. Callers are then automatically routed to the correct extension. However, this is not always good news for people making a call. Queuing systems mean that the caller is paying for the call the second the recorded announcement (and the music) starts to play. IVR systems can cause frustration for the caller who can't work out which button to press but desperately wants to speak to a human voice – especially where the system seems to loop back on itself endlessly like an electronic maze. If you work in an organisation where you receive complaints from external callers about your system, make a polite internal call to customer services and tell them!

CHECK IT OUT!

1 How well do you know the phone system in operation in your organisation? Do you know how to redirect your calls or whether you can make a conference call? Check out and list the features available on your phone and learn how and when to use those you have previously been ignoring!

2 Assess the telephone systems – and some of the telephone techniques – when you call external organisations yourself, either personally or on business. Write down your opinion of queuing systems, music on hold and interactive voice response systems. If you are studying this as a group, discuss the advantages and disadvantages for both organisations and the callers.

Supplying information

Virtually all callers want to know something or want to tell you something. However, giving information may not be quite as straightforward as it first appears. There are two aspects you must consider:

- whether the information is accurate and up to date
- whether you should be giving out the information – and, if not, how to deal with the situation.

The importance of accuracy

At the beginning of this unit you read about the importance of technical accuracy in communications (see page 150). This also applies to any information you give to other people. If you deal with a wide range of enquiries it is very likely that you will not have precise, detailed and up-to-date information for everyone who rings, and the effort of checking can be too much for some people who say the first thing that comes into their head. Hopefully that isn't you!

It is always better to admit you are not sure about something than to hazard a guess. However, if you are regularly not being informed about updates, you should talk to your supervisor. Someone who deals with customer enquiries, for instance, needs the latest price list and product catalogue to hand constantly.

You will normally find it easier to deal with standard queries accurately than more complex queries which relate to your company's policies – for instance, whether you will allow a discount for early settlement of a bill. *Never* guess anything in this situation – otherwise you will make life difficult for everyone. Simply say you will have to refer the query to your supervisor and call back.

Similarly, if you handle a complaint, be careful how you respond. Simply find out the facts and say you must pass them on. Saying you're sure the customer is right and you're certain the company will replace the purchased item is allowable *only* if you work for a company such as Marks and Spencer which has a clear, stated policy to cover customer returns.

The importance of confidentiality

If you are asked for any information which you think may be confidential or sensitive, check with your supervisor before giving it. If you are being pressurised for an immediate response, simply say you 'don't know' but will get back to the caller as soon as possible. This should apply regardless of whether the caller is internal or someone outside the company.

Broadly, the type of information you should normally never disclose includes:

- personal information about your colleagues (e.g. someone's home address or telephone number)
- information about other customers or your dealings with them
- information about your organisation's future plans
- financial information about your company.

However, that is a very general list and you will find there are more specific types of information, linked to any job you do, which you should not disclose. Often this will depend upon the style of the organisation as well as the business it is in. For instance, if you work in a company where all the managers are extremely competitive, you may find that your boss is very keen that you keep internal plans and discussions in your department to yourself as well.

It is usually fairly easy to cope if you are asked outright for information you cannot divulge. Occasionally, though, you may have to be on your guard from people who will use more devious methods – as you will see below.

It is, of course, possible that you are *told* confidential information over the telephone, rather than being asked for it. If this is the case then you have two things to remember:

- don't repeat what you have been told to anyone except the person who should receive it
- if you write the information in a message, put this in a sealed envelope.

TEST YOUR KNOWLEDGE AND UNDERSTANDING

Rachel has received a call for information at Acme Car Hire. Read through the transcript and then answer the questions.

'Good morning, Acme Car Hire.'

'Hi, is that Rachel? It's Matt Simmonds here, from Peters and Woods – your accountants. You might remember me – I called in last week to see Bob Jenkins.'

'Oh, yes I remember you now. You brought back the accounts for last year.'

'Yes. Well, I was wondering – I'm thinking of going on holiday with some friends but there will be too many of us to fit in my car, so we were thinking of hiring one. It'd have to be quite large though – a six-seater at least. Do you do cars of that size?'

'We have people-carriers if that's what you mean, and one large estate car which I think holds five or six.'

'A people-carrier might be better, though I hate the look of those things. How much would one cost for a week?'

'It would probably be about £120, no, wait a minute (*Rachel hunts on her desk*) – sorry, no, that's last year's price list. I'll have to get back to you on that.'

'OK, if you would. Finally, I'm 25 and my friends are all between 22 and 27. Could we arrange for everyone to drive or is there a minimum age limit?'

'I'm not sure. Again, I'll have to check and get back to you.'

'Whilst you're on – I was just wondering – given the fact we do work for you and so on, do you normally give discounts on these occasions? Bob said, last time I spoke to him, to let him know if ever I needed a car and I think Alex who works with me got a discount when he booked a car from you recently. Could you let me know if he did?'

'I'm afraid I don't have that information, Matt, any discounts have to be agreed personally by Bob Jenkins, but I can pass on your request to him.'

'Er, no. Don't do that just yet. If you let me know the answers to the other queries I'll have a word with him personally later on. Oh, incidentally, you remember the guy who came with me last week – Peter Tomkins?'

(*Rachel vaguely remembers another man who was talking to Susan Knowles a lot*)

'Yes, well, your colleague Susan did him a big favour providing some duplicate information for the accounts that he'd mislaid. Without her help he could have been in quite a bit of trouble. He wants ➡

to send her some flowers as a gesture of thanks but would prefer to send them to her home than to work. Is there any chance you could let me have her address?'

'Well, we don't normally let anyone have employee addresses, it's against the company rules.'

'Oh, I know – I can understand, we have a similar rule here. But it's not as though you don't know me, is it?

'No, I know that but ...'

'It's only to send her some flowers as a thank you. If Peter sends them to her at work it might come out that he lost the papers Bob Jenkins gave him. Go on, be a sport.'

'Well, all right then, but don't say you got it from me. It's 25 Holbrook Drive, Whiston.'

'Thanks. That's smashing. Don't forget to get back to me with that other information will you, my number's 392898.'

'Will do. Goodbye.'

a Which of the information do you think Rachel *should* have to hand or know instantly, given her job?

b Which information is she less likely to know, as a matter of routine?

c Which information was she correct to withhold?

d Which information should she have withheld and what tactics were used to find this out?

e What should she have done to cope with Matt's final request?

Discuss your ideas with your tutor or supervisor.

EVIDENCE COLLECTION

On page 168, your evidence collection included providing information in response to a request. It would be useful if you could include an example of at least one occasion when you had to check if information was accurate or up to date, or had to find out further details on your own. This proves you can use your own initiative.

You cannot expect people to ask you for confidential information you are not expected to give, just for evidence for your portfolio! However, you can expect your assessor to be confident that you know about this. One way of proving it would be to make a short list of the *type* of specific information related to your job which you would never divulge over the telephone without permission. However, do make sure your list doesn't include actual details that are truly confidential.

Coping with problems

You may think that coping with callers like Matt is enough of a problem, without any more. However, for your NVQ evidence you have to prove you can cope with the following kinds of problems:

- dealing with a caller if the person they want is not available
- handling a call if the information you need is not available
- coping when your telephone equipment is not working properly
- dealing with a caller who doesn't know who they want to speak to.

In addition, you also have to know how to deal with hostile callers as part of your knowledge and understanding requirements.

From everything you have read so far, you should have a fairly good idea how to cope in most of these situations. However, the hints and tips below provide more specific information on each of these problem areas.

People who are unavailable

A person may be unavailable because he or she is out of the office, involved in a meeting or has asked not to be disturbed for a time. If your supervisor is desperate to finish an urgent report before the end of the day she may ask you to 'screen' all her calls and take a message wherever possible. If you are ever asked to do this it is worth checking who you *can* still put through as your supervisor may, without thinking, automatically expect you to know that she would still want to be connected with any senior manager who rang or any member of her family.

It is not normally recommended to give any more details than you need about a person's whereabouts – particularly to outside callers. This is another 'sensitive' issue, and you may inadvertently give an outside caller information about your company's business by doing so. Equally, if your friend has just nipped to the bank or the dry cleaners for five minutes and has asked you to cover, she won't think too kindly of you if you tell everyone who rings where she has gone. Simply say that person is 'out of the office at the moment' or 'not available to take the call at the moment'.

It does help you to handle the call if you know when the person is likely to return – particularly if you suddenly find a senior manager on the end of the phone demanding immediate contact. It also makes a difference to the action you should take if your colleague will be back in five minutes or in five days. There is a world of difference between what you should do if your colleague is at lunch and if he or she has gone on holiday for two weeks!

If a person is unavailable then you have the following options:

- try to help the caller yourself

- put the caller through to someone else who can deal with the matter – this is essential if the person will be away a long time
- arrange for the caller to ring back later or arrange for your team member to return the call later (depending upon your organisation's procedures)
- take a message.

If your team works together effectively, you will know who is dealing with specific items when someone is on leave or away ill. This will help you to identify the best person to deal with such calls during a person's absence. Finally, if your manager or supervisor will be away for a time, it is helpful if you are warned in advance about any important expected calls and told who should deal with them.

Information not available

You already know that if you are asked for information that is not available, you should arrange to call back later when you have obtained it. You should not keep callers holding on for more than a minute or so.

The worst-case scenario, of course, is when you arrange to ring someone back and then can't find what you need. This often happens if there is an internal crisis and all of a sudden something is required urgently by another department, but the essential piece of paper is missing from the file!

If this happens, don't panic. Look in all the normal places you would expect to find it. Then ask if anyone has borrowed it or has a copy. Finally, think about checking your computer system – you may have an electronic copy even if you haven't a paper copy. If all else fails, have a word with your supervisor before you ring your caller to say you haven't got it. If the information has gone missing, your supervisor may want your response phrased rather differently, especially if you are talking to an important customer or a senior manager!

Faulty telephone equipment

Telephone equipment today is very sophisticated and is unlikely to fail completely. Even if there is a power cut many phones still work because of a back-up battery system. These even protect most of the functions and features on the system and retain numbers programmed in.

You may, however, have a fault on your own extension which means you cannot use it properly, or perhaps cannot hear callers distinctly. Do check your handbook carefully (you may have turned down the volume by accident, for instance) and then follow your company's procedures for reporting a fault. This is usually to notify the switchboard operator or the person in charge of the phone system in your organisation. Then tell anyone else who might try to put calls through to that extension. If you work in a large organisation with e-mail, you may want to notify everyone that your phone is out of order for a short time and provide an alternative number to ring.

A variation on a faulty telephone system is a bad connection. Again, these are rare nowadays but still occur, especially if you are speaking on an international call outside Europe and America. If the connection is really bad, the best thing to do is to ring off and try again. However, if you make international calls there are two other points you should note. Firstly, the tones used abroad are different from those in the UK – so hearing an unusual tone doesn't mean there is anything wrong. The ringing tone is often different, as is the engaged tone. If you need advice on this, contact the operator for information, or consult the back of your phone book. Secondly, if you ring a very distant location, such as Australia, you may find you have a 'time lag' on the line. This is only a matter of seconds, but there is a slightly longer delay between speaking and your voice being heard than you are used to. You can often see this on television news broadcasts when someone is being interviewed over a satellite link-up. It doesn't matter at all, provided you *allow* for the gap – and *don't* interrupt the other person mid-sentence – which causes confusion for both parties.

Finally, if you are disconnected for any reason remember that the person who made the call should be the one to call back. If you both know this it saves you trying to resume contact unsuccessfully because both your phones are engaged whilst you each dial the other's number!

Uncertain callers

Many people ring an organisation with an initial enquiry and, in this case, obviously do not know who they should speak to. They know only what their call is *about*. This is where your knowledge of your organisation as a whole and of your team in particular is invaluable.

The first point to note is not to jump to conclusions. If the enquirer has managed to tell you only half a sentence and you assume they want a certain thing and put them through, the chances are you will be redirecting them to someone else within two minutes! This gives a very bad impression of your organisation. There is nothing more annoying for callers than to be shunted from one extension to another before someone who is found who can actually deal with them.

Listen carefully to what the caller is saying and ask appropriate questions to find out exactly why they are ringing. Some people are less specific than others and you may have to probe gently to get your answers. Only when you feel you can summarise back to them, accurately, what it is they want should you decide who can handle the call best.

If you have no idea who could deal with it, *don't* guess. Ask another person or your supervisor for advice – and remember the answer. Then next time you will know how to deal with that particular type of query.

A final, but related point. If you have two or three members of staff with the same name and a caller asks to speak to one of them, do check which one they want before you connect the call. If the caller doesn't know the person's first name or department, check what the call is about before you make the connection. It should then be quite clear whether they want Mr Brown in Finance, Mr Brown in Purchasing or Mr Brown in Sales.

Hostile callers

The vast majority of callers you speak to will be quite reasonable and pleasant people. Today, even in business, people are more informal on the telephone than they used to be. First names are often used by everyone as standard and, if you go out of your way to help people and to speak clearly and politely to everyone, you will have few problems.

Occasionally, though, everyone has to deal with a 'difficult' caller. Usually, but not always, this is a person with a complaint or grievance. Or it may be someone with a particularly poor telephone manner – or someone who thinks that the best way to achieve anything is to shout at other people. Such callers can be difficult to handle but a few simple strategies can help.

Golden rules for dealing with hostile callers

1 If a caller is angry for some reason, *never* respond in the same way. You are paid to stay professional.
2 Try to keep calm. Remember the call isn't directed at you personally – or shouldn't be – unless you have done something very silly.
3 Don't interrupt the caller whilst you are being told what the problem is. This will make matters worse. Let the caller run out of steam before you speak.
4 Try to remember your assertiveness skills from Unit 201. Respond positively so that the caller knows you've got the message (e.g. 'Yes, I understand you're very annoyed, Mr Bishop'). This confirms to the caller you realise how upset he is, and he can stop trying to convince you!
5 Then deal with the call in the normal way. However, a word of warning. Irritated callers get even worse if you keep them holding on, or if you can't find anyone to deal with their business. If you do offer to take a message, stress that this will be the best thing *for the caller* because you want the most appropriate person to handle the matter. Then make sure that person gets the message as quickly as possible and, for their sake, warn them about the caller's attitude.
6 If you receive a call that is particularly distasteful, report it immediately. No one should have to listen to bad language as part of their job. In this case, interrupt the caller, say that you have an urgent call on another line and will get back to him or her in a second, and get a more senior colleague to take the call.
7 Finally, don't irritate callers yourself! An individual who is normally very calm and reasonable can become annoyed if the person speaking to them has to hunt for a paper and pen, can't seem to understand them, and then

keeps them hanging on for ages or keeps transferring them to the wrong extension. Good telephone technique and everything you have learned in this unit should help you to avoid that.

CHECK IT OUT!

A useful skill is to be able to judge the mood of callers accurately from the way they speak over the telephone. When you receive your next calls at work (or even at home), try to identify whether the caller is impatient, depressed, nervous, excited, anxious, worried or annoyed. This will help you to respond more appropriately. It can also be invaluable for your colleagues if you are transferring a call or even taking a message, if you convey this additional information.

As a demonstration, imagine how you would first react when you actually spoke to the person if your team member had made the following statements (easy to do if you just delete the last sentence in each case to see the difference):

- 'It's Mrs Stephenson, she wants to speak to you. She sounds really annoyed.'
- 'It's your sister, she wants you to ring her back. She sounded worried about something.'
- 'It's Tom, can you speak to him. He sounds as if he's in a hurry.'
- 'It's your brother. He sounds really excited about something.'

Of course, do make sure you 'read' the signals correctly before you start passing on this type of additional information. Telling someone that your boss sounds excited when he's really worried, or pleased when he's really annoyed, can do more harm than good if your colleague promptly says the wrong thing on picking up the receiver!

TEST YOUR KNOWLEDGE AND UNDERSTANDING

If you were Rachel at Acme Car Hire, how would you deal with each of the following situations?

1 Bob Jenkins is in a bad mood. He has had three crises this morning and has now found out that one of the top cars booked out for tomorrow has developed a serious fault. He says that under no circumstances must he be disturbed for the next hour. Five minutes later his teenage daughter phones saying she must speak to him urgently.

2 On the same day, Susan Knowles has taken an extended lunch break to have her hair cut. You receive a call from an important customer who wants to book a car for tomorrow. Although ➡

you look all over her desk, you cannot find tomorrow's booking sheet anywhere so cannot see what is available.

3 Bob Jenkins leaves at about 3 pm to meet his bank manager. At half past three you receive a call from him on his mobile asking you to fax a copy of a document on his desk to the bank immediately. You can't find the document he means and when you try to get him back he appears to have switched off his phone.

4 A customer who has hired a car rings from a motorway service station on his mobile. He has broken down and wants to know what to do, but reception must be poor because the call keeps fading and you can't hear him properly.

5 You receive a call from the local paper who are doing a feature on car hire firms in the area and want to include Acme. They ask to speak to someone who can authorise this.

6 You receive a call from a very angry customer on his mobile. He collected a car from you at 3.30 pm and drove only four miles before it stopped. There appears to be no petrol in the car and he is furious. Obviously someone on your forecourt forgot to fill the car – which is normal practice at Acme – before the customer collected it. The driver is now stuck on a main road in fairly busy traffic and Rizwan, the one person who could help you, is nowhere to be seen.

EVIDENCE COLLECTION

You have to provide evidence that you have dealt with at least *two* of the following problems and discuss how you would deal with others:

a coping when a colleague is not available
b coping when information required is not available
c taking appropriate action if the telephone equipment is not working properly
d handling a caller who doesn't know who they wish to speak to.

If you can identify, from your log sheet, occasions when you have coped with these problems, that is ideal; but it would help your assessor if you also gave a more detailed account of what actually happened and what you did. If you can provide more than one example, then that is even better. If, on any occasions, you followed organisational procedures to deal with a problem, then give details.

Finally, ask your supervisor to countersign your log sheet(s) and your accounts of how you dealt with problems, for authenticity.

Element 203.2 Send and receive faxes

Fax machines are a standard item in virtually all offices. They enable text, graphics and photographs to be transmitted rapidly to another fax machine anywhere in the world for the price of a telephone call.

The range of fax machines on the market varies from small, desktop devices which can 'double up' as the office telephone, to much larger, free-standing machines which have a wide variety of features. All fax machines can be used to produce simple photocopies, and a combined multi-function device, which also includes an answering machine, computer printer and scanner, can be a boon for many people who work from home or who run a very small business. Larger organisations often have several fax machines, such as one in every main office or department and perhaps a larger 'central' machine as well. This is more economical, given that the price of small fax machines is very reasonable, than making people walk around a large building just to send a fax.

Fax machines work by scanning a black and white document and converting the dark images it sees into digital pulses. These are transmitted down a telephone line to the receiving machine which reproduces these images – hence a replica of the original is produced in an average of about 20 seconds per A4 page. There is very little difference in the time taken to transmit a fax to Australia or to the next building, which means that faxes are ideal for rapid, global communications.

When the sending and receiving machines connect, there is a brief 'handshake' period when the machines identify one another and determine their speed. The slower one of the two will dictate the speed, as will the speed of the modem – a device through which digital impulses are transmitted. The higher the speed, the lower the cost of sending the fax. Other factors which influence the speed and the cost include the density of print on a page (dense print takes longer), the amount of detail and the number of pages.

Today most fax machines use plain copying paper. If you operate an older, cheaper model you may find the paper is in a roll instead, which means it is specially coated. Those models are declining in popularity, however, as the paper is more expensive, it can be difficult to straighten out when a fax is received, and the image fades over time.

Learning how to use a fax machine is normally very easy indeed. Learning how to deal with problems and maintain the machine is slightly more complicated but nevertheless essential as part of the job.

Before you start, you need to know something about the fax machine you use, and a useful starting point is to make constant reference to your own handbook in relation to the issues covered in this element. Then practise your skills whilst they are still fresh in your mind.

The importance of sending faxes correctly and as requested

Fax machines are used to send *urgent* messages, and information which would take too long to send through the ordinary mail. For that reason both incoming and outgoing faxes should be dealt with promptly, otherwise it defeats the purpose of owning such a machine in the first place!

Incoming faxes are discussed on page 203. For now, we will concentrate on the skills you need when sending a fax.

Your organisation may have a system whereby outgoing faxes have to be placed in a special basket and are sent at regular intervals, or you may operate a 'fax on demand' service whereby they are sent as requested – or you may have a mixture of both systems, depending upon the urgency of the fax. Routine faxes, such as a branch office's weekly sales report to head office – especially if these are long documents – can be sent during quiet periods or out of hours if your fax machine has a timer facility. This is useful as otherwise you are prevented from receiving incoming faxes, because your fax is busy sending messages, during a considerable part of the day.

It is important that you know the system used in your organisation. If there doesn't appear to be one, it is sensible to check, every time someone gives you a fax, whether it is urgent or not. In the first case you should send it immediately, in the second you should send it when you have finished the job you are currently doing.

One of the most fundamental abilities, of course, is to be able to send the fax to the right person or organisation. The action to take will depend upon whether:

- the person is someone to whom you regularly send faxes
- the person giving you the fax has also given you the number
- you don't know the number and have never faxed this person before.

Regular fax numbers

On most fax machines there is a memory facility for storing commonly used fax numbers and for using an **abbreviated dialling system** to call up the receiver. Quite obviously it is essential these numbers are entered accurately into the machine's memory. Machines which allow you to do this will also print a report of all the numbers in memory, which you should check carefully whenever you add or change any numbers. It is also vital that you keep the numbers up to date. Phone numbers and codes can change – Britain has had two major phone code changes since 1995 and foreign codes can also change. Businesses also move offices or may obtain additional fax machines and additional lines. If ever you are given information to update, make sure you do the job promptly, before someone sends a fax to the old number.

A known fax number

This case is easy because all you have to do is key in the number. Make sure you do this carefully, as one of the disadvantages of fax machines is that there is no way you can confirm that you are through to the right fax machine unless you signal them that you want to talk to them – which is normally done only in special circumstances (see page 202). If you want to listen to the sequence of events, then depending upon the machine you are operating – and whether it has a loudspeaker facility – you may have to listen through the handset. At least then you can check you are receiving a fax signal and not a telephone signal. However, beware! A telephone signal may mean you have connected to a multi-function line which will change to a fax signal automatically after a few seconds. If it does not, and no one picks up the telephone to change it over manually – or to confirm the number – then you are wise to check the number with the person who gave it to you.

An unknown number

You have several options here. You can ring the person or organisation and ask them for their fax number. This is usually the surest and quickest method. If you have a copy of the *British Fax Directory* you can check if they are listed. If you are trying to contact an overseas fax machine, you can telephone the operator on 153 and ask for assistance.

EVIDENCE COLLECTION

The obvious way to prove you can send faxes correctly is by starting a file in which you keep copies of faxes you have transmitted. Do check with your supervisor, however, as you may not be allowed to keep copies of any which contain sensitive information. Alternatively, offer to use correcting fluid to blank out any minor details which may otherwise prevent you from keeping a copy.

Do note that your evidence should include more than just one or two fax messages. Ideally you need a variety, to different recipients. In addition, you must include both single-sheet fax messages *and* multiple-heet.

If you send several faxes every day, keep a selection of messages but also substantiate your evidence with a log kept over a short period of time and countersigned by your supervisor. On this you can record the date and time of each fax, the recipient's name and the number of pages transmitted.

An alternative to these approaches is to ask your assessor to visit you on a busy day when you have several faxes to send and to deliver. That way, your assessor can check your skills personally.

Setting up your fax machine

Your handbook will give you full details of how to do this, as well as advising you on the positioning of your machine and how to take care of it.

The location of the machine is important. It needs to be near a power socket and a telephone point and on a firm surface, such as a desk or table, where it won't get knocked. Never plug a fax machine into a power socket which is controlled by a wall switch or timer – otherwise the machine will be turned off accidentally and you could lose valuable information stored in the memory. There needs to be space nearby for paper supplies and the handbook should also be readily available. You will never remember all the different operations you may have to carry out or how to remedy all the problems that can occur, and the last thing you want is chaos because paper is stuck, the machine is bleeping, your boss is tapping his foot and you can't find the handbook.

Once the fax machine has been installed it needs to be set up properly. This means entering information about your organisation so that all the faxes you send will be printed automatically with the correct information at the top.

The first stage, normally, is to set the date and time. You don't just need to do this when the machine is first delivered, you will also have to change the time twice a year when the hour changes. Do check carefully the format you have to use to enter the date (e.g. DD/MM/YYYY) and make sure you use the 24-hour clock when you enter the time.

The second stage is to tell the fax machine where it is located (i.e. the name of your organisation) and its number – as it won't know this automatically. You may find this information under 'Station ID' in your handbook, particularly if the handbook was written originally for the US market. The ID is important as this information is printed on the top of every fax you send and tells your receivers who you are and the fax number that is calling them. On most machines you need to key in this information and often have the option of including your telephone number as well.

Two points to bear in mind:

1 To enter the name of your organisation you will have to key in letters on the *numerical* key-pad of the machine. Be careful, because each key is designated up to three letters. You choose the one you want, usually, by depressing each key a specific number of times for each letter. If you send text messages on your mobile phone you will be used to doing this, but if not, take your time and check the letters *very* carefully before you store the name – otherwise you will have to start all over again.

2 To enter your fax number and phone number you must use the international code and not the UK code. You may have to preface these with a '+' sign. Therefore, if you work in Manchester and your number is 0161 237 4972 you would enter +44 161 237 4972, as the international standard for the UK is '44', and then the regional code without the initial zero.

There are a range of other options you can set on most fax machines. For instance, how loud do you want the beeper and/or loudspeaker, do you want to use automatic redial if a number is engaged, and do you want a cover-page to be printed automatically? (See page 190.) One of the most important options is the ability to print a **verification report** after every transmission. This report confirms whether the transmission was OK or if a problem occurred at any stage. It is usual to set this option to 'on' and to attach the verification report to any faxes you send. Other options can be chosen when you are actually transmitting a particular fax and are dealt with on pages 191–192.

Finally, find out if you should set your machine for tone or pulse dial. Usually the correct choice will be 'tone', but do check compatiblity with your local telephone exchange.

EVIDENCE COLLECTION

You may be working on a fax machine which has been set up for some time. As evidence, therefore, you may have to talk to your assessor about the operations you would carry out if you received a new machine or if the machine were sent for repair and had to be reprogrammed.

An ideal and relevant piece of evidence would be to change the time in October or March when the hour changes and to obtain witness testimony from your supervisor to prove you have done this. As further evidence, attach a header sheet which shows the time both before and after you made the change.

Preparing faxes for transmission

Faxes can be prepared in many ways. Some organisations use pre-printed fax forms, others use headed paper. Some of the more sophisticated fax machines will receive and transmit messages that have been prepared on a computer (see also Information update on page 197).

There are five aspects you have to consider when preparing a fax:

1 the format for faxes sent by your organisation
2 whether a cover page or cover sheet is required – or whether the information on the header page or header sheet is considered sufficient (see below)
3 the quality and type of documents you are transmitting
4 the number of pages you are transmitting
5 the style and tone of the fax message if you are composing one yourself.

Fax formats

Faxes often look more like a memo than a letter – even if they are sent on headed paper. The key information which must be provided is:

- the name of the recipient – and department if it is a large organisation
- the name of the sender
- the date (although this is also printed on the header sheet)
- the subject (so the recipient can quickly see what it is about)
- the number of pages being transmitted.

The final item is usually worded 'page 1 of 4', 'page 2 of 4', etc. This helps the recipient to check that the document has arrived in its entirety.

Faxes are often signed, but check whether this applies in your organisation.

Header sheets and cover pages

All fax machines print a page header or header sheet and most give you the option to attach a cover sheet or cover page.

The header sheet is the small area at the top of each fax you send. It contains all the information you input when you first set up your machine. The type of information it contains and the amount of detail is likely to be specified by your organisation. It will look something like the following (although the information may be in a different order):

| 06/11/2002   15:20   +44 161 237 4972   BAKER'S TRAVEL   PAGE 01 |

You must remember that this takes up a little space at the top of each fax message – so it's no use trying to transmit beneath it a full A4 page or you will lose the last few lines!

A cover page or cover sheet allows you to send even more information, automatically, before each document you transmit. This can be very useful if you are just sending a copy of a document to someone, as it saves you preparing a brief fax message for courtesy to explain what you are sending. On most machines you have the option whether you want to send a cover page and you make this decision at the time of transmission. A cover page may look something like the one illustrated here.

You may wonder how your fax machine can do this automatically, but the answer is usually quite simple.

- The 'TO' information can be obtained from your abbreviated dialling system or any other facility you have for storing commonly used numbers in your machine. On many machines, if you are dialling direct this line would be left blank.

```
┌─────────────────────────────────────────────────────────┐
│                 A FAX COVER PAGE                        │
│  06/11/2002        15:20                                │
│  COVER SHEET                                            │
│  TO:            OXFORD BRANCH                           │
│  FAX:           +44 1865 302988                        │
│  FROM:          BAKER'S TRAVEL                          │
│  FAX:           +44 161 237 4972                       │
│  TEL:           +44 161 237 2000                       │
│  TO FOLLOW:     05 PAGES                                │
│  COMMENT:       COPY OF ITINERARY FOR JOHN MARSDEN     │
│  ATTACHED. PLEASE RING SUE CAMPBELL UPON RECEIPT      │
└─────────────────────────────────────────────────────────┘
```

- The 'FROM' information is the same as would normally be printed on your header page – either with or without your phone number.
- You would be prompted to enter the number of pages you are sending when you tell the machine you want to send a cover page.
- You would be asked what comment you wanted to put at the same time. Often you have a choice of some standard options (e.g. urgent or confidential) or you can write your own. Make sure, though, that you don't exceed the number of words or characters you are allowed.

The documents you are transmitting

The basic rule to remember is that the clearer the documents you are sending, the easier they will be to read. A standard, black and white, printed A4 page is therefore usually straightforward. However, the situation is rather different if:

- the document has been printed in colour (fax machines recognise only black and white)
- it is on flimsy or coloured paper
- it is in a book or folder and cannot be fed into the machine (or be laid flat on the glass)
- the margins are very narrow (either side to side or top to bottom)
- the document is a valuable original which may be damaged if you feed it into the machine
- you are transmitting a photograph.

Your options are as follows:

1   If the document is flimsy, cannot be laid flat or fed into the machine, photocopy it first – and transmit the copy, not the original.

2   If the margins are very narrow, then again photocopy it, but this time reduce the document slightly so you have wider margins. This prevents any text being lost when you transmit the document. Alternately, if your fax machine has the facility to reduce, you can choose option 4(d) below.

3   If the document is on coloured paper you can photocopy it and adjust the settings on your copier so that the background is lighter. Or you can select option 4(c) below.

4   If your fax machine has the capability, you may be able to make many adjustments on the machine itself. The main ones to know about are as follows:

   a   **Resolution**. This is normally set as 'standard'. You can select 'fine' if the document has small print or 'superfine' if the document has very small print or artwork. There is usually a separate 'photo' resolution. The higher the resolution the slower the fax is transmitted, so more detail is included. However, this also increases the cost, so choose these options only if you need to.

   b   **Grey scale**. This setting increases the different shades of grey which can be identified on the page. It helps for coloured photographs and coloured print. However, there is one snag. If the machine receiving your fax is very basic, it will ignore all your fancy settings and print the document in basic black and white!

   c   **Contrast**. Use this to lighten or darken documents. Normally you will have a 'standard' setting but can choose light (if your document is light) or dark (if your document is dark) to help to compensate.

   d   **Reduce**. You may be able to reduce the print ratio on your machine and this is advisable if the print is very long on the fax you are sending. Otherwise, the recipient may receive two pages when you thought you were only sending one (if your fax machine 'carries over' print automatically) or some print will be missing from the bottom of the page.

The number of pages

It is obviously easier to send a one-page fax to someone in the UK than a 20-page fax to someone in India – for a variety of reasons (read about overseas faxes on page 201).

However, the main point when you are sending multiple pages is to check that:

* all the pages are the right way up
* they are in the correct order
* they are numbered properly.

Then check your handbook carefully to make sure you know:

- whether the print should be facing up or down
- which side of the document should go first (top or bottom)
- whether the first page should be on the top or the bottom.

Failure to get this right can mean your fax being sent upside down, which isn't too bad; in the wrong order, which is rather worse; or not at all because the receiving fax pages are blank, which is disastrous!

The style and tone of fax messages

You may be asked to write a brief fax message yourself. This will often be the case if you don't have the facility to add a cover page, or if rather more information should be included than you would state on a cover page. You will also have to compose a brief message if there are no other documents being transmitted – you simply want to pass on information quickly.

Fax messages are normally:

- short and to the point
- relatively informal.

However, you should still make sure you include all the key points. It is sensible to get your supervisor to check the first ones you write before you transmit them.

CHECK IT OUT!

Rather than just transmit messages without thinking, read those you send. This will have several benefits. You will get a better idea of the way faxes are worded in your organisation, you will remember the layout, and you will also gain a better appreciation of the business activities going on around you.

A word of warning, however. Just because your boss or supervisor sends a very friendly or informal message to someone doesn't mean that you can do the same thing. The tone you use depends upon how well you know the other person and whether they work at the same level as yourself or are senior to you.

TEST YOUR KNOWLEDGE AND UNDERSTANDING

Tasnim works for Tara Kershaw, a computer consultant, who travels regularly around the UK. One of Tasnim's regular jobs is to send and receive faxes, and Tara is trying to train her to write her own when she can.

➡

1 Tasnim has been asked to confirm by fax a booking for a hotel in Dublin. She has made three attempts at drafting this, shown below. Which do you think is the most suitable for transmission – and why?

2 Tara is going to speak at a conference in Dublin on the second day of her stay. She has asked you to help by preparing a fax to the organiser, Cherie Phillips. The key facts to include are given below – but need rearranging into a slightly more logical order. Draft out your message using an appropriate format and check your finished work with your supervisor or tutor. Remember that you are writing this *for* Tara and she will sign it.

- Say I will bring my own laptop but will need a data projector for my talk.
- Confirm I will arrive at the venue at 0930.
- Ask if they know how many are due to attend, then I know how many information packs to take.
- End by saying I look forward to meeting her again.
- Confirm I will be delighted to join them for dinner in the evening.

TASNIM'S DRAFT FAXES

TK COMPUTERS
15 Brier Road
LANDSBURY, LD3 4MP

FAX MESSAGE

TO   Reception, Queen's Hotel, Dublin

FROM   Tasnim Akhtar, Administrator

DATE   7 October 200-

PAGE   1 of 1

RESERVATION FOR TARA KERSHAW

Thanks for your help when I rang to book a room. I confirm we need this for two nights, 20 and 21 October, and your rate is £75 per night + VAT.

Regards

Tasnim

TK COMPUTERS
15 Brier Road
LANDSBURY, LD3 4MP

FAX MESSAGE

TO   Reception, Queen's Hotel, Dublin

FROM   Tasnim Akhtar, Administrator

DATE   7 October 200-

PAGE   1 of 1

RESERVATION FOR MS TARA KERSHAW

Further to our telephone conversation this morning I have pleasure in confirming our reservation of one single room with private bath for two nights, 20 and 21 October, at the rate of £75 per night + VAT in the name of Ms Tara Kershaw.

Yours sincerely

Tasnim Akhtar

TK COMPUTERS
15 Brier Road
LANDSBURY, LD3 4MP

FAX MESSAGE

TO   Reception, Queen's Hotel, Dublin

FROM   Tasnim Akhtar, Administrator

DATE   7 October 200-

PAGE   1 of 1

CONFIRMATION OF RESERVATION FOR TARA KERSHAW

I confirm the booking made this morning for one single room with bath for two nights, Wednesday and Thursday, 20 and 21 October, at the rate of £75 per night + VAT.

Tasnim Akhtar

Knowing your equipment – and using it properly

Every fax machine is delivered with an owner's manual, or handbook. Some are clear and easy to follow, others less so. The more functions there are on your machine, the more likely it is that the handbook will be quite long. It is important, however, to take note of what it says and use your equipment in accordance with the manufacturer's instructions. If you do not, and your machine develops a fault, your employer might have to to pay for its repair because it has been used incorrectly.

You will usually find that your handbook covers the following areas of use:

- suitable places for siting the machine (see below)
- setting it up on delivery (see page 188)
- understanding the keys, and the information you need before you use the machine
- basic operations and how to undertake these
- more advanced operations
- problem solving – often called a 'troubleshooting guide' – and routine maintenance (see page 198).

Unless you are very unusual, it is likely that you will skim the handbook the first time you need it, learn the basics and then never look at it again unless you have to. Few people sit and plough through it page by page, and even those who do cannot remember operations they use only rarely. The danger with skimming the manual is that you can miss some vital items you really do need to know, such as:

- that your fax should be kept away from heaters, water and direct sunlight, and be kept as dust-free as possible
- that you have to 'fan' the paper before you put it into your document feeder and that the paper must be of a certain thickness and weight, otherwise it will jam or slip
- that some documents are unsuitable for transmission, such as papers that are curled, folded, ripped or wrinkled, or if they contain paste, tape,

staples or paperclips (cardboard, newspaper and fabric is also usually unsuitable)

- the correct method of replacing the printing cartridge and paper or paper cassette
- the type of printer cartridge you need to keep in stock
- what to do if someone bleeps to speak to you at the end of a transmission
- what an alarm signal means (usually that you are out of paper or your print cartridge is exhausted) and what will then happen if a fax is about to be transmitted
- how to keep your fax machine clean – and not just the outside!

Basic operations

The first thing to check is the sequence of operations required to send a basic fax. You may have the choice between sending faxes manually or automatically – you should learn *both* operations.

Secondly, you need to know how to tell the machine to redial the number automatically if it is engaged. This saves you time, as you don't have to stand over the machine and keep trying yourself. Often you can set **automatic redial** so that it happens automatically.

The third thing you need to know is how to **cancel** a transmission if you suddenly realise you have dialled the wrong number or have the wrong document in your hand!

Finally, it is useful to know how to take a simple copy of a document. This can be handy if your photocopier is some distance away and you need a copy urgently.

More advanced operations

If you master only the basic operations, you may not realise some of the more advanced functions your fax machine can do. Knowing these can be useful – as you may be able to make appropriate suggestions to help your supervisor and colleagues – and this type of initiative usually impresses everyone. The next section helps you to develop these skills yourself.

 INFORMATION UPDATE

Technological developments are likely to mean that any fax machine you use today will be decidedly old-fashioned within the next few years. Current developments include much faster machines, mainly because they incorporate high-speed modems and faster scanning operations. Transmission is therefore much quicker. However, in the future you are not only likely to be sending information more quickly but also in colour. One new machine can print in black and white or colour and can hold up to 540 pages in memory! In addition, it will automatically send and receive e-mails with attachments and will transmit to either fax machines or direct to PCs via the Internet.

The link between fax and the Internet is growing all the time. A wide variety of organisations offer fax services which will allow computer users to receive fax messages on their e-mail or transmit a fax from a desktop or via a website. Fax software is now available which links PCs to fax. In this case, you simply prepare the message on your PC and then instruct your PC to transmit the message. You can also access fax messages sent to your company from your computer.

If your organisation already uses fax software and you have the option of sending and receiving faxes from your computer, then you should note that Option Unit 214 will enable you to count this towards your award (see page 467). In addition, you will also have to prove that you use other types of electronic communication facilities, such as e-mail and remote information services.

CHECK IT OUT!

1 The table on pages 199–200 lists the main features on modern fax machines. Check the list against the machine you use regularly and note down how many you have and how they work. Finally, think of occasions when some of these may be useful for your employer.

2 Find out more about the link between fax and e-mail and the type of fax services available for businesses. If you have Internet access you can do this easily – contact www.fax.com/ and www.swiftnet.co.uk/ for details.

Dealing with problems

For your NVQ level 2 award you have to prove that you can deal with *five* types of problem which may occur when using a fax machine. From everything you have read in this unit, and from your handbook, you should be able to cope in most of these situations. However, the main points to bear in mind are summarised below.

Machine out of paper

It is sensible to check that there is always enough paper in the cassette or paper tray. If stocks are running low this will be signalled to you (see page 197).

FAX FEATURES

Abbreviated dialling.   Allows regularly used numbers to be stored in an abbreviated format.

Activity log or journal.   Prints out a report on all faxes sent and received since the last report was printed.

Anti-junk option.   Enables the user to block calls from unknown machines to reduce the number of 'junk' faxes received.

Automatic dialling/redialling.   Transmission is automatic once the connection is made. If the number is engaged the machine automatically redials the number.

Broadcast facility.   Allows you to send the same fax to several different numbers automatically.

Call reservation.   Allows you to automatically signal the receiving fax machine that you want to speak to the operator as soon as transmission has ended.

Delayed transmissions.   Allows you to program your machine to send a fax at a later time. May be linked to a **timer** function to send certain faxes *every* day at a specific time. (See also **transmission reservation**.)

Dual access.   Enables faxes to be sent and received at the same time.

Duplexing.   The machine has the ability to transmit a two-sided document.

Memory.   Usually, the more expensive the fax, the greater the memory capability. Used to store incoming faxes if the paper or cartridge runs out. On some machines, incoming faxes will be stored in memory if the machine is currently transmitting.

Network capability.   The machine can be linked to a computer network and can receive fax messages for transmission direct from any PC.

Number search.   Enables you to search quickly for a stored number.

Overseas mode.   An option to improve the quality of faxes sent abroad. Transmission is slightly slower than usual.

Paper-out warning.   Signals you when the paper is running low.

Password.   A system whereby the sending and receiving fax machines both recognise a specific password and will transmit only if these agree.

FAX FEATURES contd.

Polling.   The ability to call another machines and 'collect' messages left for it. Now sometimes called **fax on demand**.

Signature storage.   Enables a previously stored signature to be reproduced on a message at a specified point.

Smoothing.   A feature which helps to improve the appearance of incoming faxes by 'smoothing' out the lines of print.

Transmission reservation.   Allows you to program the machine to send a fax when it is free, rather than waiting.

Turnaround polling.   Enables your machine to send a fax and poll the called machine at the same time.

Verification mark.   A small mark printed at the foot of each transmitted page.

Verification report.   A report which confirms whether or not the fax was transmitted without problem.

Try to keep a small stock of paper near to the machine. There will be less reason to panic if your machine has a memory capability, so that any incoming messages are stored automatically.

Check your handbook carefully so that you know how to refill the cassette or paper tray correctly. It is usual to fan the paper before putting it in, to help separation. Practice doing this during a quiet period so you can do it routinely and without thinking. Finally, no matter what the crisis, *never* be tempted to use paper which isn't meant for the fax machine.

Document jams and misfeeds

There will often be a warning alarm if your document either jams or misfeeds when you are transmitting, or if the paper on which a message is being recorded jams. The first thing to check is which type of jam you have to rectify, as the remedy will be different in each case.

Documents being transmitted can jam or misfeed if they aren't inserted properly, if they are of unsuitable paper type, if they are the wrong size, or if they did not feed though properly. Your handbook will tell you how to open the machine, if this is required, and how to remove the jammed papers. *Never* just pull and tug on a document which is stuck part-way into the machine or you could cause considerable damage. Before you restart your operations examine the papers to see if you can identify the cause and check that the guides on the document feeder are correctly positioned.

A paper misfeed when a message is being received means you have a problem between the paper tray or paper cassette and the printing mechanism. Again, check the handbook carefully. You will normally have to remove the paper cassette or tray to get at the paper, but do check if you also need to remove the printer cartridge. Again, follow the instructions carefully and don't just pull or tug paper which is stuck.

EVIDENCE COLLECTION

You must include evidence which proves that you can deal with *at least* two of the problems described above and below, and be prepared to discuss what you would do if the others occurred.

You can help yourself by having a strategy for collecting evidence.

a   Make sure that on the next few occasions when the paper needs refilling that *you* are the person to do it.

b   Keep a list of occasions when a number was engaged and state what action you took, and why, in each case.

c   If you never have a paper jam, then great! But check in your handbook what you should do if one occurs. Tell your colleagues to let you know if there is one and then rectify it.

Either write a brief report to summarise the problems you have resolved and ask your supervisor to countersign it, or ask for witness testimony from someone who has seen you do all these operations.

Finally, do be aware that your assessor may ask you to discuss how you use the equipment in accordance with manufacturer's instructions. If, therefore, you can link the problems you have solved with reference to the handbook, this would be useful.

Receiving number engaged

This may be because the machine is currently busy, or because you cannot get a connection (especially if you are trying to send a fax overseas). Set your machine to retry the number automatically – and check back in 5–10 minutes to see whether the fax has been sent. If the message is urgent and you still can't get through, warn the person who gave you the message that you are having difficulties. Other strategies to try include:

- telephoning the other organisation to see whether there is a fault with their fax machine – and checking the number at the same time

- setting your machine for delayed transmission, if you can

- ringing the international operator on 153 to see whether there is a connection problem to a foreign country.

Receiving number not a fax machine

If your fax is transmitting automatically you will normally simply get a 'no response' error message. Switch to manual and listen to the sequence of operations, to check whether you are receiving a fax signal when you dial. If you hear only a telephone signal, then wait to see if it is answered – the fax may be switched off or faulty on a dual-purpose line. If this is not successful, check the number, either with the person who gave you the message or by ringing the recipient on another line, if you have one. The most important point is to warn the person who gave you the message that you are having problems, so that an alternative method of contacting the recipient can be considered.

Confirming receipt

When a fax is transmitted, the sender can obtain confirmation that there has been no breakdown in communication by checking the **verification report**. However, there are occasions when you may still wish to check that the fax has indeed arrived. Such occasions include:

- if you are transmitting to a small organisation and the person may be out, yet the matter is urgent
- if you are transmitting to a large organisation with a central machine and you want to check the fax has actually been delivered to the recipient
- if you or your supervisor wish to discuss the contents of the fax with the receiver immediately after transmission
- if the document is extremely important and you have been asked to speak to someone to double check
- if you are concerned about the quality (perhaps your fax machine has been causing problems or you have transmitted a photograph or very detailed document) and you want to check the document is clearly readable
- if the verification report indicates a problem (e.g. transmission cut off part-way through a multi-page fax) and you need to establish which pages are missing.

Your machine will usually have the facility to speak to the person on the other end. However, note that this will be the person operating the fax machine – who may be different from the person who will actually be commenting on the document or the recipient in a large organisation. In addition, because fax machines usually have their own dedicated telephone lines, the fax operator will not be able to transfer you to someone else. Therefore, contact the fax number if you are querying the quality, actual receipt or how to remedy a particular problem, but contact the actual recipient if you need to discuss the document. In that case it is sensible to allow a few minutes for the fax message to be delivered to the person's desk!

Handling and delivering incoming faxes

Within your own organisation you may be responsible for handling incoming faxes. Incoming faxes will normally be received automatically unless your fax is dual purpose and operates also as an incoming telephone line. In this case, you will receive a telephone call first and then will have to switch to a fax receive mode. If your fax machine has a dedicated telephone line, your major task is to check the received tray regularly.

Some very basic machines don't have a tray and then messages are likely to slither off the desk and on to the floor. The danger then, of course, is that someone walks past, thinks someone else has dropped some rubbish on the floor and puts this in the nearest waste bin!

If your fax machine is in the office with you then you will hear it start. You will also hear it beep if the sender wishes to speak to you – and you need to know which keys to press to be able to do this. After speaking to the sender, do make sure you replace the receiver properly – otherwise your machine will give the 'busy' signal to anyone else who calls.

Wait for the message to finish transmitting before you remove it from the tray and then collate the pages. Check they are in the right order and none is missing. Put the cover sheet, if there is one, on the top. Fasten them with either a staple or a paper clip, depending upon the type of document and/or your boss's preference.

The recipient may be due to discuss the document with the sender fairly promptly, so it is important that you deliver the message immediately. Treat it as you would an urgent telephone message. If the recipient is away, check with your supervisor or a colleague whether you should leave the message on the recipient's desk or pass it to someone else to deal with.

TEST YOUR KNOWLEDGE AND UNDERSTANDING

What action would you take in each of the following situations? Discuss your ideas with your tutor or supervisor.

1 You receive a fax message which is unreadable because the quality is so poor.
2 You have been asked by your supervisor to send an urgent fax to your head office. The number is constantly engaged and when you go to tell him you find he has gone out for the rest of the afternoon.
3 You are phoning the fax number of a contact given to you by your boss, but find this is a telephone line, not a fax line.
4 You receive a multi-page fax from Australia but two pages are missing.

5   You arrive home on Friday night and realise, in horror, that after moving the machine as requested you did not replace the mains plug. You are aware that your organisation normally receives faxes from reps over the weekend.

6   You receive a fax which is addressed to another organisation.

7   An important document you were transmitting jams in the machine and tears badly as you remove it.

8   You receive a fax clearly marked 'Urgent' but there is no recipient's name on it.

9   A fax operator contacts you to say that the fax you have just sent has arrived without problem but they have no person working there with the name you have put as the recipient.

10 A member of your team, who uses the fax machine regularly, frequently leaves the area in a mess, never refills the paper tray even when the 'paper out' warning is showing, and 'guesses' how to solve problems rather than reading the handbook. Yesterday, she replaced the printer cartridge but then forgot to close the cover properly so the machine was out of order. You are tired of her behaviour and are worried you may get the blame if she damages the machine because of her carelessness.

EVIDENCE COLLECTION

The simplest way of providing evidence that you can deliver faxes is to ask for witness testimony from your supervisor. Alternatively, you can keep copies of faxes you have delivered (preferably including some multi-page ones which you have collated) and write a brief note on each, explaining when it was received and how you delivered it.

You can strengthen your evidence considerably if, on at least one fax message which is urgent, you note down what you *would have done* had the recipient been out of the office.

Unit 204   Prepare and print documents using a computer

This unit is concerned with one of the most fundamental administrative tasks you will do in an office – use word-processing software to prepare and print documents. Word-processing is an essential skill for all administrators, given the number of documents that are routinely produced every day. The ability to input text quickly, amend it as required, change the layout or format on request and print out copies quickly and easily has been a boon for everyone involved in document production. Managers can change their minds about content and administrators can adjust and improve layout without work having to be redone from scratch. Standard documents can be saved on disk and produced at the touch of a few keys, tables can be created quickly and easily and, if required, text can be imported from other documents and inserted at a particular point.

Your ability to use word-processing software to undertake a variety of tasks quickly and effectively will be absolutely critical to your future career development. At any job interview you are likely to be asked to specify and prove your skills in this area. There are a range of qualifications you can take to enhance your profile. These include specialist RSA word-processing examinations from level 1 to level 3 (Advanced), and a variety of other awards covering other types of business packages in addition to word-processing – such as CLAIT (Computer Literacy and Information Technology), IBT 2 (Integrated Business Technology) and ECDL (the European Computer Driving Licence). So if you are very keen and interested in this area, you may find it both enjoyable and rewarding to develop your WP and IT skills in the future.

This unit covers the fundamental aspects of using word-processing software. There are three elements. The first relates to inputting and editing text, the second to formatting text and making sure the layout is as required, and the third to printing documents. You are likely to find that the evidence you produce will probably cover more than one element at once, particularly if you are printing documents to include in your portfolio.

Please note that, throughout this unit, it is assumed that you are using Microsoft's Windows® 95, 98 or 2000 system software.

This section covers all the knowledge and understanding you will need for this unit. To start, however, we will concentrate on the key features which encompass all three elements and cover the main aspects of using word-processing in a commercial organisation.

KEY SKILLS SIGNPOST

There are obvious links between this unit and the Key Skills unit **Information Technology**. However, you will find your Key Skills unit easier and more interesting to achieve if you also operate other software – such as a database or spreadsheet package, and use the Internet to find information. You will find these alternatives covered in Units 206, 210, 213, 214 and 215. N.B. Units 210 and 215 can be found on the Heinemann website (see page 357 for details).

The activity below assumes that you can use the Internet and covers some of the areas required for your IT key skills award at Level 2.

IT2.1

You have been asked to use your IT skills to help to solve the following problems.

1   Your manager frequently travels to your branch offices in Glasgow, Newcastle, Manchester and Bristol from the head office in London. She prefers to travel by train and likes to travel on a Monday evening, stay away all day Tuesday and return Wednesday afternoon. She dislikes having to look up departure and arrival times for each journey and would like a quick reference guide to help her.

2   There have been several complaints by staff lately about discomfort caused by operating computers. It has been decided to create a short leaflet for staff giving guidance on correct posture and good practice.

In both cases, search the Internet to find relevant information on:

a   train departure and arrival times for the above locations

b   health and safety related to computers to supplement the information given in this book.

Useful starting points may be www.railtrack.co.uk or a search engine such as www.ask.co.uk. You can also refer to relevant websites for health and safety on pages 20 and 22. Either print out or download and save appropriate information for later reference.

List the searches you do and the criteria you used to find your information.

IT2.2

Use the information you have obtained on train times to prepare a table which includes *two* options for each journey your manager regularly makes. Select the options you think would be most convenient for her in each case.

Use the information you have obtained on health and safety to design a simple leaflet for staff. Decide which information would be the most relevant and how you can present this in a user-friendly manner. Include a brief list of recommendations to staff to help to prevent future problems.

IT2.3

Prepare a memo to accompany your table. Explain briefly the information you have included and why you selected it.

Create your draft leaflet. Use borders and margins effectively and include at least one image. Save your work so that it can be recalled easily if your supervisor wishes you to make some amendments to the draft before the leaflet is issued.

The importance of professional documents

Organisations are judged by the quality of documents they produce and send to other people. A prospective customer is hardly likely to be impressed if a letter contains three errors and is printed at an odd angle on slightly crumpled paper. This gives the impression that goods produced or services offered will be similarly slipshod and careless. For this reason organisations invest a considerable amount of money buying up-to-date computers, printers and software to benefit from technological advances in document production. This investment is completely defeated if those creating and printing the documents take no pride in their work – or don't know the functions well enough to take advantage of the powerful tools literally at their fingertips.

There are four checks you need to bear in mind for *any* document which you produce.

1 **Is it technically accurate in every respect?** Obviously you may be somewhat dependent upon the author of the original document, but you can destroy even the most careful and conscientious writer if you:

   - cannot read someone's writing and guess a word
   - don't check your own facts when you are writing a document
   - mis-key a word to give an entirely different meaning (for instance, 'complete the bank form' instead of 'complete the blank form')
   - don't ask for assistance if you have a query about something you have been asked to do
   - don't check your work properly before it is printed.

2 **Is every word correctly spelt?** Unless you possess absolutely superb spelling and keyboarding skills then you will need to use your spell-checker before you print out a document. However, spell-checkers – although wonderful – have their limitations so you still have to check your work yourself and look up words you do not know – as you will see on page 237.

3 **Is the layout of the document appropriate and suitable?** Does the layout enhance the document, or spoil it? Have you followed the correct layout and style for your organisation? Is the format as requested by the author of the document? If not, do you know how to make the changes required?

4 **Does the printed document look professional?** Is the print aligned properly on the page or is it slanted? Is the print quality as good as it can possibly be on your printer? Is the positioning of the print on the page correct? If you need to make any adjustments can you do this, regardless of whether you need to make adjustments to the document on screen or adjustments to your printer?

Only if you can *routinely* produce professional documents can you claim to be a professional at word-processing!

The importance of clear instructions

You will save yourself a considerable amount of time and reduce inconvenience for yourself and other people if you are:

- clear about what you are doing before you start
- willing to ask questions if you are uncertain about anything
- always mindful of the requirements of the person asking you to do the work.

Being clear about what you are doing

If you are involved in a routine task that you have done many times before you may be able to do it almost automatically. The situation is different if you are given new work to do or a complex or involved task – or if the instructions are not absolutely clear. It is therefore sensible to do a few quick checks before you start any piece of new work, no matter how experienced you are.

a Have you been given clear instructions, either in writing or verbally, on what needs doing?

b Do these include informing you:
  - whether the document is already on disk or has to be prepared from scratch

- exactly what text needs to be input
- whether any text or tables have already been keyed and saved
- if text or tables have already been input, whether any editing is required
- if information has to be updated, where you can find the latest information
- the preferred layout for this document
- how much flexibility you have over deciding the layout yourself, if you have problems with the suggested one
- how many copies are required
- when the finished document is needed?

Asking questions

It is far, far better that you clarify any issues about which you are uncertain *before* you start work. Nothing is more annoying (for you) than to key in two pages and then to be told that the first six pages are already saved on disk! If the work is very complex, it is sensible to check whether the person who gave you the work will be available later to answer any queries. You don't want to start an urgent complex task, find three serious problems you can't solve yourself, and then discover that the person who set the task won't be around for the rest of the day!

Many new administrators hesitate to ask questions because they are worried they will be perceived as being poor at their job. In fact, the reverse is true! You cannot imagine a professional painter coming to your house and just starting the job without checking your exact requirements. In fact, it is more reassuring for *both* of you if the details are checked at the outset. Similarly, professional administrators also check anything they are not certain about. They can then guarantee being able to meet the person's requirements – which enhances their reputation.

The best time to ask questions is when you are first given the work. Simply say 'Can I just check through this with you so I know exactly what you want?' Few people could take exception to that! The trick then is to repeat the instructions *back* to the person to check you have understood them. This is also a tactful way of handling the situation if you can't understand what you are being told! Asking the person to repeat it and then repeating it back yourself will usually highlight any misunderstandings.

A more difficult situation is if you forget instructions, or have a problem later, when the person is busy with something else. Again, if you apologise for the interruption and explain why you have a query you will normally have few problems.

TEST YOUR KNOWLEDGE AND UNDERSTANDING

Consider what you would do in each of the following situations. Then discuss your ideas with your tutor or supervisor.

1 A manager in your department frequently gives you documents to produce just as he is rushing out to a meeting, with only very sketchy instructions. He then becomes annoyed if the document is not completed to his liking when he returns.

2 A technical manager is excellent at his job but his spelling and grammar are poor. You have just been given a three-page document to input, with some appalling errors.

3 You are typing an important document for your supervisor which you know she has spent several days preparing. Just as you finish keying it in, you notice that one of the requirements for this document is that it must be no longer than 2000 words – but you are fairly sure it is much longer than this.

4 Your boss is insistent that a letter to a customer must be on one page of A4 only. When you key it in you find you have extended to three lines on a second page.

5 You have been preparing an urgent document for your supervisor for most of the day. She wants it finished by 4 pm. At 3.45 pm, when you are on the last page, your screen freezes and none of your alpha-numeric keys will function.

6 For several days you have been producing a very long sales proposal for a customer. It is required for a presentation this afternoon. At 10 am your manager is in a panic because he has found that two technical terms used throughout the document are incorrect. He has given you the right words but needs the changes made and the document re-printing within the next half hour.

7 You are asked to make some changes to a complex table. You are not too sure how to carry out this operation but do your best. After one particular key stroke the whole table goes awry and looks a complete mess.

(Some of these questions test how well you know your system and the facilities you have. You may therefore like to check your own ideas against some of the features mentioned on page 215.)

Meeting individual requirements

If you produce documents for people regularly then you get to know their individual requirements. One person may prefer one style of document and someone else may prefer something different. As an example, one manager in an organisation liked all his documents justified (all the text is aligned at the left *and* right margins) whilst another didn't like the gaps this created in the middle of lines, and a third didn't mind – as long as the document looked professional. Capitalisation and punctuation are two other areas where people often differ. One may prefer many capitals and hyphens (e.g. Co-operative Societies) whilst another may prefer the more modern version (cooperative societies).

You may find that some of the people who give you work appear to be very decisive and rarely make changes after a draft document has been produced. Others may seem to want endless alterations. Do bear in mind this isn't because they are being awkward! Sometimes new information comes to light at a later stage, whilst a very technical or involved document may need several redrafts – or it is only when the document is in print that it is obvious that it could be adjusted to read better or look more effective. The wonderful thing about word-processing is that such alterations are very easy to make – if you know what you are doing. Comfort yourself with the fact that if you had been doing that job on a typewriter twenty years ago you would have had to start afresh every time.

There are two ways in which you can note people's alterations. The first is to make a list yourself, the second is to read the notes which have been written on the document. Do check you can read these clearly and go through them all with the originator of the document if necessary.

Using your system and your software

Quite obviously, before you can count yourself as an expert at word-processing you need to be familiar with your computer system and the software that is used in your organisation. This section provides an overview of the type of systems and most commonly used word-processing software currently found in business. Even if you know your system backwards, this may prove helpful if you change your job in the future and have to use a different system.

Computer systems

All computer systems are a combination of **hardware** and **software**. Hardware is the equipment you use and can touch – and includes your VDU or monitor, keyboard, processing unit (which will include your floppy disk and perhaps a CD-ROM drive) and mouse. You may also have your own printer – normally either a desk-jet or a laser (see page 264). If you access the Internet or send e-mails over the Internet then your computer will have a modem inside to enable you to communicate externally. Other items

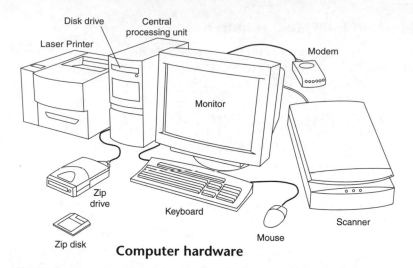

Computer hardware

classified as hardware include a scanner (for scanning documents into the system rather than keying them in) and sound speakers. If you study option unit 213, you will also learn about other types of hardware, such as Zip drives.

The software includes your **operating system** and **applications programs**. Without software a computer is simply a potentially clever but empty box! Today over 90 per cent of organisations use the Windows® operating system, developed by Microsoft. The operating system tells the hardware how to behave like a computer. The version of Windows you use will depend upon how up to date your system is and whether you operate a stand-alone computer or whether your organisation has **networked** (linked) computers. Network users have shared access to the operating system and software programs which are held on a **file server**. To offer these legally the organisation purchases a site licence from the software house and also buys a version of the software which is often configured differently from the software you would buy for a stand-alone system.

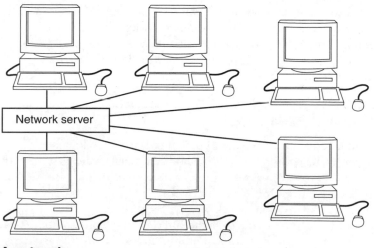

A network

Understanding Windows®

It is amazing how many people use Windows without understanding what they have on their computer! On Windows, the first thing you see is the **Desktop**. This has a **Taskbar** at the bottom with a **Start** button in the left-hand corner and the current time at the right-hand side. On the screen itself will be a number of icons showing what is available. Your system will have been configured (designed) to give access to certain facilities. This will be done by the organisation's network specialist, or by the supplier if your organisation has purchased a stand-alone system. Most large organisations also employ computer specialists who will help users to get used to their system.

Windows gives the opportunity to reconfigure the Desktop to suit oneself. You can move the icons around the screen and add icons for new programs. You may be somewhat limited as a user of a network system, but if you do not like the Desktop configuration on your screen – or find it difficult to use – it is worth finding out how it can be changed.

 INFORMATION UPDATE

Microsoft's Windows has been upgraded several times since it was introduced, to enable users to benefit from technological developments, new features and more powerful software. The version currently installed in most offices is Windows 98, but this has now been updated with Windows 2000. There are three versions – Windows 2000 Professional, Windows 2000 Server and

CHECK IT OUT!

Windows gives access to My Computer and Windows Explorer. You can use Windows Explorer to manage the files and folders you create in any software you use – including word-processing. Explorer will help you to create new files and folders quickly and easily, delete files and folders, move files to a new folder, copy files from one disk to another, examine the content of any folder quickly, and check how much space is available on your disk drives – to name but a few of its features.

Further details on My Computer and Windows Explorer are given in the notes on Option Unit 213 on page 448. Even if you are not intending to do that option, it is worth checking whether you have Explorer on your system and, if you have ignored it so far, learning how to undertake basic file and folder operations. You will find that this effort pays dividends in managing files in the future – *particularly* if you use more than one software package.

Windows 2000 Advanced Server. To run Windows 2000 you need a computer which has a fast processing speed and a minimum of 32 megabytes of RAM (random access memory). So if your organisation updates its operating system, you may find you get a new, faster and more powerful computer as well!

Word-processing software

The most commonly used word-processing software is Microsoft's Word for Windows. Other commonly used programs are WordPerfect, WordStar and ClarisWorks. In addition to different makes of software there are also different **versions**. The latest versions of Word for Windows in common use at the time of writing are versions 7.0 and Word 97 – although Word 2000 is now available.

Most word-processing software is bought as part of a suite of packages – e.g. Microsoft Office, Lotus SmartSuite and Corel WordPerfect Suite. Again these come in versions – so whilst you may have an earlier version of Office installed, version 2000 is also available. Similarly the latest version of SmartSuite is 9.5 and the latest version of Corel's product is WordPerfect Office 2000.

A suite of software means that the packages within the suite are integrated, so that each one is compatible with the others. You can therefore create a document in one package (e.g. a table in a spreadsheet) and easily transfer it to another (e.g. a word-processed document) using standard commands.

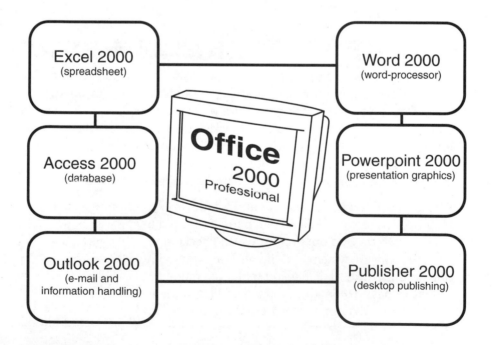

Word-processing functions

Word-processing software – regardless of which make or version you use – is designed to undertake the following main operations.

- Text can be changed and manipulated on screen, for instance by inserting and deleting, cutting and pasting.
- A page size can be selected and different formats and layouts chosen, including the style and size of the print and the size of margins. On many packages you can shrink a document (within reason) to fit a specific number of pages.
- There are various advanced features, such as headers and footers, page numbering and mail merge – so that standard letters can be personalised.
- Any document created on screen can be saved and/or printed. Printing can be either by page or as a complete document.
- File management options enable you to create, delete, move and search for files and folders you need.
- The software will give assistance to the operator in various ways: through the inclusion of a spell-checker or a thesaurus (which gives alternative words); an 'undo' facility – to go back a stage if the operator makes a mistake (probably the most valuable feature of all); a word count feature; a search and search/replace facility so that certain words can be found and changed quickly even in a long document; and a help facility in case you get stuck.

The more you understand your software and its facilities the more choice you have about what you do – and how you do it. One problem is that most people get used to the main functions and then ignore the rest. Try to rise above the standard of the 'average operator' by continually developing your skills.

CHECK IT OUT!

Understand your screen when you are into your word-processing package – not just so that you know where everything is, but also so that you can describe it properly to someone. Otherwise you will use the wrong terms.

The illustration on page 216 shows how a typical word-processing screen looks before text has been inserted. Check the main definitions in the glossary at the end of this unit.

Starting up and closing down

There are correct and incorrect ways to do even these simple operations!

Start up your system by checking, firstly, that you haven't left a floppy disk sitting in your 'A:' drive. If you have, press the small button on the front of

Windows screen in Office 2000

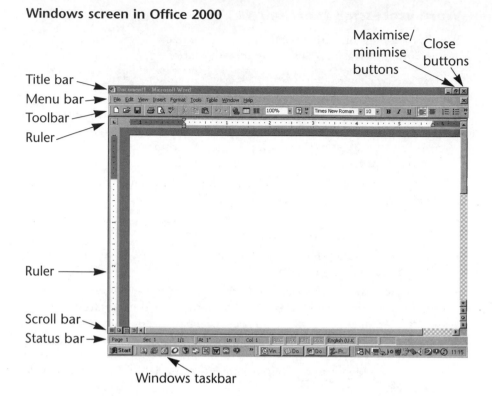

Maximise/ minimise buttons

Close buttons

Title bar

Menu bar

Toolbar

Ruler

Ruler

Scroll bar

Status bar

Windows taskbar

the drive to release the disk (otherwise your computer will not be able to start Windows). Now press the 'On' button on your computer unit. If this is linked to your monitor you will not need to depress a button on that as well – but if the monitor has a separate 'On' button, press that before the computer's button.

Allow time for the system to 'boot up'. If you operate on a networked system you will have to key in your user ID (identification) and your password – which will show on screen only as a row of stars (*****) – otherwise anyone standing behind you could read it. *Never* disclose your password to anyone and try to remember it without writing it down. If you must write it somewhere try to do it in code (e.g. adding or subtracting two letters or digits for each character). If you forget it then you will have to ring your computer help-desk for assistance. Note whether your system is **case-sensitive** or not – if it is, then it will matter which letters are upper case (capitals) and which are not. An intelligent system will remind you if this is the case.

Once Windows has loaded you will need to access your word-processing software. How you do this will depend upon your system and the layout of your computer Desktop. Normally you will use the mouse to move the pointer arrow either to Start (and read from the menu that appears) or to the appropriate icon on the main Desktop or button on the Taskbar and then click the left mouse button (once only on the Taskbar). Sometimes you may have several access options – choose the one that is easiest for you.

If you have to leave your desk for a few moments it is not necessary to switch your machine off. If the work is confidential, there are several tactics you can use to prevent people reading your screen (see page 227). Normally your **screen-saver** will come into operation after a pre-set time. This may generate a swirling pattern on your VDU. A screen-saver is intended to prevent stationary images 'burning' on to the screen, which is why screen-saver patterns are forever moving. You can probably change the design of your screen-saver – if you don't like it – and the length of time before it comes into operation by means of **Control Panel** in Windows (select Display and then the Screensaver option).

Switch off your system by the recommended method. Firstly you need to exit your word-processing software. Before you do this *always* check that you have saved your work properly – although the package will prompt you at this point if you have not saved your work. Then close the file or files you have been working on and exit the software. This action will return the screen to the Desktop. On a stand-alone system you will now opt to shut down, while on a network you will 'log off'. It is important you undertake these operations as instructed as this enables the system to close itself down properly. There is usually a short delay before you see a message on screen saying that you can now switch off the machine.

Never switch the system on and off again quickly or repeatedly or you are likely to cause a considerable amount of damage – and never shortcut the proper shut-down procedures just because you are in a hurry! Occasionally, particularly if you are on a stand-alone PC, you may find your computer 'hangs' during shut-down. If this happens regularly, notify your computer experts. Immediately, you can do an emergency close down. How to do this is described below.

If you are ever in the unenviable position of your computer 'hanging' or 'freezing' – failing to respond to any keystrokes or mouse actions – then don't panic. It is to be hoped that you have been sensible enough to save your work frequently, in addition to perhaps having the 'automatic save' option set on your system – particularly if you are creating an important document (see page 243).

Sometimes during a 'freeze' your egg-timer will remain fixed on screen or you will see a blue warning screen. Never be tempted to try every key you can think of to see if that will help. It could be simply that your computer is just struggling to do something and needs a little time.

Give the computer a couple of minutes before doing anything. If nothing has happened after that time, there are basically three choices:

a   You can ring your computer section if you are on a network, to see if there is a network fault.

b You can try your Start button on the Taskbar to see whether that is still functioning. In the unlikely event that it is, you will be able to shut down your system properly.

c If you cannot get any response it will be necessary to do an **emergency close down** (by depressing the Control/Alt/Delete keys simultaneously). This should result in the 'Close Program' dialogue box appearing. Here you will see all the programs that are currently running – and you are likely to see a longer list than you expect as these are Windows programs that run in the background all the time. Highlight the program that is causing problems (you should see the words 'not responding' after its name) and click on End Task (sometimes you may be asked to wait a while and then try again). You can then shut down your computer completely or reboot. However, you will lose any work you have input since you last did a save. If you have your automatic save function set properly and save regularly yourself, this shouldn't cause you any problems.

Error messages

If you operate on a networked system you may see a warning occasionally instructing you to close down. Don't ignore such warnings – they are put there by your computer staff to prevent you being 'caught out' if they are aware that there is a network problem which may cause it to go off-line shortly. In this case, save your work and log off properly before that happens.

On any computer, if there is a problem you may suddenly find an error message appearing – either when you switch on or when you are trying to load something. Some relate to problems with your programs or files you have deleted, others can occur if you are short of memory or if the program considers it has attempted to carry out an 'illegal' operation. Memory problems are dealt with on page 248, but it is worth noting now that you can often simply follow the instructions on screen (usually to log off) and then reboot to solve the problem. If the error message recurs think about what may have caused it by noting down the file or folder you were using or opening, what programs you had in use and the key strokes you had recently done. All these will help your computer staff to diagnose and solve the problem.

CHECK IT OUT!

Many hackers (people who access computer systems without authorisation) consider that part of their success is due to the carelessness with which people choose and use their passwords. Studies show that most people use fairly obvious passwords – the month of their birth; the name of their partner, child or pet; the name of their house or road – or a word associated with the time of year. One organisation discovered in December that over 90 per cent of its staff had passwords relating to Christmas! ➡

Your system will prompt you to select a new password after a certain period. This is to enhance security. Even if it does not, you should change your password yourself from time to time. However, all security measures are defeated if your password is so obvious anyone could guess it! Apparently the best method is to think of a word only you would know – such as your favourite place to visit at the moment, or a flower you saw last week, or some other word associated with your life. This way, the only way someone could access your system would be to read your mind!

Check back through the passwords you have used in the past. How obvious were they? Now try to think of one which no one else would guess and use *this* one next time.

Conventions for naming and saving files

File management is an important part of word-processing. Without it you might create hundreds of documents and not be able to find any of them again. Just as in a manual system, documents become files, files go into folders (which are also referred to as 'directories'), and both files and folders need labelling and putting in a logical order.

Your PC disk drives prefer order to chaos. They use a very methodical way of creating files and folders – and this is graphically represented by means of a **directory tree**. You can see this for yourself if you access Windows Explorer. Click on the small + sign to the left of a folder to see all the branches of your sub-directories. The files will then be shown in the right window (see illustration on page 220).

Understanding disk drives

One of the first things you will see listed is the **drives** on your computer. Before we look at files and folders, let's look at your options for saving your documents. You have a number of choices.

a   You may save on to floppy disks (in your **A: drive**) – although these are mainly used for back-up documents these days. The word 'floppy' may seem to be a misnomer as the disks appear to be quite rigid – but if you slide the metal plate to one side, inside lies the disk itself. The first rule is to label all your floppy disks clearly, whether they contain original or back-up documents. The second is to remember that there is a small button on the back you can slide if you want the disk to be **write-protected**. This means you cannot by accident wipe off important documents that are saved on it.

Directory tree in Windows Explorer

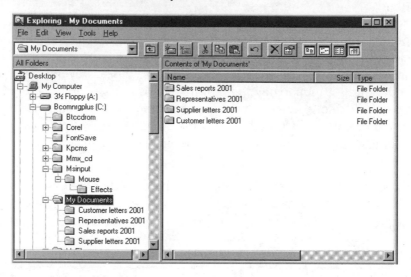

b   You can save on to your hard disk (the **C: drive**), this being the most usual method. There can be a problem if your computer breaks down, which is why important documents need backing-up on to a floppy disk or other type of medium.

c   If you operate on a network, you can save on your home area (this may be your **H: drive**, **S: drive** or any other appropriate letter designated by the network administrator). This is the area on your network file server sectioned off for your use alone. Again, this doesn't mean you shouldn't back up your work – servers can 'go down' and lose data, just like your computer.

When you are saving documents and creating files and folders you need to know where you are working – quite simply because keying in the wrong drive letter will put you in the wrong place. You could spend a long time looking for something on your C: drive if you stored it in your home area, for instance (although Windows does have a file-search facility – see page 246).

Understanding and creating folders and files

Needless to say, your system needs your help to create files and folders – they won't just magically appear. In most word-processing packages, such as Word, all the files you create may be saved in a special folder called My Documents or My File. You can find this out by starting a new document, selecting Save and seeing what your default is in the 'Save In' part of the **dialogue box** which appears.

Let's assume you have a brand new computer with a new word-processing package and you want to have an orderly system. First you need to think about all the different types of documents you will be creating. If you work for Sales, for instance, you may write letters to customers and suppliers, communicate with reps and prepare sales reports. You would then want to create four folders, one for each of these types of document. It is sensible to put the year after each folder name and start a new folder each new year to prevent them becoming overcrowded.

The easiest way to create a folder is to go to the Start button and access Windows Explorer (which may be listed under Programs). Now scroll down the list in the left-hand window and find My Documents. Click on it so that it highlights and click on File on the menu bar, go to New and select Folder. A new folder appears in the right-hand window which you can name – just type in the name you want and press enter. You can create any number of folders this way.

Every time you create a document you create a new file. This is why you can access documents through the **File** option on the **menu bar**. After you click on File you have the choice of whether to start a new document or open an existing one. If you create a new document, then at the point it is saved you will be prompted to give it a name. There are three things you need to remember.

a   Save the new file and give it a name straight away, or after you've typed one or two lines, rather than wait until you've finished the whole thing. If you are interrupted you might forget to save your work.

b   When saving a new file for the first time, check that you are putting it in the correct folder by looking at the Save In box. You can access all the directories you saw in Explorer through this window. Find My Documents (if that is where your folders are located) and then select the correct folder.

c   Name your file so that you can recognise it quickly. Modern word-processing systems allow you far more characters than in the past – although you should check those which are not accepted by your system. Often these are special characters (such as /, \ and *). If a file name is rejected, remove the offending character and try again. Your system will prompt you if you try to give a file the same name as another one.

Try to be logical and descriptive in your choice of names. These may be determined by your organisation, in which case you have no choice. If not, don't abbreviate names so that you cannot tell later what they are. If you do a number of drafts of a document then you can identify them easily if you suffix them with v1, v2, v3 (version 1, etc.). Try to avoid labelling anything 'latest' as you may end up with several 'latest' versions!

If you click on Open to access an existing file, again a dialogue box will appear on screen. Again you need to check you are in the correct directory and the right folder to be able to open a file.

The dialogue box will display all the folders in a directory in the window in the middle of the box. If you have several, use the **scroll bar** on the right-hand side to view all of them. If you double-click on the folder you want all the documents inside it appear. Then you double-click on the document you want.

If you save a document in the wrong folder by accident, you can move it – either via the dialogue box or by using Windows Explorer.

WARNING: Do be careful if you delete *folders* in Windows Explorer, as some contain programs that are required to keep the system operating. Stick to deleting files that you are certain you do not want. Many systems will warn you if you try to delete important systems files – but you cannot rely on this. If you delete a file, wait a little while before you empty your Recycle Bin – then you may be able to retrieve it if you find it was important.

CHECK IT OUT!

How well do you know your file management dialogue box? Have you *really* investigated all the options for displaying or listing your folders and files and finding folders and files quickly?

Bring up your dialogue box on screen (select Open in the File menu) and *read* it! Click on the buttons or menus and try to find out what the options are. Use your on-screen help to assist you. You may get a few surprises and find an even easier way of creating new folders on your system than the one described above.

File Management dialogue box (Windows 2000)

House styles

Organisations have house styles for documents that are produced regularly. This is to prevent people outside the organisation receiving documents which vary tremendously in format and style depending upon who wrote or who produced the document. The traditional method is to produce a reference manual with a copy of each document prepared in the house style and to place one manual in every office. You can then refer to it easily, even if you produce a particular document only on odd occasions.

If you work on a computer network, however, you may find that your house style is available on your system as a **template**. In this case many of the required features will have been pre-set.

If there appears to be no specific house style in an organisation you join, it is still useful to look at the existing files to see how letters, memos, reports, etc. are *usually* laid out and use them as your guide.

The house style may specify:

- the size and type of paper used (e.g. A4 headed paper for letters)
- the layout and line spacing
- the typeface and font (see page 253)
- the way continuation sheets must be set out
- any headers and footers which must be included.

If you have problems with a specific requirement and cannot understand how to do this on your word-processing package, then check the manual – you may find instructions are included. For example, some organisations insist that their logo be incorporated into certain documents – and you may have to ask someone how to do this on your system.

EVIDENCE COLLECTION

1 Start your evidence for this unit by obtaining information about the house styles used in your organisation. Select three types of document you regularly produce and identify what requirements must be followed. If you also have specific requirements with which you must comply when you save files and name documents or folders, include these as well.

Prepare a brief summary – preferably on your word-processor – which covers these areas, sign it and ask your supervisor to countersign it for authenticity.

2 Explain to those people for whom you often create and print documents that you will need evidence that you meet their requirements. Ask them if they would be willing to put more complex requests in writing to you (a handwritten note is sufficient). Add a summary of any questions you have asked to determine their requirements exactly – and the answers you received. Attach a copy of the finished document and then ask the person to confirm (in writing) that you fully met their request.

If you do this for all the more involved documents you produce over, say, the next month, you will obtain evidence which will count against several requirements of this unit.

Computers and health and safety

There are two ways in which you can think about health and safety – one is your own, and the other is your computer's!

In Unit 102 you learned about the Health and Safety at Work Act. You also learned about the Display Screen Equipment Regulations (on pages 13–14) and the dangers of RSI (on page 37). Turn back now and refresh your memory about the DSE Regulations and how they affect you.

Various concerns have been expressed by people who use computers regularly. Some of these are important – and have influenced the introduction of laws such as the DSE Regulations. Others have been more alarmist and have little substance. Test out your own knowledge by doing the quiz below – and compare your answers with those on page 276.

However, if your health is important so is that of your computer! Unless you look after it you can hardly expect it to give you good service. Taking care of your equipment means:

- remembering to turn it off at the end of the day, if that is what you have been asked to do
- using it only according to the recommended instructions – for instance when starting it up and closing down the system
- keeping drinks and other liquids *well* away from all your hardware
- cleaning the screen and keyboard regularly, using appropriate products such as screen wipes and keyboard sprays
- keeping connecting wires at the back of your desk and not moving or pulling your computer into a position where the wires are stretched
- not losing your temper if the system doesn't respond to you and repeatedly striking keys in anger or (heaven forbid) hitting the computer.

According to one survey – called Network Rage – 83 per cent of computer users experienced a violent reaction to their computer problems. Some had even smashed their keyboards or thrown their mouse across the room. No doubt most of them were looking for a new job as well as a new computer by the end of the day!

TEST YOUR KNOWLEDGE AND UNDERSTANDING

How much do you know about your health and safety as a computer user? Test yourself by identifying whether each of the following twenty statements is fact or fiction. Then check your answers with those on page 276.

1 Staring at a VDU screen for long periods causes serious eye problems.

➡️

2 A range of upper limb disorders – also known as repetitive strain injuries (RSIs) – can be caused by using a computer, resulting in pain in the hands, wrists, shoulders, neck and back.

3 A person suffering from epilepsy should obtain advice before using a computer.

4 VDUs emit radiation which can be dangerous unless a screen filter is fitted.

5 A copy or document holder can help to reduce posture problems at a stroke.

6 Computer users who request a footstool must be provided with one.

7 Pregnant women shouldn't work on a computer.

8 Special ergonomically designed keyboards can be purchased to reduce wrist and hand strain.

9 Computerised offices can cause excessive 'dry heat' resulting in dry eyes, sore throats, skin problems and cold/flu-like symptoms.

10 Touch typists are less at risk from possible upper limb disorders than users who 'hunt and peck' around the keyboard.

11 The height of the VDU screen should not be above the horizontal eye height of the operator, and the centre of the screen should not be more than 800 mm above the work surface.

12 Computers can give users an electric shock.

13 The weight of your head is significant in relation to posture, head and neck problems.

14 Your VDU should not be positioned in front of a wall or other fixed point.

15 Crossing your legs can reduce many of the problems associated with sitting at a computer.

16 Many computer users suffer from stress which affects their health.

17 Emissions from VDU screens cause skin conditions, such as dermatitis and acne.

18 Most people who suffer from work-related upper limb disorders (such as RSI) are typists or computer users.

19 Computer users can buy software which gives them stretch and exercise programs to relieve their shoulders, neck, hands and back.

20 Virtually all the health threats from computer use can be completely eliminated by a few easy procedures.

Dealing with sensitive or confidential information

Most networked computer systems operate with some type of password system, and individual packages may also require the keying in of different user passwords to prevent anyone who is unauthorised from accessing confidential or sensitive information. As a first step, you should make sure you know and understand the official security systems which are in place in your organisation to protect certain types of information. Normally, however, the problem for administrators is more basic. For instance, you work in a busy office. You've been asked to prepare a document which contains confidential information which your supervisor has stressed she doesn't want the other staff to know about just yet. You know it will take you some time to key it in. How do you ensure no one sees what you are doing during this time?

Some of the main points about dealing with confidential or sensitive information have been dealt with in other units. You should keep the hard copies in a special folder and lock this away when you are not using it. Another useful strategy is to keep other papers on your desk, so that you can cover up the original document unobtrusively by sliding another paper over it if someone approaches you. The main problem for most computer users, however, is preventing other people from reading the text showing on their VDU.

Administrators who regularly deal with confidential work usually position their desk well away from the door and any major traffic routes, to minimise the number of people who walk past their computer screen. They will also place their computer screen so that people approaching them see the back of it first – not the screen itself. All organisations which use computers in front of members of the public (such as building societies and banks) do this. They also use special 'flat' screens that can be read only when the screen is directly facing the user. If you regularly deal with confidential or sensitive material and you think your desk or screen position could be improved, then suggest this to your supervisor. You have no need to explain your actions to other members of staff – simply say you want a change, or use your new-found knowledge of health and safety requirements as an excuse!

Even with all these precautions, you may have to be vigilant if you are keying in sensitive material over a period of time. Strategies to protect your screen include:

a   saving and closing the file if you are leaving your desk for any length of time

b   switching off your monitor *only*

c   turning down the brightness on your screen

d   having another document in another window – and switching to this one if someone comes up to talk to you.

To find out if you can do (d) on your system, check the Window option. If you have this option, which enables you to work on more than one document at once, this is the best choice as you can do this quickly and easily without anyone realising!

Finally, if you back-up the work on to a floppy disk then make sure that this *also* is locked away with any hard copies. There is little point in guarding your screen all day if you then leave your floppy disk on top of your desk when you go home!

ℹ INFORMATION UPDATE

In addition to protecting sensitive data, you also need to be wary about protecting your computer. Most people today are aware of computer viruses, yet fail to take even the most elementary precautions with their own computers. A virus is a rogue program which has been designed to cause a malfunction within an existing system. The growth in the number of people sending information over the Internet has increased the danger of viruses being downloaded – the 'I love you' virus which affected many computers across the world in May 2000 cost businesses an estimated £3 billion to put right. However, you don't need to be on the Internet to import a virus to your machine. Simply using a borrowed floppy disk from *outside* your organisation or system could do it, if the disk contains a virus and your computer is not fitted with virus detection software. Even if it is, this doesn't totally solve the problem, as viruses are constantly being developed to *outwit* such software. Currently there are around 60,000 known viruses circulating, and with 200 new ones reported each month it is doubtful if any detection software could cope with every one.

You can do your bit to help to keep your computer data secure from viruses by complying with all your company's procedures and regulations on using disks. This may mean that any unknown floppy disks must be screened before they can be used on the company computer systems. *Never* think it doesn't matter if you ignore these rules just once – many viruses don't give anyone a second chance!

EVIDENCE COLLECTION

Be prepared to discuss with your assessor how you name and save files in your organisation and how you deal with sensitive or confidential information. If you can, identify specific occasions when you do this and make a note of these.

Prepare a brief summary – on your word-processor – of the times when you have had to consider how to name and save files and/or take special care because you were handling or creating a sensitive document. You can give this to your assessor as additional evidence of your knowledge and understanding of this area.

CHECK IT OUT!

At the end of this unit (page 277) is a glossary of all the Windows and word-processing terms used in this unit. You may find it useful to refer to this to refresh your memory of what various terms mean.

Element 204.1 Enter and edit text

The first stage in the creation of any document on a computer is to enter text. If you use word-processing software, an associated skill is being able to edit text, save it and take the appropriate action if you meet with a particular problem. This element requires you to enter text using a keyboard – which is still the standard method despite the advent of computer scanners and voice recognition software.

Your evidence for this element must prove that you can input printed and handwritten text, can carry out basic checks and corrections, and deal with specific problems.

Keyboard layout and usage

One of the most fascinating aspects of computers is that, despite all the advances in technology, everyone is still using a keyboard based on a design over 125 years old! The difficulty, of course, is that touch typists are now so used to its layout that suggestions for changes (and there have been a few, over the years) are always discounted because of the problems it would cause existing users.

The standard keyboard contains:

- **alpha-numeric keys** (in other words, letters and numbers), which you use all the time
- **function keys**, which you use relatively frequently
- a **number pad**, which you will probably use very rarely, if ever.

Alpha-numeric keys

You will find your way around these much more easily and quickly if you learn to touch type. It is amazing that today all school children aren't taught this skill on reduced-sized keyboards at about 10 years of age. Rather like riding a bike or learning to swim, keyboarding is an indispensable skill that would then be with them for life. Instead, people learn to hunt and peck their way around the keyboard relatively quickly and then dislike the idea of 'unlearning' all their skills whilst they are taught to touch type. Yet everyone is still impressed if they see text being input at about 60 words a minute by someone who continually looks at the copy and never at the keyboard!

The advantages to touch typing are so great that, if you have not achieved this skill, it is well worth taking the time to do so. Within a month you could have reached your current speed, increased your accuracy and then you *will continue to improve* for some months to come. It is a decision you will never regret. There are a few things to consider.

a   Identify the best way of learning for *you*. This may be attending a short course or booking in for special keyboarding sessions at your local college, or buying yourself a typing tutor program to use on your home computer.

b   Practice little and often. Two one-hour sessions are better than a two-hour session, practising for an hour a day is better than practising for three hours on two days. Keyboarding is like driving – your brain needs time to establish the links between the movements you are making.

c   Even though it is difficult, resist the temptation to go back to your old ways during the initial weeks. Use every keyboarding session as an opportunity to develop your skills. This may mean talking to your supervisor as your speed will initially decrease, before it starts to speed up again.

d   Don't worry if you find the numeric keys harder to master. Even the most experienced touch typists often still glance at these to check they are entering figures correctly.

You will find there are numerous benefits. You will be more accurate, faster and have less danger of developing hand and wrist problems – and you will also have an extremely valuable and marketable job skill.

Function keys

There are two types of function key. The first are the keys which are assigned to the same operation on all computers. These include Control (Ctrl), Alt, Delete (you have already learned that these three keys combined will exit your system even if it has frozen), Insert, Home, End, Page Up/Down and the arrow keys. Other function keys are the F1 to F12 keys which will be specially assigned depending upon the package you are using.

Spend some time familiarising yourself with the differences between some of these keys and what they can actually do on your word-processing package. For instance:

* **Home** may have no effect or may take you to page 1 of your document or to the beginning of a line (and note that Control plus Home will take you to the top of page 1 on some packages or let you select the page you want to go to on others).
* **End** will take you to the end of a line.
* **Insert** – most word-processing packages are automatically set so that as you type new words they are inserted and the rest of the text automatically 'moves along'. It is possible to alter the setting so that new words instead *overwrite* existing text. Watch what you are doing, however, or you may take out whole lines in error!
* **Delete** will remove the character on which your cursor is positioned, whereas the **back arrow** key will remove the character to the left of your cursor. Delete will also remove – at a stroke – any text that is highlighted (selected)!

- Your **Control** and **Alt** keys can often be used for shortcuts to access menu options. These are denoted after the menu option. Touch typists who usually prefer using the keys to a mouse find it much quicker to learn several of these shortcuts and use them habitually.
- **Page up** and **Page down** may seem obvious – but it is amazing how many people don't bother using them!
- **Esc** usually cancels a particular function – for instance, you can close a dialogue box quickly using this key.
- The **tab** key will help you (or your text) to move quickly across screen by a pre-set number of spaces at once.
- The **Windows** key on the more modern keyboards will open the Start menu no matter where your Taskbar is or what you are doing.
- The **arrow keys** are invaluable for moving through a document – although you should also learn the quick way to move from one page to another specific page in a long document on your system.
- The **Return** (or **Enter**) key is used to enter hard returns (to force a new line or paragraph). It is also useful for agreeing 'OK' to a request – and to save you the trouble of using your mouse.

If you do not know whether your **F keys** have any function on your package you could always try depressing each one in turn to find out. F1 will usually start the Help function in any program, but thereafter the functions do vary. For instance, with Word, F7 will start the spell-checker, while with WordPerfect you will exit your document immediately! With WordPerfect each F key is a valuable shortcut which is depressed in conjunction with Control, Alt or Shift to access different options. All word-processing packages have key combination shortcuts (which may be shown on the menu, in brackets). If you are experimenting, you may learn some useful speedy ways of doing things without always having to use your mouse; but don't choose a time when you have an important document on screen!

CHECK IT OUT!

Sometimes you may be required to enter a character that isn't on a standard keyboard, such as a fraction or mathematical symbol (e.g. ‰) or a foreign word with a special accent or punctuation mark (e.g. garçon). All these symbols or characters are available on your computer and are usually found under the Insert menu.

One of the skills you need to possess to obtain this unit is the ability to use your program's help files when necessary. Assume you have typed this sentence for your boss: 'It is no use being blase about this problem.' He informs you that you should have typed 'blasé' which means 'uninterested' and asks you to edit the text. Use your program help files to find out how to do this on your system.

The number pad

Only if you regularly input numeric data into your computer are you likely to use this pad – which has made several people query why computer keyboards are not normally available without them, so that the mouse would be nearer and easier to use (for a right-handed person). Keyboards without a number pad – or with the number pad on the left-hand side for left-handed people – are available but you would probably need to ask if your company just bulk orders its keyboards from its usual supplier.

CHECK IT OUT!

One of the biggest critics of standard keyboards is AbilityNet, a charity which aims to assist any computer user with a disability to use their equipment more effectively. Computers are a tremendous boon for many people with disabilities who want to develop work-related skills and who also like to use computers as a means of communication with the outside world. The charity will also give advice to users with posture problems or who fear they may be suffering from RSI.

The information provided by AbilityNet is so good it is invaluable for able-bodied users as well as anyone with a disability. You can find out about this yourself if you have Internet access by bringing up their website on www.abilitynet.co.uk. You can obtain:

- information on different types of keyboards – including ergonomic keyboards – plus names of suppliers as well as other devices, such as trackballs, which are better than a mouse for people who can't grip easily
- details of additional aids for computer users with visual or hearing impairments
- information on RSI and links to other sites which are concerned with this subject plus other health-related issues
- a range of factsheets and skillsheets which you can download free.

You will need Acrobat Reader software on your system to read the factsheets, but this too can be downloaded from the AbilityNet site. If you are using someone else's computer, do consult them before you do this. Information includes useful hints and tips for shortcuts – and you can also obtain the latest on voice recognition systems if you can't wait for the day the keyboard is defunct for ever!

Roll-up keyboard

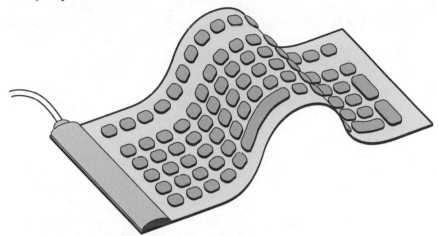

Ergonomic keyboard

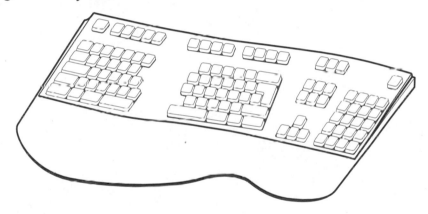

Positioning original documents

To comply with the Display Screen Equipment Regulations, your workspace should be sufficiently large for all your routine paperwork as well as all your computer hardware. Most people place the hard copy from which they are working to the left or right of their keyboard, flat on the desk. Although this may be the most common option it is not the best one – simply because you are turning your head to one side and bending it down for long periods of time. The result can be a crick in the back of your neck at best, or problems with your neck and shoulders which need the help of a physiotherapist to put right.

Ideally, text should be positioned at eye level, particularly if you are keying in for long periods. Document holders can be purchased which can be positioned so that the text is in front of you. This is preferable to having the VDU in front of you – particularly if you are a touch typist. Many document holders have a sliding horizontal clip which slightly magnifies each line, making difficult documents easier to read. If you buy a document holder make sure it is stable and easily adjustable to different positions, heights and angles and large enough to fit all the document sizes you regularly handle.

Correct posture for sitting at a keyboard

①   Appropriate lighting with no glare or distracting reflections
②   Adequate leg room
③   Window blinds
④   Software: Appropriate to task, user trained to use it properly without undue stress or pressure
⑤   Adjustable screen with stable image, glare and reflection free and at appropriate height
⑥   Adjustable, detachable keyboard
⑦   Spacious work surface to allow flexibility
⑧   Adjustable chair
⑨   Footrest
⑩   Copy holder at eye level

For your award you will have to prove you can input text both from typed documents and from handwritten documents. If you are visually impaired you can input from Braille instead. If you are preparing a draft document which you know will be altered and returned to you later, it is sensible to check whether you can print this out in double line spacing. It is then easier for alterations to be made and easier for you to read these. If you are dealing with a handwritten document where the handwriting is very small or you are struggling to read it, you may find it is easier to read if you photocopy and enlarge the original a little.

A final tip. Always keep multi-page originals clipped together. Or if you must separate them, clear your desk of everything else. Otherwise – especially if you are not a naturally tidy worker – you may easily find you've lost a page or thrown one away in error!

CHECK IT OUT!

Check how many you score when you are sitting at a computer. Give yourself one point each time you can honestly say 'yes'.

1 You are sitting up straight with your back slightly arched – you are *not* learning forward.

2 Your head is held erect and your chin is tucked in.

3 Your feet are flat on the floor or on a footrest.

4 Your knees are lower than your thighs.

5 The edge of your chair does not press against the back of your knees.

6 Your elbows are almost at right angles and there is a gentle downward slope from your elbows to your fingers on the keyboard.

7 You get up and change your activity *regularly* (for at least 10 minutes every hour).

8 You have experimented with your computer's colour combinations to get the best ones to suit your eyes.

9 Your desk is uncluttered so that you don't have to reach further than is necessary for what you want.

10 Your computer screen was cleaned within the last two days.

If you didn't score 10 out of 10 you may need to learn a few techniques to help yourself if you are feeling any discomfort. Try this:

• Massage the small muscles of your hands and fingers twice a day.

• Drop your hands down to your sides occasionally and gently shake your hands and fingers.

➡

- Blink regularly to keep your eyes lubricated.

- Refocus your eyes regularly by looking out of the window or at a far wall. Ideally your screen should be placed where you can do this easily. Looking at a distant object and then a close one and alternating quickly between the two helps to revive tired eyes. Then visually trace a horizontal 8, first in one direct and then the other.

- Massage the small muscles at the bottom inch of the back of your skull if you think you are getting a headache. Take a break and stretch your head and neck upwards. Then slowly rotate both your shoulders forwards in a full circle four times – first together and then separately. These will help to reduce muscle tension and are better for you than painkillers!

Finally, the importance of changing position regularly cannot be over-emphasised. Sitting down in one position for long periods puts tension on the whole of your body. Take a break – do another job. Make a telephone call or do your filing. Anything is better than ending up with serious posture problems.

EVIDENCE COLLECTION

A new member of your team has joined the organisation straight from school. He uses a computer only infrequently but will do so more often in the future. He has never learned to touch type and is apt to think such sessions are more for girls. He has no idea about posture, nor about having his copy in the correct position. Last week he had more work to do than usual and complained about neck ache all day Friday.

Either discuss with your assessor the arguments you could put forward to persuade him of the benefits of learning to use a computer properly, *or* write him a short memo, on your word-processor, giving suggestions in writing.

Checking and correcting

Checking text

Checking a document – '**proof-reading**' to give it its proper title – is an essential skill. However, many people who use a word-processor are either so keen to print out the document they can't be bothered to check the document at all, or they confuse checking with giving it a 'quick read', or they rely totally on their spell-checker to do the job for them. In all these cases the result is likely to be an unusable document.

This is because proof-reading is a *skill* – just like keyboarding – which you can learn and develop. People who are really good are often called 'eagle eyes' by the rest of the staff, as they seem to be able to spot an error from the other side of the room! However, such vigilance is invaluable as it prevents silly mistakes remaining in a document which may cause confusion, annoyance or hilarity when it is read elsewhere.

Before we look at how you develop proof-reading skills, it is important to understand how spell-checkers work and why you can't just rely on them – no matter how sophisticated your software package. If you use Word, you will find the package tries to help you by highlighting words it doesn't recognise and correcting straightforward mistakes as you are keying in. This is its AutoCorrect feature and you can see how it works by investigating this on the Tools menu. However, AutoCorrect alone should not be relied upon; you will still need to run a complete spell-check at the end by clicking on the ABC button on the Toolbar. If you use a different package from Word and are not sure what is available, access the Help screen, enter Spell and see what choices are given.

A spell-checker is good only for basic spelling errors. It will still leave errors in your work, for a number of reasons.

- It may not know some technical words or proper names (e.g. the correct spelling of a customer's surname) unless you have added these to the in-built dictionary.

- It cannot tell when you have mis-keyed a word that results in another genuine word (e.g. form/from or word/work).

- It cannot differentiate between homonyms – words which sound the same as another one (e.g. principal/principle or councillor/counsellor).

- Unless you have a grammar checker, there will be no warning that you have used punctuation incorrectly (e.g. it's/its or who's/whose). If you are using Word, the grammar checker may highlight such errors in green – but that is still not to be trusted in all circumstances.

- Believe it or not, some spell-checkers contain the *wrong* spelling for some words!

So you still have some work to do yourself. The best way to develop proof-reading skills is to do the following.

1 Decide whether you really can check work better on screen or on paper. If the latter, then print out a copy in draft print setting when you have

finished and check this, rather than reading the screen. Mark up any errors in red so that you can find them easily when you are making the amendments.

2 Read *word by word* – not in groups of words. The easiest way to check you are doing this is to ask yourself one question. Are you reading your work as you would a magazine article or are you reading the text as if it contained instructions for dyeing your hair, when you would be desperate not to get it wrong? Skim reading is *not* appropriate when you are proof-reading.

3 If there are figures included, ask someone to read the numbers to you while you check your work.

4 If you have any doubts about spellings, punctuation or the meanings of words, you have several options. You can use an ordinary dictionary (although this is often of little use if you have no clue at all how the word is spelt); you can access a thesaurus on screen if you have one; or you can ask for help from a colleague who you know has excellent English skills. If the problem is over the meaning of a sentence or a technical word then you are better referring the problem to the person who gave you the document in the first place.

 INFORMATION UPDATE

If you fear your spelling and word skills are really bad, you could lobby your supervisor to buy a CD-ROM called the *Bookshelf British Reference Collection* (produced by Microsoft). This contains a number of reference books, including Chambers Dictionary. If you use Word and have a CD-ROM drive, you can keep the disk in the drive and access the dictionary direct from Word. If a few people in your office are poor spellers it may be a good buy – it currently retails for about £30.

TEST YOUR KNOWLEDGE AND UNDERSTANDING

A colleague has keyed in the letter opposite. Highlight in one colour all the errors which would be identified by an on-line spell-checker, and in another colour the errors which would *not* be identified by a spell-checker. Then rewrite the letter so that it is as perfect as you can get it. (You can assume the names of the recipient and sender are spelt correctly.)

Dear Mr Pickard

Thank you for your recent order which we recieved on 22 September for a Sony 17 inch moniter, reference CPD-E4928E. We confirm that this moniter is compatable with your computer system as specified in your letter.

Unfortunately we must advice you that we are out of stock of this particular model at this time. We can, however, supply you with an alternative VDU which has a slightly hire specification at a cost of an additional £35 plus VAT. In this case, please let us know and we will arrange for immediate despatch.

However, if you would prefer to weight, then no further action is neccesary. As soon as we recieve further supplies we will arrange delivery.

We regret the inconvenience caused by this delay but are sure you will appreciate that some matters are outside our control. We would aim to delivery the original model no later than 31 October but please note that this date is our best estimate and does not from a contract to supply by this date.

Yours sincereley

John Barker

Sales Admin Office

CHECK IT OUT!

1   How good are your dictionary skills? You can test these by seeing how long it takes you to (a) find a word you know and (b) find a word you don't know! You should also know that a dictionary can give you more information than just the spelling of a word. In a good dictionary you will find advice on spelling and spelling variations, guidance on the usage of words, hints on pronunciation, and reference pages relating to abbreviations and other useful facts.

The quick way to look up a word is to focus on the top right-hand corner of every page, which gives the final word on that page. This will help you to quickly find the initial letter of your word and then find a word near to yours in spelling. Then look at the tops of other columns, which again have the final word highlighted. This helps you to find the appropriate column quickly. You can then look down it for the word you need. Try to avoid being distracted by reading about interesting words you meet as you go!

Many people who are poor spellers consider dictionaries useless, especially if the spelling isn't obvious from the pronunciation. When searching for words such as lieutenant (pronounced 'lef-ten-ant' in this country), subtle (pronounced 'suttle') or charismatic (pronounced to rhyme with Paris), you might be looking under the right first letter but that's about it.

If you do find the word you want, do check you are not looking at a word which is very similar – but incorrect – by reading the meaning. So you wouldn't mistake 'compliment' and 'complement' or 'definite' and 'definitive' for instance.

If you know the meaning of the word, but haven't a clue how to spell it, another source of information may be a thesaurus. You may have one on your computer but the book versions are normally superior. A thesaurus is a dictionary of synonyms, or words similar in meaning. So if you wanted to find out how to spell 'aggravate' and knew it means 'to annoy' you may be able to find it out by checking in the thesaurus.

Check your own dictionary skills now by listing five words you know how to spell and five which you struggle with. Then try to look up each one and see how quickly you can do it.

Finally, check out a thesaurus – either on screen, or in a book (preferably both) and identify how this could help you in an emergency.

2 Another source of assistance on your computer is your program's Help files. These will help you to find a file or folder (see also page 246) or learn how to carry out a particular operation. People have mixed views about Help files – some are very user-friendly and easy to understand and others are less so. However, it is worth developing the habit of trying your program's Help files *first*, and asking for clarification from someone only after you've tried to solve the problem yourself!

Editing text

You will often have to edit text, either because you have spotted errors which need correcting when you are proof-reading, or because the author of the document wants some changes made before it is printed and distributed. The ability to edit text is one of the greatest benefits of word-processing, so it is important that you know how to make the required alterations.

a   When altering characters, odd words or a short sentence you can use either the delete or the back arrow key – whichever you prefer – to remove the wrong items and then insert the correct version.

b   You can **overtype** text if you switch this option on, but be careful you don't overtype too much. This is a more hazardous option than deleting and then inserting.

c   You can use automatic **search and replace** for a word or phrase which needs amending throughout a document. You will have the option to replace this with a different word or phrase at the same time, either automatically or by approving each alteration before it is made.

Two tips:

- The search feature can also be used to find something quickly in a multi-page document, no matter what your reason for needing to find it.

- Do be careful to add spaces properly when you are entering the word or phrase to search for. For instance, if you want to find where the word 'opt' appears then key in 'opt[space]' – otherwise your computer will find and stop at every word starting with the letters 'opt', such as optimum, optimist, option, etc. The situation is easier if you have the option to 'match whole word' – when you can clearly differentiate whether you want to look for whole words only or not – or 'match case' option. In this case you can insert capital letters where they apply and the package will look only for this specific combination.

If large amounts of text need moving around in the document you should do this by using the '**cut and paste**' facility. Click your cursor on the start of the text you wish to move, using the left button on your mouse, hold down the button and drag the mouse until the end of the text you need and release. All the text you need will then be highlighted. Next access the Edit menu and select Cut. This moves the text to the **clipboard**, which is a spare temporary storage area on your computer. Next find where the text needs inserting and click your cursor at this point. Finally access the Edit menu again, select Paste and your text will appear.

Four tips:

- It is useful to know the size of your clipboard. If you use Word 2000 you can hold as many as 12 items of text or graphics simultaneously. However, there are few people who can remember what they are doing with such a large number! It is better to cut and paste one section at a time no matter how sophisticated your word-processing package.

- Unless you are very good at thinking in advance, you may find that the line spaces are odd after you have moved a paragraph (or spaces after a full stop at the end of a re-positioned sentence). Always check these are correct both in the original position and in the new position of the text and delete or insert spaces as required.

- On many packages you can use keystrokes to highlight blocks of text, instead of using the mouse. This option gives more control, especially when selecting large amounts of text. With most packages, for instance, Shift + either the right or left arrow key will highlight one character at a time, Shift + the up or down arrow will highlight one line at a time, while if you depress Control at the same time you will select a paragraph at a time and Shift + Page Up/Down highlights a page at once. Alternatively you could ask your supervisor for a new 'wheel' mouse which is usually easier to control.

- Before and after doing any major change it is a good idea to save the document.

Finally, learn how to use the **Undo** facility, which is usually found under Edit on the menu bar. Then if you do make a mistake (e.g. by changing or cutting the wrong text) you can quickly get back again to where you were. Your package may also include an 'Undo History' feature which will not only take you back 'one step' but several. If you have a limited clipboard this can be used to retrieve text you forgot to paste before you did another cut – but only if you remember quickly, usually within about the next 10 command keystrokes.

EVIDENCE COLLECTION

Start a folder in which you save documents you have produced.

You must include at least one (preferably more) you created from printed text and one produced from handwritten text (not your own handwriting!). In this case, save both the original *and* your final document. Include also some examples of documents that have been corrected and amended *first* as a draft and *second* in their final version. These must include examples where you have checked text using at least *two* of the following methods. You must also be prepared to say how you would use the third.

a   used a dictionary to look up words
b   had to check something with the person who gave you the document
c   used your program's Help files or on-line spell-checker to make corrections

and edited text in all the following ways:

a   manually deleted and replaced text
b   used automatic search and replace
c   moved blocks of text to a new place in the document.

One document could, of course, contain several of these – you don't need a separate document for each one. But it should be clear from the difference between the draft and the final version that the alterations required needed you to undertake these actions.

Saving text

You have already read about naming and saving files on page 220 and will learn about different file formats on page 244. Return to pages 220–222 now and check that you can remember the key points about saving files which have already been mentioned.

Most systems have an automatic save function which can be set so that your system 'backs up' your work at regular intervals. As a first check, find out how this works on your system and make the delay as short as you can. It is useless if your automatic back-up occurs only every half hour. In this case, if your system crashed, you could have as much as thirty minutes' inputting to do to get back to where you were. Ideally, you need it set it at between three and five minutes. You also need to check where the back-up documents are located, if the system doesn't tell you automatically.

In addition, you need to save your work yourself at regular intervals on the basis that it is better to be safe than sorry! If ever you lose a large amount of work because of a computer problem, you will never doubt this philosophy again.

Good times to save are:

- just before you make major editing changes or try anything new – so you can always go back to where you started
- regularly, during major editing changes, if you are worried you are going to get confused if you are interrupted for any reason
- before you access Help or switch into another document via your Window option
- just before you go into another part of your system (e.g. to find a spreadsheet in another package, send an e-mail or access the Internet)
- before you leave your computer (in case someone leans on it, switches it off or there is a power cut)
- almost every minute if you have workmen in the office – especially if what they are doing may affect the electricity supply.

Look upon the saving of your work as an insurance policy. The more frequently you habitually save, the safer you are if anything goes wrong, and there is less chance you will ever have to own up to making a major mistake which will take some time to sort out.

You also need to ensure that you have important programs and important documents on more than one drive, particularly if you have a stand-alone computer, otherwise if your C: drive becomes corrupted you will lose everything. Most organisations have a system for ensuring that start-up sequences and programs are backed up – but this is no help to you as none of your document files and folders will be included. For most text-based work, the ideal method of backing up documents is to save them on floppy disks as well as on hard disk. A useful method is to make a habit of regularly copying the content of your folders to floppy disk and labelling the disk with the date – preferably daily. The next day you can repeat this procedure. The following day you can overwrite your first disk.

File formats and extensions

On page 214 you read about the types of word-processing software that exist and the various versions on the market. One aspect of these variations is important if you are ever saving text to be used on someone else's system, or sending text (e.g. attached to an e-mail) to someone else.

Each system uses a slightly different **file format** and this is shown by the file **extension** – which is the three- or four-letter code following the 'dot' in the file name. Its function is to tell Windows which program the file relates to. For instance, all documents you create in Word will end in '**.doc**'. Opening a file with this ending automatically triggers the system to launch Word (if it is not already running) and to display the document. Other commonly seen word-processing extensions include '**.wpd**' (WordPerfect), '**.lwp**' (Lotus WordPro) and '**.wmw**' (Word for Macintosh users).

There are two points you need to understand about file formats and extensions:

a You can open a file with a different extension only if your software recognises this and can convert it. Most modern word-processing systems will automatically give you the option to convert a file you receive with a different extension from yours – or tell you quite simply that the file cannot be opened.

b You may not be able to open a file which was saved on a *later* version of software than the one you are using. If you use Word 6.0 and your friend uses Word 2000, he or she will have to convert her files (by saving them as a Word 6.0 document) before you can read them. Alternatively your friend could save them as plain text files. These will be simpler versions of the files which remove all the formatting commands (bold, italics, paragraphs, etc.). Such files are denoted by the extension '**.txt**'. Another alternative is to try rich text format which ends with the extension '**.rtf**' – this will preserve some of the formatting, but not all.

CHECK IT OUT!

You can check out the options on your own system by clicking on the **Save As** option on the File menu and then reading the dialogue box in front of you. Either by reading one of the windows, or by accessing the choices in your drop-down menus, you will find the different ways in which text can be saved.

Simply selecting Save on the File menu means the document is saved automatically (i.e. by default) in the file format required by your own word-processing software.

INFORMATION UPDATE

Everyone knows that computer crashes cause problems. A recent survey has shown that 44 per cent of company data is lost this way, and 14 per cent through software corruption. However, another major cause is human error: 32 per cent of data is lost through computer users accidentally deleting or overwriting files or saving them in the wrong place.

The company which carried out the survey, DataSafe Services, has estimated that 57,000 small businesses in the UK would face total collapse if they lost all their computer data. It offers a service for storing data securely off-site. However, you cannot rely on your company using this type of service if you make changes and then forget to save your new version to disk!

Always be very careful and *think* before you press the delete key or try to close your system down, especially if you are working in more than one package simultaneously. In a word-processing package you will be prompted to save a file if you have made changes since your last 'save'. However, on some systems you may not see this if you are exiting from another program and it won't help you either if you save your document in the wrong place. Don't lose 32 per cent of your computer data through sheer carelessness!

EVIDENCE COLLECTION

The easiest way to prove to your assessor how you name and save files – and that you back up your work – is to print out the file list from different folders on your C: drive and to print out a list of files stored on your floppy disks. One way of doing this is to open Explorer and use the Print Screen command. Alternatively you can type out the lists.

Dealing with problems

There are three types of problems you need to be able to deal with as part of this scheme:

- accidental loss or corruption of data
- duplicate file names
- not enough storage space.

Whilst the answers to many of these problems have been referred to in earlier sections, below is a short summary to help you when you are explaining these issues to your assessor.

Accidental loss or data corruption

The first and most obvious point is that if you save regularly, have your automatic back-up operating properly *and* have recently backed up your hard disk folders on floppy disk, then this is likely to be far less traumatic than if you do not!

Accidental loss can be a floppy disk that is missing, a file you cannot find on your system, or missing pages from a document when you access it.

You will minimise problems with floppy disks if you label them clearly, keep them in a disk box and look after them. If you lose a disk, search your desk drawers, desk top and cupboards, or ask if anyone has moved it. Hopefully your floppy disks contain only your back-up files so you will have other versions of the documents you can access on your hard disk or home area. Again, good working habits make all the difference!

If you cannot find a file or folder, check that you are searching on the right drive – especially if you have C:, H: and A: to choose from. Again, being methodical makes all the difference. Read your screen carefully. Try to remember any similar titles you may have used. If you still have no success, use the Help facility to investigate what type of assistance you can obtain from the program. Some word-processors have features such as a QuickFinder to help you to locate lost files or, if you are using Word, for instance, you can access Find through the 'Open file' dialogue box. Otherwise, access the Help facility, key in the word Find and see what happens. Read any related trouble-shooting screens and follow the instructions carefully.

If you are still struggling, use Windows to help you:

a   Click the Start button and select the Find option – if this gives you several options, then you want the one relating to Files and Folders.

b   If you know the name of your lost file and have some idea where it was saved, enter the details. If you know it must be in one of two folders, then enter one of these in the Look In box. You can use the Browse option to help you make a choice. If you have no idea, search the whole drive.

c   If you know the type of document but cannot remember its full name, use the wild-card option (*). This character, the asterisk, can be used to replace one or several characters you can't remember. For instance, letter*.doc will find all the files which start with the word 'letter' that you have created in Word.

d   If you can remember when you last modified or when you created the document, use the Date Modified tab to narrow down the choice.

e   If you can remember any key words in the document, enter these using the Advanced tab.

f   When you are ready, click Find Now and keep your fingers crossed!

Finding a file in Windows

```
┌──────────────────────────────────────────────────────────────────────────┐
│  ┌─Name & Location─┐ ┌─Date─┐ ┌─Advanced─┐                                │
│  │                                          │              ┌─Find Now──┐   │
│  │  Named:      │recent                  ▼│              └───────────┘   │
│  │                                          │              ┌─Stop──────┐   │
│  │  Containing text: │                    │              └───────────┘   │
│  │                                          │              ┌New Search─┐   │
│  │  Look in:    │🖴 (C:)                 ▼│              └───────────┘   │
│  │                                          │                  🔍          │
│  │      ☑ Include subfolders    │Browse...│                              │
│  └──────────────────────────────────────────┘                            │
│                                                                            │
│ ┌Name──────────┬In Folder────┬Size┬Type──────┬Mod──┐                      │
│ │ 📁 Recent     │📁 C:\WINDOWS\... │    │File Folder│ 21/(│                │
│ │ 📄 mostRecent[1]│📁 C:\WINDOWS\...│1KB │GIF Image  │ 18/'│               │
│ │ 📄 b-lrecentchanges[1]│📁 C:\WINDOWS\...│1KB│GIF Image│ 01/'│           │
│ │ ◀                                                    ▶│                 │
│ │3 file(s) found        │Monitoring New Items          │                 │
│ └──────────────────────────────────────────────────────┘                 │
└──────────────────────────────────────────────────────────────────────────┘
```

Occasionally a file may have become hidden for some reason – in which case the only way you can find it is through Windows Explorer. Select View, then Options and then Show All Files. This will show every file on your computer – if it isn't here, it doesn't exist!

If you access a document with the last few pages missing, it is likely you have opened a previous version of the document – or forgot to save the last one. You either need to search for the one you updated yesterday or, if this doesn't appear to exist, re-enter the text and be careful to save your update properly.

Data corruption occurs if there is a fault with your system. System faults are less significant in terms of your own work if you have back-ups on floppy disks. If your computer is faulty, however, don't risk loading your floppy disk in case this also becomes corrupted. Report the problem and use another machine or wait until yours has been given the 'all-clear'.

Duplicate file names

Your system will not allow you to save two files with the same name in the same folder. If you try to do this you will receive a message which warns you that the file already exists and asks if you want to replace it. Do stop and think at this point. Replace it, by all means, if you have undertaken editing changes which have improved the document. If you are working on a draft which might be changed *back* to the earlier version – or if it is likely that the author will want to refer to the original version at any time – then use the 'version 1' (v1), 'version 2' (v2) method described on page 221.

If you have been specifically requested to save the file under an existing name, you can change the name of the existing file by opening your file management dialogue box, highlighting the file name, clicking the right-hand mouse button and chosing the Rename option. You can then re-use the title you were instructed to use without problem.

Insufficient storage space

You will receive an error message if the amount of space remaining on a floppy disk is insufficient for the size of file you are trying to save on it. You may even receive a message if your C: drive has become very cluttered.

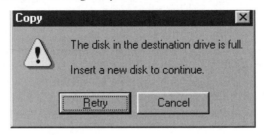

You can check the amount of free space remaining on any disk through Windows Explorer. Highlight a drive in the left-hand window and then select File and Properties. Click on the File menu to read what each option says. You will also see a reminder of when you last backed-up your file – as well as the amount of free space existing on the disk.

The action to take will depend upon whether you are concerned about space on your C: drive or a floppy disk in your A: drive.

Hard disk problems are caused because, over time, new programs and files are created and – even if you delete those you don't need regularly (see below) – the space on your C: drive won't be used as effectively as it was in the beginning. This is because 'fragments' of deleted programs and files are left behind. There are three ways to resolve a space problem on your hard disk.

a Check the Recycle Bin and empty it. The correct term here is **purge** as you will be *permanently* getting rid of these documents.

b You can **compress** the existing data on a disk to make more room. This option is available in Windows Explorer.

c You can **defragment** your hard disk. Defragging is a housekeeping task that 'cleans up' your disk and finds available space. You will probably find that the system runs more quickly afterwards.

However, don't try either compression or defragging on your own. Check with your supervisor and ask for help from someone who has more experience. Select a suitable moment, too, as defragging a hard disk can take some time.

Floppy disk problems are caused because the file you wish to save is too large for the remaining space – even if at first glance there seems to be sufficient space available. This is because, to save a file on a floppy disk, you need about *double* the space of the largest file saved on it still available. This is because the system always assumes it may have to resave the largest file again before it is deleted (think about this for a minute if you're not sure why). So if you've a very large file to save it is preferable to use a new disk.

CHECK IT OUT!

One of the most neglected housekeeping jobs of all amongst computer users is deleting historic files which will never be needed again. If you 'tidy up' your folders and delete old files regularly you will rarely be stuck for space – and your computer will feel better for a spring clean! However, remove only your own files and *never* anything with a file extension you don't understand, as many will be programs that are essential for the operation of your system. This is why it is dangerous to delete anything via Windows Explorer. Instead, use the dialogue box in your word-processing package which controls your files (the one you access when you want to open a file). If you don't know how to delete a file, find out via the Help option.

Windows sends any files you delete from your hard disk to a Recycle Bin. If you make a mistake you can restore the file again, provided you have not emptied the Recycle Bin. If you don't know how to do this, find out yourself by accessing Help when you are on your Desktop. If you delete files from a floppy disk by mistake, there is no fall-back – the files have gone for good.

EVIDENCE COLLECTION

Your assessor will not expect you to *create* problems just to prove this section of the unit! You can answer questions if no problems do occur during the time you are taking your award. Obviously, however, if a relevant problem occurs and you solve it, make a note of it. Better still, ask your supervisor – or a colleague – for witness testimony to confirm the actions you took.

Element 204.2 Format and lay out documents

It used to be said that anyone who creates a document has to have excellent keyboarding skills, an eye for detail and an artist's appreciation of balance and form. We have already covered keyboarding skills, and you will clearly be better at proof-reading if you have an eye for detail. But what about the artistic element? This relates to the way the document looks on paper – and word-processing has probably made this even more important because of all the options now readily available.

This element covers many of the standard operations you need to know to be able to format and lay out documents effectively. However, you can also make a valuable contribution to the process if you *care* about how your documents look on the printed page and if inconsistency – say between spacing or margins – annoys you. An eye for balance is important and can never be under-estimated. As you become more experienced, people who give you documents to produce will ask your opinion about layout and format, rather than simply tell you what they would like.

At this point, though, we will assume that you are usually given instructions on how a document should be set out. If you are not, then do ask the originator if he or she has any preferences and/or check to find out if there is a house style you must follow (see page 223). You need to check whether:

- the text must be formatted in a particular way
- any specific layout must be used
- you need to transfer any data from other files into your document.

All the main aspects of these three requirements are covered in this element.

Placing data from other files

For your award you need to prove that you can place existing text, tables of numbers and graphics into a file. You have already learned how to cut and paste text in word-processing files (page 241), and how to track down files (page 246). Technically, therefore, it would appear to be a straightforward operation to put these skills together to access data and place it in your word-processing document. However, the following points should also be borne in mind.

Begin by creating your new document and saving it with a suitable name, before you start on any operations at all. Keep this document open on screen whilst you look for another file. Remember you can use the special Windows key to find another program if your Taskbar isn't visible on screen all the time.

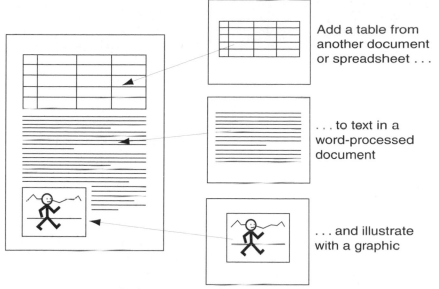

Importing text into a document

- Add a table from another document or spreadsheet . . .
- . . . to text in a word-processed document
- . . . and illustrate with a graphic

If you are accessing *text* which is in another file created by your word-processing package you obviously don't need to change to another program. Simply select the correct folder and open the file. Then highlight the text you need and *copy* it to the clipboard. *Do not 'cut' it* – otherwise it will disappear from its original location whereas you want it in both locations. Click on the Window option on the menu bar to return to your first document, select the point at which you want the text to appear and paste it in. Then make any spacing adjustments that are needed. You may like to note that if you are operating with more than one package showing on your menu bar – because you are **multi-tasking** and switching between packages – then you can move from one to another quickly by pressing Alt and the tab key simultaneously.

A numeric *table* may be in a word-processed document or in a spreadsheet or database package. Either open the relevant document or use the Start button to open your spreadsheet package and find the file you need. Then, using copy and paste as before: highlight the text you need, copy it to the clipboard, then close the spreadsheet package (click the small cross at the top right of the screen). Put the cursor at the insert point in your document and paste the table into position.

Graphics may be in an existing document (such as a graphic created in a spreadsheet package) or may be stored as a 'clipart' file. You can find out about the graphics already stored on your system via the Help screen. If the graphics exist in a current document you will use copy and paste. If they are stored in a clipart file, then you will need to select the graphic image you require and insert it where you want it. The exact sequence of operations to carry out will depend upon your system and where your clipart graphics are stored.

Problems and concerns

Identifying the text or graphic you need, copying it and then pasting it where you think it should go is normally the easy part! The problems start if you find, for instance, that:

- the text or data was stored in a completely different format from your current document
- the size of the table or graphic is out of proportion when it is moved
- the imported graphic or table spills over into one or more of the margins
- your existing text splits at a peculiar place to make room for it
- the table or graphic is wide rather than long, so you need to put it on a page which has a different orientation (e.g. A4 landscape instead of A4 portrait).

First, remember that you can always select Undo and start again. This is much better, if you have had a complete disaster, than trying to play about with your new document. And as you saved your document anyway before you started, if your Undo goes wrong you can always close and reopen the file and start again.

Solving problems

Changing the format of imported text or data is often the easiest of all problems to solve. You can normally highlight the whole thing and then select the formatting options you want to apply throughout. In this way you can alter the font type, size, line spacing, etc. (see page 253).

You can usually resize a table by clicking on the outer edges and moving them inwards or outwards. You can then adjust any interim columns in the same way. If you have problems because a table has gone into a margin and you can't seem to reach it, go back into the original document and copy and paste the table into an empty new document. Then play about with it to your heart's content. Only when you are satisfied should you import it into your source document. In that way you keep your source document intact and don't risk messing it up whilst you adjust the table to fit.

Graphics can usually be sized quite easily be clicking on a corner and dragging. This keeps the graphic in balance. If you click on a vertical or horizontal line you will stretch the graphic in a particular direction and, unless you are very lucky, it will never look the same again! If you click on the whole graphic you can normally reposition it on the page – so that it is in the middle or to the left- or right-hand side. If you are using Word 97 or a later package it is easy to position the graphic, or instruct the package to wrap the text around it, so that it looks balanced. With earlier packages, expect the text to split above and below the graphic.

If you have problems, consider the following options:

- move the graphic image around the page until the text flows in an acceptable way
- use the View option (if you are using Word for Windows) so that you can see what the page will look like when it is printed.

If a table or graphic needs to be on a wider page, then you will need to alter the orientation of the page (see page 259).

CHECK IT OUT!

Many word-processing packages now have some quite advanced drawing tools and features that used to be available only on expensive desktop publishing packages. Therefore, if you know what you are doing, you can modify any graphic you import into a document. You could crop some of it, for instance, if you want to show only part of a drawing, or you could change the size, or flip or rotate it.

You may enjoy developing your skills in this area. To see what's available on your package search the Help facility for Graphics or Drawings and see what you find. Then experiment!

EVIDENCE COLLECTION

Begin by collecting examples of any documents where you have had to access and place text or data from another document or package. You need examples of text, tables *and* graphics. If you are really lucky you may obtain an example of all three in one document, but this is unlikely.

Ideally, print out the *original* document (before you imported the data), the document where you accessed the text, table or graphic, and the final document where they were put together.

Formatting text

Text formatting refers to the way that text looks on the page.

Fonts and point sizes

The appearance of the text is determined by the **font** you use. There are a range of fonts to choose from, and they can be used in different sizes (e.g. 12 point or 16 point). The larger the number, the larger the text. Normally, the font style should be the same throughout a document. However, you may select different sizes and/or fonts to denote types of headings. Very important (main) headings could be 16 point, lesser headings could be 14 point or 12 point.

- Comic sans MS may be used if you want a plain but different appearance – say for younger readers

- Times New Roman is a traditional, serif, font which is used by many business organisations

- Ariel is a clear font which is commonly used these days for business documents

- *If you wish to make a document look as if it was hand-written, you could use a font such as Caflisch Script.*

The main thing to remember is *consistency* – all the headings of the same importance should be the same size.

There are several standard fonts, but you may have the font determined by your organisation's house style. Fonts are either **serif** or **sans serif**. The latter are plainer – they do not have the 'fancy endings' to characters you find with serif.

You may wish to vary the font if you are producing a document for a specific reason. Some alternatives are shown in the illustration above. Can you identify the two which are sans serif?

No matter which fonts you use, you can still use other features to emphasise headings or words, such as:

- **bold** to differentiate an important heading or word
- *italics* to indicate a word is stressed – or for some references
- underscore – although this is infrequently used nowadays in most word-processed documents (you could use it for a side heading if you have used up all your other options!).

Many people prefer to use keyboard *shortcuts* for these features – Control + b for bold, Control + i for italics and Control + u for underscore.

CHECK IT OUT!

As a first step, test out a few of the fonts – and the sizes – you have available and compare them. Now type in a paragraph of text (you could copy one from this book) and try highlighting it and adjusting the font style and/or size.

Now check that you can use bold, italics and underscore without any problems.

INFORMATION UPDATE

Modern documents are designed to look *simple*. You only have to compare the type of documents which are produced today with elaborate historic manuscripts – or even letters or newspapers produced 20 years ago – to see the difference. The wording, punctuation and design are all more straightforward and streamlined.

A document which appears fussy or cluttered does not look professional. Neither do a variety of fonts, lots of changes in spacing or paragraph styles, too much text on one page, text that is so small it is difficult to read or so large as to look alarming, or a mixture of enhancements which 'overgild the lily'. As a simple test, try creating a large heading (16 point) in a fancy font, in bold and using underscore. Hopefully you will think it looks dreadful!

Paragraphs

Today most paragraphs are blocked to the left margin. However, you can vary this. On many packages you will find some of the options displayed as icons on screen buttons, although a greater range is available if you access Format on the menu bar and then click on Paragraph.

If you wish to indent a paragraph, you can select this option *or* you can use the tab key. However, with this method you must remember to depress tab at the start of each paragraph.

Pressing the tab key will indent the first line of the paragraph at a fixed distance. Every time you press the tab at the start of a paragraph you will achieve the same indent. Each subsequent time you press tab, the first word will move across another fixed distance. The second and subsequent lines still start at the left-hand margin.

If you **justify** a paragraph, then you are entering a command to ensure that the text starts and ends so that both the left and right margins are aligned.

You will have other options available, so it is well worth spending a few moments testing them out. However, again remember that a mixture of

CHECK IT OUT!

The correct term for a paragraph where only the first line is indented is a **hanging indent**. The right name for a paragraph where all lines are indented is a **normal indent**. A **double indent** is where both sides are indented. Knowing these terms is useful if you work for someone who uses the correct phraseology, or if you have a package which uses these terms when you refer to the Help screen.

styles in one standard business document usually looks awful – so choose one style and stick to it!

Bullets and number lists

In addition to standard paragraphs you may be expected to produce a number of points which are listed either numerically (1, 2, ...) or prefaced with bullet points. Both methods have been used below. The main difference between this option and an indented paragraph is that now you want *all* lines of text to start at a particular inset point.

One way to produce a list is as follows:

1   Type the paragraphs or sentences first.
2   Then highlight the text.
3   Select either bullets or numbers (again displayed as icons on buttons in many packages or within the Insert or Format menu).
4   At this point the bullets or numbers will be entered at the start of each paragraph. If there are any you want to remove – because there is more than one paragraph under a particular bullet or number – you can do this by using the delete key *or* (in Word) click on the paragraph which doesn't need a bullet or number and click on the bullet/number button again. You should find any numbers adjust automatically.

An alternative way is as follows:

• Begin by clicking on the bullets or numbers icon.
• Then start your first paragraph. Don't worry if your paragraph returns to the left-hand margin at the second line – this happens with some packages.
• When you press Enter to start the next paragraph (and put in a hard return) you should find your paragraph adjusts.
• Click off the bullets or numbers option when you reach the end of the list.

One problem with the second method is that on some earlier software packages it is difficult to put a double space between the paragraphs, and you may also struggle to remove unwanted bullets or numbers. On more modern programs the package tries to be intuitive – and you should find that after you have done one or two paragraphs the package assumes it knows what you want to do and sometimes does it for you. This is very helpful when it gets it right, but is agonisingly frustrating when it doesn't! The ideal is to practise on text that isn't important.

Do remember to keep the spacing between paragraphs the same throughout. This will often depend upon the length of the paragraphs. If you are typing only a line or two then you may just continue with the next numbered point or bullet immediately below. If the paragraphs are quite long, it can be better to leave a space between them. If there is more than one paragraph for some numbers or bullets, it is essential.

Line spacing

Most business documents are prepared in single line spacing. However, when producing a draft upon which people will write comments, you may want to allow space for these by using double line spacing – or even greater. You can select line spacing either throughout the document or just for specific lines of text.

To select a specific line spacing throughout a new document, set this before you start to type. Through the Format menu, select either Paragraph or Line (it will depend upon which package you are using). A dialogue box will give you the options available and on some packages you will also see a useful graphics box which shows you how your text will look. Again, it is worth experimenting to find out the options.

If you want your spacing to apply only to a specific part of a document you have already created, select this text first (by highlighting it) and *then* access the Format menu and select the change you require. The change will then be applied only to the highlighted text.

Note that in Word, depressing Control + 1 or Control + 2 enables you to toggle between single and double line spacing.

Tables

You will usually find the Table option on the Menu bar. When you access this you are given the option to 'insert' a table or 'create' a new table (again it depends upon your package). You will next see a dialogue box. Your main choices are:

- how many columns you want (this option creates lines *down* the table)
- how many rows you want (this option creates lines *across* the table)
- the format you want for the table.

<table>
<tr><td colspan="3">EXAMPLE OF A SIMPLE TABLE. THIS CELL HAS JOINED COLUMNS AND IS IN BOLD, AS A HEADING</td></tr>
</table>

Columns can be different sizes	Or equal . . .	. . it's up to you
You can adjust columns by clicking on the vertical line and dragging it . . .	. . . and vary the number you have in a row by joining or splitting cells	

In Word you can select from a range of several pre-set formats by selecting AutoFormat. On some other packages you have to begin by creating the table before you can format it. Formatting relates to the type of lines which surround the table and are drawn within it, and features such as shading.

If you select one column and one row then you end up with a box – called a **cell** – which can be quite useful for displaying a heading or an important sentence or paragraph. You can create the table and then type the text or, if the text has already been prepared, you can create the table and then cut and paste the text into it. The table will adjust in size accordingly.

When entering material into the columns you will need each one wide enough to take the information. You will also need enough rows. Don't worry if you don't calculate these accurately at the start – you can add or delete rows or columns, and widen and reduce the size of any cell as you go. You can also join or split cells – so if you want to put a title on your first row, you simply join all the cells together by highlighting them and selecting Merge Cells or Join Cells (depending on your package) in the Table menu. Alternatively, if you want to divide a cell, you can do so by clicking on Split in the same menu.

You can also move a table if you put it in the wrong place – by cutting and pasting it. In Word, make sure your cursor is within the table, select Table from the menu bar, then Select Table to highlight it and, finally, cut and paste it. On many packages you can also simply highlight the table with your cursor and then select cut and paste from the Edit menu. However, if you use that option, do check you don't start *within* the table or you will leave out the table and just move the data!

Finally, you will find your table is automatically placed to extend from the left to the right margin. You can shrink it by clicking on the outside vertical lines – but it is always a good design feature to make sure it is placed centrally on the page so it looks balanced.

EVIDENCE COLLECTION

You need to collect documents which prove you can undertake all these operations. If you are desperate, you could copy out the previous section on your word-processor, but it is much better if you can produce actual documents which occurred as a natural part of your everyday work. Remember you will need documents that include:

a   bullets *and* numbered lists

b   changes to the font you normally use

c   indented and justified paragraphs

d   different line spacing

e   a table

f   an occasion when you have used the tab key (which could be for indented paragraphs).

Don't expect to produce all of them in one document! A selection would be much better as evidence of your abilities.

Document layout

Whereas you will usually choose most of your text format options either at the start or during the production of your document, your document layout will sometimes be selected at the end – as some of your choices may be determined by the document itself – and you will discover this only as you progress.

The correct layout adds the finishing touches to a document – particularly one which is formal, long or needs to be appropriate for an external presentation.

Page orientation and size

The orientation of your page relates to which way the paper will be held for the text to be read. Will the short side be at the top – or the long side? The default on your system is **portrait** orientation – where the short side is at the top. If you wish this to change you must select **landscape**. On Word you select this option through the File menu and then access Page Setup. On some other packages you access the options through the Format menu (e.g. Page and Page Size in WordPerfect) and a small graphic may illustrate the orientation you have selected.

You may want the whole document to be in the same orientation, in which case select it at the start. On the other hand you may wish specific pages to be in that orientation. You can select a specific orientation at the start of a particular page – so that you can have, for instance, a table on landscape orientation in the middle of a document which is otherwise portrait orientation. However, you must remember to reselect the original orientation when you have finished on that page – otherwise all the remainder of your document will be on landscape paper!

If you want to change several pages to a different orientation it is often best to highlight these and then select your orientation – but packages do vary in their ability to sort themselves out afterwards – so check it yourself. One package is renowned for getting muddled up to such an extent that it is often easier to put A4 landscaped pages at the back, all together, rather than keep changing the orientation throughout one document.

The normal paper size used in British business is A4. However, you may have other options available on your screen – such as Letter or Envelope sizes. You can choose only options your printer can cope with – otherwise your document will look good on screen but you will have serious problems when you start to print it.

Margins

Margins provide the empty space around the material on the page – both top and bottom and left and right.

Left and right margins are adjusted in Word through the File menu and Page Setup. On some packages where the margins are shown as dotted lines on the screen (which are never printed) you simply move the pointer arrow to the pre-set right and/or left margin lines, wait until it turns into a small cross and then drag the lines to where you want your margins to be. If these methods don't work on your package, access the Help screen and type 'margins'.

Your package may let you choose whether you want to apply the new margins to the whole document, or only from this point forward, or to text you have already highlighted. If it does not allow this, it is likely that you will change only the margins from the point you are now. Brief changes can be effective, such as choosing a double indent for a piece of text you want to look different; for instance:

> if you want to start and end a particular piece of text – or a table – between two different margin points, like this.

Top and bottom margins relate to where the text starts and ends on the page. You can make changes to these margins through the menu bar – for instance through File and Page Setup or through the Format option. On some packages you have the option to drag the bottom margin (as you did the left and right margins) to include a final line of type. Again, however, do check whether the command will be applied to the whole document or only certain pages – and make sure you enter this properly for what you want.

Try to use your imagination and judgement in relation to margins, rather than creating every document using the pre-set positions. A very short document on A4 paper looks better if it starts lower and has wider margins –

it is more balanced on the page. If you are trying to fit a considerable amount of text on one page, then you will need narrower margins. They normally look better if they are equal – but if you are short of space then narrow the right side before the left. If the document will be bound you also need wide margins, otherwise some text may be lost on the side where it is bound. Finally, again do aim for consistency in one document – with all your margins.

CHECK IT OUT!

Other features of margins are useful to know. These include knowing how to insert a **page break** because you want to 'force' a new page. Also, does your package have an option whereby the text can be resized automatically to make it fit on a particular number of pages? If it doesn't you can always highlight the text and reduce the font size yourself.

Does your package automatically help you to avoid orphans and widows, or do you have to look for them? An **orphan** is where the first line of a paragraph is placed as the last line on a page, and a **widow** is where the last line of a paragraph appears as the first line of a new page. Both are incorrect and should be adjusted so that the paragraph stays 'together'. If you use Word or WordPerfect, check you can turn this feature 'on' or 'off' as you desire.

Page numbers

It is always sensible to number the pages of a long document. Apart from helping the reader, you have an immediate double check when you are collating, and extra insurance if you drop the document on the floor at any stage!

You can start page numbering at the beginning of the document or, if you have a title page you may wish to start it later, say at *your* page two – which will be page one when you number it.

Select either the Insert or Format menu (it will depend upon your package) and find the Page Numbers option. You will have two main choices:

- the style of numbering
- the position of the numbers.

The style option may allow you to choose between standard (Arabic) numbers or Roman numerals, for instance. You may be able to choose whether to have the numbers in faint print or bold. You also have to choose the position of the numbers on the page.

It is useful to learn how to paginate two documents so that the numbers are sequential (i.e. 'run on') – so that if you are creating half of a long document and a colleague is creating the other half you can link them together by their numbers. In this case, whoever is doing the second part will select a specific page number for their first page as it obviously won't be number one! You will find guidance how to do this in the Page Numbers dialogue box *and* in the on-line Help facility.

Headers and footers

- A **header** is a specific piece of text which is put at the top of every page or specific pages (usually all odd or all even pages).
- A **footer** is a specific piece of text which is put at the bottom of every page or specific pages (again, usually odd or even pages).

Page numbers can count as headers or footers, but usually the term is used to refer to more specific items of text. In this book, for instance, you will see that the unit title is a footer on every even page and the element title is a footer on every odd page.

Your package will help you do this automatically so you don't have to keep entering the text yourself. It also doesn't matter if you insert or delete text on a page – pre-set headers and footers always stay in the same place.

The best way to experiment with headers and footers is to start a new document, type a few lines of text and then access Headers and Footers through the View or Format menu. Then read your screen and practise with a few ideas of your own, or try these:

- Create a header with the name of your organisation to go at the top of a page.
- Create a footer with the file name of the document and the creation date to go at the bottom of the page.

Both Word and WordPerfect contain shortcuts to help you to do this, and you can investigate these through the Help screen. Using these techniques will help you to locate printed documents in your file folders more easily.

Once you have done this successfully, you can develop your skills by creating more than one header, or more than one footer – and then specifying where you want them. However, do be careful if you are combining a text footer with a page number – and make sure there is enough space for both.

Finally, remember to double-check the page length. Adding headers and footers can affect both the top and bottom margins. Be aware that you will not see the headers and footers on some screens (it depends on your package). You may have to access Print Preview before you can see them – or take a print out to see what they look like and how your page actually appears.

1 Identify the formatting and layout aspects you would consider if you were asked to produce each of the following documents:

   a a short, snappy information sheet for some school children who are visiting your organisation.

   b a letter to an important customer which contains several specific points in response to a complaint

   c a long memo to your sales staff which includes the sales figures for last year and this year

   d a new staff handbook which will contain graphics prepared in another package and health and safety information which is stored in a different folder (it must be easy to read)

   e a formal report of 20 pages to be sent to shareholders with a title page and an index page (it will be bound before it is dispatched).

   Check your ideas with your tutor or supervisor.

2 Throughout this unit you have met several terms related to Windows and word-processing. A new member of staff has asked you what the following terms mean. Can you help her? Check your answers with the Glossary on page 277.

   a What is the difference between a Taskbar and a toolbar?

   b What is a button?

   c What is meant by an orphan and a widow?

   d What is a dialogue box?

   e What is a header and a footer?

   f Is there any difference between deleting and purging?

EVIDENCE COLLECTION

By now you should have quite a range of documents in your collection, so you may wish to start by checking if any will already 'count' towards this section. Your final set needs to include an example of a document in which you have:

a changed the page orientation and size

b altered the margins

c added page numbers

d added headers and footers.

Again, don't expect to do all these operations in one document. It is better to have a range of examples. However, if you have had to create a complex document which *did* involve all these operations, that should be sufficient.

Element 204.3 Print documents

The main reason for producing most documents is, of course, to have a printed version in your hand that you can send to the correct recipient. This means that in addition to knowing how to enter the correct commands to print a document you also need some mastery over your printer. Printers can be temperamental. If you share an expensive laser printer with several other users you may have to wait your turn, but you do gain several benefits. Firstly, the print quality is normally excellent and it prints quickly. Secondly, if there are any problems you may be able to refer them to a colleague or to a technician. No one will want you to be messing about with a very expensive piece of equipment unless you know what you are doing.

If, however, you have your own printer it is likely to be an ink-jet costing around £200. In this case, if it goes awry it will usually be up to you to put it right. Ink-jet printers are ideal for producing good-quality copies, are very inexpensive but operate more slowly than laser printers. However, they can cause problems, and for this reason you need to make friends with your printer and get to know it – otherwise it may sorely try your patience on occasion. There is nothing worse in an emergency than producing a perfect document and then finding you have a problem with your paper feed! This element covers the key points you need to know and may help you to develop a certain rapport with even the most troublesome printer.

Accessing documents

At the most basic, you may be asked to find an existing file document and to make a printout. There are various points to note.

Check that you have the necessary authority to make a printout, particularly if the document contains sensitive or confidential information. You could find yourself falling foul of the law, for instance, if you make a printout which contains a customer's name and address or a member of staff's name and address and give it to an unauthorised person. On a more fundamental level, don't print one of your supervisor's or manager's files for a colleague unless they have agreed – there may be something within the document they don't wish the whole office – or that particular person – to read. So, first rule, check that the person requesting the printout is allowed to receive it.

Check how many copies are required. If you have an ink-jet printer and multiple copies are required it might be quicker and cheaper to print one copy and then photocopy it, particularly if there are several pages. If you have a speedy, modern laser printer then you may make multiple copies on that instead. Don't, however, tie up a shared printer for a long time without first consulting your colleagues who use it.

Check whether all the pages in the document are required or just an extract. You don't want to print out a 50-page document for someone who only wants a copy of the table on page 4!

If you are busy, it is sensible to check whether the printer has sufficient paper before you start, so that you don't have to break off from doing something else half-way through. It is also sensible to do this if the job is urgent and if you are going to leave your desk (or the printer) for a while – otherwise you may return some time later, hoping to find the job complete, only to discover everything stopped half-way through and with an error message showing on your screen.

Ask the person who wants the printout whether there are any specific requirements, such as special paper to be used or a set deadline for the printout.

If the document is in one of your own files you should be able to find it easily – particularly if you have already covered Element 204.1. If the document is on another person's hard disk, you will need either to use their computer or ask that person to save a copy on to a floppy disk for you. Then make sure you know the file name under which the document is saved. You can bring up the document on your own computer and print it out. Another option is to ask the person to e-mail it to you if you have an internal e-mail system.

CHECK IT OUT!

There are a number of ways in which you can view a document in a word-processing package.

- The Normal or default view is the way you usually see the document on screen as you are creating it. This will show you the text without any formatting commands.

- In Word, you can view a document in Outline only – where you will see only the main headings. This is useful if you are moving or copying text over a large document and want to see quickly where you are.

- Another option is to see the document *including* the formatting commands. This is essential if something has gone wrong with the document and you can't understand why.

- On most packages you can use a 'zoom' facility to see parts of a document in more detail or to look at the whole page on screen.

- Other options link to the way the document will look when it is printed. Options may include print preview, page layout or full screen.

Check out *all* the options available. Knowing how they work helps you to check your formatting and layout far more quickly and easily and saves time and effort printing a document which contains an easily solvable problem.

Checking the document is ready for printing

Before a document you have created is printed you should have:

a   proof-read it *thoroughly* (see page 237)

b   made sure it is complete – and you haven't forgotten to add anything that was required

c   checked that the formatting is correct and consistent throughout

d   checked that any page formatting commands are correct

e   viewed the document under Print Preview (if you have this option) to see what it looks like – and have made alterations if any are required.

Printing a document to the required specification

Before you access the print options, you need to know:

• whether you are just printing a particular portion of text

• whether you are printing just a few pages

• whether you are printing the whole document, and if so, whether you want the document to be printed in reverse order (which saves you the trouble of re-ordering it)

• the page orientation that may be required

• whether you must use special or headed paper and, if so, whether you need to make any adjustments to allow for this – such as moving the text further down the page (or increasing the top margin) to allow for a printed heading

• whether you need to make any adjustments to your printer that are controlled from your computer.

We have already covered page orientation on page 259. If your computer is configured correctly and the **printer driver** is correct (the program which sends instructions to your printer), then your printer should *automatically* select the correct orientation for each page – according to your pre-set instructions. If it does not, check the Help screen on your computer and refer to the printer manual. If you have any doubt, take a test page before printing out the whole document.

If you are printing only a particular portion of text the easy way is to highlight this before you select Print. However, if the text is short and split over two pages, this is how it may print – on two sheets of paper. To prevent this you would have to copy and paste your highlighted text into a new document and print that.

The Print dialogue box will allow you to select other options, such as whether you just want:

• the current page printed (i.e. the one on which your cursor is currently placed)

- a specific range of pages to be printed (e.g. 15 to 22 or 1, 2 and 6)
- the complete document to be printed (this is the default setting if you don't enter anything different)
- the number of copies you need.

If you have any doubt at all that the document will look as required then take one copy and do multiple copies only when you are satisfied.

Printer adjustments

These are usually controlled from your computer, but will depend upon the printer you have installed and the options available. It is worth checking, for instance, whether you can select different quality modes, such as 'best', 'normal' or 'draft'. The draft setting prints much more quickly and uses less ink or toner, so is useful for internal documents. Remember not to touch a page printed in 'best' on an inkjet printer for a few moments – until the ink has dried. Select 'colour off' if you have a colour printer and just want the text printed in black.

Most printers allow the operator to make adjustments for printing envelopes, labels or different sizes or thicknesses of paper.

Finally, if you have a sophisticated laser printer you may be able to print on both sides of the paper automatically.

Printer dialogue box

Printer problems

Understanding printers

Solving printer problems is always easier if you know what is happening when you want to print. Your document file, and the settings you have selected, are sent to the printer by two pieces of software – the word-processing program and the printer driver. Both need to be working properly for the information to be transmitted.

Because the printer cannot print as quickly as it can receive the file data, it uses a **buffer** to store the data. The amount of information that can be held in the buffer, and the speed of printing, will determine how fast a document is produced. If you send dozens of documents to print very quickly, they will be held in a **print queue**. When this is full, you cannot send any more until the queue has decreased. (For information on accessing your print queue, see page 272.)

The other feature you need to know about is **spooling**. This enables your computer to do two things at once – it lets you continue working with a new document whilst it is printing out your old one.

Your printer speed will depend upon the type of printer, the complexity of the job and the print quality you have chosen. Coloured graphics, for instance, take longer to print than black and white text.

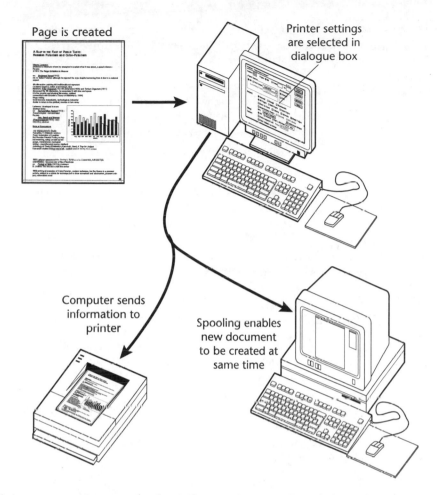

Page is created

Printer settings are selected in dialogue box

Computer sends information to printer

Spooling enables new document to be created at same time

The way your printer works depends upon its type. An ink-jet printer shoots very fine jets of ink on to the surface of the paper. A laser printer shines a laser beam on to a special, photo-sensitive drum and then uses toner to create an image on the paper.

If a problem occurs your printer will send a message to your computer and that will be displayed on screen.

Sorting out problems

At the beginning of this element the difficulties of managing a troublesome printer were mentioned. However, you have to prove you can do this to achieve your award. You need to be able to cope if:

a   the printer is off-line
b   it is out of paper
c   it is out of toner (or ink, if you are using an ink-jet)
d   there is a paper jam.

However, some other common problems are mentioned at the end of this section, just in case you have other difficulties which you need to rectify quickly.

Finally, you have to be able to remedy any problems and still avoid waste. This means being vigilant so that you are not caught unawares if your ink or toner cartridge runs out (see page 265) and not using half a ream of paper after remedying a problem to test if the printer is working properly!

Printer off-line

If your printer is off-line there is no communication between your computer and the printer. This is usually quickly remedied by depressing the 'on-line' button on your printer. If nothing happens, check the cable connections. Then check your screen to see whether you are receiving an error message. Occasionally your system may lose communication with your printer. If so, shut down Windows and restart and try again. If you still cannot achieve a link then report the problem.

Printer out of paper

The printer handbook will tell you the recommended type and weight of paper to use, and how to replenish the paper tray. Do remember, also, that when you open a new packet of paper there is a right way and a wrong way to put it in the printer. One side of the paper is slightly 'fluffier' and may cause misfeed problems. Most paper packets say on them somewhere 'this way up' or have an arrow pointing to the side to be printed. Fanning the paper, to separate it, is always a good idea. Never overload your paper tray.

Keep a small stock of paper near the printer so that you don't have to walk a long way every time the paper needs replenishing, and learn how to replace paper in your printer as soon as you start to use it – don't rely on other people to do the job for you.

Finally, remember that if you alter any paper guides to insert the paper you must put them back to their proper positions before you start to print.

Printer out of toner

Laser printers use toner cartridges, ink-jet printers use ink cartridges. Dozens of varieties are on the market so if you need to reorder cartridges do make sure you specify exactly the right make and reference number.

Depending upon your printer, you may receive a warning that the toner is low. However, on some basic models – and most ink-jets – the first warning you will have is that the copies are becoming fainter and fainter. This can be extremely annoying if you find out only when you return to collect a large document that the last 40 pages are unreadable! In addition, of course, you will have wasted 40 sheets of paper. On many printers, if you need to replenish the cartridge part-way through a long document you first need to press the 'off-line' button to stop printing. When you press it again, the printer will start from the point at which it paused.

If you use a colour printer, you may also have special cartridges to replenish for colour prints in addition to the normal ones for black print.

The handbook will tell you the procedure to follow to change the cartridge. The first time you do this, ask a colleague to observe you if you have any doubts or worries. Then check how you should dispose of the used cartridge. In some organisations these are recycled by being sent away for refilling.

Paper jams

Paper jams always seem to occur when you are in a hurry! They can be caused for a number of reasons:

- the paper is unsuitable for the printer
- the paper is damp
- the paper guides have been set incorrectly
- there is too much paper in the paper tray
- there is a problem with your printer mechanism.

The first thing to learn is how to cancel printing immediately if there is a problem. Usually the best – and quickest – response is to turn off the printer. If an error message appears on your screen you are safer to 'cancel' the printing session than to try to keep going. At least you know where you are when you have rectified the jam and can send a new instruction to print.

Then check your handbook and use the manufacturer's recommended procedure for releasing the jammed paper. You will find that this instructs you *never* to forcibly tug paper in the wrong direction. You should remove it in the direction of travel, wherever possible. If it tears, make sure all the small fragments are removed. Then take a test page if you are worried about the problem recurring.

CHECK IT OUT!

Learn how to communicate with your printer on screen! Click on the Start button and then select Settings and Printers. If you now double-click on the printer icon you will see your print queue dialogue box. This lists all the jobs waiting to be printed and the status of each one. You can highlight any jobs in your queue and press the delete key to cancel them if you have a problem.

Printer error message

Other problems you may experience – and action to take

- *The printer does not start as expected.* Check your screen in case there is an error message, such as Printer Not Responding; then check that all the covers are closed, the printer is switched on and on-line. Then re-try.

- *A blank page comes out of the printer.* You may have put in a new cartridge without removing the protective tape. Or the wrong printer may have been selected on your printer driver program. Or you need a new cartridge.

- *Gobbledegook is printed.* Your printer driver program is wrong or incorrectly set to another printer or has corrupted. If this has never happened before it is worth trying one quick check. Turn the printer off, cancel the print job on screen (see above), turn the printer back on and try printing just one page. If the situation is no better you can access Windows Help if you want to investigate further or report the problem to a computer technician.

- *The printer is suddenly very slow or erratic.* There may be a problem with the spool setting on your computer. Ask a colleague who understands these things to check it for you.

- *The text is slanted on the page.* You have loaded the paper so that it is skewed. Take the paper out and reload it – and check all the guides are set correctly.

- *The text runs off the page.* Check your margins and check you've selected the right page on your print menu. This can also happen if two pages stick together. If printing is continuing without problems, wait until the end of the job, remove the paper, fan it and print out the two incorrect pages again.

- *Print quality is poor.* This will occur if your paper is of inferior quality or you need to replace the cartridge. It can also signal that your computer needs cleaning – on ink-jet printers the printer head can become blocked.

- *The print is smearing or blotchy.* You touched the page whilst the print was still wet, or your printer needs cleaning. If you are printing in best quality then it is worth checking if there is a 'pause' feature on your print screen which slows down the printer. If you think your printer is dirty you may be able to use a self-cleaning routine – the manual will tell you. Otherwise, carefully remove the cartridge and use either a special cleaning kit or a lightly moistened cotton wool bud to *gently* clean the head. Be careful! Sharp objects and heavy handling are likely to damage it.

Finally, remember to keep the rest of your printer clean and to check the manual for how to undertake this safely.

CHECK IT OUT!

Find your printer manual and *read it*! Make notes on how to:

- correctly rectify paper jams and replenish the cartridge
- use different sizes and types of paper
- stop printing quickly if there is an emergency
- keep the printer clean and well maintained.

If you read the manual carefully – even after some months of use – you are likely to find one or two functions you can carry out which you did not notice the first time you started using it. This is normal. When getting to know a new printer you are naturally concerned with the key tasks you have to perform every day, and the extras follow later.

Finally, check that you know where the **trouble-shooting information** is to be found if you need it quickly. If you are completely stuck, note that most printer manufacturers have excellent websites which include advice on problem areas – check your handbook.

 INFORMATION UPDATE

Traditionally, offices used two types of machines to produce documents – printers and photocopiers. The latest developments include all-in-one machines that link them together.

The range is impressive, from small, one-per-desk devices – which may even include a scanner and fax facilities. These save space as well as cables, plugs and sockets. Prices currently range from about £250 to £400.

Organisations that are prepared to spend greater sums of money to equip a number of network users with such facilities can buy a digital photocopier which receives print commands direct from a computer and will automatically recognise users and send final documents to a nominated 'mail' tray for that person. Long, routine jobs can be programmed to be printed overnight to leave the machine free during the day for urgent or special documents. To meet user needs there are usually two or three differently sized paper trays as well as other features such as collators, document sorters and a stapling facility. These options, and others such as reduction and enlargement, are set on screen. There is normally more than one toner cartridge in the machine – so the machine automatically switches to the spare if it senses the toner is low.

However, administrators can rest assured they will still be needed. Someone still has to check the paper trays are full regularly or the whole point of rapid printing at any hour of the day or night is soon defeated!

TEST YOUR KNOWLEDGE AND UNDERSTANDING

1 A new member of staff has joined your team. Your printer is unfamiliar to her.

   a What functions would you consider she must learn *immediately*?

   b What functions would you show her after she has worked with you for about two weeks?

   c Select any three of the functions you have identified and check that you could show someone how to carry them out *without* having to refer to your printer manual!

   Check your answers with your tutor or supervisor.

2 Your supervisor is considering purchasing a new printer for your office. Could you answer her queries below? (If you can, supplement your knowledge by researching some of the latest printers on the market.) Check your responses with your tutor or supervisor.

   a What is the difference between an ink-jet and a laser printer?

   b Which would be best in a busy office where the work has to be top quality?

   c How much does each type of printer cost?

d If one administrator undertook a lot of colour printing and worked in a separate office, which type of printer would be best for her?

e What is the cost of replacement cartridges for each type of printer?

f What is the best way to keep the printer clean?

3 You are aware that your rather old printer is slightly cantankerous and can cause problems. However, you are horrified to find that a new member of staff has used nearly a full packet of paper to print out a 20-page document properly. You look in the waste bin to see what has gone wrong.

a What problems are you likely to find on the discarded pages? (If you are studying this as a group, you could brainstorm this for ideas; alternatively, you could look back through the last few pages for inspiration.)

b What advice would you give the member of staff concerned?

c Why do you think the prevention of this type of wastage is so important?

EVIDENCE COLLECTION

Again, you are not expected to create problems with your printer just to provide evidence. However, unless you are very lucky, it is unlikely that you will *never* have to undertake any actions to maintain your printer whilst you are taking your award. If necessary, make sure you are the person to refill the paper and replace the cartridge next time this is required. And volunteer to fix the next paper jam!

Your assessor will expect you to provide evidence, or answer questions, on the following problems:

a   printer off-line

b   printer out of paper

c   printer out of toner

d   paper jam.

If you have solved other problems too, so much the better! You can obtain evidence if you ask your supervisor or colleague to provide witness testimony that you have undertaken these operations as part of your job and can deal with these problems without difficulty.

Answers to quiz on pages 224–225

1   False, although using a computer frequently can make existing visual problems worse, which is why users can ask for a free eyesight test.

2   True.

3   True, but note that computers cannot *cause* epilepsy.

4   False – the radiation emitted is minimal.

5   True (see page 234).

6   True – the feet must be properly supported (but a large book can be just as effective as a footstool).

7   False. However, pregnant women who have concerns about using a computer should be able to talk to someone in private.

8   True (see pages 232–233).

9   True. Fresh air and de-humidifiers can help to reduce this.

10 True.

11 False. 800 mm is far too high (measure it!). There is much debate as to whether a VDU should be positioned at eye level or so that the user is slightly looking up or down. Find the position that's best for you – even if it means separating your VDU from the processor.

12 False, except in very rare circumstances. You are much more likely to get an electric shock from a plug or socket.

13 True. Your head weighs between 12 and 14 lb and supporting it for long periods can cause discomfort if your posture is incorrect or your chair back doesn't support you.

14 True. You should be able to exercise your eyes easily by looking out of a window or across the room.

15 False. Never cross your legs (at all, if possible). It is very bad for your blood circulation.

16 True. If you are pressurised to produce documents quickly (or if your keystrokes or work rate is measured in some way), then this will cause stress which can be detrimental to your health if it is above the level you can cope with.

17 False. In very rare cases they can make some existing conditions, such as eczema, slightly worse.

18 False. In a government survey only 38 per cent were computer users. People involved in routine repetitive assembly work and packing were more vulnerable.

19 True.

20 True – so make sure you follow them!

Windows® and word-processing glossary

Applications software. Programs such as word-processing and spreadsheets which do a specific task

Buttons. Small buttons on a Windows program which undertake specific functions, such as close, maximise or minimise

Clipboard. A temporary storage space for sections of a document you have cut or copied

Control Panel. Part of Windows Desktop which gives access to how the program functions, such as setting the time and day or screen-saver options

Delete. Removing text which is no longer required. Deleted text can usually be undeleted via the Undo facility

Dialogue box. A box which either gives or asks for information on screen. Windows packages denote options which are followed by a dialogue box by a series of dots after the menu option (e.g. File Open ...)

File. A document created on a software package

File extension. The suffix at the end of a file which denotes the format of the document, such as '.doc' or '.wpd'

Flush. To align text along a margin – left flush is aligned along the left margin, right flush along the right margin. Text that is flush at both sides is justified

Folder. An electronic folder into which documents can be stored for ease of access

Font. The style of characters which combines the typeface, the pitch (see below) and spacing (e.g. Times New Roman, Ariel or Helvetica)

Footer. Text that appears at the bottom of every page in a document

Graphics. Pictures that are stored or can be changed on a computer system. They include freehand drawings, clipart, charts and graphs

Header. Text that appears at the top of every page of a document

Icons. Small pictures of programs (on a Windows desktop) or frequently used functions (on a program) – such as a small printer for 'print' and a disk for 'save' on word-processing packages. Clicking on an icon gives instant access to the function

Indent. Text which starts to the right or left of a margin or to the right of existing text. Sometimes called 'inset'

Keyboard shortcuts. Key combinations which will access a particular feature or function without any need to use the mouse

Layout. The way that text and graphics are arranged on a page. This determines which parts are emphasised and also affects the appearance of the document

Menu bar. The horizontal bar at the top of your screen with your menu options

Orphan. The first line of a paragraph that is positioned as the last line on a page

Point. The height of a typeface (its width is called pitch). Common point sizes are 10 and 12

Pop-up window. A window which suddenly appears in association with a particular function or request – such as Help

Pull-down menu. A menu at the top of your screen which enables you to access commands or options. When you click on the key word (or use the keyboard shortcut) the menu 'drops down' as if you have pulled it down

Recycle Bin. A directory on your desktop where deleted files are stored temporarily. Purging the bin will free up space on your hard disk – but then the documents will be gone forever

Returns. Word-processing includes both hard and soft returns. A hard return is inserted when the Enter or Return key is pressed and this forces a new line regardless of the position of the margin. Soft returns are entered by the program and enable the text to reflow automatically when insertions or deletions are made

Screen-saver. The moving design that pops up on screen after a pre-specified period of inactivity

Scroll bars. Bars at the side and bottom of the screen with arrows at each end used to move up, down or across a document

Start button. The button used to access programs on a Windows Desktop

Status bar. The bar at the bottom of the screen, but before the Windows taskbar which gives basic information, such as page number and current mode of operation

Systems software. Software which drives your computer, i.e. your operating system and the utilities that help your computer to function

Taskbar. The bar at the bottom of your screen in Windows Desktop with the Start button to the left and the time at the right (unless you chose to change their positions)

Template. A pre-designed document layout that can be stored on disk or on a network and used for specific house styles

Title bar. The bar at the top of your screen which states the program you are using

Toolbar. A bar containing buttons with icons to enable quick access to commonly used functions, such as bold or italics

Typeface. The design of characters. The two main categories are serif and sans serif. The latter are plainer and have no decorative edges

Widow. The last line of a paragraph that is positioned as the first line on a page

Windows Desktop. The screen which is displayed when Windows loads and which contains all the program and document icons

Windows Explorer. A program for managing files, folders and disks across all the programs stored on a computer using Windows

GROUP A OPTION UNITS

Unit 205 Record, store and supply information using a paper-based system

This unit is one of two in Option Group A.
Select *either* this unit *or* Unit 206 – but not both!

A vast amount of information is stored every day in organisations. Much of this is still kept in paper format, although today more and more information is being stored on computer systems. Storing paper-based information has a more basic name – and is commonly referred to as 'filing'. Even if you work for an organisation which has advanced electronic filing systems (see page 294), it is very doubtful whether everything you ever need to store can be scanned into your system and retrieved at the press of a few keys!

In the 1980s, when computerised systems were becoming increasingly popular, there was much talk of the 'paperless office'. Ironically, the opposite has occurred. Surveys have shown that computers have actually increased the number of documents handled in offices because obtaining and printing information from a variety of sources is now so much easier. Many people also prefer hard (paper) copies of documents to reading information on screen. They can take the documents with them to a meeting, write notes on them, use them for reference, take them home to read. All of these options are less feasible – or impossible – if the document can be viewed only on screen. This may be one of the reasons why organisations in the UK have been slow to convert to electronic filing – in the year 2000 over 70 per cent of companies still kept their document records entirely in paper-based systems, according to a survey by Toplevel Computing.

Therefore, the emphasis in this section is on the traditional methods of recording, storing and supplying paper-based information. Whilst some people either actively dislike filing or simply tolerate it as a necessary evil, others have different views and get satisfaction from knowing that everything is where it should be and can be found quickly. Certainly, most people will agree that life is much easier and less stressful if a document can be found rapidly, without having to hunt, panic stricken, through piles of papers.

This unit comprises two elements. The first is concerned with storing information properly and the second is related to retrieving and supplying information when it is needed from a paper-based system. You may, of course, store and retrieve information on your computer system or in an electronic filing system, and supply information you have found on the Internet. However, note that those systems are covered in other units of the scheme. Finding information saved on your computer system is covered in Unit 204, and electronic storage and retrieval and using the Internet is covered in Option Unit 214.

Before you can learn about storing and supplying information in more detail, you need some basic knowledge and understanding of the type of systems you will be working with and how these operate. The first part of this section, therefore, is concerned with the essential information you need to cover for the whole unit.

CHECK IT OUT!

In some organisations, filing clerks are now being renamed 'data storage specialists' and filing is being renamed 'document management' or 'information handling and retrieval'. How much happier would you be if your organisation adopted any of these ideas?

 KEY SKILLS SIGNPOST

If you are taking your Key Skills award, you will find there are opportunities in this unit to obtain evidence towards the **Problem Solving** key skills unit at Level 2. These are linked to the problem-solving issues described on pages 322 and 324 and the evidence you have to collect on this topic on page 325.

PS2.1

The following problems can occur with storing and retrieving information.

- A manual filing system has expanded to the point where there is insufficient room for all the documents.
- There are many new users of a paper-based filing system who do not understand how the indexing system works. The result is a number of missing documents which have been placed in the wrong files.
- There is no proper system for borrowing file folders in a system with the result that several go missing and cannot be traced.

- There is no system for storing magazines and/or press cuttings which are used by staff. You are asked to suggest a system to solve this problem.

For *any two* of these problems (or for an alternative problem you have agreed with your tutor or supervisor):

a explain the main features of the problem and why it occurs

b identify what would be the ideal situation you would want to achieve

c suggest different ways of tackling the problem

d decide which would have the most chance of success, bearing in mind factors such as health and safety, time, resources, the expertise required and the views of other people.

PS2.2

Do the following for each of the problems you have selected.

a Obtain approval for either your chosen option to solve the problem, or for an alternative option, with your supervisor or tutor.

b Prepare a plan, showing the sequence of tasks you will undertake and the time, resources and assistance you will need.

c Carry out your tasks, but be prepared to make changes to your plan to show you are responsive to suggestions to overcome unforeseen difficulties.

d Obtain and use support from other people when it is offered, whether it be your supervisor, tutor or colleagues.

PS2.3

Do the following for each of the problems you have selected.

a Decide and agree the methods you can use to check if the problem has now been solved.

b Apply these methods to make your checks, and describe the results.

c Explain the decisions you had to make when you were implementing your plan, and any changes you had to make.

d Identify what you did well and assess anything that went wrong. Summarise these as the strengths and weaknesses of your approach. Use them to conclude what you would do differently next time if you had to solve a similar problem.

Data protection and other relevant legislation

Data Protection Act 1998

Much of the information stored by organisations concerns individuals. These may be private customers or staff. As an individual yourself, you may be concerned about the type of information you would like any other organisation to hold about you – regardless of whether this is the school or college you have attended, your past or current employers or companies where you have bought goods in the past. The law is aware of this and protects individuals through the **Data Protection Act 1998**. This regulates the type of information that can be held and what it can be used for. It also gives everyone the right to find out what is held about them and to have inaccurate information corrected. All organisations have to comply with the requirements of the Act.

The original Data Protection Act, in 1984, covered only information held on computer. The 1998 Act, which replaced it, covers both information held on computer *and* manual data held in structured filing systems. A structured file basically means that there is a set of information about an individual – a **data subject** under the Act – such as a personnel file or a customer file. Between March 2000, when the Act was introduced, and 23 October 2001, all organisations must check that their data and manual files comply with the Act. However, manual data stored before 24 October 1998 won't be completely covered by the Act until October 2007. This is to give organisations – called **data controllers** under the Act – time to check which files must comply with the law and take appropriate action.

If an organisation fails to comply or breaks the law, the **Data Protection Commissioner** has the power to issue an enforcement notice or an information notice against that data controller. An enforcement notice instructs the data controller what action is must take (or what activities it must cease). An information notice is a request for information. The Commissioner also has the power to apply for a warrant to enter and search premises if there is evidence of contravention. Failure to comply with a notice or to obstruct a search are criminal offences.

Defamation

Defamation relates to written or spoken words which malign the reputation of another person. If, for instance, a memo is written alleging that a member of staff is dishonest, then the writer could be accused of libel. (Spoken defamation is called 'slander'). For that reason, most organisations are very careful about what is written about other people and what is stored in their filing systems. This has become doubly important now that the Data Protection Act has given rights to individuals to access and read information that has been written about them.

Copyright legislation

The **Copyright Designs and Patents Act 1988** limits what you can copy and distribute to other people. This may affect you when you are supplying information to other people (see also the photocopying Option Unit 218.

People obtain the copyright in material when they create it. So an author of a book, such as this one, 'owns' the copyright. You can, therefore, supply material produced *within* your organisation to anyone, because your employer holds the copyright. However, if you store information that was created and published by someone else in your filing system you cannot simply make multiple copies of it without thinking, and distribute it around or outside the office. Neither can you use chunks of it in your own documents without acknowledging the true author. You should do this by acknowledging who wrote the original item, the title, the date it was published and the publisher's name.

If you wish to circulate your own document more widely, or have it published, you may need to obtain specific permission to use the information. As an example, many organisations keep 'cuttings' libraries containing press clippings about the firm. Yet the copyright for these cuttings belongs to the newspaper or magazine in which the article appeared. If your boss wanted to use these cuttings in a brochure about the company, he or she would need to obtain permission to do that from the copyright holders.

THE DATA PROTECTION ACT 1998

The Act requires all organisations and businesses which process personal data on individuals (a **data subject**), to give notification that they should be included in a register of **data controllers**, unless they have already registered under the 1984 Act. They must state:

- their name and address and the name of their representative, if any
- a description of the personal data being processed and the types of data subject which it covers (e.g. customers, employees, students, etc.)
- a description about why the data is being processed
- a description about any recipients to whom it may be disclosed
- a description of any countries outside the EU to which it may be sent.

The term 'data' which is covered by the Act relates to:

- information recorded or processed by computer
- information which is part of a relevant filing system or forms part of an accessible record (e.g. health records, social services records, etc.).

All data controllers must comply with the eight Principles of the Act in relation to the handling of personal data.

- Data must be obtained and processed fairly and lawfully. Normally this means the individual has given his/her consent. Explicit consent is required for 'sensitive' data relating to religious or political beliefs; racial origin; trade union membership; physical or mental health or sexual life; criminal convictions.
- Personal data must be held only for one or more specified and lawful purposes and should not be processed for another reason.
- The data should be adequate, relevant and not excessive.
- Personal data must be accurate and kept up to date.
- Personal data must be kept no longer than is necessary.
- It must be processed in accordance with the rights of data subjects (see below).
- It must be stored to prevent unauthorised or unlawful access, loss, destruction or damage.
- It must not be transferred outside the EU unless the country to which it is being sent also protects the rights of data subjects.

The rights of individuals (data subjects) include:

- the right to access data held about them
- the right to prevent processing which would cause damage or distress
- the right to prevent processing for direct marketing purposes
- rights in relation to automated decision-taking (e.g. evaluating job performance or credit worthiness on the basis of personal information)
- the right to take action to correct, block, erase or destroy inaccurate data
- the right to compensation if damage is suffered through contravention of the Act.

Exemptions

The Act allows for certain exemptions, although in many cases specific conditions are attached. Broadly, the categories of exempt data include that held for:

- purposes of national security
- crime detection and taxation purposes
- health, education and social work
- research, history and statistics
- domestic use only.

TEST YOUR KNOWLEDGE AND UNDERSTANDING

Details of the Data Protection Act are given in the table on pages 287–288. Read this carefully and then answer the questions below. Check your answers with your tutor or supervisor.

1 What is the difference between a data subject and a data controller?

2 Police records on individuals are one example of a structured file which is not covered by the Act. Can you suggest why?

3 You buy a home computer and set up a database of your friends and contacts. Would you need to tell the Data Protection Commissioner what you are doing?

4 Three of the following are an offence under the Act. Can you identify them?

   a You enrol at college to improve your word-processing skills and are asked if you will voluntarily identify your ethnic origin on the enrolment form.

   b Your employer provides information about your income to the tax office without your consent.

   c Your employer sells its personnel records to an insurance company so that it can contact each person to try to sell its products.

   d You write to your bank and ask them to give you details of the information they hold on you in their files but they refuse, saying it is confidential.

   e Your brother has a small business and employs 16 people. He says he doesn't need to give notification as the Act covers only businesses with more than 50 employees.

5 Your boss has written a reference for a former employee which says he was idle, incompetent and probably dishonest. You see the copy when it arrives in your filing tray.

   a What risk is your employer taking by writing such a reference?

   b Why is this situation even more risky since the Data Protection Act 1998 was passed?

6 Your boss, who is a health and safety specialist, is producing materials for a talk he is giving next month. He has asked you to find several booklets and reports in the files and wants to use these as a basis for notes and handouts.

  a If he wanted to quote some information from a published report in his notes, what must he do to avoid breaching copyright legislation?

  b He is thinking of having his notes published as a short handbook to sell to everyone who attends. He wants to include an illustration he has seen in a magazine. How can he do this without breaking the law?

Filing systems and procedures

Any organisation which stores items and retrieves them regularly needs a system that all users must follow. You can see these systems in operation if you visit a library, where books and journals are classified into subjects, or in a local video store, where videos are categorised into subject areas with probably a special section for new releases or 'top twenty' popular films.

In the same way, a **filing system** is the method and equipment used to store documents. Many organisations operate more than one system because, as you will see, some are more appropriate for certain types of documents than others.

Procedures are the recommended sequence of activities which you must follow when you use the system. These are known to all users and staff. Library staff or video store staff will help new users to 'find their way' around and tell them what they must do if they wish to borrow or hire an item – although the exact procedure may vary slightly from one place to another. Similarly, for administrators, filing procedures will vary slightly from one employer to another. However, they are important because they ensure that everyone uses the system in the same way and in the best way for the needs of the organisation.

You need to know what types of system you are likely to meet and what types of procedure you will have to follow. If you have a good understanding about this, then no matter where you work you will find it easy to adjust quickly. When you become more experienced, you may even be able to make suggestions for improvements.

Filing systems

Filing systems may relate to:

- the types of equipment used
- the types of storage method employed
- the way in which the information is classified – or ordered within the equipment.

Classification systems are dealt with on page 297. In this section we will look at types of equipment and storage methods. You may find these differ, depending upon the *types* of files stored. The most usual types are listed in the table below.

THE MAIN TYPES OF FILES

Active office files	Usually found in each department. Active files are usually kept in a central area where they can be accessed by many people. They contain the latest and the most frequently used information.
Active personal files	Contain the information each person needs to do his or her own job. They are kept as near to each person's working area as possible.
General departmental files	Contain information which is not accessed as regularly as the active files. They may be kept in a separate area to save space in the office itself.
Archived files	Usually situated in the basement or some other area away from the main working area. They contain information which must not be thrown away but which is historic and required only infrequently.

Standard equipment and storage systems

Vertical filing cabinets are the most common type of filing equipment. They consist of a metal or wooden cabinet with a number of large drawers – three or four being the most usual. Inside the drawers there are usually suspension pockets, which hang from side to side, often in a continuous row. Each pocket has a tab at the front giving the name of the file folder it contains.

Many cabinets are designed to be resistant to fire and impact, so that if there is an accident the documents inside should still be safe. The cabinets can be locked. You will also find that they are fitted with a safety feature to stop you opening more than one drawer at once – as otherwise you are in danger of the whole thing tilting towards you.

Lateral filing cabinets are large (open) cupboards, but instead of shelves you will see suspended pockets hanging in rows from one side of the cabinet to the other, with tabs on the side. The file folders are also inserted sideways – usually to the right of the identifying tab. A sliding door or blind can be pulled down when the cabinet is not in use to protect the files from dust.

A variation is a multi-purpose lateral cabinet which contains some rows of pockets and some shelves. On these shelves may be placed other types of storage systems, such as lever arch or box files (see page 293).

Horizontal filing cabinets are used for storing either small quantities of documents or very large documents. They consist of a series of shallow drawers in a metal cabinet. A variety of different sizes are available – from drawers which store A4 paper to those which store A0 size. You are apt to

CHECK IT OUT!

You won't get very far when you are trying to match folders and storage systems to your documents unless you know the main paper sizes used in an office. You also need this information if you are photocopying, faxing or ordering stationery – to name but a few jobs which involve paper.

The standard paper size in Britain is A4 (210 x 297 mm). If you double that it becomes A3, double again and it becomes A2, and so on to A0 which is obviously huge! If you halve A4 it becomes A5, halve again A6, and so on. Envelopes have a similar system, but use the letter C – so a C4 envelope is the same size as A4 paper. The exception is a DL envelope – which holds A4 paper folded three times – so is the standard size for inserting business letters.

Check all these sizes in a stationery catalogue and list which sizes of paper you use and need to file in your office.

find the latter if you work for an architect or surveyor who needs to keep large plans and drawings flat and safe.

Rotary filing systems are becoming less common but are similar to the circular rotating stands you may see in a shop. The stand is designed to hold A4 lever arch or box files, or special folders, and spins round to give all-round access to the files.

Types of storage

Documents may be stored in a variety of ways and you are likely to find your stationery cupboard contains a variety of products for this purpose.

- **Ring binders** are used for storing small quantities of documents on a particular topic.
- **Lever arch files** are a larger version of ring binders, for greater quantities of documents on a particular topic.
- **Box files** are used to store documents which cannot or must not be hole-punched. These include important legal documents, presentation documents, catalogues and bound reports.
- **Document wallets** are used for transporting small quantities of documents (e.g. to a meeting) or for storing them on a temporary basis.
- **File folders** are used for storing papers within a filing system. They are available in a variety of colours and with optional fastenings. The type used by your organisation will depend upon whether any colour-coding system is in operation and whether papers are fastened inside the folder or put in but not secured to the folder itself.
- **Expanding wallets** (sometimes called 'concertina files') are used to store documents in alphabetical order on a temporary basis, such as just before transfer to the main filing system.
- **Index pages** or **dividers** are used to separate documents filed in ring binders or lever arch files.

CHECK IT OUT!

Lateral cabinets take up less space than vertical cabinets. Some manufacturers claim the contents of over five 4-drawer cabinets will fit easily into the new types of lateral cabinets which will rotate or revolve within a cabinet. They also argue that these filing systems are more versatile and, because the files are visible, labelling is clearer and colour-coded filing is more effective. Despite these claims, most offices still appear to contain a large number of standard vertical cabinets!

List the type of equipment and the systems operating in your office. Find out, too, whether your office has archived files and, if so, state where these are kept.

1 Look through a stationery catalogue and identify the different types of filing supplies that are available. Ideally, select a catalogue which also contains a good range of filing equipment – and compare the prices of cheaper cabinets and the more expensive fire-resistant and shock-proof cabinets. What difference do you think you would find between the types of document stored in both styles of cabinet?

2 Solicitors and accountants are two examples of firms where client papers are likely to be kept in folders with a built-in fastening, so that papers are always secure.

   a Why do you think this is the case?

   b Can you think of any occasions when it would be acceptable to simply place papers in a file folder, without fastening them?

3 Some people prefer to work at desks where one drawer has been designed to be a filing drawer and hold suspension pockets. In other offices – and in hospitals – certain types of files are stored in mobile trolleys.

   a What type of files do you think administrators keep in their desk drawer?

   b What do you think are the advantages and disadvantages of storing files in a desk drawer?

   c What type of files do you think would be kept in a mobile trolley – and why?

 INFORMATION UPDATE

Electronic document management system (EDMS) is an important-sounding name for a system whereby documents are scanned into a computer and stored in files or folders controlled by special software. Systems range from basic ones which can be used by small businesses, up to those costing many thousands of pounds.

Filing procedures, and gaining access to the system

In this unit you will meet a variety of filing procedures. However, most organisations also need to have some controls over who can access the system. These controls vary, depending mainly upon:

• whether the organisation has a *centralised* or *decentralised* filing system

- the different types of documents that are stored, and the extent to which some are confidential or contain sensitive information
- whether the system is manual or electronic – or both.

Centralised filing is where the majority of the documents are kept in one area of the organisation and controlled and operated by specialist staff. If there are many thousands of files, special equipment may be purchased – called **automated filing systems** – to enable the files to be retrieved by means of a control panel. An example would be a building society which stores the deeds of all the properties on which it has allowed mortgages. In this case you would have to follow set procedures for requesting access to a file and, unless you worked in the centralised area and had received training, you would not be able to operate the system yourself.

Decentralised filing is more common. This is where each department or section keeps its own files. The sales department keeps customer records, the purchasing department keeps supplier records, the human resources department keeps personnel records, and so on. In this case the departmental staff will do their own filing and, as soon as you have been shown how the system operates, you would most likely be expected to do this job.

No matter where you work you will find that some documents will be stored separately. This is because they contain sensitive or confidential information. Senior managers in an organisation will often have their own files which contain detailed financial data or information on future company developments which they do not want to be public knowledge. Access to such information will be tightly controlled, as will access to sensitive personnel information and payroll figures.

As your career develops and you take on more responsibility, you may be given greater access to sensitive information. Senior administrators are used to dealing with it daily and keeping what they read to themselves. Until you have proved yourself as being both conscientious and discreet, you are unlikely to be given the same privileges. This is sensible. After all, you wouldn't like your own personnel file to be available to anyone to read, would you?

INFORMATION UPDATE

According to one research report, companies in Europe produce over 5000 million documents every 24 hours, and 95 per cent of this is stored on paper. In the future, many organisations may have to seriously consider faster ways in which to store and retrieve all this paper, and one method being promoted is automated or **robot filing**. One company, Kardex, can supply a unit called DataStack which will hold 250,000 documents and is operated from a control panel. The code number of the document is entered, the robot selects the right shelf and in less than eight

One method of robotic filing

seconds the document is in your hands! Whereas previously such units were very large, this one takes up four square metres – so you may find you could fit it into one corner of your office. You may even find it would take less space than the system you have at present.

The importance of effective and efficient information systems

There are times when everyone needs to provide information quickly. This may mean simply referring to a document for some basic facts or actually having to produce a particular document. If you want to apply for a passport, you have to produce your birth certificate; if you want to hire a car, you have to produce your driving licence; if you apply for a job you may be asked to take with you all the certificates you have gained.

In a busy office, information and documents are received, referred to and required constantly. Any information system, therefore, must be able to cope with constant storage and retrieval by a large number of people – and unless this is controlled in some way it is likely that havoc will ensue! For instance, if there were no set procedures for storing or borrowing papers:

- no one would know where information could be found
- people would be operating with different sets of information and no one would know which was the latest version
- documents and files would go missing and no one would know who had them
- an important document which related to two or three files would be put into only one
- delays would occur as people looked for missing papers
- wrong decisions would be made as no one would have the full picture about a particular situation
- customers would be given incorrect information and might take their business elsewhere as a result.

Imagine for a moment you have started work in a very small firm and have been asked to design a filing system that will operate effectively and efficiently. You must obviously ensure it meets the needs of everyone who will use it. In this case you would have to make sure that it was:

- **easy to use** – so that people who used the system only occasionally could still follow it without difficulty
- **logical and consistent** – so there was never any confusion as to where a file could be found
- **appropriate for its purpose** – so that documents are stored according to their type, how often they are required, whether they are confidential, etc.
- **flexible** – so that it could grow to meet future as well as current needs
- **kept up to date** – to prevent delays finding the latest information
- **regularly 'pruned'** – to remove old or outdated papers.

If, as an administrator, you have *your own* files on particular aspects of your work they should be organised according to these criteria, too. Then you and your information system will both be effective and efficient.

Classification systems

The first step in setting up a filing system is to decide the order in which you will keep the files. Basically, you have four main choices. Documents can be stored alphabetically, numerically, alpha-numerically or chronologically. In each case there are certain rules you have to follow to make sure you are using the system properly.

Alphabetical filing

In this case files are kept in alphabetical order. However, they may be stored:

- by name
- by location
- by subject.

The choice will depend upon the type of files being stored.

Alphabetical by name is used when *the name of the person or organisation* is the most important factor, such as for customer files or personnel files. This is the system used in the *Phone Book* – which is a good reference guide if you are ever puzzled about where a particular file should be placed.

Alphabetical by location is sometimes known as **geographical filing**. It is used when the *place* is the most important factor, for instance if you had files relating to branch or sales offices or if you had overseas agents in different parts of the world.

Alphabetical by subject is used when the *topic* is the most relevant aspect. Many managers prefer their files kept this way as they can have one file for each area of work with which they are involved. Purchasing offices may keep information by product, which is a variation on this (e.g. computers, office furniture, printers, etc.). If a particular topic is very broad, you may find files sub-divided under a heading. For instance, the heading 'office furniture' could be sub-divided into bookcases, desks, chairs, filing cabinets, etc. *Yellow Pages* is an excellent example where information is classified alphabetically by subject.

Alphabetical filing – the rules to follow

You may think that using the alphabet is so simple that no rules are needed, but you would be wrong! For instance, do you:

- put Brian McDonald's file before or after Bill Maguire's
- put TM Products before or after Tate and Jones
- put St Peter's School before or after Salisbury Council
- put Wellington in Shropshire before or after Wellington in Somerset
- place a file labelled 'IT services' before or after one labelled 'Inkjet printers'?

Rules are needed so that everyone who uses the system will do the same thing. New files will be stored in the right place and anyone looking for a file will know immediately where to look. So it is important that you not only understand the rules but know how to apply them. The exercise below should help you to develop your skills.

TEST YOUR KNOWLEDGE AND UNDERSTANDING

The chart on page 300 summarises the rules of alphabetical filing. Study these carefully and then do the three exercises below. Check your answers with your tutor or supervisor.

1   You are rearranging files into alphabetical order by name. Rearrange the list below into the order the files should be placed in your filing cabinet:

123 Nursery	MPH Supplies	Tradewise Ltd
McDermott & Sons	James O'Connell	The Oz Shop
Thomas Marsden	The Traders Corner	St Stephen's Hospital
Smith Electrical	M & J Supplies	Department of Social
The 6 Stars Hotel	OTZ Publishers	Security
Martin & Jackson		Department of Trade
		& Industry

2   You work for a supermarket which has stores around the country. The files are ordered by the location of each store, firstly by county and secondly by town (e.g. under Hampshire the stores in Havant, Portsmouth and Southampton follow in alphabetical order). You have just purchased a new filing cabinet and the following files are lying on the floor. Into which order would you put them back?

Sussex	*Suffolk*	*Surrey*	*Somerset*
Worthing	Ipswich	Guildford	Taunton
Brighton	Stowmarket	Epsom	Bridgewater
Eastbourne	Bury St Edmunds	Woking	Wells

3   An administrator in a college keeps her files in subject order. From the list below, identify how her files should be ordered.

Health and safety	Admissions
Careers office	Examinations – general
Applications	Marketing – advertisements
Examinations – regulations	OHP supplies
Awards evenings	Examinations – results
Awards and presentations	Marketing – leaflets
Course fees	Office technology courses
Examinations – entries	

Numerical filing

A numerical system is used when there are so many files the system would quickly become congested under frequently used letters of the alphabet, such as B or S, as this would mean constant rearranging of the files. Instead, each file is given a number. This may be a customer number, employee number or supplier number. There are two types of numerical filing systems.

RULES FOR ALPHABETICAL FILING

Rule to follow	Example
PEOPLE	
Surname first	Low Alan
Short names before long	Low Alan Lowe Alan
For identical names, follow first names or initials	Low Alan Mark Low Alan Steven Lowe Alan
Nothing always comes before something	Patel H Patel Hussain Patel Hussain Z Patel Hussain Zafir
Mac and Mc are both treated as Mac and filed *before* M	McDade B MacFarlane J McGowan M Madden T
Ignore apostrophes	Ollett T O'Malley M Ormerod S
ORGANISATIONS	
Ignore the word 'The'	Old Mill Restaurant, The Open University, The
Numbers change to words	Five Star Fitness Four Seasons Garden Centre
If names are identical, street or town is used to determine order	Blakes Travel, Lindhurst Road Blakes Travel, Watery Lane
Initials come before full names (but ignore the word 'and' or '&')	BB Security B & B Motors BEL Systems Bacchus Engineering
Treat both 'Saint' and 'St' as Saint	Sainsbury's J plc St Vincent's Housing Association Salad Bowl, The
File public bodies under town or city or by name of department	Lancashire County Council Leigh Borough Council Liverpool City Council Employment Office, Barnsley Employment Office, Bradford Environment, Department of

- In the **numerical by sequence** type, each new file is simply given the next available number. If earlier numbers become available as files are removed, these may be reallocated to new files. This will depend upon company policy.
- In the **alpha-numeric** type, files are sub-divided first under the letters of the alphabet, e.g. A1, A2, A3, B1, B2, etc.

In both these cases a special index is required as it is impossible to go straight to a particular file unless you know its number off by heart. Indexes are dealt with in the next section.

A variation on numerical filing is storing documents in chronological order. This is used when the date is the most important item of information. Travel agents, for instance, always file tickets under the date of travel and finance departments file bank statements under the date on which they were issued.

TEST YOUR KNOWLEDGE AND UNDERSTANDING

1 Match the most appropriate filing system from those mentioned above with each of the following sets of files:
   a personnel records kept in a small firm
   b your own pay slips
   c patient records kept by a large hospital
   d reports sent by publisher's representatives, each of whom visits schools around the country
   e information on different types of training courses available.

2 A large college has operated a numerical system of recording students for several years. It has now decided to change to an alpha-numeric system with the first letter determining the department where the student has enrolled; i.e. B = Business Studies, A = Art, H = Humanities, C = Catering. The enrolment number will be 01, 02, 03, etc. followed by the current year. Therefore, in 2001, the first student to enrol in Business Studies will be B012001.

   The following is a list of students whom you are enrolling this morning. Allocate the correct number to each one.

   0930: Karen Alstead – Business, David Slater – Business, Anne White – Catering, Susan Lloyd – Art, Amina Coudrey – Business, Guiseppe Parente – Humanities

   10.30: Michael Parr – Humanities, Safik Alli – Business, Joanne Loughlin – Art, Paul Haydock – Humanities, Catherine Betts – Catering, Alan Turner – Humanities

   11.30: Aled Evans – Business, Francesca Kerr – Art, Tahzim Akhtar – Humanities, Mohammed Malik – Art, Lee Wozniak – Catering, Amjed Javed – Business

   12.30: Emma Brook – Art, Andrew Stirrup – Catering, Khalid Hamadeh – Humanities, Paul Wright – Business, Tracie McCruden – Business.

Advantages and disadvantages of different methods

No system is perfect but some methods of classification are more appropriate for certain types of files than others. A major consideration in choosing a system will be its size and whether it will be expected to grow quickly in the future.

The chart opposite summarises the advantages and disadvantages of the different classification systems used.

However, do bear in mind that any system is only as good as the people who use it!

- Alphabetical systems by name will fail if you do not check the spelling of some surnames, e.g. Ayers and Eyres, Akeroyd, Ackroyd and Akroyd, Allan and Allen!

- Alphabetical systems by location or subject will fail if you 'guess' where a file should be stored or don't read properly the various sub-divisions that may exist, e.g. under a country, county or topic heading.

- Numerical systems will fail if you transpose figures and write 652 instead of 562 or L231 instead of L321 *or* if you lose an index card and so can't locate the file at all – as you will see in a minute.

Index systems

An index system is the method used to guide users to files stored in numerical or alpha-numerical order.

- **Index cards** are stored in a small cabinet with the key information written at the top. Guide cards usually help the user to quickly locate a card under a particular letter. The size of the cards means that additional reference information can be included on them.

- **Strip index cards** are much smaller strips which fit into a special holder. Different colours are available which can help to differentiate particular types of file. Strips can easily be removed and new ones added. The holders normally rotate for ease of use.

- **Visible edge cards** fit into plastic wallets which are ordered one upon the other with the key information visible at the bottom edge of each card. Again these cards are quite large and so additional information can be included.

- **Rotary index cards** are slotted on to a small drum in a metal cabinet. The drum is rotated by means of a small handle at one side. The cards and the cabinet are both small and so can fit easily on a person's desk.

You use an index system by looking for the name and reading off the number alongside. This is the number under which you will find that

Classification method	Advantages	Disadvantages
Alphabetical by name	Easy to use A miscellaneous file for each letter can be created for 'one-off' papers	Popular letters become congested Difficult to expand Names can be confused
Alphabetical by subject	Easy to add new topics Easy to sub-divide main topics Sensible grouping for finding out information or writing summaries and reports on a topic	Can be overlaps between subjects resulting in duplication, much cross-referencing or confusion May be several files on a particular topic
Alphabetical by geographical area	No need to know complex foreign names Simple and easy if location is known	Expansion can be difficult Similar place-names can be confused, eg Boston Lincolnshire and Boston USA
Numerical by sequence	Capable of infinite expansion Each file has a unique number The file number can be used as a reference number in correspondence	An index is essential for files to be found Transposition of figures can cause problems Miscellaneous documents are difficult to store
Alpha-numerical	Easy to expand under each letter Numbers can be used as a reference number	Can be confusing unless the system is understood Index essential to find files
Chronological	Useful when date most significant item Easy to use and understand	Too specialised for general use Additional information required if several items filed under the same date

particular file. A major danger is cards being taken out of the system and then misplaced. If the number is too long to remember, make a note of it. *Don't* be tempted to remove the index card from the system.

Taking care of files

Lost files (or lost papers within a file) cause havoc in an office. Their loss is usually noticed in an emergency – such as when a customer is waiting or while the managing director is waiting on the telephone for an immediate answer to a query. If a file is missing and never found again, extreme difficulties can be created – and a lot of work for someone – especially if it contains valuable or original documents.

Damaged documents also cause problems, particularly if part of the text is missing or some pages have been removed from a multi-page document.

Problems can be minimised if:

- there is a proper loan system in operation, to prevent people casually 'borrowing' files (see page 319)
- people are refused permission to borrow odd documents from folders – they have to take the whole file
- there is a proper filing system in operation
- everyone who uses the system understands how it works and the classification system used
- any torn papers are mended promptly
- filing is done promptly – preferably daily
- files containing queries are stored in a separate basket and these, too, are dealt with promptly
- missing files are rigorously searched for.

The latter means checking all the places the file may have been put by accident, everyone's desktop and all the filing baskets and trays. After only one incident like this, it will convince you that keeping files safely is important for your sanity!

How to solve this type of problem and others is dealt with in more detail on page 319.

CHECK IT OUT!

In addition to taking care of the system, you should also work in such a way that you take care of yourself when you are filing – and other people! How safe are you when you are filing? Can you honestly say that:

- all your filing cabinets are positioned so that open drawers aren't a hazard
- all the heaviest objects are to be found in the bottom drawer of your cabinet
- you always close filing cabinet drawers when they are not in use
- you never carry too many file folders at once – so you can't see where you are going
- you always stand on a safety stool if you are reaching files on high shelves?

If not, then now's the time to review your working habits, before someone gets hurt.

Finding and returning files

Files may be missing from a system because:

- you have already removed it from the system for some reason, but have forgotten
- someone else is filing with you, and they have just removed it
- someone has borrowed the file
- the file has been (temporarily or permanently) misplaced.

Procedures for lending files are dealt with in Element 205.2. At this stage you simply need to remember some key points.

- The more methodical you are when you are filing, the less chance there is that you will forget you have removed a file for some reason (such as updating the name or replacing the folder if it is damaged). If you take a file out of the system, try to deal with it straight away and immediately return it.
- The better you work with your colleagues in a team, the less chance you will worry each other by removing files unexpectedly.
- A useful strategy is that any files that have been removed for repair or for any other reason are stacked in *one place* – then you know where to check if you are searching. Otherwise you will have to scour the office looking on desks and in cupboards!

Dealing with confidential information

Even if you are not allowed access to files which are strictly confidential, it is likely that you *will* handle some documents containing sensitive information even at the start of your career. No matter where you work there is likely to be a certain amount of information which your supervisor would not like to be general knowledge or to be talked about outside the organisation. If you work for a doctor, solicitor or accountant, for instance, you would be expected never to discuss details of patients or clients at all when you are away from work.

Generally, types of information likely to be confidential include:

- personal information on individuals, such as their age, address, medical history and details about personal relationships or problems
- financial information about individuals, such as how much they earn or how much money they owe
- financial information about your organisation or department
- future business plans of your organisation
- other customers, clients or contacts and their business to anyone outside the organisation.

Basically, if you even *think* information might be sensitive or confidential, assume that it is. It is far better to err on the side of caution than to have to apologise later for a mistake.

Golden rules for dealing with confidential documents and files

1 Never leave a confidential document or file lying on a desk.
2 Never take a confidential document or file into a public area, such as reception.
3 If you are working on a confidential file and someone comes up to your desk, either close it or move another piece of paper over the documents.
4 Never discuss anything you have read with other people unless, obviously, you are working with a colleague on the matter in question.
5 Never lend out confidential files without first checking that the borrower has the right of access. This is the one exception when your supervisor may agree that a particular (non-sensitive) document may be borrowed but not the whole file. In that case photocopy the document for the borrower so that the file remains intact.
6 Lock all cabinets containing confidential files after use and don't leave the keys lying on your desk!
7 Destroy confidential documents or files which are no longer required by *shredding* them – don't just put them into your waste or recycling bin.
8 Assist your organisation by cooperating fully with them over all the requirements of the Data Protection Act (see pages 286–288).

CHECK IT OUT!

Check that you are completely familiar with all the systems and procedures used by your organisation to maintain and control all the filing systems in operation.

 INFORMATION UPDATE

According to a survey by office equipment manufacturer Rexel, only 25 per cent of large companies are satisfied that their confidential material is properly disposed of. Most had serious worries that sensitive documents were thrown away carelessly and without consideration for the contents. This is despite the fact that safe disposal of confidential information is now a legal requirement under the Data Protection Act!

Today there is really no excuse for any office not to have some type of shredding system available for staff. Tiny handheld ShredStiks cost less than £50 – and can even cope with staples or paperclips! Larger versions for shredding entire files and massive computer printouts cost much more, but are usually transportable so they can be moved from one office to another. A third alternative is to use a shredding service. Shredit, which operates in the north west of England, will collect confidential files which have been placed into sealed containers and claim they can shred 10 hours' of office material in just 15 minutes. Why don't you check to see if anyone operates this type of service in *your* area?

EVIDENCE COLLECTION

When you begin collecting evidence for this unit, be prepared to discuss any problems you encounter when you are storing information and what improvements you can suggest. A useful starting point is to keep a log of problems which routinely occur and how you solved them. You may find it useful to wait until you have read pages 319–324 before you submit evidence – as this may provide you with more ideas.

You will also need to say how you have dealt with confidential information. If, therefore, you actual handle confidential documents or files from now on, make a note of this so that you won't forget. You do not have to provide any confidential details, simply keep a record of the *type* of documents or files and what you did.

Element 205.1   Record and store information

For this element you have to prove that you can follow established procedures when recording and storing information. This does not just mean placing documents in files properly, but also any occasion when you are amending or updating information *relating to* the system. Therefore, if you are keeping a file diary, amending index cards, changing the names on folders or keeping any other related records you must make sure that you:

- write clearly
- copy information accurately
- update records promptly
- keep related information together
- look after documents, files and records for which you are responsible.

You will also be expected to demonstrate that you can use at least two types of filing system from the following list: alphabetical, numerical, alpha-numerical, chronological. If you use only two of these, be prepared to answer questions and answers from your assessor on the remaining two. You are also likely to be asked how you would identify and report any problems with the filing system and perhaps to make suggestions for improvements. You will also be expected to know how to deal with confidential information.

Most of the knowledge and understanding you need for this element has already been covered in the previous pages. This short section, therefore, gives you guidance on evidence collection and covers the remaining knowledge and understanding you need.

EVIDENCE COLLECTION

You can produce evidence, using the established procedures in your workplace, in a number of ways.

a   You can write a summary of the procedures to follow and the systems you use, and how often. It is sensible to ask your supervisor to countersign this for authenticity.

b   You can ask your supervisor, or colleagues, to provide you with witness testimony that you store information properly and promptly.

c   You can arrange for your assessor to visit to watch you in action. Do be prepared to answer simple questions about what you are doing at the time.

Recording and storing information accurately

Everyone who uses a filing system has certain responsibilities which must not be ignored. Even if you know a system well, and file all the documents in their correct places, there are still several other considerations you need to bear in mind.

a Can you put documents neatly *into* a folder, so that they are all punched squarely and the edges of each are aligned in the file – or do you generally create a higgledy-piggledy mess?

b Are the folders you write clearly – and correctly – labelled?

c If you had six documents to put in a file would you check they were inserted so that the most recent one is at the top – or would you be more likely to put them in random order?

d Would you keep putting papers into a folder until it was so bulky it could hardly be lifted out of the cabinet without ripping?

e If someone wanted to borrow a file, what would you do – make a note of it or just hand it over? And what if they just wanted to borrow one document out of a file, what would you do then?

f What would you do if a document could be filed in more than one folder because it relates to two people or two topics?

g What would you do when there are so many folders in a drawer that you can no longer get them out one by one because they are all wedged together?

Even the best-designed filing system in the world will soon be a complete shambles unless everyone who uses the system knows what to do to maintain it *properly*.

Earlier we assumed you were setting up a new filing system in a small firm. If you had done that, what else would you need to think about for the system to operate efficiently? The easiest way is to consider this in the stages you would have to go through when you were storing and retrieving documents.

Stage 1: Papers arrive for filing

You will need a place where documents can be kept before they are filed – ideally a large basket or tray, near to the filing cabinets. Some organisations ask staff to put a 'release mark' (such as a small tick or cross) on the document so that papers still being used are not filed by mistake.

Stage 2: Papers need pre-sorting

The idea here is to save yourself from having to access the same file folder six times during one filing session – or keep having to walk backwards and forwards if you have a large system. If you have an alphabetical system, you sort all your papers into alphabetical order, grouping papers for the same file folder together. Ideally, you will then store these in an expanding or concertina file. If you have a numerical system you need to put the file number on the top of each document and then order them numerically. Some organisations routinely use the file number as the reference in outgoing correspondence, which will save you work, but you will still have to put the number on all incoming documents.

Remember: even if you can't file every day, you should pre-sort every day. Then you can still find any document quickly if necessary.

Stage 3: Papers need preparing for filing

Check the documents for paperclips or pins which could trap other papers behind them. Replace them with staples so that associated documents are still fastened together. Repair any torn documents. Punch the documents squarely using the guide rule on the punch or align the arrow in the centre with the centre of your document (*gently* fold the document in half first).

Stage 4: Actual filing

Locate each folder and pull it out gently – *never* tug it by the tab or you are likely to end up with the tab left in your hand and the job of having to replace the folder with a new one! Double check the name to make sure you have the correct file. Put the documents in the folder in chronological order with the most recent at the top.

Replace the folder – but be careful. If your suspension pockets are not continuous, do make sure you don't drop a folder between two pockets – otherwise it will simply slide down to the bottom of the drawer and may be lost for months. And do make sure, also, that you always replace folders *behind* their identifying tab – not in front of it.

Stage 5: Solving problems

It is wise to deal with problems as they occur, rather than saving them all up for another day, when tackling them becomes overwhelming or even depressing. Every time you are filing you are likely to find:

*   some documents which don't seem to go anywhere
*   some documents which could go in more than one place
*   the file folder you need is missing.

A 'one-off' document may go in a miscellaneous file *or* a new file may have to be started (see pages 316 and 319–324).

Updating records

There are a variety of records you may need to update as part of your job. Organisations change their name, their address, their telephone number (or dialling code). These may be recorded on index cards linked to your filing system. If the name changes, you will also have to change the name on the folder – and move it to a new location if it is in an alphabetical system. People borrow files and return them – they will not think much of you if you forget to update your records so that a file they have returned still shows as 'outstanding'. If you have a master list of files, then this will need updating whenever you start a new file (see page 317).

The worst thing you can do is jot down important information on scraps of paper with the aim of updating the records in a day or two. You will be lucky if you can find the scraps of paper by then and in the meantime the records are out of date. Confine yourself to using a proper notebook and clearly cross out information you have transferred. Check names and spellings if you are ever in doubt. Write with a suitable pen and print letters on folders and tabs – in particular, if your writing is difficult to read.

In some organisations there is no need to record every document placed in a file. However, that is not always the case. There are some types of file kept by certain types of firm which have a 'file log' detailing, literally, every single bit of paper in the file. This system is often used when a series of documents are required to complete a particular transaction or piece of business.

The aim is usually to provide a brief summary of the file contents so that progress can be determined quickly without having to read through the whole file. An example is when your doctor writes on the front of your record folder a summary of your visits and the actions taken. Other examples include:

- solicitors logging documents placed into a client file so that they can check quickly how far they are through a legal process
- insurance brokers logging when quotations are received from insurance companies and sent to clients
- estate agents logging the progress of a sale, such as the number of enquiries, viewings and then the whole process of the sale
- accountants logging when financial information has been received from clients, when the tax return has been completed and sent to the Inland Revenue, and when the tax owing has been agreed
- doctors logging when responses have been received from consultants or when test results have arrived.

If you work for any of these types of organisation you may find that you have to complete a summary to identify every single item you place into a file. The summary is often clipped to the front, or inside the front cover.

If this system operates in your workplace, the skill you need to learn is how to summarise the information so that it is clear to the reader, yet still succinct. You will not be expected to make a lengthy entry which uses up most of the log sheet, nor will you be expected to be so brief that the entry is meaningless! The easiest way to develop this skill is to read examples written by other people who have more experience, or to ask for specific guidance if you are holding a document you don't understand.

Another occasion is when information is logged for particular types of files in a department. Most finance departments log all the invoices that have been received, human resource departments log the applications that have been received in response to an advertisement, any administrator will log replies that have been received to invitations – whether to a meeting or to a special event.

INFORMATION UPDATE

Today, many organisations log information electronically rather than by hand. Large insurance companies, when dealing with claims, immediately give each claim a reference number and then *all* documents related to it are stored in a computerised filing system. Standard letters are produced by the system, received documents are scanned into the system, and the whole file can be accessed on screen at any time.

At a more basic level, many finance departments record invoices generated and received using a spreadsheet package, so that the total amounts owed and owing adjust automatically with each new entry.

TEST YOUR KNOWLEDGE AND UNDERSTANDING

1 You work in the human resources department and progress with all applications is logged carefully. Firstly, all vacancies are given a code and all applications are allocated a number and listed on a sheet. Those applicants who are shortlisted are signified as SL on this sheet. A list is then prepared of all shortlisted applicants and a note is entered against each when references have been received and placed in the file.

a Your colleague, Royston, had been filling in the sheets for an Administrative Assistant vacancy but completed only the first sheet before he was asked to do something else and hand over the job to you. Make out a list of the shortlisted applicants from the information given on page 314.

b Your supervisor informs you that two references have been received for Mick Yates, Shamila Choudrey and Karen Watts, and only one reference received for Jackie Bryant. Update your sheet with this information.

c What do you think is the purpose of logging all applicants and then all references?

d Discuss your ideas and check your shortlist sheet with your supervisor or tutor.

2 You work for Sarah Dover who is the Customer Services Manager of a large retail store. All complaints are logged but serious complaints also have a file summary on the front so that progress can be constantly monitored.

The first stage, always, is for the company to send a standard letter acknowledging receipt of the complaint. Sarah will then answer the letter or send a further letter, saying the complaint is being investigated.

Mrs Jane Bradley complained because a pair of jeans bought for her son had frayed within a month. The summary on page 315 shows the entries on the folder so far.

a This morning, 4 July, Sarah gives you the following documents to place in the file:
  i a laboratory report dated 30 June stating that the fabric had a substantial flaw
  ii a copy of a letter she has written today to the suppliers asking for an explanation
  iii a copy of a letter she has written to Mrs Bradley today enclosing a voucher for £50.

b Write down the entries you would make for each of these documents.

c Why do you think you would be expected to write your initials alongside each entry you make?

Check your ideas and your summaries with your supervisor or tutor.

HUMAN RESOURCES DEPARTMENT
VACANCY FOR ADMINISTRATIVE ASSISTANT

Ref no: 203   **Closing date: 31/10/01**

Name of applicant	Ref. no.	Shortlisted (Y/N)
Deborah Ainsworth	203/1	N
Allan Bold	203/2	N
Jackie Bryant	203/4	Y
Shamila Choudrey	203/5	Y
Tamira Khan	203/6	N
John McIntyre	203/7	N
Rachel Osborne	203/8	Y
Petra Stevens	203/9	N
Karen Watts	203/10	Y
Mick Yates	203/11	Y

FILE SUMMARY

File title: Mrs Jane Bradley, 50 Windermere Road, Chelmsford

Document date	Summary	Date filed	Initials
20 June	Complaint received about rapid fraying of jeans	25 June	JA
25 June	Acknowledgement letter sent	26 June	JA
25 June	Request for laboratory report on fabric	26 June	JA

Procedures for cross-referencing

You may have difficulties deciding where to store a document which could go in more than one place. This is when the **cross-referencing** system is used. This means you put the document in the most likely place and put a reference in the other files. In some organisations the document itself is copied and put in all the files. However, this can create problems as it is costly to keep photocopying documents and file folders are apt to become full much more quickly.

Another time when cross-referencing is used is for associated companies and, in this case, if you use a numerical filing system you will also have to put a cross-reference into the index system. For instance, if you have a file already for Downham Supplies, no. 3002, and they expand their business and start up Downham Direct where goods can be ordered on-line, your supervisor may still want all documents stored in the original file. In this case, in the index you would insert a reference strip or card:

Downham Direct See under Downham Supplies, 3002

Procedures for opening new files

Unless there are proper procedures for opening new files it is very easy to create one of the following problems:

- there are numerous file folders containing only one or two documents
- there are *duplicate* file folders for similar things, with important information split between different folders.

Avoiding 'tiny' files

Tiny files waste space and materials, given you need to use a new document folder each time you start a new file. This danger occurs when you have a new customer or topic and start a new file and then find that after an initial enquiry or document nothing else happens.

For this reason, most supervisors prefer you to check whether a new file should be started or whether the papers should go into a 'miscellaneous' file. The procedures will vary from one organisation to another.

- In some organisations, such as a hospital, all files must be kept separate. Therefore a new patient would *always* have a new file, even if he or she visited only once.
- In commercial organisations, there may be a system whereby new customer files are started only after an initial order has been placed – or even later.

Some people consider that **miscellaneous files** are a nuisance because everyone forgets to look in them when searching for a document. Others consider that miscellaneous documents should be kept completely separate, such as in an A4 lever arch file. Yet others consider that miscellaneous files are useful and there should be one for each letter of the alphabet, and papers should be transferred only when there are six or more on a related person or topic.

It will therefore depend very much upon the type of organisation you work for and your supervisor's opinion of miscellaneous files!

Avoiding duplicate files

Duplicate files most commonly occur when you are filing by subject. This is because names cannot be considered in more than one way but topics certainly can! One person may therefore file all information on employees under 'staff' and another may file it under 'personnel'. Worse, both people use the same system and some information is in one folder and some is in another.

The most sensible course of action is to have a printed list of all the files currently in use and to check this carefully before starting any new file. It is always worth checking with your supervisor before you think of starting a new file, to find out if it really is necessary in this situation. If it is, remember that you will have to make out a new folder *and* also make out a new visual tab for the drawer or cupboard and add the name to any existing file list.

EVIDENCE COLLECTION

1 Either keep a record of the type of information you have recorded, *or* ask whether you can take a photocopy of file logs or other documents you routinely update. Alternatively, if your assessor visits you, have available some examples of recent paper records you have made to confirm that information has been stored.

2 Obtain witness testimony from your supervisor to prove that:
   • you regularly keep information safe and intact
   • you update and store new information promptly
   • you store information only according to the established procedures for your filing system.

3 Write a brief account of the cross-referencing system you use and the procedures you must follow for opening a new file. Be prepared to discuss these with your assessor.

4 Remember that although you may be using only one filing system at work (alphabetical, numerical, alphanumerical or chronological) you will have to prove to your assessor that you understand how to use the other three systems, both for this element and the next.

Element 205.2 Retrieve and supply information

The opposite task to storing information is, of course, to find it again. This is when all your good work pays off. The more up to date, neat and orderly your system, the easier it is to find what you have put away.

For this element you will again have to show that you can use at least two of the following types of filing system: alphabetical, numerical, alpha-numerical, chronological. If you work with only two systems you may have to prove to your assessor that you could deal competently with the others. You will also have to provide evidence relating to:

- the records you keep when information is removed
- what you do if items are missing or overdue
- the action you would take if you provided information which was not what was really wanted.

All these topics are dealt with in this section.

Retrieving and removing information

There are two main reasons why you will need to retrieve a file, or a document contained in a file:

a   You are adding to the file yourself, and need to find a particular file to put a document away.

b   Either you or someone else wants the file – or some information it contains – for a particular purpose. Fundamentally, this is the main reason for keeping files in the first place. If no one ever needed to access them, the filing system would be, quite literally, a waste of space.

Virtually all organisations have established procedures which must be followed if a manual file is borrowed or removed from the system for any reason. This is important, otherwise other users who may need the same information urgently will have no idea where to find it.

Golden rules for lending paper files

1   *Never* lend individual documents from a folder if you can possibly avoid it. The only possible exceptions should be:

   a   if the file is large and someone wants to take some specific information home or to a business meeting out of the office and obviously doesn't want to transport a large file

   b   if the file contains information that is confidential and yet a person needs access to a document which is not (in this case they may be given permission to have just that document).

To prevent confusion, in most organisations you would have to photocopy a document that was required, rather than remove it from the file, so that the file as a whole remained intact.

If an original document must be removed, then write a note in its place in the file and clearly state who has it, when it was borrowed and when it will be returned. Put another entry in your diary or in the file log (see below) so that you remember to remind the borrower if it isn't returned on time.

2 When a file is borrowed it is usual to record this on a log or list. Some organisations use a log book or file diary. Others use a card index system. The usual headings are shown below:

Name of file	Date borrowed	Borrower	Date returned

3 Put a marker or 'out card' where the folder is normally kept. Ideally you will also record the agreed date of return on this.

4 Files should not be lent for an unspecified time. Agree with the borrower when the file will be returned *at the time it is lent*.

5 Check the log regularly and chase up any outstanding files not returned. If the borrower wants to extend the loan period you can ask for the file to be returned temporarily if you have documents waiting to go into it.

Identifying and reporting problems

A nightmare scenario, as you saw on page 304, is an important file or document going missing. Although you may have instructions that you should report missing items immediately, this does not mean you shouldn't use your own initiative at all to try to solve the problem first – and sometimes some simple detective work can work wonders.

First step – don't panic. The calmer you remain the greater likelihood of success! Second step – don't blame anyone else. If you later find the file on your own desk you will feel silly and may have made a few enemies!

a Start by checking the file diary or log to see whether someone has borrowed it and hasn't returned it.

b If a recent entry shows the file has been returned, check whether this is accurate information or if, for some reason, the borrower still has it.

c If there is no recent entry in the diary or log, check all the obvious places where the file might be – tops of filing cabinets and desks, your boss's 'out' tray, in the drawer itself (i.e. *under* the suspension units or in the wrong section).

d Check whether there is a cross-reference entry under which the folder could have been placed.

e Try to find out when it was last seen and/or who may be working on it.

f If you operate an alphabetical system, try to think of similar names the file may have been stored under. If you operate a numerical system, look at the file number carefully and then assume someone has read it wrongly, or transposed the numbers. For instance, could file 631 have been filed under 637 or 831 or 837 or even under 136 or 316 or 361?

g Ask your colleagues (or e-mail them) to find out if anyone has borrowed it.

If the missing item is a document you can still follow the same course of action – but don't forget to check the filing tray, any pending trays and your concertina file, too, if you routinely use one for pre-sorted documents.

If the missing item is found, try to find out why the system isn't working properly. Was the cabinet left unlocked so that anyone could help themselves, did a new member of staff borrow the file who perhaps didn't know how the system operates? Then see if you can make an appropriate suggestion to improve the system and prevent the problem recurring (see below).

If the missing item is still not found, then you will have to report it – even if you dread the thought. You will actually feel better if you own up to the problem than if you keep it to yourself for days, hoping against hope it will turn up before someone needs it. You may even find that the person to whom you must report the problem actually has the missing item – you never know!

Do bear in mind, however, that although a single document may be more difficult to find, it is easier to replace than a whole file full of documents.

EVIDENCE COLLECTION

In addition to evidence that you can retrieve information without difficulty, your assessor will also require evidence that you keep a record when information or files are removed. If you have a file log or diary, ask whether you can photocopy this for your portfolio – however, do make sure there is some proof that the entries on this have been made by you! For instance, you could ask your supervisor to confirm this if the entries are not in handwriting.

You will also need to show that you know what to do if an item is missing *and* that you could tactfully remind borrowers who are holding on to overdue files to return them. If either of these situations occurs, write a brief account of what you did and the outcome. If you send a written reminder to a borrower, put a copy in your portfolio. If neither situation occurs, don't worry – but remember your assessor will want to discuss these types of problem with you.

INFORMATION UPDATE

A new invention is the Trans-action file which is made by a company called Rackline. These are lateral files which are fitted with a special hook which means that not only can the file be removed easily, but any working papers can easily be clipped to the actual file folder. If people regularly want to keep certain active papers separate from the file in your workplace – or if people are regularly borrowing files – you could suggest that this type of system might be more appropriate for the active files in your office.

Solving other problems

A variety of problems can occur with a filing system, no matter how well it was set up in the first place. Some of these are related to the people who use it and others are related to the system itself.

Problems with the users

These may include:

- users who don't follow the procedures laid down
- users who don't understand the system
- users who are careless or try to rush the job because they don't like it.

In the first category will be people who try to borrow files without asking, don't return files which are overdue, or ask for information to which they are not entitled. These people may include your colleagues or your supervisors. Normally, however, senior staff are keen to ensure that important information is protected and will support you if you have a problem with a particular person.

In the second category are users who perhaps don't need files very often, such as representatives or others who are often out of the office. They may visit you infrequently and think they can just help themselves. They may even be helpful and offer to put back information for you – and then put it back in the wrong place! The trick here is to identify who are the problem people and keep them away from your system by offering to help. It may create work initially but will save you time in the long run. New staff may also present problems – the obvious strategy is to make sure new staff can use the system only after they have been informed about the procedures to be followed.

Users who are careless may be colleagues who dislike filing and try to do it quickly. They may hope that if they make a complete mess of the job they will no longer have to do it! This is not advisable for anyone, as the impression they are giving of their overall abilities is very poor. Filing may be tedious at times, but it is not usually difficult. However, it is a good measure of a person's ability to concentrate, take care and be methodical – all invaluable administrative skills! If you have a serious problem with a particular colleague, have a quiet chat with your mentor or supervisor in confidence.

Problems with the system

Most problems with paper-based filing systems occur over a period of time. They include:

- folders becoming too full so that no more documents can be added
- cabinet drawers becoming too full with no more space for new files
- as the filing system is expanding, files are more difficult to find
- congestion in particular areas of an alphabetical-by-name system
- duplication of files in an alphabetical-by-subject system
- too much filing to do, so that it is taking up an immense amount of time.

Folders which are becoming too full must be divided into two. It is sensible to put the start and end date on the first folder and then to just put the start date on the next one. This helps to guide people who are looking for a particular document. It is also worth checking with your supervisor whether all the documents in a general folder must be retained, or whether some can be thrown away. A general folder which has been in operation for several years may easily contain outdated information. It is also worth checking your cross-referencing system – to make sure people aren't routinely copying documents into several files simultaneously – which will contribute to them becoming full much faster.

If a cabinet drawer is becoming overcrowded, a first step is to see whether you have space in the rest of the cabinet to rearrange the folders – but this may mean re-labelling the drawers themselves. Periodically you will find that your supervisor will want to prune files to make more room, but you should do this task only *under instruction* – otherwise you may accidentally throw away something important.

Most companies operate some type of **retention policy** – especially as some documents must be kept for a specific length of time by law. Accident reports, for instance, have to be kept for 30 years and tax assessments for 12 years. If you work in a human resources or finance section, or for an accountant or solicitor, you will find that a considerable number of documents must be retained for very long periods. Normally these are not kept in the main filing system but are **archived** and stored in another area, such as the basement.

If you work in an expanding company, where the filing system is growing, there are several problems you may encounter, in addition to the above. You may find that the sheer number of files makes it difficult to retrieve information quickly. A sensible step is to think about introducing colour coding (i.e. different coloured folders for different categories of documents) – so that certain files show up immediately.

If you operate an alphabetical system using, say, customers' names, you may have problems with common letters such as B, S and T. Therefore the spacing you originally allocated in the drawers is no longer appropriate. Before you start moving all the files around, it is worth considering whether another system might now be more appropriate, such as numerical or alphanumerical, and you could suggest this to your supervisor.

Subject files are probably one of the worst types for becoming disorganised. Often documents will be received which could be put under more than one heading – especially internal documents. There is a danger, if several people use the system, that new folders are made out for a topic which already exists, but under a slightly different name. Every twelve months it is worth going through such files to check whether they are still current or whether there are any duplications. You will know if this is a possibility because the system will have become more and more unworkable and documents will have become very difficult to find!

If the actual number of documents to be filed is increasing dramatically, this is another problem for staff – particularly if it is taking up increasing time simply to keep on top of it. This is a problem to discuss with your supervisor, who will want to identify whether this is a continuing trend or a minor blip, because of some special event or occurrence. If people routinely put every document for filing, then a first step could be for them to be more selective over the items they want to keep – especially as recent studies have shown that over 80 per cent of filed information is never looked at again! Items stored on disk, for instance, could be retained in electronic format rather than in hard copy. Staff should also be discouraged from printing out and filing dozens of e-mails, or only marginally relevant information from the Internet, and then filing these.

If, however, all the items are important and the situation is continuing, your supervisor may wish to consider reallocating duties or getting you some help, rather than risk the filing getting out of date. Or you could try to talk your supervisor into obtaining information on converting to an electronic filing system. If you already use Windows software on your computer and have a scanner, you could argue you're already part-way there!

Passing on information

You will often have to pass on information for someone who has asked for it, such as 'Can you find me the results of the customer survey we did last year?' You will be expected to do this promptly – particularly if the information is needed urgently – and may be asked to provide it in a certain format. Your success will depend upon the following factors:

- how well you know your system
- the degree to which the request is precise or accurate
- whether you ever received the document in question!

If you know your system very well you may be able to go immediately to the file which contains the correct document. If you do not, then your first thought may be 'Customer surveys, customer surveys – where on earth do we keep them?' Rather than hunt high and low, ask someone else who may know, to save time.

If, however, your company didn't do a customer survey last year – or did six – you will need to go back to the person who made the request to find out what is wanted. It would be sensible to take the whole file with you, so that he or she can decide whether there is anything similar contained in it.

Equally, if you can find only the survey itself, but not the results, this may be because you never received them. Again, you would need to inform the enquirer of this fact – and again it is useful to take the file with you when you do.

If nothing in the file is suitable, and your colleague is still desperate for information, there are several alternatives to suggest:

- If the document is internal, will anyone else have a copy?
- If it was external, could the source be contacted for another copy?
- If it was prepared on computer, might a copy be held electronically on disk?
- If it was an e-mail, is it still in the mailbox or was it saved?
- If it was a press clipping or the result of research, will the library have a copy or could you obtain one on the Internet?

In addition, if you really know your system well, you may be able to think of:

- other files in which similar information may be found
- other documents in which similar details are given.

If your suggestions are rejected, don't be downhearted. You may have triggered a few ideas in the mind of the other person as to where some useful information could be found. In addition, you will have proved that you can take a positive and proactive approach when you encounter a problem – which is far, far better than simply shrugging your shoulders and walking away!

TEST YOUR KNOWLEDGE AND UNDERSTANDING

You are responsible for helping Deepa, a new member of staff, to learn how to file properly. Although she can do routine jobs she still refers to you when she has a problem. How would you advise her in each of the following cases? Discuss your suggestions with your supervisor or tutor.

1 She has mistakenly punched a set of documents in the wrong place so that they aren't aligned in the folder.

2 She has made out a folder with the wrong name but there isn't room on the tab to correct it. ➡

3 Even though she can remember putting some documents into a file this morning and putting the folder away, she now can't find it in the cabinet.

4 A memo from a senior manager needs to be filed which refers to four customers. She doesn't know which file to put it in.

5 There are ten documents waiting to be put in one file which is out on loan. Although she has telephoned the borrower twice as the file is overdue, it still hasn't been returned.

6 Your supervisor needs to take one file to a meeting this afternoon. This was borrowed by another colleague yesterday and today he is having a personal day's holiday.

7 An important document had to be filed in file 76071 this morning. Deepa remembers filing it, yet the supervisor has now looked in the folder and asked her where it is. To Deepa's horror, she can't see it. Her supervisor has given her ten minutes to find it.

8 Deepa has been asked by a colleague for a copy of a blank appraisal form but she can't find one. She asks you if she can have access to the personnel files where a completed appraisal form will be kept, so she can give him this instead.

EVIDENCE COLLECTION

The final type of evidence you need to provide is to prove that you are thoughtful, positive and proactive if problems occur and that you can suggest alternatives if information you have obtained does not match a person's requirements.

For this reason, if you do have to deal with problem situations and make suggestions, do make a note of this (see also the Key Skills signpost on page 284). It is even better if you can make your suggestion to someone in writing (even if this is only an e-mail or brief note) and include a copy of their response. However, no one is asking you to invent problems just to gain the award. Your assessor will be able to ask you questions on this topic if you haven't encountered any problems so far.

The same applies to being asked for information. If you have passed on information which is not in the correct format and then made some useful suggestions, either write a brief account and ask the person to countersign it, or ask the person for witness testimony. Otherwise, your assessor can again assess your abilities in this area by question and answer.

Unit 206 Enter, retrieve and print data in a database

> This unit is one of two in Option Group A.
> Select *either* this unit *or* Unit 205 – but not both!

You may not realise this, but you have actually been handling databases for some time! The only difference between those databases and the ones you will read about in this unit is that many databases with which you are familiar are in paper form. They include:

- any address books you may have
- your telephone directory or *Yellow Pages*
- any lists you keep of videos, records or CDs you own.

These are all databases because they are **structured** sets of data. 'Structured' means that they are organised in a particular way, so that you can find what you want as well as add new items of information easily.

Today when we talk about databases we are usually referring to data stored on a computer. Computers have revolutionised the type of information that can be stored – in terms of its volume, complexity, flexibility and ease of access. Therefore, whether you work for a small firm which wants to keep a list of its clients or customers on a simple database, or for a large national organisation which has databases for thousands of customers and products, there is a useful application for a database for your employer.

You should select this unit, rather than 205, if you regularly work on a database to enter, retrieve and print data. It does not matter if this is on a large or small scale; you can use any computer program capable of processing data to achieve this unit.

Note that if you have permission only to read database records and print reports then you will *not* be able to generate the appropriate evidence for this unit. The first element specifically requires that you input data.

 KEY SKILLS SIGNPOST

If you are taking your Key Skills award, you will find there are opportunities in this unit to obtain evidence towards the **Problem Solving** key skills unit. The list opposite relates to Level 2.

PS2.1

The following problems can occur with entering, retrieving and printing information in a database.

- There are a number of details you would like to record on a particular form but there are no fields for this data. This also limits the type of reports you can produce.
- There are many new users of the system who do not understand how it really works. Some people are simply careless, and inputting errors are causing considerable problems. Yesterday, several customers received reminders for non-payment because payments had been logged into the wrong records. In other cases, you are finding that users are ignoring the problem when they can't find a record and simply not bothering to update the record or report their difficulty. The overall result is that the data is becoming too inaccurate to be usable.
- You update the database as part of your job but find it difficult to do this regularly when you are very busy with other tasks. You are worried that people are using out-of-date information simply because you haven't been able to update the records quickly enough.
- You work in a sales department and are frequently asked for reports on sales by your boss, the Sales Manager, and various representatives. Often these are 'duplicates' in that different people may request a copy of the same report several times during a week. You think there must be a better way of issuing reports which are regularly required – and sometimes wonder why some staff cannot print off their own from your networked system as it is taking you so much time.

For *any two* of these problems (or for an alternative problem you have agreed with your tutor or supervisor):

a explain the main features of the problem and why it occurs
b identify what would be the ideal situation you would want to achieve
c suggest different ways of tackling the problem
d decide which would have the most chance of success, bearing in mind factors such as health and safety, time, resources, the expertise required and the views of other people.

PS2.2

Do the following for each of the problems you have selected.

a Obtain approval for either your chosen option to solve the problem, or for an alternative option, with your supervisor or tutor.

b Prepare a plan, showing the sequence of tasks you will undertake and the time, resources and assistance you will need.

c Carry out your tasks, but be prepared to make changes to your plan to show you are responsive to suggestions to overcome unforeseen difficulties.

d Obtain and use support from other people when it is offered, whether it be your supervisor, tutor or colleagues.

PS2.3

Do the following for each of the problems you have selected.

a Decide and agree the methods you can use to check if the problem has now been solved.

b Apply these methods to make your checks, and describe the results.

c Explain the decisions you had to make when you were implementing your plan, and any changes you had to make.

d Identify what you did well and assess anything that went wrong. Summarise these as the strengths and weaknesses of your approach. Use these to conclude what you would do differently next time if you had to solve a similar problem.

Computerised databases

If you use one as part of your job, you should already know what a database is, why they are used and their main benefits. You should also know the correct terms to use for the various routines you carry out.

On the other hand, if you have been carrying out these database tasks as routine operations, without thinking much about what you are doing, use this unit as an opportunity to extend your knowledge and understanding of databases as a whole. Then if your job is changed – or you change employer – you will be better able to describe your skills and use them in a different situation.

For that reason, before we cover the requirements of each element of the unit, we will start by looking at the main features which apply to all databases.

Understanding databases

What is a database?

A database stores information in a structured way electronically. It is like a giant electronic filing system. Each database record contains relevant information – like a card record which can be viewed on screen. Today, databases range from the very small (for instance, to keep a record of your friends' names and addresses or details of your CD collection) to vast on-line databases such as Britannica.com, which gives much of the information from the *Encyclopaedia Britannica* on-line. Your organisation may have internal databases for:

- customer records
- product lines
- spare parts
- staff records.

The type of database system in use will depend upon whether you work on a computer network or a stand-alone PC and whether there are single or multiple users accessing the system simultaneously. However, certain basic principles apply to most databases:

- Each database is a set of information relating to a specific topic or subject (e.g. customers, products, suppliers).
- A database comprises **forms** which are designed to hold certain information.
- Each form is comprised of **fields** under which one piece of information is stored.
- Some fields must be completed but others can be left blank.
- The size of each field may be limited.
- Data in a field can be edited or changed.
- When the fields are completed each form becomes a database **record**.
- Data is organised in such a way that it is simple to find information by searching for it.

Benefits of databases

The main advantage of a database is the speed with which information can be found and sorted. All databases are designed to enable the user to search for information and to produce reports which order and display the information in a specific way. The following are some examples:

- On a customer database, you could search for a customer if you knew the name but not the address or if you knew the customer code but nothing else, and you could print a report listing all the customers in a particular area.

- On a product database, you could search for details by product code, by type or by price, and you could print a report listing all your products which sell for less than, say, £10.
- On a spare parts database, you could search on criteria such as availability or model of appliance and print a report listing all the items currently in or out of stock.
- On a staff database, you could print reports listing staff by department, by age or by salary.

Another major benefit is that more information is available to users – although access is likely to be controlled for security reasons (see page 338). This helps managers who need information to make decisions, and helps administrators who regularly need information to deal with enquiries.

The database can be set up so that important information must be entered on each record before it is 'accepted' by the system. This improves the accuracy and reliability of the information contained in the database. For instance, you are unlikely to be able to create a customer record unless you enter the full address and postcode. In addition, the postcode itself can be checked against a special 'postcode' database which stops anyone making an invalid entry.

Finally, a large database would be structured for the needs of the whole organisation and controlled by a Database Administrator, who would also be responsible for its development and the creation of new reports that users need.

Types of database, from the simple to the complex

The simplest type

A simple database used to store information on one topic is a **flat** database. Think of it as a set of electronic index cards which you can search through very quickly to find the particular records you need. You may hear this referred to as a **file management system**, because such a database is a set of files on one topic.

Among the simplest types of 'ready-made' database are electronic address books, which are provided with many software packages, including e-mail. These have many of the features of complex databases in miniature, so they are a useful way to learn about the fundamental principles of a database.

In an address book there are pre-designed forms and specified fields into which you enter data, so they are quick and easy to use. One disadvantage is that there may be several fields you do not need, or some you would like to have which are not available. This is why it is an advantage to be able to create or use a database designed especially for your own needs.

Jenny is setting up an address book for her main customers. She starts by entering information on each one on a blank form. She checks each one carefully to make sure it is correct. The record she has created for Jane Scott is shown below.

When Jenny wants to find an address she looks at the index. This shows all her records in a columnar table. Jenny can decide which columns she wants to see when she looks at the index, and the order in which they appear. She can also choose how to list records by 'sorting' them. She has started by sorting them in order of town or city.

However, she decides later that she would prefer customers in alphabetical order. She therefore accesses her 'sort' facility and changes the order in which they appear.

Column Sort

Column to sort by first:

- E-Mail Type
- Facsimile Number
- First Name
- Greeting
- Home Phone Number
- **Last Name**
- Mailstop
- Name
- Organisation
- Phone Number

OK

Cancel

Help

Sort order
- ● Ascending sort
- ○ Descending sort

Corel Address Book

Book Edit View Address Help

My Addresses | Frequent Contacts

Search List (F2)

Name	Phone Number	Address	City	Postcode	E-Mail Address

Name	Phone Number	Address	City	Postcode	E-Mail Address
James Bryant	0161-530-6000	Waterside	MANCHESTER	M25 4KL	jb@starfish.co.uk
Riaz Hussain	0121-467-9021	Albany Heights	BIRMINGHAM	B15 7KP	riaz@tradewind.co.uk
Rehana Patel	01253-785988	Talbot Road	BLACKPOOL	BP3 4KK	RehanaP@towerent.co.uk
Jane Scott	0161-247-398...	Pinehead Road	MANCHESTER	M60 4YB	janescott@fenner.co.uk
Ben Watson	0151-350-2998	Jerrard Way	LIVERPOOL	L12 6SM	benw@benson.co.uk

Close Dial... Add... Remove... Edit... Address List >>

Jenny is pleased with the start she has made, and knows that it is easy to amend data if necessary, by bringing up any record and editing the entry in a particular field. She also likes the fact that she can search for any name she knows using the 'search' facility.

Databases created for a purpose

Databases can be created on a PC by using a program such as Microsoft's Access or Corel's Paradox. These use exactly the same principles as Jenny's address book, although they have more sophisticated features.

The designer normally *starts* with a columnar table and specifies the fields required, by deciding first the number of fields. A field is required for *each* separate piece of information, so first names and last names, for instance, require *two* fields. Then each field is given a title or name. The length of each field is now determined – it must be sufficient for the number of characters or digits required. Finally, the type of data which will be input is decided – this is so important it is dealt with separately below.

Once all this has been done, the design of a blank form is decided. The form should be designed with the user in mind – to make it logical and easy to complete.

The designer will then consider three other aspects:

- the type of searches users will wish to make
- the ways in which the information on screen will need to be sorted
- the type of reports that will be required.

As an example, Joe works for a vet. He is designing a database which will enable the practice to keep customer records and record when pets visit the surgery. He wants to use the database to remind people when their pets are due to be inoculated. He starts by creating a table and entering his first record. This is shown in the illustration above.

Key field and data types

The first column in Joe's table is simply a number. This is inserted automatically by the package. It is very important because it will be the key field for the database. This means it is the only field which is *always* going to be unique for each record. Joe could have renamed this 'customer number' had he wished, or given it any other unique identifying title.

Joe now decides which type of data must be entered into each field.

- **Text entries** are for fields containing text and numbers – such as an address.

- **Numeric entries** are for fields containing numbers used in calculations.

- **Date/time entries** are obvious. These fields will accept entries only of dates or times. Joe used this for his final column 'date last inoculated'.

- **Currency fields** will accept only monetary values (e.g. £45).

- **Yes/no fields** will accept only one of two options, either yes/no, true/false or on/off.

- **Memo fields** for long text entries such as general comments.

Joe knows that specifying the correct data type for each field will help to prevent users making errors when updating a record, because the system will prompt them if they try to enter the wrong type.

Complex relational databases

Large organisations may have several databases, each designed for a particular purpose. If you work for a large company you may use a customer database which also links to the product database and the sales database, from which all invoices are produced. This would enable you to find a customer record when an order is received, and immediately check whether each item requested is in stock.

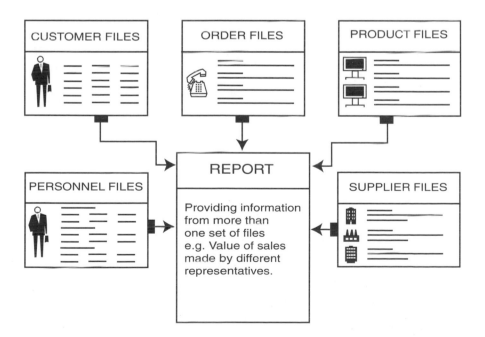

CUSTOMER FILES

ORDER FILES

PRODUCT FILES

PERSONNEL FILES

REPORT

Providing information from more than one set of files e.g. Value of sales made by different representatives.

SUPPLIER FILES

A database which is linked to one or more other databases is called a **relational database**. For instance, if you took an order for a customer and used a relational database, the goods requested would be:

- logged on the customer record
- logged as a sales record to produce an invoice
- automatically deducted from the stock database.

Further, if an item is updated on one database, which is common to others, this will be updated automatically on all the related databases at the same time.

A relational database is a centrally designed and controlled system which you may find is referred to as a **database management system** (DBMS). The relationship is illustrated in the diagram on page 335.

EVIDENCE COLLECTION

Which type of database do you use regularly? How complex is it? Was it designed within your organisation or bought from a specialist provider? Is it a relational database? What features does it have to help prevent you making errors when you enter data?

Find out the answers to these questions to help you understand more about the database you will use to obtain your evidence for this unit. Your assessor will find it helpful if you write a brief description of the database to put in your portfolio, as this helps to explain the type of evidence you will be producing.

Element 206.1 Enter and find data

Obtaining clear information on data to be entered and found

Information on data to be entered

Information to be entered may be given to you in various ways.

- You may transfer paper records on to an electronic database.

- If you speak to customers over the telephone, you may ask them questions to enable you to complete the record during the conversation.

- You may be given an amended database printout as a source document.

- You may be given verbal instructions on the changes to make.

- You may be responsible, as part of your job, for keeping a database up to date – for instance, by entering price changes on a product database and simply be given a basic instruction (e.g. 'increase all sales prices by 3 per cent').

You must check carefully that you have all the information you need and query (not guess!) any data which is unclear or ambiguous. For instance, an incorrect entry on a product database could result in additional stock being ordered when it is unnecessary, or items being listed as 'out of stock' when they are not.

Information on data to be found

You will waste considerable time and effort in searching a large database without knowing what it is you are supposed to be looking for or how to find it. More typically, however, you may *think* you know what you are looking for, but the reality may be somewhat different. If you have 36 customer records under the name Patel or Smith, then knowing this basic fact is insufficient (as you will see on page 341). You would either have to obtain more information or run the risk that you access the wrong record or then enter data into the wrong record. In a 'worst case scenario' this could result in the wrong Mr Patel or Mrs Smith receiving a cheque as a refund or a bill.

Therefore, accessing the wrong record can cause considerable problems. Depending upon why your database is used, you may:

- spend a tremendous amount of time looking for non-existent records

- print out dozens of records for someone when only one is required
- enter new data into the wrong record
- amend correct data – so that it is now incorrect
- cause inconvenience for customers or employees if they are contacted because of the incorrect entry.

It obviously helps if you know how to search and sort your records to find what you need quickly and easily. You have already seen how Jenny did this (page 332) and will find further details on pages 341–342.

Permission to access database files

Quite obviously, not all database files are available to everyone in the organisation. You are unlikely, for instance, to be able to access the staff database to find out how much your line manager earns! Quite apart from the restrictions of the Data Protection Act (see pages 286–288), there are other good reasons why access to databases is restricted, such as confidentiality issues.

- Sensitive company and financial information will not be accessible to anyone except senior managers.
- Routine information (e.g. on customers and products) will be available to most staff to *read* on screen, but cannot be changed. They will, however, be able to print routine reports.
- Data input and amendments will be restricted to trained staff so that changes and amendments are controlled and can be checked.

Database form and report design – and the type of reports available – will usually be undertaken by specialist staff – such as the Database Administrator.

Even the simplest database, produced on a PC, can be 'protected' by means of a password. Complex databases operate a more sophisticated system, based on a system of 'user groups'.

Depending upon which user group you are in, you will find you have a specific 'view' of the database, depending upon how access has been structured. You will normally be able to read more than you can alter (or 'write'), and won't be able to see everything that is stored. This is controlled by assigning access rights to different groups, as you will see below.

TEST YOUR KNOWLEDGE AND UNDERSTANDING

An access table for a personnel database is shown opposite. This specifies which user groups can read the various fields of the database and which user groups can read and write (i.e. alter) certain fields. Study this and answer the questions which follow. ➡

1 All staff belong to user group 1, but only the switchboard operator and a few other selected people belong to user group 2.

   a What key information is provided to all staff through this database?

   b Why do you think the switchboard operator belongs to user group 2?

2 User group 3 includes all staff in the personnel department and some managers. Give *two* reasons why all staff should not be able to read all these items.

3 User group 4 is all senior managers. To what additional information do they have access and why do you think they need it?

4 User group 5 includes selected members of the personnel department. Why do you think they do not need 'write' access to item 4?

5 User group 6 is highly restricted and comprises two senior staff, one in personnel and one in salaries. Why do you think this restriction is necessary?

6 The items denote fields on the database record.

   a Can you think of any additional fields which would be useful on a personnel database?

   b For each new item you suggest, what read or write access rights would you give to each user group?

EXAMPLE OF ACCESS RIGHTS FOR A PERSONNEL DATABASE

User group	Item 1 Staff name	Item 2 Staff address	Item 3 Extension no.	Item 4 DOB	Item 5 Date started	Item 6 Salary
1	Read	–	Read	–	–	–
2	Write	–	Write	–	–	–
3	Read	Read	Read	Read	Read	–
4	Read	Read	Read	Read	Read	Read
5	Write	Write	Write	Read	Write	Read
6	Write	Write	Write	Write	Write	Write

There are various ways in which you can check the type of fields or files to which you have access.

a   You can try accessing them on your system. If they are restricted, the system will probably not show them to you! This is one of the benefits of a database system – those who devise it can include safeguards to ensure confidentiality of sensitive information.

b   You can check the user manual see whether it confirms your lack of access – just in case you suspect your system is faulty.

c   You can ask your supervisor.

Then note these down.

Remember that you may be able to read more information than you can change – so you should check both your 'read' access rights and your 'write' access rights. If you need to obtain a higher level of access than normal, for a particular reason, it is likely that specific procedures will have to be followed before this is allowed.

Locating and retrieving database files

The way in which you locate and retrieve database files will vary, depending upon the system you use.

If you know which record you want to find, then you should check:

*   whether there is a Find option on the toolbar (or equivalent keyboard shortcuts)
*   whether you can use the Search facility under a specific, known criterion.

On many databases these two operations are linked, so that when you click on Find you are asked to specify the fields you want to search. The more of these you identify, the slower the search but the more accurate.

If you have only general information, you will have to enter as much as possible into the 'field' possibilities and then assess the records displayed to select the correct one.

On a very complex database, you may have several variations of similar data stored in different parts of the package. In this case the first task is to identify the specific area in which you should be searching. Usually the options are displayed in a list of folders and you can click on these to see the options in each one.

Using standard queries

A **query** is when you ask the database to provide you with information. You can usually:

- display all the records, one by one
- just specify the specific information you want displayed by limiting the number of fields to be shown
- specify certain criteria to limit the number of records displayed.

The search routines you can use will be determined by your system and the way your database has been structured. As you saw on page 334, records are designed so that they contain key fields, which may represent one or more fields of data, which uniquely identify that record. This means that no two records can have the same key field value. For instance:

- in a personnel database, there will be a staff reference or code number for each person
- in a college database, each student will have a unique student number
- in a customer database, each customer will have his or her own customer code number
- in a national bank database, each bank can be identified by its unique sort code and each account in each branch by the sort code *plus* the account number.

If you know the unique identifier then you can bring up each record you want instantly by keying this in. Unfortunately, you may often have no idea of the identifier, even though you know which is your key field! For instance, customers may contact you but may not know their reference number – so the database has to be structured to provide other methods of finding information. You may even find an electronic index has been constructed to help you. This means that the sorting and retrieval of different records is much faster.

The first thing to find out is what standard queries are provided by your database. These often cover the most routine searches that are envisaged by the designer. For instance, a customer database could be searched quickly by inputting surname and address which *together* are likely to be unique to each customer. A further check could be to ascertain when the customer last placed an order and what it was for, to check you are looking at the right record.

In addition, you need to be aware of:

- how records can be sorted on your system, to change the order in which records are displayed (see pages 331–332 and below)
- whether you can save queries you use regularly – so that you can access them again at the touch of a key
- whether you can reduce the number of records displayed by using **filters**, which are devices that hide records with certain characteristics so that you can work on a selected subset of the data

- what **wild-cards** you can enter to search when you do not have specific information to hand.

There may be other features the database designer has incorporated to help. For instance, you may be able to click on a drop-down menu giving you specific options when you are entering a query – such as a personnel database which is structured so that you can select from a menu of the different departments in the company to refine your search from the outset.

More about sorting

Sorting changes the order in which the database records are displayed. Depending upon how sophisticated the database is, a range of sort options may be available to you, including:

- alphabetical order (e.g. A to Z) or reverse alphabetical (Z to A)
- the date when the record was created (most recent either first or last)
- a geographical sort, so that all customers in a particular area are listed
- a numerical sort, so that all customers who are high- or low-spending are listed.

It is extremely useful to be able to sort on multiple criteria. For instance, if you operate a library database and are asked to print out a list of the oldest books on geography because these are going to be scrapped or sold, you will need to sort both by date of purchase (or date of publication) and by the category 'Geography'. If you use a large company database, it should have been designed to allow you to do this (or put in a polite request to your Database Administrator!). If you use a database on a PC then you will normally be able to do this by using the advanced filter/sort option.

TEST YOUR KNOWLEDGE AND UNDERSTANDING

1 On a leisure club database, which of the following would be the unique field in each member's record: the member's name, his or her address, the membership number, or the date of joining?

2 You are booking a holiday in a travel agency and the flight reservation is being made on a database. Which of the following is the key field which must be correctly showing on the confirmation printout: the departure time, the departure airport, the destination airport, or the flight number?

3 A customer is claiming that you have posted to him the wrong item. Which of the following combinations of items of information

would enable you to check this instantly: the customer's name and the date the item was sent; the customer's account number and product code number; the supplier's name and product number; the customer's account number and product cost?

4 Your company is introducing loyalty awards for staff and you have been asked to print a list of all personnel who started before a specified date, in alphabetical order. What facility would enable you to do this?

5 You are entering information on all your CD collection into a database. On which criteria do you think you would like to be able to sort your data, and why?

Using automated facilities to check data entries

There used to be an expression commonly used in relation to computers: garbage in = garbage out. In plain English, if you input rubbish then the result will be useless. This is particularly appropriate in relation to databases. As an example, if you were inputting student records in a college, and entered some dates of birth mistakenly as the current year, then any report which listed students by age would be incorrect. You may think it would be acceptable to argue that you were simply *copying* information the students had mistakenly written on their enrolment forms – but this would be no excuse. You therefore need to *think* when you are inputting. It is not just a case of hitting the right keys but mentally checking whether everything you are keying in is 'sensible' or 'rational' – and querying it if it is not.

On some packages you will have facilities to help you – but these will mainly relate to text entries. A spell-checker can help only with common words but not proper names (such as the name or address of a customer). If you are fortunate, the database will be designed so that you are prevented from making some silly errors, such as the following.

• You will be prevented from entering text in a numeric field (but not vice versa – as numbers are often required in a text field, such as a house number).
• All postcodes may have to be of six or seven characters.
• Some fields may 'autofill' – for instance, with the current date.
• some numeric fields may limit you to numeric entries between a specified range.
• Many fields may limit you to 'yes/no' options.

You will also find that you are unable to leave key fields blank – you will be prompted to complete these.

Using program help facilities

All databases have help facilities. If you use a Windows-based database then you will find the Help screens and options are similar to those you see when you use Word or other packages.

On some database systems, the help facilities are very user-friendly and easy to follow. Wizards can be useful, as can any other device which actually undertakes a miniature demonstration on screen. On other packages help facilities are harder to follow. Much will depend on your fundamental understanding of how your system operates and your knowledge of the terms used. It is well worth trying to understand how your help facility operates and to access it first to test out a procedure which you already know how to do. Then you can see how the information is structured. Next, try it for a simple query before you try it for anything more complicated.

Finally, if you need to ask for help to understand your Help instructions, don't be dismayed! Use this as a learning opportunity. Ask an expert for assistance and then go *back* to your help facility and see if it is clearer once you know what you are supposed to be doing.

Maintaining data integrity

Much of the data entered into databases is sensitive or confidential, as you have seen already. Consider it a privilege if your organisation allows you to enter and view this type of information. Your supervisor will be concerned that all data be handled in such a way that the requirements of the Data Protection Act are met (see pages 286–288). In addition, your employer will need you to do your part in ensuring that the data you enter is complete and accurate (see pages 345–346).

Finally, it is up to you to ensure that data is secure. This means using your computer system properly, complying with organisational requirements for its use, and *not* discussing any sensitive items you read in your electronic database with other people or taking and distributing printouts containing sensitive information to people who are not allowed to receive them.

1 All databases are usually protected by a user ID log-in system and/or password. Why do you think this is necessary?

2 Some commercial companies sell their databases of customer names and addresses to other organisations, who can then use the information to promote their own goods. To comply with the Data Protection Act, forms often have a 'check box' at the bottom that customers must 'tick' if they don't want this to happen. Most people never notice the little box so it stays unticked. They then wonder how other firms know about them and have managed to send product information through the mail without being asked.

a What is your opinion of this practice?

b Discuss with your supervisor whether your company does this or with your tutor whether your college would pass on its student database to anyone.

3 You regularly use the personnel database at work and have a high level of access. State what you would do in each of the following situations:

a A friend in another office thinks she is paid less than her colleagues who do the same work. She asks you to tell her the salary earned by each of her colleagues to help her case.

b A new colleague really likes your friend and wants to send her a Valentine card. He asks you for her address.

The limits of your responsibility and checking data

Your ability to read data and enter or amend data is controlled by your access rights. You may also have the ability to create new files and delete those which are no longer needed.

If you work for a small organisation and operate a simple, flat database you may be able to do even more. You may be able to design forms or reports if you are proficient with the software. However, if you are operating a large, relational database which has been developed by a Database Administrator you will not be allowed to undertake any operations relating to the structure or design of the database, but will have to make your requests to a specialist.

However, whereas the operation of the database is not your responsibility, the accuracy of your data most certainly is. A well-designed database will prevent some fundamental errors, but nothing can be built in to stop you spelling someone's name wrongly or transposing the house numbers in the address. This is where good, old-fashioned proof-reading comes in! In addition, try to stay alert when you are entering data so that you never enter 'garbage' just because it's there! If you know that Marsha Fields left the company last month but you are asked to enter a leaving date of yesterday, then check it. Don't simply key data in blindly.

Reporting problems

You should have few problems using the organisation's database if your computer system is working properly, the database itself has been well designed, and you are complying with instructions. Problems may arise, however, if:

- there is a problem with your computer hardware or network
- the database is 'off-line' for any reason (probably for maintenance or for the addition of new reports or facilities)
- a record you need has been deleted or corrupted
- the data you have been asked to input is incompatible with the way the field has been structured
- you need to search on specific criteria but the system is not designed to allow you to do that
- you cannot find a particular record no matter how you search.

Before you report the problem to the relevant person you may wish to make a few checks yourself.

a   If the problem appears to be with your own computer or with the network, first check all the cable connections and the power supply. If they seem to be intact, next determine whether the database is still available on a colleague's system. If it is not, find out whether the problem has already been reported, and how long it will be until the system comes back on-line.

b   If the data is incompatible with a field structure, you may be able to adjust the entry if you are an experienced user – but adjust the source document too, so that the data matches on both.

c   If you cannot search on a particular criterion, check your manual, handbook or Help screen to see whether other options are available. If not, then your supervisor may be able to arrange for this search option to be made available.

d   If a record is corrupted or missing and you have tried every search you can (and checked your handbook or manual and Help screen), find out whether there is any good reason why the record should have been removed (e.g. it was input in error, was a duplicate, the product is no longer stocked, or someone has specifically asked for it to be removed).

EVIDENCE COLLECTION

1   You need to prove that you can find and input both numbers and text into a database. Check the records you have printed out so far as evidence to ensure that you can prove you do both. It will help if you can also show examples of instructions you have been given to enter new data into the database.

2   Obtain a copy of any procedures you have to follow when using the database. 'Personalise' these by identifying which are the most important to you in relation to your own job and responsibilities.

3   As obvious evidence that you can find, enter and amend data in a database, take a hard copy of database records you have accessed and updated, both before and after the operation has been carried out.

4   You also need to prove that you can find data by using both types of routines – sorting records and using standard queries provided by the database. Do this by keeping a record of the searches you undertake over a short period and explaining how you found the required information. Do check that your evidence covers both types of routines. If it does not, you may be expected to answer questions from your assessor on how you would undertake the other type of routine.

5   Prove that you can use your program's Help by writing a brief description of two occasions when you have accessed the facility. Say why you needed to do this, the information you found and how you applied it. You may also want to say how user-friendly you find the Help facility.

Element 206.2 Generate reports from a database

A database **report** is a list of specific information, in a particular order. For instance, on a customer database there could be several report options available:

- a list of every customer in alphabetical order
- a list of all customers in a specified locality
- a list of customers who spend more than a specified amount each month or year
- a list of all customers who regularly buy a particular product.

In addition, these options can be *combined* so that you could request a report listing the customers in a particular area, in alphabetical order, who spend more than £5000 a year and who regularly buy toiletries from your company.

Reports are usually designed to be **columnar** – that is, the information is produced in columns with headings. The headings on a report are determined by the designer. You cannot have a heading on a report which doesn't represent a field on your records – because this information would not be known to your system. You are also limited to a specific number of headings because of the size of your paper! However, if you are working on a relational database, you can have a report which combines headings from different databases.

As an example, a school keeps a database of all its pupils and records their name, address, emergency telephone number and contact name, and tutor group. It also has a database of examinations taken and the results. A report could then be designed which listed the name of each pupil as well as his/her examination results and these could be printed out for each tutor group and/or for each subject. Or a report could be run for all the results for one subject or even all the results for the school. The example on page 349 shows a report for one tutor group and for one subject, in alphabetical order of pupil.

Obtaining information on the type of report required

If you use a complex database you are likely to have the option to produce a number of reports which have been pre-designed by the Administrator and his/her staff. People who ask you for a report may know all these better than you do, and state exactly which report they want. This type of request is easy. A more difficult request is from someone who *doesn't* understand your system and what is available. They simply know what information they would like to have!

REPORT ON STUDENT EXAMINATION RESULTS BY TUTOR GROUP

EXAMINATION RESULTS   Report run: 22/08/02 15.12

Tutor group: Mr M Marney – Group 2

Subject: GCSE Business Studies

Name	Grade
Susan Ainsworth	A
Naseem Ali	B
Uzma Begum	A
John Cummings	C
Richard Diaferia	E
Adam Fielden	D
Richard Gill	A
Nicola Goffin	B
James Hargreaves	C
Laura Hartley	E
Iftikhar Kasim	B
David Lee	D
Sobia Malik	B
Dawn Oliver	C
Neelam Rani	B
Tracey Simpson	C
John Taylor	D
Mohammed Sirtaj	C
Sahid Umarji	A
Kevin Watson	E
Carrie Woodward	C

c:/examreport.tg2.22Aug02

Before you can suggest the best type of report, you need to know:

- what information is crucial to the report
- what information would be good to have, but isn't essential
- what information is definitely not required.

It will help if you also know what the report is being used for! You can then suggest the different versions that you know are available and which would be most appropriate.

It is useful to remember that if you are regularly asked for information which is not available in report format (or which takes two reports to list) then you should ask the Database Administrator to design a report which does provide it. If you work on a PC, you may be allowed to do this yourself if you understand the software fully. For instance, in Access, you can use the Report wizard to help, or you can try AutoReport. However, you need to be taught how to do this properly and you can *only* do it once your basic database has been constructed and some records have been created.

 INFORMATION UPDATE

Large superstores have immense customer databases which are created from different types of customer information. Customers who own Loyalty Cards complete a form when they apply for their card, and this provides the source information for their database record. This will be amended, over time, to include information from sales. The amount the customer spends, the type of products bought, how frequently and where they shop will all be recorded.

This information is put to good use. Mailshots can be targeted at particular customers. Customers with young children will receive details of toys and baby items, high-spenders will receive information on top-of-the-range products, males will receive information on car accessories and females on beauty products – and so on. Discount vouchers can be sent to tempt people to buy more of their regular items and to try new items which link to their shopping patterns.

Next time you receive a mailshot through the post, think about the type of data that organisation holds about you, and why they think you will be interested in certain items!

Choosing a report format

Obviously, it is important that you do not access data files and produce reports without the necessary permission, as described on page 338.

Before going ahead and producing the report you must make certain checks to ensure that it will meet the requirements of the person requesting it. The main checks relate to the **format** of the report:

a   what information is required
b   how it should be grouped or organised
c   in what order the information is required
d   the amount of detail needed
e   the layout and 'look' of the report.

Some of these options may be **pre-set** in the organisation's database, so reducing the choices. In particular, you are likely to find that the format has been set up by those who constructed the database. As you have seen, reports are usually columnar, so that you see a series of headings across the top with the relevant data under each one.

The headings will be determined by the *type* of report you run, and the grouping of the data will be determined by the *order* in which you require the information. You do, however, often have discretion in relation to *how much* information to provide. Usually it is best to give just enough rather than too much information, so that the key data are not hidden somewhere in a long list.

TEST YOUR KNOWLEDGE AND UNDERSTANDING

You operate a school database which records the following information on all pupils in separate fields: first name, middle name, last name, address, town, postcode, date joined, date left, current year group, and current tutor. In a separate (but related) database are attendance details. From this combination, identify which requests for reports are possible from the list below, and which are not:

a   names of all pupils who left last summer

b   names of all pupils in Year 10 who live in a specified town

c   the number of pupils in Year 9 who have a less than 90 per cent attendance record

d   the attendance of all pupils in a specified class

e   the names of all pupils who are over 150 cm tall

f   the names and addresses of all pupils who started last September

g   a summary of the punctuality record of each pupil.

Modifying a report format

Reports can be designed to be viewed on screen and can be printed as hard copies or transmitted electronically (see page 353). You can run a report and view it on screen to select a particular item of information (e.g. to find out the telephone number of a customer). However, if someone wants to study a report in detail away from a computer, then you obviously need to make a printout.

You may be given the opportunity to modify the format to make it easier to read or more attractive, such as by:

• adding a title header, and perhaps including the date the report was run

- changing the font size or typeface
- selecting design features such as bold or italics
- printing out only selected sections
- changing the orientation for the printout (e.g. portrait to landscape or vice versa).

The final point in that list is important if the report as shown on screen would not fit on a standard piece of A4 paper in the portrait orientation (i.e. short side at the top).

It is a good idea to make your changes and then check these with the person who asked for the report to see if it meets their needs. A useful tip, if the report will be very long, is to ask that person to check it on screen before you start to print *or* to print off just one page as an example. You can do this by selecting Print and Current Page or a specific page to print. Otherwise you are likely to be in danger of wasting both time and paper, waiting for a long but unusable report to print out in full.

CHECK IT OUT!

1 Look back at the report shown on page 349. Identify the header and the footer used. Now say why you think a footer which refers to the file name and date the report was produced would be useful.

2 Select a report you have printed and experiment with all the modifications you can make in relation to headers and footers, font size and typeface, design features and so on. If you take several printouts of different variations, this will provide useful evidence that you can make modifications when requested.

Final checks

Once you have made any modifications required, you are well advised to check your work again before you print it in full. Again print a selected page or ask the person who made the request to view it on screen. Do a 'double check' that all the information you were asked for is there – or you know something is missing but can't do anything about it!

If you are not very impressed yourself with what you are viewing, it is likely you could make some changes or suggest some amendments to improve it.

Finally, even if you think everything is fine, and the information is complete, you may still be asked to make changes – either because the person making the request has thought of something else he wants, or because his views on design are different from yours. If this happens, curb the urge to sigh loudly and be prepared to do as you are asked with good grace. You never know, you may learn something as you do!

Setting up the printer

If you regularly produce reports you may have your printer set up appropriately. However, changes may be required if you use the same printer for other types of work and/or you are running a report in a different type of format, such as landscape.

Today, most printers are controlled from the computer. Access the File menu, select Print and view the alternatives available on your system. For instance, in addition to changing the paper orientation you may also have the option to print an internal report in draft mode or to print in colour.

It is very important that you check all your settings carefully before you start to print a very long report – for obvious reasons.

Problems when printing

Occasionally you may encounter problems when you try to print a report. These may relate to:

- computer hardware or software issues
- problems with the design of the report or database
- problems with the printer.

Your printer must be connected properly and the computer system must recognise the type of printer you use before you can print anything! However, if you can normally print without problems and you are having problems when you use the database, report the situation to your supervisor.

A report that is too wide will have information missing at the right-hand side of the printout. You may be able to get round this by changing the type size and adjusting the margins, and/or by changing the orientation of the paper. If this does not work, you need help as it may be that your printer cannot cope with the report format you have requested.

The printer, of course, needs to be fully operational and loaded with the correct paper. If the printout is faint or unreadable, first check that it is not set to 'draft' mode. Alternatively, the ink or toner cartridge may need changing. If the paper jams, then try reloading it. Always consult the printer handbook and carry out basic checks yourself, before you ask for expert assistance!

Transmitting electronic copies

If you are connected to a computer network, you will be able to use your company email facilities to send the report electronically. You do this by 'attaching' the report to your email message. Simply click 'attach' and then locate the computer file for the report and double click on the name. This method is often quicker than sending a report through the internal mail and saves paper – particularly if you are sending it to several people. It is also frequently used to send reports over the Internet, such as to branch offices or other staff working away from the office.

EVIDENCE COLLECTION

1 Keep a log of the reports you are asked to run over a period of time. Identify why you were asked to run each one and state which you transmitted electronically and which ones required a hard copy to be made. Remember that if you use only one of these methods, you must be prepared to prove to your assessor that you understand the other.

2 If possible, include examples of various formats – or show you can change the format by taking two or three different versions of the same report.

3 Ask one or two people for whom you regularly input data and produce reports to provide witness testimony to prove that you can input data completely and accurately, that you follow organisational procedures, maintain data integrity at all times, and produce reports that meet their requirements.

4 Finally, keep a log of any problems you have to deal with when printing and state what you did in each case.

GROUP B OPTION UNITS

Introduction to Group B Option Units

There are 15 Group B Option Units in the NVQ level 2 Administration scheme. You have to do only **two** of these. Eight of these units are covered in the following pages and the remainder are freely available on the Heinemann website (for details, see below). You can therefore obtain information on all of these quite easily.

Making your choice

Although the units in this book are in numerical order, don't let this influence your choice! You should select those which are most appropriate to your job so that you have no difficulties in obtaining evidence. If you are studying your award on a full-time basis, do talk to your tutor about which of these option units would be the easiest to do. You can then select those for which appropriate facilities are available to you, or perhaps those which link to a skills award you are taking.

Thinking in 'groups'

Important guidance on choosing your options was given in the Introduction, pages xvi–xix. You may wish to turn back to these pages now, to refresh your memory. This section told you that the options can be thought of in groups – and this, too, may help your choice. For instance, there are:

- four admin support options – photocopying, stock control, doing the mail and arranging events

- two 'people' options – providing customer service and dealing with visitors.

- four computer skills options – providing IT support, using e-mail and the Internet, using spreadsheets and producing mail merge documents

- two communications skills options – producing documents from own notes and producing documents from recorded speech

- three financial units – receiving and making payments, processing financial information and helping to collect debts.

However, do remember you can choose *any* two – so you have a very wide choice!

Important note – computer skills option units

It is assumed that you will not be undertaking any of the computer skills option units – Units 213 and 214 in this Student Handbook and Units 210 and 215 on the website – unless you *already* possess a good working knowledge of your organisation's computer systems and software. The information given for these units therefore focuses on additional points relevant to the knowledge and understanding requirements for the option units as well as specific guidance on evidence collection.

If you are concerned that your skills in any area may be insufficient there are a variety of ways in which you can improve. You can:

- purchase a simple 'user-friendly' guide to the software you are using
- find a variety of relatively inexpensive books at all good booksellers
- attend an in-company skills training course on the software package you are using
- develop your skills through careful use of manuals, the use of 'help' screens and by asking for assistance from experts in your workplace
- take a short course (flexible options are often available) at a nearby college to improve your skills in a particular package.

Units available on the Heinemann website

Guidance on the following skills and finance option units is freely available on the Heinemann website at www.heinemann.co.uk/vocational/NVQ:

Unit 210 Produce and distribute mail merge documents (ADMIN210)
Unit 215 Produce simple spreadsheet documents (ADMIN215)
Unit 216 Produce documents from own notes (ADMIN216)
Unit 217 Produce documents from recorded speech (ADMIN217)
Unit 219 Receive and make payments (ADMIN219)
Unit 220 Process financial information (ADMIN220)
Unit 221 Support the collection of debts (ADMIN221).

Each of the units above has a password, which is given in brackets after the unit title.

The last lap

If you have worked through the scheme methodically, you may have already completed six of the required eight units. You are now on the last lap to achieving your award. You are also used to finding evidence and building your portfolio. For that reason, the notes given for the Group B Option Units are shorter than for the other units. The focus is on the knowledge and understanding you must know and the evidence you need to collect. Hopefully they will answer all your queries and enable you to obtain your last two units without any difficulty. Good luck!

Option Unit 207 Provide effective customer service

FOCUS OF THE UNIT

To obtain this unit you must be able to:

- **communicate** with customers, on the telephone and face to face
- **provide services** to meet customer requirements
- **help** customers with problems and complaints.

EVIDENCE COLLECTION

It will make your evidence collection easier if you can obtain copies of the following:

a   customer service policies or standards with which you have to comply when dealing with external customers

b   procedures you have to follow when dealing with customers, whether internal or external

c   telephone messages you take on behalf of customers (either internal or external)

d   completed job request forms upon which internal customers ask for administrative work to be carried out

e   any complaints logs, complaints procedures or copies of documents relating to problems or complaints you have handled.

Key facts on customer service

The importance of effective customer service

Why are organisations keen to provide effective customer service? You can answer this by considering why, if you owned a business, you would want to provide customer service. Or you can think about what you want from organisations where *you* are the customer. Your answers may include:

a   to keep customers happy

b   to ensure anyone who wants information or advice obtains it promptly c to help retain customers – so they come back again and again

d because customers will then tell their business contacts, friends or relatives about your business – and you will obtain new customers

e to reduce the number of complaints and problems you have to deal with.

In fact, effective customer service is about all these and more. In a customer-focused business:

- the customer comes first
- customer needs are identified quickly
- customer expectations are exceeded
- customers are 'delighted' with the service they receive – consistently.

Remember that *your* 'personal' customers are not just those people who want to buy goods or services from your organisation. They include all those people who need your help or cooperation to achieve something themselves, and these include your internal customers. If *you* are 'customer focused' therefore, you will do all you can to help to meet their needs.

Is this the case with your customers? Or are you annoyed when the telephone rings when you are in the middle of the job or someone appears in your office? Do you try to get rid of people as quickly as possible, or spend time finding out what they want and trying to help them?

KEY NOTES ON THE BENEFITS OF EFFECTIVE CUSTOMER SERVICE

- It enhances the reputation of the business.
- It helps to promote customer loyalty.
- It attracts new customers (word gets around).
- It reduces staff time dealing with problems and complaints.

Who are your customers?

If you listed all your customers you would be likely to include:

- existing external customers
- internal customers
- prospective customers
- other visitors and callers (e.g. delivery people and tradespeople).

The list would include every group in which people needed your help or assistance.

Organisational procedures

Most organisations have customer service standards. These may give target response times, such as:

* all telephone calls must be answered within six rings
* all letters must be acknowledged within three working days.

However, setting standards is a waste of time if the person answering the phone is abrupt or discourteous, or the person writing the letter doesn't answer the customer's concerns properly. In both these cases the customer would be dissatisfied with the service.

Procedures try to avoid this. You may find procedures which state:

a   how to greet and address customers (see also page 363)

b   how to deal with visitors to your organisation

c   how to answer telephone calls (see also Unit 203)

d   how to respond to routine enquiries

e   how to respond to customer complaints

f   the returns policy for goods brought back by customers.

Procedures give details about the way staff must respond to a situation. These reduce the need for staff to ask a supervisor how to deal with individual situations and ensure that all staff respond in the same way. There may be a standard method for listing callers, arranging appointments or handling routine enquiries. Staff may have to log all customer complaints so that common problems can be identified and solutions sought to avoid them in future.

Written complaints may have to be handled by a specific supervisor or manager. If the organisation sells goods to private individuals, staff need to know whether faulty goods can be returned for a refund or whether goods can be returned (unused) if the buyer has changed his or her mind about the purchase.

Customers and their 'special needs'

Your customers may have special needs because:

- of their own personal circumstances
- of a physical impairment or disability
- they cannot speak or read English very well
- they have particular requirements linked to their culture or religious beliefs
- they have an individual or unusual request.

For example, an internal customer may be under tremendous pressure to complete a complex job to a deadline and needs your immediate assistance. An external customer may have a visual or hearing impairment or may use a wheelchair and need access to another floor, or have recently arrived from abroad and understand little English. An Islamic customer may be on a day visit to your company during Ramadan and may be fasting, or a Jewish customer may be staying for lunch. A customer may request highly detailed technical information or ask for a financial agreement to be reviewed because an accident or illness means he cannot work for some time. The variations on this theme are endless, as you can see.

Although you cannot prepare for every eventuality, the following tips can help:

1 Find out the type of special needs you are most likely to meet in your current employment, and obtain advice on how to cope with those.
2 Make sure you know what special facilities are available in your organisation for anyone with a disability, such as wheelchair access, disabled toilet facilities, etc.
3 Keep an open mind and *never* assume that something 'cannot be done' because it hasn't been done before! Ask someone for advice who you know will be helpful and positive if you have a problem.

If you do your best for all your customers, and treat them all as special people, then you will be doing your best both for them and for your organisation.

CHECK IT OUT!

Investigate the facilities for people with a disability in your college or workplace. Then decide how you would assist each of the people with special needs in the examples given above. Discuss your ideas with your tutor or supervisor.

Key facts on communicating with customers

Meeting and greeting

Many organisations have a specific style for greeting and addressing customers – either face to face or over the telephone. Often this varies in formality, depending upon the 'style' of the organisation. A solicitor's office, for instance, will have a more formal style than your local radio station. Whether you are instructed to greet people with your organisation's name, your own full name or simply your first name (e.g. 'Hi, I'm Debbie, can I help you?'), do make sure you know the correct approach to use. Similarly, you may be expected to address all your external customers formally – Mr Sharples or Mrs Martinez – unless you know them well or they have specifically told you to use their first name. Today, most organisations call internal customers by their first name but there is always the exception. If a senior executive expects you to address him by his surname, you are advised to do so!

Finally, don't make assumptions about names. Just because two people arrive together this does not mean they are husband and wife. Similarly, a woman talking about her adult daughter may well have a different surname from her (for instance, if the daughter has married), and may even have a different surname from her son, if she herself has remarried. You are always safer to ask, rather than to assume.

Promoting a positive image

Next time you visit a supermarket, study each checkout and decide which operator looks the most approachable. Which would you aim for, if all the queues were the same length? Which would you go to if you had a problem and wanted some advice – and why?

We often judge people on their appearance – not just whether they are smartly dressed but by how friendly or approachable they seem. If someone smiles frequently, makes eye contact with us, seems to have time to help us, then we receive a positive image. If they are also knowledgeable about the goods sold or services offered and give us correct information promptly we are doubly impressed.

We cannot judge people by appearance on the telephone, so we listen for clues in the way they answer. We want someone to sound pleasant, friendly and helpful.

If you think someone is unapproachable, unpleasant or has little time for you, you might try to avoid them. If you meet them when you are a customer you may even take your business elsewhere in future. This is the effect of projecting a negative image on customers.

KEY NOTES ON POSITIVE IMAGE

- In person you need to look smart and cheerful, be approachable and friendly, smile at people and have time to *really* listen to them.

- Projecting a positive image also means being loyal to your organisation *and* to your team – *never* 'rubbish' them to someone else.

- On the telephone, your voice is your image – you need to sound approachable and friendly.

- Keeping people waiting projects a negative image. If there is a delay, explain why and get help.

- Your positive image is enhanced if you know basic information about your products and services so that you answer queries accurately.

- What you don't know, find out, and know who can help a customer if you cannot.

- Always keep your promises to a customer.

- A positive image is vital to retain customers.

- A positive image means you can retain customers even if you can't satisfy all of their needs.

Communications standards and skills

There are several aspects to communicating effectively with customers:

a   the speed with which customers receive a response
b   the manner, or tone of the response
c   the message you give them verbally
d   the other signals you project, non-verbally
e   how good you are at *listening* to a customer
f   your non-verbal communication skills and ability to interpret body language
g   problems you may encounter when communicating and how to deal with these.

For your evidence for this unit, you need to prove you can communicate with customers effectively face to face *or* on the telephone. Face-to-face communications and internal telephone communications are covered in Unit 201. Dealing with customers over the telephone is covered in Unit 203.

The most important reason for having a positive image is that it can help you to retain customers – even when you cannot meet their needs! This is shown on the diagram below.

	Positive image		
Needs not met	RETAIN	RAPTURE	Needs met
	RUIN	RISKY	
	Negative image		

Look first at the horizontal line. At the right-hand side, the customer is delighted. Whatever was wanted you have provided. However, this is not always possible. At the left-hand side we have a dissatisfied customer, whose needs have not been met. This may be no one's fault. You may not stock a product the customer wants, the product may cost too much, your opening hours may not suit the customer, or the customer's order may be delayed for some reason. So even though you have tried to help, it has been impossible to meet the customer's needs.

Now look at the vertical line. At the top is the person who projects a positive image of the organisation by being helpful, friendly and trying to assist as much as possible. At the bottom is the person who projects a negative image by being abrupt, unhelpful or uninterested in the customer.

The four squares of the diagram show the results.

Above the horizontal line – a positive image has produced success:

- **Rapture** – the customer is thrilled to get excellent service and have his/her needs met.
- **Retain** – even when needs cannot be met, your efforts have meant the customer will stay loyal to your organisation

Below the horizontal line – a negative image has either lost the customer or is in danger of doing so:

- **Risky** – you have met the customer's needs – but your attitude may have meant he/she will try elsewhere next time.
- **Ruin** – you have failed to meet your customer's needs and annoyed him/her with your attitude. You have lost that customer and will lose many more in future.

Improving your communication skills

Customers vary tremendously. Some know exactly what they want, some are unsure. Some are in a hurry, others have time to kill. Some are easy-going and patient, others are perfectionists or impatient. Some external customers have a lot of money to spend, others have not. How can you respond appropriately to each different type of person you may have to deal with?

It helps if you have a tried and tested approach for dealing with customers. The most usual stages are shown below.

*   Approach a customer positively, with a smile and a pleasant greeting. As you have seen, some organisations have a standard greeting they prefer staff to use, others allow you choose your own.
*   Build a good relationship with your customer. Learn to identify clues to the customer in his/her body language *and* by listening carefully (see below).
*   Ask questions to check you have the right information (see page 376).

- Sound confident and give accurate and precise information – but *never* make promises you cannot keep.
- Remember that customers judge you on your tone of voice and body language, as well as what you say!
- Never assume you know what a customer wants – find out!
- Be prepared to vary your approach when necessary and use different methods to improve your communications with them, such as using simpler words or examples and taking your time.

CHECK IT OUT!

The tone of voice we use can change the 'message' in the words completely. Try saying 'Yes, all right' in four different ways:

- The first time be angry, as if you are in the middle of an argument and having to give way.
- The second time be resentful, as if you are being forced to do something – and sound sulky
- The third time be sincere and reassuring.
- The fourth time be enthusiastic, as if you are agreeing to a wonderful idea.

The importance of body language

You send messages to customers you meet face to face by the way you stand, your facial expressions, gestures and tone of voice – and they send messages to you. Realising the power of body language helps you in two ways. You can project a more positive image to your customers and you can 'read' the messages they are sending to you – and respond accordingly. For instance:

- We turn our body (and feet) towards something in which we are interested – not just our head.
- We feel comfortable standing close to people we know well but need more personal space with a stranger.
- If people make 'eye contact' with us, we think they are more honest – but we will look away if we are disinterested or bored.
- We walk more quickly and may tap our feet, or drum our fingers, or check our watch frequently if we are in a hurry or impatient.
- If we are confident we stand straight, or sit up straight; if depressed or dejected we hunch our shoulders and look down.
- When we are interested in what someone is saying we concentrate on them and tilt our head and/or nod at appropriate points. We will also lean slightly towards them when they are speaking.

The importance of listening skills

Could you repeat what someone has said afterwards or did you spend most of the time waiting to say something yourself? **Active listening** occurs when you are concentrating more upon the other person than yourself – so much so that you can summarise their attitude as well as the content of their message. Remember that when you deal with customers on the telephone you cannot assess their body language to help you – so your listening skills become even more important.

KEY NOTES ON LISTENING

- Recognise when your listening ability fluctuates – such as when you are bored or uninterested in what the customer is saying, distracted, in a hurry, annoyed or uncomfortable, or when you think of something you want to say in reply.
- 'Switch yourself back on again' when you feel your mind wandering.
- *Never* interrupt – wait until there is a 'natural break' in the conversation.
- Focus on the person who is speaking.
- Make notes if the information is complex or important.
- Keep an open mind until the conversation has ended – don't jump to conclusions.
- Repeat the information back to check you have understood it correctly.

Ensuring understanding and dealing with problems

A customer will not understand you – nor you them – if the communications 'cycle' between you breaks down. This is shown on page 369. The breakdown results in a number of possible problems.

The sending stage

You cannot 'send' a message to a customer if:

- you don't know what you are talking about
- haven't 'thought through' what you are going to say
- are vague or imprecise
- are trying to do something else at the same time.

Recognise the **symptoms**:

- You are concerned you do not know enough to deal with a customer.
- You struggle to express yourself properly.

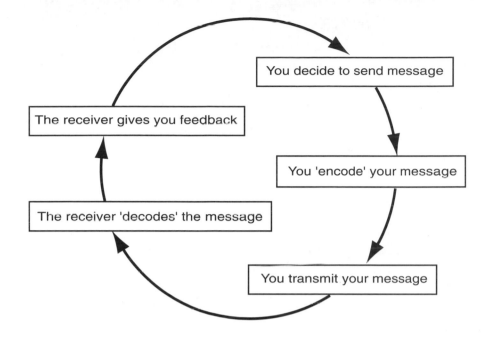

- You are very nervous.
- You are trying to work and deal with customers at the same time.

The solutions:

- Check facts before you start and make sure you have all the information you need.
- Practise your verbal communication skills.
- Take a deep breath, relax and smile. You can only do your best!
- Stop working if a customer arrives. If all your customers leave, you'll have no work to do!

The encoding stage

A customer cannot understand your message if:

- you use words or terms they do not understand
- your message is confused, vague or incomplete.

Recognise the **symptom**:

- You do not know what to say or how to say it clearly.

The **solutions**:

- Think about what you are going to say before you say it.
- Speak clearly and concisely.
- Use a vocabulary they will understand.

The transmitting stage

Your customer won't get your message if:

- your message is distorted or interrupted (such as being disconnected when you are on the telephone)
- there is too much external 'noise' or other distractions.

Recognise the **symptom**:

- Your receiver cannot hear you properly.

The **solutions**:

- Make sure the time and place is appropriate. In a noisy area ask the customer to follow you to a quieter place.
- If a customer has a hearing impairment, don't shout (that's pointless). Enunciate your words so they can lip-read more easily and slow down!
- If you have a bad telephone connection, say you will disconnect and ring back – and do so.

The receiving stage

Your customer won't understand your message if:

- they cannot understand the words you have used
- your tone and attitude distracts them
- *they* are too angry or annoyed to listen
- they are trying to do something else at the same time

Recognise the **symptoms**:

- You don't seem to be 'getting through' to your customer.
- Your customer is becoming annoyed – or getting more annoyed.
- Your customer is losing interest.

The **solutions**:

- Never interrupt a customer who is annoyed. Wait until he/she has finished speaking (see pages 371 and 384).
- Rephrase your message if the customer doesn't understand you – don't just repeat yourself.
- Check your tone and attitude is appropriate.
- Learn to 'read' your customer's body language (see below).
- Don't expect your customer to listen to important information when they are doing something else, such as signing a cheque!

The feedback stage

Feedback is essential so that you understand a message has been received correctly. There will be problems if:

- you do not listen to feedback or do not respond to it appropriately
- you do not give someone the opportunity to give you feedback.

Recognise the **symptom**:

- If someone asked you to 'sum up' how the customer felt at the moment, you couldn't do it.

The **solution**:

- Learn to listen at each stage in the conversation, then adapt your approach accordingly.

Dealing with other types of problem

There may be occasions when you have an unreasonable, angry or excited customer to deal with and feel you cannot cope. Try the techniques below and, if you feel you are losing control, don't hesitate to refer the matter to a more experienced team member or to your supervisor and ask them to deal with the person. Listen to what they do and how they do it – then you will be better able to deal with the situation next time.

Someone is angry, annoyed or excited

- Remember that they are annoyed at your organisation, not at you personally.
- Stay calm, and take a few deep breaths if necessary.
- Look sympathetic and interested – remember your body language skills!
- Suggest a face-to-face conversation is continued away from any main public areas.
- *Really* listen – and make notes if the situation is complex.
- *Never* interrupt, say the customer 'must be mistaken' or do anything to make the situation worse.
- Use your questioning skills to find out what the customer wants your organisation to do (see page 376).
- Check with your supervisor before you make any promises.
- Make sure whatever is agreed is done. Quickly.

Someone is impossible to please

- Use your listening and questioning skills to find out what the person wants.
- Suggest only solutions and actions that are in accordance with your company policy and procedures.
- Explain carefully why you cannot comply with the person's request.
- If they still won't accept this, ask your supervisor or another team member to speak with them.

Remember that the most awkward or angry customers do not necessarily have the most cause to be so! Some customers may have a valid complaint or problem and have to pluck up courage to talk to someone about it. They should not get worse treatment just because they are polite or do not shout – in fact, it is arguable that they should get *better* treatment! Listen to the facts, rather than the 'tone', and respond fairly to everyone.

Finally, you should never have to deal with a customer who is threatening, intimidating or of whom you are afraid. If you are ever in this type of situation, get help immediately.

KEY SUMMARY NOTES ON COMMUNICATING AND CUSTOMER SERVICE

- Always comply with your organisation's standards for customer service, including the speed and manner in which you should deal with customers.

- If you cannot deal immediately with a waiting customer, acknowledge his or her presence and give an estimated time when you will be available. If it is longer than five minutes, try to get someone else to help them. Never say you 'won't be a second' if you will obviously be much longer – better to say five minutes and take only three! Always apologise later for any delay.

- Become familiar with the type of requests and enquiries usually received and have the information at your fingertips. This helps to give you confidence.

- Smile when you approach someone, and if there is a standard company greeting, use it.

- Never assume you know what someone wants before they have told you!

- Don't 'gush' when customers look important or be casual with customers who do not. Appearances can be very deceptive! Treat everyone with respect and *always* be polite.

- Don't use 20 words when 10 will do. Speak in a language your customers will understand. Don't use jargon with external customers (unless they are technical specialists) or 'fillers' such as 'er' and 'um'. Say what you mean (politely) and mean what you say. Speak slightly more slowly if you are nervous.

- Treat difficult requests as a challenge. Don't rest until you've found a solution or have a very good explanation as to why you cannot help.

- Learn to be a good listener.

- Try your best to help everyone, no matter how unusual their request or need. But if a customer is very angry or unreasonable, refer the matter to a more experienced team member or your supervisor.

EVIDENCE COLLECTION

For this element you need to demonstrate that you can communicate face to face *or* on the telephone with both internal or external customers and can discuss how you would communicate using the other method. You can expect your assessor to want to observe you when you are communicating with customers – either face to face or on the telephone. You can also expect to answer questions which show you understand the importance of projecting a positive image and that you know how to solve customer problems. This also means you need to be able to project a positive image to your assessor!

You can provide evidence yourself if you:

a obtain witness testimony from internal customers with whom you deal regularly to prove that you can communicate with them clearly, politely and confidently

b obtain witness testimony from internal customers if they have a problem you have solved

c obtain witness testimony from people to whom you have referred problems which you cannot solve yourself.

Don't approach external customers for witness testimony without your supervisor's agreement. However, you can write an account of the external customers you deal with, and how you communicate with them, and state any problems you have solved. Ask your supervisor to countersign it for authenticity.

Key facts on providing services to customers

As an administrator, you are expected to prove you can supply the following services:

- provide information
- take messages
- provide other forms of support, such as administrative services.

There are certain important skills you need to learn to do this. You must be able to:

- find out exactly what the customer requires
- record their request accurately
- give information accurately
- check that you are not offering to do something which is outside your area of responsibility
- provide the required service to the standard and in the time scale required, so that the customer is satisfied
- check whether there are any other services you could provide to meet other needs the customer has.

Taking messages was covered in Unit 203, and different types of admin support operations are covered in Option Units 208, 209, 211 and 218. This element focuses upon how you deal with customers requiring such services.

Assessing customer requirements

Even if you have practised your communication skills so that you can say what you mean, that doesn't mean all your customers will be able to do the same! Some customers know exactly what they require, others do not.

Before you can agree to providing any service you need to establish who the customer is, what they want, and whether you can provide it. If you cannot provide it, what alternatives are available?

Who is the customer?

Knowing who is making the request is vital as this can affect the service you agree to provide. Normally a request from a senior manager takes priority over one from a junior team member. Equally, a request from an important external regular customer may take priority over a request from an unexpected caller.

What do they want?

Is the customer request simple, routine and easy to fulfil – or is it difficult, complex and outside your area of responsibility? Never make promises you cannot keep, such as agreeing your department will take on more work during a busy period! Say you will check with your supervisor and call back. And do so.

Does your team provide the srvice?

Is the request for a service your team is responsible for providing? Do you know all the services you do provide and can provide? If not, check with a more experienced colleague before you give a negative response.

What alternatives are available?

If you cannot provide the particular service requested, can anyone else in the organisation help? Or is there any similar service you can offer that may be acceptable? This may mean, for instance, providing information in a slightly different format, or providing administrative support but slightly later than the date by which it was originally requested. Remember you may have to *negotiate* alternatives – and you need to make certain that the final alternative is agreeable to both you and your customer.

What additional services can you supply?

Many organisations offer 'extras' which the customer may not even know about. For example, the ability to 'collect by car' or have a free delivery, a gift wrapping service and help with packing are just some of the services offered by large stores. Suggesting these can help your organisation to retain a customer and assist the customer considerably.

INFORMATION UPDATE

Identifying customer needs can be difficult because all customers are different. One person may simply want reassurance (for instance, that a delivery will be made on a certain date), another may want information, someone else may want you to solve a problem.

Internal customer needs are usually easier to identify. Your colleagues will tell you what they want. In many of the units in this book you have become familiar with the importance of establishing exactly what people want when they give you a job to do. Sometimes internal customers confuse wishful thinking with needs! They ask you to do a job in two hours whereas tomorrow would do. Your job may include trying to separate wishes from needs.

External customer needs can be more difficult to ascertain. Many customers don't know they need something until someone suggests it! Excellent sales staff are skilled in asking questions to find out exactly which product would be most suitable for the customer. Finding out about customer needs – and how good the organisation is at meeting them – is often done through customer surveys. Find out if your organisation ever issues surveys to establish customer needs and, if so, what the results were.

Today, your internal customers are also considered very important. This is because they, too, are trying to satisfy an external customer. If you let down your colleague, the ultimate customer will be disappointed. Some experts see this as a 'chain' in which internal staff may be linked, but at the end there is always an external customer whose satisfaction depends upon strong links in the chain.

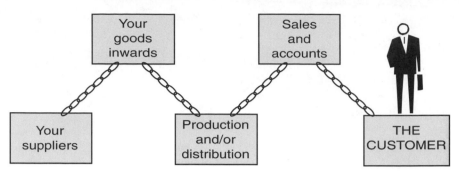

The customer service 'chain'

The skill of questioning

If people are unsure about what they want, or what you can provide, you may have to ask questions to find out their exact requirements. However, there is a skill to asking questions so that you don't irritate or annoy people and yet still obtain all the information you need. People who do this for a living (such as journalists) often 'set the scene' by explaining that they will have to ask a few questions first. If you explain that this helps you to provide a better service most people will be more than willing to answer.

Remember to write down the answers so that you don't have to repeat the questions again because you have forgotten what was said!

 KEY NOTES ON QUESTIONING

- Ask one question at a time, otherwise you will confuse people.

- Ask questions in a logical order.

- Avoid personal or 'direct' questions (if a customer tells you 'I'm sorry, I can't collect it on Wednesday' you should *not* respond with 'Why not?')!

- Recognise the difference between a question and an interrogation. Use pauses in the conversation and moderate your tone of voice.

- Ask 'open' questions which begin with 'who', 'what', 'when', 'how', 'why', 'which' – these will give you the most information.

- Ask 'follow-up' questions when you need specific information.

- Ask difficult questions – and respond to them – tactfully. For instance, a suitable response to 'Will it be ready on Friday?' is either 'Yes' or 'No, I'm sorry, we can't complete it until Tuesday' – and *never* 'By Friday? You must be kidding! We're far too busy to do it for then.'

Recording the information

Once you have established the customer's exact requirements, *write them down*. Remember your communication skills, and the importance of feedback by checking the details whilst the customer is still available. Full details should be recorded – even if you think you are providing the service yourself. If you wake up with 'flu tomorrow, someone else will have a serious problem if you have made only rough notes.

The information should include:

a who requires the service (name, address or department, phone or extension number)

b the exact service required

c the date by when it must be provided.

Note down also any information you have already given to the customer, so that they don't receive it twice. You have already learned about the importance of providing accurate and up-to-date information in various units in this book – it is just as important in this situation, otherwise you can seriously mislead a customer and create problems for other people.

photocopier is being repaired. What information do you think you would need to fulfil each customer request promptly and effectively?

3 You receive a request for an emergency job which will mean that other people's work will be delayed.

    a   Would you agree to this? Give a reason for your answer.

    b   Do you think it would make any difference if the request was from the managing director's office?

Check your ideas with your tutor or supervisor.

EVIDENCE COLLECTION

Obtain a copy of your own job description or write a brief description of your job role. Then list the types of service you are expected to provide (to internal and/or external customers) and those you are not. In each case identify the information you require to be able to provide the service promptly and effectively.

Finally, list examples of requests you would have to refer to your supervisor, because they are outside your own area of responsibility.

Providing services and checking satisfaction

Customers will be satisfied (or delighted) with the service you provide if:

- it is as agreed beforehand
- it meets their needs (or goes one better!)
- it is delivered by the agreed date
- it is to the required standard.

If you fail to meet any of these criteria, the customer may be entitled to be displeased with the service provided. If you fail to meet several of them, expect a complaint!

- **As agreed**. This means you noted down the request and then fulfilled it properly (for instance, you provided 50 photocopies as requested and not 15).

- **It meets their needs**. This means it is complete and what the customer wanted. For instance, you were asked for information on train times and you have 'thought through' the request so it covers the right stations and a range of times, and does not include options which would involve many changes. This is why good questioning skills at the outset are invaluable.

- **It is delivered by the agreed date**. Exceed a deadline, where you can, rather than disappoint people. You can do this if you slightly overestimate the time it will take, rather than under-estimate. If you think there may be a delay, you will find your customers are more reasonable if you warn them in advance and renegotiate the deadline date.

- **It is to the required standard**. Photocopying which is crooked, back to front or wrongly collated won't meet anyone's needs. Neither will incorrect information or messages given to the wrong person. Take your time, concentrate on the job you are doing and set yourself high standards.

Checking customer satisfaction

A friendly call to an internal colleague to check that they are happy with your service will always be appreciated, as will a call to an external customer that they now have all they need. If you have done your job properly, then the majority of your customer service checks will give you a positive response.

If, however, a customer is not happy with the service – what then? Firstly, you need to put matters right. Secondly, you need to identify what went wrong, and try to prevent it happening again.

Putting matters right

Apologise to the customer – even if it wasn't your fault. You are apologising for the inconvenience if the service wasn't up to standard. Then find out what you can do to put matters right. If a job has to be redone make sure you know exactly what is required, and by when.

Identifying what went wrong

If the job wasn't as agreed, why not? Was the information recorded inaccurately or incompletely – or not at all? Who made the error and how can this be avoided in future?

If the job didn't meet the customer's need, why not? How much effort was made to find out what the customer really wanted? Who talked to the customer and did the person doing the job use initiative and common sense and check any queries with the customer?

If the job was late being completed, why was there a delay? Was it a mistake or unavoidable? If the latter, was the customer warned in advance. If not, why not?

If the job was of poor quality, then who completed the work? Was the problem due to lack of training or experience, or because the person couldn't be bothered to do the job properly? If the job has to be redone, should it be given to this person or someone else? (This is likely to be your supervisor's decision.)

Keeping records of services requested and provided

Many organisations keep detailed records of external customers to enable them to 'target' customers more precisely. A typical example is superstores who issue customer loyalty cards. Every single purchase is recorded on a computer database so that mailshots promoting particular products and discount offers on these goods can be sent to tempt customers to increase their spending. What such databases don't record, however, is the number of times a customer has been disappointed because the service or item required wasn't available. The only way to obtain this is by carrying out a survey of shoppers.

As an administrator, however, you are better placed to 'track' and record what you did and what you couldn't do – for both your internal and external customers. This is important because:

- if you are regularly asked to do or supply something, you may need to give this higher priority or keep more stock
- if you regularly can't supply a particular service, then your supervisor may wish to consider changing the provision so that you do.

Feedback and information such as this enables your organisation to continually improve its customer service and keep it in line with customer requirements – even though these constantly change.

You need to prove you can provide all of the services listed on page 373 to either external or internal customers (and explain how you would provide them to the other).

You can also provide evidence by:

a keeping a list of the services you have agreed to provide to different customers – and records of those you were asked for but couldn't provide

b noting any *additional* services you suggested to a customer

c keeping the notes you made when you were agreeing and recording the service you should provide

d keeping copies of written information you have provided to customers

e obtaining witness testimony from internal customers that you have provided the service they required within the agreed time and checked they are satisfied with what you have done

f asking your supervisor for witness testimony that you have provided services to external customers and checked their satisfaction.

Key facts on helping customers with problems and complaints

To obtain this unit, you must be able to prove that you can deal with *two* of the following types of problem:

• the need for information and advice
• the need for a service or product to be changed
• complaints about your products or services.

Information and advice

There is a difference between giving information and giving advice. Information must be accurate and must be complete. Advice is something you offer to a customer to help with a specific request, such as assisting someone to find something, or to complete a form or to solve a problem. Giving advice properly is a skill. You need to be sensitive to the customer's needs and careful not to assume you know more about them than you do. You must also be careful not to patronise customers – which means treating them as if they know nothing!

The need for changes

An external customer may return a product that is faulty or ask for a service to be delivered differently (e.g. on a different day). An internal customer may want changes made to documents you are producing or alter their original request in some way (such as increasing their order for photocopies by a certain number).

Complaints about services or products

These are received when something was sub-standard or faulty, or when promises made by staff have not been kept. External customers have a legal right to products that are not faulty, which match their description and are safe to use. They have a right to quality services which are reasonable value for money. Your internal customers may have no 'legal rights' as such, but they do have expectations about the quality and standard of services you will provide – and these should also be as agreed.

Basic legal requirements relating to customer problems and complaints

The law affecting customer service is considerable, particularly if you are selling goods or services to external customers. For this unit, you are not expected to become a legal expert, simply to know that customers have certain legal rights. A basic understanding is extremely useful, however, as you are frequently a customer yourself and knowing what rights you have is invaluable if a purchase doesn't work or falls to bits the second you get it home!

The basic legal requirements are given below. Read this carefully then carry out the 'Check it out' on page 383 to become a greater expert at customer rights – including your own.

 KEY NOTES ON BASIC LEGAL REQUIREMENTS

Contracts of sale

If your organisation agrees to supply a good or service to a customer at a pre-agreed price then it enters into a legal contract of sale. Each contract may have special **express** terms – such as an agreed date for delivery. However, certain terms are **implied**. For instance, if you buy a computer you do not have to say it must work properly – that is an implied term. If it does not work, you could reject the contract and claim damages. If it works, but an 'extra' you ordered is missing, such as speakers, that is less serious. You could not reject the contract but could claim damages and therefore pay a lower price for the computer.

Legislation

Legislation can also introduce implied terms into a contract of sale.

The **Sale of Goods Act 1979 and 1995** means that goods must be:

- as described (e.g. if a wallet is described as leather it must be so)
- of satisfactory quality, in relation to the price paid, the description and its age
- fit for the purpose for which they are intended (e.g. an umbrella must open and be waterproof!).

The **Supply of Goods and Services Act 1982** covers repair and maintenance services and protects buyers against shoddy workmanship, delays and exorbitant charges. Under the Act, all services should be carried out:

- for a reasonable charge and within a reasonable time
- with reasonable care and skill
- using satisfactory materials.

The **Consumer Protection Act 1987** relates to price and safety. Customers must not be misled about the price, price reductions must not be exaggerated, and all supplied goods must be safe to use.

The **Trade Descriptions Act 1968** protects customers against false and misleading descriptions of goods, including illustrations which give false impressions.

The **Consumer Credit Act 1974** protects people who buy on credit in their own home by giving them a 'cooling off' period during which time they can change their minds.

The **Unfair Contract Terms Act 1977** prevents suppliers from limiting or taking away a customer's legal rights, such as through notices which disclaim any responsibility if goods are lost or damaged.

CHECK IT OUT!

Either visit your local Citizens' Advice Bureau and/or Trading Standards Office and obtain leaflets on customer protection, *or* (if you have Internet access) surf the Net to find out more. Useful websites are the Office of Fair Trading at www.oft.gov.uk, the Institute of Trading Standards Administration at www.tradingstandards.gov.uk, The Advertising Standards Authority at www.asa.org.uk, and the National Federation of Consumer Groups at www.nfcg.org.uk. Finally, two other informative sites are www.bbc.co.uk/watchdog and www.consumerworld.org.

The importance of collecting information

Before you can respond to a problem or a complaint you need to obtain as much information as possible. Otherwise you may make the situation worse! Customers with a problem or complaint often feel that no one has really listened to them or understood what they need – you must be the first person to show them that the opposite is true. Such situations are a key test of your listening and questioning skills. Only when you know exactly what the problem is, or what the complaint is about, can you hope to try to put matters right.

The need for empathy

Don't confuse 'empathy' with 'sympathy'. Your customers don't want you to make nice noises but to understand how it feels to be in their shoes. You **empathise** if you can identify with the customer and feel what he or she is feeling. You then start to understand their problem or complaint on a different level (i.e. from *their* perspective), and can more accurately identify the type of help they need and suggest more acceptable solutions.

Dealing with customers politely and calmly

You have already seen how to deal with angry or annoyed customers (page 371). Remember:

- never argue with an angry customer
- don't raise your voice or get upset
- don't make excuses
- don't interrupt someone in 'full flow' – wait until they 'run out of steam'
- don't hesitate to apologise – for the inconvenience your customer has suffered
- get help if you need it.

Identifying solutions

Some people consider that there are no such things as problems, only opportunities! If you think this way, you will see every problem as a chance to show your customer how keen you are to put matters right and meet their needs. However, the solutions you offer must be in accordance with your organisational procedures and capable of being delivered!

Some problems are easier to solve than others. This will depend upon:

a the type of problem or complaint

b what the customer actually wants

c   how reasonable (or angry) the customer is

d   what you are capable of suggesting and delivering.

If you offer a customer several alternatives, it proves you have thought about the problem or complaint and are trying your best to help. It is also more difficult for a customer to turn down several options than to reject one! You therefore have a better chance of reaching agreement with your customer.

However, if the 'gap' between what the customer wants and what you can do is huge, and all your alternatives are rejected, you need to refer the problem to a more experienced team member or to your supervisor. For instance, if a customer is demanding a large discount because a product or service was not as expected, then it is likely to be outside your area of responsibility to agree to this.

If the 'gap' between the customer's demands and your alternative solutions is only small, then you should try to negotiate with the customer to reach a compromise that suits you both. For instance, the customer wishes to collect an item on Tuesday and you will not have it ready until Thursday. In this case, for instance, is there any way you can bring the date forward to Wednesday and/or have the item delivered?

Keeping the customer informed

Customers get frustrated and annoyed if they are left wondering what will happen next. And customers who had a problem or complaint are often doubly annoyed! At each stage of the process, always keep the customer informed.

 KEY NOTES ON KEEPING CUSTOMERS INFORMED

When you have negotiated a solution:

- agree with the customer what you will do
- do it
- confirm you have done it.

When you have to refer the matter to another team member:

- tell them what you are doing and why
- remember it's still your problem until the other person actually takes it over
- if you are really efficient, you will check with your colleague later that everything went smoothly.

When you have to find out more information:

- fix a date and time for re-contacting the customer

- never keep them waiting any longer
- if there is a further delay, keep them informed – and give the reason
- if the delay is prolonged, keep in regular touch
- remember, the problem isn't solved until the customer is satisfied.

Following up your actions and recording the problem or complaint

It is very important that you check that any customer who originally had a problem or complaint is now satisfied. You should also record or report the problem in accordance with your organisational procedures.

Most organisations have standard procedures for recording customer complaints – although you may find there is a difference between the procedures for minor and major complaints and those made by internal and external customers. The aim of recording complaints – particularly those from external customers – is to identify areas where customer service could be improved. For instance:

- If customers have complained about long delays at reception, then more staff might be employed.

- If customers have complained about delivery problems or damaged goods, the organisation could tackle its haulage contractor.

- If staff have complained about the quality of photocopying, then either the operator needs more training or the copier itself needs servicing or changing.

- If customers regularly have a problem finding their way around your organisation, the signs should be improved or clear, internal maps produced.

- If customers always need help completing a particular form, could the form be changed or simplified to help them?

At regular intervals, senior staff should check the type of complaints being recorded to see whether there are common areas where improvements could be made. You can also add to this process yourself. Alarm bells should sound if you find yourself saying 'No, I'm sorry, we're always being asked for that but don't do it' or 'I'm sorry, yes I understand, we're always receiving complaints about that.' In both these cases you are constantly disappointing your customers – and your supervisor should be informed. Improving customer service is in everyone's interest in an organisation – including yours!

EVIDENCE COLLECTION

If you deal with customer problems or complaints, you may need to record them as part of your organisational procedures. If that is the case, include in your portfolio copies of several of the documents you have completed.

Remember that your assessor will need evidence that you can deal with *two* of the types of problems listed on page 381, with either internal or external customers, and explain how you would deal with the others.

If you are able, collect evidence which includes:

a   notes you have made when recording a customer problem or complaint

b   copies of any written responses that have been made to a customer, offering alternative solutions

c   witness testimony from any internal customers that you have dealt to their satisfaction with a complaint they had

d   witness testimony from your supervisor that you have dealt with problems and complaints and followed organisational procedures when recording and reporting these.

Unless you have specific permission from your supervisor, do not contact external customers who have made a complaint, asking them to provide witness testimony.

Option Unit 208 Maintain and issue stock items

FOCUS OF THE UNIT

To obtain this unit you must be able to:

* **maintain** stock levels
* **issue** stock items on request.

EVIDENCE COLLECTION

It will make evidence collection easier if you can obtain the following information:

a a list of the internal and external suppliers with whom you are allowed to place orders

b a copy of any organisational procedures you must follow when you are ordering or issuing stock items

c copies of internal or external orders for stock for which you have been responsible

d copies of stock records you have been maintaining

e copies of any other documentation with which you have been involved, such as stock-taking records, inventories, requisitions for internal orders, etc.

f examples of any communications you have had with suppliers relating to delivery problems, such as damaged or returned items, non-delivery, late delivery, etc.

Key facts on stock

Requirements for ordering, taking delivery, storing, stock-taking, issuing and disposing of stocks

All organisations have procedures in relation to the above – although they will differ slightly from one to another. Standard practices are usually similar to the following:

Requirements for ordering

There are usually some controls over what goods can be ordered. These controls may include:

- who is allowed to sign an official order
- which suppliers may be used
- under what circumstances items may be ordered
- the maximum quantity that can be ordered
- when items can be ordered.

These are necessary to prevent people ordering whatever they want, when they want – and the result would be chaos! The *aim* is to control:

- overall spending on stock
- the amount of stock held (normally through restrictions on storage space)
- the amount of money tied up in stock at any one time
- the amount spent on stock in a particular month.

Towards the end of the financial year, for example, large orders may be 'held over' or encouraged – depending upon the financial situation of the organisation.

You may have specific instructions that the maximum stock level for photocopier paper is, say, 100 reams and that new stock cannot be ordered until there are 30 or fewer reams in stock. The minimum level is calculated to allow for the *average* needs of users during the **lead time** between an order being placed and delivery. If a very large job requires additional stocks then you may be instructed to order more to cope with that.

Taking delivery and storing

Taking delivery includes checking the new stock against the order and **delivery note**, and the physical task of unpacking it and dealing with any problems (see pages 394–395).

Storing stock properly is important to prevent accidental damage which would make it unusable (see page 395).

Stock-taking

Stock-taking involves counting the stock and checking the result against the organisation's records. Any discrepancies must be reported and investigated. In a well-run system, these are likely to be minor and relatively easy to track. Computerised stock-control packages can print reports which list all the stock received, stock issued and adjustments over a period so that stock movements can be checked. This will remind you, therefore, that you disposed of some items last November – provided you entered the information accurately. On a manual system it is important to keep clear records so that any investigations can be undertaken speedily.

Pilferage is a key reason why stock-taking is carried out. If security to the stockroom is lax, some people may be tempted to help themselves to items. Allowed to go unchecked, the cost to the company can be considerable.

For that reason, if you found that several items regularly went 'missing', you could recommend that security needs improving.

Issuing stock

Stock can be issued to users 'on demand' or only on specific occasions, unless there is an emergency. Whereas the on-demand system is more flexible, unless you work near the stockroom you could find yourself spending a considerable time each day issuing stock items. For that reason, some organisations restrict the issuing of stock to certain days or times. However, there should be a procedure for dealing with emergency requests. Your sales manager wouldn't be pleased if he cannot have folders for an urgent presentation to a customer because they weren't ordered last week!

Usually, stock is issued only against a signed authorisation – often called an internal order or **requisition**. This is a further check that the person making the request is allowed to have the items.

Disposing of stock

This is necessary for several reasons:

- to remove items which are out of date (e.g. letterheads with your old company phone code or previous logo)

- to remove items which are obsolete (e.g. fax rolls when the fax is replaced with a plain paper model)

- to get rid of damaged items

- to get rid of surplus items which will never be used but are taking up space (however, this type of disposal indicates there may be a problem with the ordering system – see page 401).

Never dispose of any stock without the authority to do so from your supervisor. Rather than simply throwing things away, items may be able to be put to some use, such as:

- finding out if another department can use the item
- selling surplus items to staff at a discount
- using out-of-date or obsolete paper products as scrap pads.

If you have a good relationship with your supplier, and a surplus item was ordered recently, you may be able to arrange for the item to be returned. However, this will be as a favour – the supplier is under no obligation to accept it.

 INFORMATION UPDATE

If you think ordering and maintaining stock is a very unimportant job, perhaps you should think again. The total amount of stationery ordered each year in Britain is valued at £3,100 million!

Current figures show that a company with 100 employees spends, on average, £84,000 on stationery of which 15 per cent (£12,600) is wasted, stolen or never used because it is out of date (source: Netstationers, *Mind Your Own Business,* August 2000). This works out at £126 for every employee. You might want to multiply this by the number of employees in your firm to see what your wastage figure could be!

Reporting discrepancies or damage and recommending improvements

You will be responsible to your supervisor or line manager for maintaining adequate stock levels and issuing stock items on request to your colleagues. This is usually the person to whom you should also report any problems – unless there is another authorised person with whom you have to liaise over stock control.

You may be able to suggest improvements to prevent problems recurring. This will be the natural outcome of any investigation and you can usefully contribute to this process (see page 400).

KEY NOTES ON REPORTING PROBLEMS IDENTIFIED WHEN CHECKING STOCK

- Don't be alarmist. Check the extent/seriousness of the problem before you report it. Getting hysterical about a box of paperclips or claiming that two camcorders have been stolen and then finding them in the cupboard where you locked them away last week won't make you very popular!
- Once you have the facts, report the problem promptly.
- Don't accuse anyone or make wild assumptions – stay calm and simply state the facts.
- If you know *why* the problem has occurred, then say so. If it was your fault, apologise (and don't repeat the mistake!).
- If you don't know why the problem has occurred, then be prepared for an investigation if the matter is serious.

Methods of keeping stock records

There are two basic systems used for keeping stock records, manual and computer-based.

Manual systems

Most manual systems include **stock record cards** – one for each item held (see below) – usually stored in alphabetical order. An entry is made for every item received or issued and the new balance is calculated. If the balance shows the stock is below the minimum or re-order level, the item is usually 'flagged' to ensure it is included on the next order. The card is updated when the delivery has been unpacked and checked. If deliveries are awaited the card should state this, to prevent the goods being ordered twice in error. This also helps to show which orders are delayed so that you can 'chase up' the supplier (see page 398).

STOCK RECORD CARD

Item Post-It Notes **Unit** Packs of 12 **Maximum** 40 packs

Supplier Statline Ltd **Minimum** 10 packs

Date	Received	Issued	Dept.	Req. no.	Balance
3 Dec					18 packs
7 Dec		6 packs	Sales	3028	12 packs
8 Dec		4 packs	Finance	3039	8 packs
14 Dec		4 packs	Admin	3142	4 packs
16 Dec	34 packs				38 packs
17 Dec		2 packs	Personnel	3180	36 packs

There will be some kind of **ordering system** so that you have a record of:

• the official orders that have been sent to suppliers for new stock

• internal orders or requisitions you have received, against which you have issued stock items.

The second type of record is important as it helps you to prove *why* you issued certain items, and to whom, if this is necessary.

There will be **documentation** relating to stock-taking. This may include a master list of all stock items held on which you would enter the physical stocks held, the stocks held according to your records, and a column for recording discrepancies or notes. Finally there will be **records** you keep in relation to authorised disposals of stocks.

Computer-based systems

Computerised systems follow a very similar format to the manual type, the difference being that the information is stored electronically and updated on screen. A major benefit is the number of reports you can produce at the touch of a key.

- A **stock valuation** is simply a list of all stock held at cost price.

- A **re-order list** is a summary of all stock that is reaching, or at, re-order level.

- A **stock inventory list** is completed during stock-taking. In this case the list of stock is complete with the amount held according to the computer – you have only to do a physical check and enter this figure.

- A **stock analysis** shows the turnover of each item, i.e. how fast it is being replaced. Those 'turning over' the fastest are your most active items (see below).

- An **audit trail** is a very useful report as it shows *all* the computer entries that have been made since the last audit trail was printed. This is a safeguard against the fact that no individual can remember everything that happens over a long period – but your computer can!

There are also certain safeguards in a computer system. For instance, you cannot make an adjustment without stating why you are changing something. In the audit trail the explanation is then printed out to remind you why you made the amendment. With a manual system you have to be more self-disciplined. If you use liquid paper to adjust a figure no one will know but you – until stock-taking time – when you will have to say why!

It is, of course, possible to thwart even the best computer system if you key in the wrong quantity. For that reason, whatever system you use, note that some criteria apply to all stock records.

KEY NOTES ON STOCK RECORDS

- All records must *always* be up to date. Otherwise everyone is making decisions using the wrong information.

- Records *must* be accurate. Entering the wrong amount received could be critical if it means that a key item may run out before it is replaced (because you think there is more than you possess). Conversely, entering too little received might look a little suspicious if you did it often!

- All handwritten records must be clear and legible. Write neatly. Print if necessary. Don't rub out or use liquid paper or – even worse – cross out and overwrite items. Remember that many entries will be figures – and you cannot guess these if they are unclear. If you are keying data into your computer, you need to be equally vigilant.

Key facts on maintaining stock levels

Levels of demand

Both the **items** kept in stock and the **levels** of stock vary, according to usage by staff. A stock turnover report produced by a computer system will show the most 'active' items – but these also change over time and because of circumstances. There are two types of trend you can identify – short-term and long-term.

Short-term demands change because of specific jobs. A large mailshot will increase the demand for envelopes, an annual sales conference may increase demand for presentation materials. Learn to spot monthly or annual trends which will affect demand for certain items at certain times – and plan accordingly. Short-term demand changes affect the *levels* of stock you hold.

Long-term demands change because of new business, technological developments or new items coming on to the market. A company which installs an internal e-mail system may find that demand for memo paper falls dramatically. One which purchases a thermal binder may have no further use for comb or slide binders – and so on. Long-term demand changes affect the *types* of items you keep in stock.

Checking deliveries

The system for receiving stock will vary, depending upon the size of organisation. In large organisations, deliveries are often made at a central point. The goods are checked and a **goods received note** (GRN) may be made out. Any discrepancies between the actual goods and those stated on the delivery note will be noted on the GRN. In a smaller organisation – or one without a central delivery point – unpacking and checking the goods may be your responsibility. In this case you must check that the items

delivered match those itemised on the delivery note *and* on the order form –
in every way. If they do not, this may be because:

- items are out of stock at the supplier (they are usually marked on the
  delivery note as 'to follow')
- items are obsolete and are no longer supplied
- items are missing (because the packer made a mistake)
- too many items are included, again because of a mistake (it is not ethical
  to keep these as bonus items!)
- items may be damaged
- the wrong items may have been sent.

There may have been a deliberate substitution if something you ordered was
out of stock at the supplier. If you do not want to accept the alternative then
contact the supplier immediately and arrange for collection.

 ## KEY NOTES ON HANDLING AND STORING STOCK

- Handle the goods carefully. Use a trolley for heavy boxes.
  Follow instructions to open the box the right way up.

- Unpack items carefully. Don't remove wrapping paper unless it
  is necessary. Many items, such as paper, remain in good
  condition longer if you leave them wrapped.

- Store stock in a special, lockable, store or cupboard, preferably
  on slatted shelves so that air can circulate freely. This prevents
  damage or deterioration through damp. The storage area
  should be away from direct heat or light – both of which can
  cause the deterioration of many stationery items. The shelves
  should be clearly labelled.

- Put new stock at the bottom (or back of a shelf) so that
  the oldest items are used first. This takes effort but is
  important.

- For safety and convenience:
  - stack items with descriptive labels facing outwards
  - store heavy items low down
  - put fast-moving items where you can reach them
    easily
  - take special care with potentially dangerous items
    (e.g. keep scissors and drawing pins in boxes, store any
    inflammable fluids on the floor – making sure the label is
    clearly visible)
  - comply with any specific storage instructions (e.g. 'this
    way up').

Suppliers of stocks

Large organisations normally have a list of supplier firms which must be used. These will have been chosen because they are reliable, reasonably priced and provide a rapid service. Many suppliers give discounts to regular customers and are more sympathetic towards replacing goods which have been ordered in error.

Today, many organisations try to keep supplies to a minimum to reduce the need for a large, costly storage area. In this case it is essential the supplier has a rapid delivery service – such as guaranteed delivery within 24 hours. This not only reduces the amount of storage space required but also prevents problems with unscheduled 'big' jobs which may otherwise deplete supplies.

 INFORMATION UPDATE

A new development is stationery suppliers who use the Internet to promote their services. Goods are ordered on-line and can often be purchased at discount rates because the suppliers have fewer costs associated with operating their business than those who need a local showroom or warehouse. Two examples are www.netstationers.co.uk and www.stationerystore.co.uk. Another alternative, for many companies, has been to hand over the whole job of monitoring and maintaining stationery stocks to a professional organisation. The official term for this is **outsourcing**.

Ordering from internal and external suppliers

If you work for a small organisation, you will simply order from an external supplier. If you are employed in a large organisation then you may order certain items *internally* – for instance from a centralised purchasing or stores department. You are likely to find a difference in the procedures you have to follow.

External suppliers normally insist upon an official, signed order before they will supply any goods. This is their safeguard against anyone placing an order without the proper authority, for which they would not receive payment. In an emergency, a signed order can be sent by fax. Internet suppliers ask the company to register as a customer and users have to go through a password/identification procedure before the order will be accepted.

When you place the order it is sensible to agree the delivery date, especially if the items are required urgently. It is also wise to note the name of the person you contacted – in case you have any queries later (see below).

Internal suppliers will usually require an internal order – often known as a **requisition**. Again this must be signed by someone in authority before any goods can be issued, as the value of the order will be set against the department or budget holder ordering the goods. Again it is worth checking when you can expect to receive the goods – unless you already know.

Although *all* orders should be checked carefully, it is crucial this be done for external supplies. Legally, if you make a mistake on the order and request the wrong items in error, the supplier has no obligation to take them back. Therefore double-check:

a   the quantity (remember these vary – paper is supplied in reams, envelopes in 100s or 1000s)
b   the reference or order code for each item
c   the description
d   the size
e   the price.

Always check you have the latest price list.

Note the date the delivery is due and ring the supplier the following day if nothing has been received. Similarly, you will have to contact the supplier if there are any discrepancies or mistakes after an order has been delivered.

KEY NOTES FOR CHASING UP ORDERS

- Be polite yet firm. Have the order to hand, so that you can quote the date and the order number.

- If you remembered to note the name of the person you first contacted about the order, ask to speak to that person.

- Briefly summarise the date and contents of the order – then enquire about delivery.

- Try to obtain a firm commitment before you conclude the call.

- If there is doubt about certain items, ask what is being done to speed up delivery.

- If you are concerned that the delivery is overly delayed – or you feel you are getting nowhere – say you will speak to your supervisor and call back.

EVIDENCE COLLECTION

For your award, you have to prove you deal with at least one supplier (internal or external) but could also deal competently with the other type. This is why you need to keep comprehensive records of your dealings with suppliers.

If you need to chase up a supplier, keep a record of what you did and when. This is good business practice – as well as providing evidence for your NVQ award! If you do not have to do this job at the time you are taking your award, be prepared to answer your assessor's questions on this topic.

Key facts on issuing stock items on request

Issuing stock items

If you work for a large organisation you may have to follow specified procedures when issuing stock – and these may differ depending upon whether you are issuing to your own team or to other parts of the organisation. In a small firm, the system is likely to be more informal, but it is sensible to have some controls and not simply give anyone anything they want – whenever they want it.

Procedures are likely to cover:

- how often stock can be issued
- the quantities of stock that can be issued at one time

- what to do if a very large quantity is requested
- what paperwork you have to complete when stock is issued.

Stock may be issued once a day, several times a week or on demand. The more formal and the larger the system the more likely it is that there will be specific times. The same is likely to apply if you are issuing stock to other departments. If you work in a small firm where stock is issued flexibly – or are issuing items only to people in your own team – you may be able to save yourself walking time by having a small supply of frequently requested items in a locked cupboard near to your desk. Don't forget to include this stock when you are completing your records or undertaking a stock check.

There may be controls on how much stock you can issue at once without special permission. Anyone can need a pen or pencil, but asking for 100 pencils or for three pencils every day is rather different! Ask for a reason if people want a very large amount or if they frequently request an item – in case you have to explain why the stock has been used so quickly.

There may be special paperwork (such as an internal requisition) which has to be authorised before stock can be requested – or such paperwork may apply only to orders over a certain value. This varies considerably from one organisation to another. If the request is from another department, there may be additional paperwork to complete to ensure that you are credited with the value of the stock you have issued.

Issuing receipts

The person requesting an item may have to sign a receipt under certain circumstances. You will make out the receipt, ask the other person to sign it, issue a copy to them and retain a copy yourself. This system may be used on the following occasions.

- Items are issued in an emergency and the official paperwork is 'to follow' – for instance, if a manager gives you telephone authorisation to issue the items. The receipt can be kept until the official requisition is received.

- Valuable items are loaned to staff – such as camcorders or laptop computers. Staff should also receive a reminder of the conditions which apply when equipment is lent – as special insurance is needed to cover equipment taken off the premises. You should also agree and log the date of return.

- Items are loaned for special events – such as folders and files for an exhibition or conference. This saves you having to book the stock out and then back in again.

- A large number of goods are being collected by someone from another department.

- Checks are being made on the frequency with which staff request expensive items – such as laser printer cartridges. If usage is higher than expected, your normal records will probably not say which *individuals* are using the items – your records will state only the department name. Often simply asking people to sign for goods makes them wary of asking too often! A company may introduce this system if they suspect some staff are taking items home to save their personal stationery bills!

The above are examples of occasions when receipts may be required, but circumstances vary between organisations. It is important to check those occasions when they may apply in yours.

Suggesting improvements

Ideas for improvements can arise in various ways, but the most obvious source is problems which you want to eliminate or reduce. Problems can occur in even the best system over a period of time. Some suppliers may become less reliable, the space available may become more cramped, you may find the number of orders has increased so that the job is more demanding or the number of emergency items being requested has increased. Rather than tell your boss you have a problem, it is always better to consider solutions and present your recommendations in a positive way.

You also need to consider *how* you will present your recommendations. Managers are busy people. They will have expected you to think through the implications of your idea. What will it cost? Who will it affect? How much work will be involved? Will it actually *save* money? (These ideas are always welcomed above all others!) Then they will expect you to summarise your ideas clearly and concisely. Finally, they will expect you to present your suggestions at the right time – not in front of half the office and not when they are about to rush to an urgent appointment.

Rather than trying to think of an improvement – which can be difficult – it is usually easier to think how you could reduce any problems or improve any problem areas. For instance:

- Are you happy with your suppliers? Are they reliable? Do you get good service? Are the items you order delivered promptly and in good condition?

- Is the storage space suitable and secure to prevent pilferage? Is it well ventilated and of an appropriate temperature so that stock is maintained in good condition?

- Is the level of damaged stock and wastage acceptable? Could anything be done to reduce it?

- Is expenditure on stock good or average for your department or is usage very high? Could anything be done to find out how to reduce it a little and save money?

- Are health and safety issues taken seriously? Are all dangerous substances clearly labelled? Are all flammable substances stored away from heat? Is there a 'no smoking' sign in the room and is a safety stool provided to give safe access to high shelves? Is there a trolley for moving heavy items? Are potentially hazardous items (scissors, drawing pins, etc.) kept on low shelves and in boxes?

- Is the stock room neat and tidy? Can you find what you want easily and quickly?

- Does the range of stock reflect people's needs or would it be useful to review the items that are held?

- Is out-of-date stock disposed of properly? Have you any better ideas for getting rid of items no longer needed?

- Do people 'stick to the rules' in terms of ordering goods properly, filling in the correct forms, obtaining authorisation, collecting items at the correct time – or are people forever asking you to 'bend the rules' and issue items on demand and without having completed the proper paperwork?

- Is there a good reason for all the forms and records you use? Are any completed for reasons that no one can remember? Is there space to store all your records so that they can be found quickly and easily?

- Do staff who are responsible for stock work together effectively as a team? Could the duties be allocated better?

- How many emergencies are there in the average week or month? Can anything be done to reduce these?

These points may give you some ideas but nothing is more effective than thinking about *your* system and how it operates. If you owned the business (and personally paid the stationery bill), would you be happy with it, or would you want it changed? If so, why?

Another tip is to jot down your ideas in a notebook. Often, when you are busy and have a problem to solve, you may have a good idea and then forget all about it – until the problem repeats itself! Making a note immediately is always useful, as you can then think about your idea and develop it when you have more time.

Once you have made a good suggestion which results in an improvement, you will find that your subsequent ideas are welcomed, as you will have proved that you can suggest changes which make a positive difference. Employees who can do this are always valued – wherever they work.

Disposing of unwanted stock

This was dealt with on page 390.

EVIDENCE COLLECTION

Make copies of stock control records which prove you have issued stock together with the request or requisition forms used in your organisation. Alternatively, ask both your supervisor and colleagues to whom you have issued stock to provide witness evidence for you.

Obtain copies of any receipts you issue and note on each *why* the receipt was issued. Or you could write a brief description of why and when receipts are used in your organisation and ask your supervisor to countersign this. If you do not issue receipts, then expect to answer questions from your assessor about why these may be used.

Make a note of any occasions on which stock is disposed of. Identify the stock, why it was disposed of and what method you used. Again, ask your supervisor to sign this document.

Try to make one recommendation which would improve your system and put this in writing to your supervisor. Attach any reply you receive. Then write a brief description for your assessor as to why you made this recommendation and the eventual outcome. If you do not make any recommendations (because your system is so good!), be prepared to answer questions from your assessor to cover this item.

Option Unit 209 Coordinate mail services

FOCUS OF THE UNIT

To obtain this unit you must be able to:

- receive, sort and distribute mail
- dispatch mail.

EVIDENCE COLLECTION

It will make your evidence collection easier if you can obtain the following items:

a a copy of any procedures you must follow when dealing with incoming and outgoing mail

b a statement which describes your own involvement with mail handling

c a copy of any routine mail handling records you complete.

If you work in a small firm the procedures may not be official but may be issued as guidelines to staff. If you have no guidelines, then, after discussion with your supervisor, you could draft them yourself (see pages 405–406), using your own experience and stating the actions you are expected to take when handling mail. Check your finished work with your supervisor or tutor as his/her approval will be required if you are using your document as official evidence.

The statement about your own involvement will say whether you work in a large, centralised mailroom, for instance, or for a small firm where only one or two people handle the mail. Alternatively, are you just involved in departmental mail duties but also liaise with staff in a central mailroom? In this case, you should describe your own duties and how you relate to other staff. Try to make your statement quite detailed so that your own role in relation to mail handling is fully and accurately described.

Key facts on coordinating mail services

Correct procedures for receiving and dispatching internal and external mail

Mail handling is important in all organisations. Every day many documents arrive by post – some important, some urgent, some routine and some, possibly, of no use at all! Similarly, documents such as letters, reports, catalogues and leaflets are sent out by post every day. Despite the increase in electronic methods of sending documents, the Royal Mail continues to handle over 70 million items of mail every day. In addition, many companies also use private couriers or private delivery services to distribute other types of documents and packages both within and outside the UK.

Large organisations often have a central mailroom with trained staff responsible for the receipt and distribution of incoming mail and the preparation and dispatch of outgoing items. A small firm may give this job to one or two key staff who do these tasks as part of their other duties. In many medium-sized organisations there will be a central point where mail is received and distributed, or received and prepared for dispatch – but most of the distribution and preparatory dispatch work will be done by departmental administrators.

Most organisations have procedures for dealing with the mail. These are, effectively, the 'do's' and 'don't's' which all staff must follow. Procedures are useful as they ensure everyone knows what to do and how to do it. If you have a problem or difficulty, then you can find out what you should do by referring to the procedures. In a small firm, without official procedures, experienced staff may know what to do and may tell more junior staff, but the system is apt to be more haphazard if nothing has been written down.

You may find that there are two sets of procedures, one for staff who work in the mailroom (in a small firm, the person who 'does' the post) and one for staff who collect mail and/or prepare mail and then deliver it to the mailroom (or post person).

An extract from both types is shown on the following pages. Check these against those in your own company. In particular try to find out the following.

a   How do the duties of departmental or general office staff and mailroom staff differ? For instance, whose responsibility is it to wrap parcels and packages or to select a particular mail service in your organisation?

b   If you needed to dispatch a large parcel by courier, whose permission would you need before you could action this?

c   Are the guidelines different on a Friday, and what happens just before a bank holiday? For instance, are *all* mail items sent by second class, given that no one will receive the item until Monday or Tuesday anyway.

d   Is the post collected by the Royal Mail, or does someone take the franked post to a postbox every day?

EXTRACT FROM PROCEDURES FOR MAILROOM STAFF

Incoming mail

1 All mailroom staff must report to work no later than 8 am each day.

2 All mail must be opened and pre-sorted on arrival apart from Personal or Private and Confidential items.

3 All mail, apart from financial or legal documents, must be date-stamped.

4 All enclosures must be checked and clipped to the main document. Any omissions must be noted on the document and initialled.

5 All envelopes must be retained for 24 hours in case of queries.

6 All staff must be familiar with the company procedures for dealing with suspicious items. These must be reported immediately to the mailroom supervisor.

Outgoing mail

1 All items are to be sent by second-class post unless marked otherwise.

2 Internal items must be placed in the special trays and sent to branch offices in *one* large envelope.

3 Queries over special services should be directed to the mailroom supervisor who has the discretion to recommend a more appropriate service if this would fulfil the requirements at less cost to the company.

4 It is the responsibility of mailroom staff to ensure that all forms and records are completed accurately.

5 Outgoing mail must be ready for collection at 4.45 pm each evening.

EXTRACT FROM PROCEDURES FOR MAILROOM USERS

1 Departmental staff must collect mail between 10 am and 10.15 each morning and 2 pm and 2.15 pm each afternoon. During these times they should also bring mail for dispatch – either internally or externally.

2 Outgoing mail must be checked by departmental staff to ensure all letters have been signed, enclosures are attached and the address is correct.

3 Any mail which has to be sent first class, by airmail or by a special service *must* be clearly marked as such on the envelope.

e   What rules are in place to try to save money – for instance, rules regarding the dispatch of personal mail, the use of special services and whether envelopes are re-used for sending internal items.

f   Do mailroom staff personally deliver mail to desks, or is mail collected by certain individuals?

The importance of meeting deadlines when distributing and dispatching mail

Incoming mail is always distributed early in the working day, as it is likely to contain important and urgent items. Staff need to receive mail promptly so that they can check it for important developments before they become involved in other activities that day – mainly because information they receive could affect their actions. A rep's report or a letter may influence a discussion with a customer, a memo about an internal development may affect a discussion in a meeting later that day. Anyone who has not received and read their mail that day – and therefore has no knowledge of the current situation – will be at a disadvantage and can easily look foolish or inefficient. Additionally, most managers and supervisors will *prioritise* their work for the day depending upon what their mail contains. Therefore, to be effective and use their day wisely, they need their mail early.

Outgoing items must be dispatched promptly as people in *other* departments and organisations also need information quickly. If the Royal Mail collects your post you will have a clear deadline for completing everything. Even if it doesn't, your local postbox will have a last collection time – missing this means walking to a main post office where the collection time is a little later. However, for national items (rather than local) you will still be limited to about 6 pm or 7 pm. In addition, special items need to be handed over the counter – so you must arrive before the post office closes. If you 'miss the post' then everything will be delayed for 24 hours – which could be crucial for very urgent items. Moreover, you can't just post special items and hope no one will know – you need a receipt. You therefore have the additional agony of having to explain the problem the following day! For these reasons most organisations have a clear routine and deadline for dispatching outgoing mail.

Key facts on receiving, sorting and distributing mail

Sorting and recording incoming mail and dealing with urgent and confidential mail

The first task is for incoming mail to be pre-sorted into specific categories.

Internal items

These are the ones received from other departments, from branch offices or from the firm's representatives. Remember to follow the correct procedure for internal items marked 'urgent' or 'confidential' (or both) – see below.

External items

External items are those received from other organisations or individuals.

Routine items are first- or second-class mail or circulars. Open first-class items *first* – particularly if there is a large amount of mail. Then if anyone needs their mail quickly you will have sorted out the most important items. Circulars, such as booklets, magazines and journals may need to be seen by several staff. You may have to deliver them to a particular office or person who will circulate them. Otherwise you may need to attach a circulation or routing slip which lists the names of those who will see it and the office to which it must be returned.

Urgent items can be identified because they are marked Special Delivery by the Royal Mail, have been delivered by courier, or the word URGENT is printed on the envelope. These are usually opened first and kept separate from routine items. If the item is delivered outside mailroom hours, it should be delivered quickly and/or the recipient asked to arrange for its prompt collection. You will be expected to sign for Special Delivery items delivered by the Royal Mail and items delivered by courier. This means you take the responsibility for ensuring the item is delivered promptly – as there is proof that you were the person who received it!

Confidential items must be left unopened. If the recipient is on leave and the item is marked urgent, the best action is to deliver the item to the recipient's line manager.

Other types of item

- **Recorded Delivery** letters must be signed for on receipt and a record made in the appropriate book.

- **Monetary items,** such as cheques, are kept separate in most organisations. In some firms every item is logged, either in a special Remittances Book or on computer.

- **Parcels and packages** may need signing for on delivery. Depending upon your organisation's procedures, you may have to open them and check the contents or deliver them unopened to the recipient. If you have to sign for anything you haven't checked, write 'contents not checked' on the form. If an item is damaged state this on the form you sign and attach a note for the recipient so that it is clear that *you* didn't damage the parcel! If a parcel is heavy *don't* attempt to lift or move it yourself. Get help instead.

Identifying and reporting suspicious or damaged items

Many large mailrooms display a poster giving staff instructions what to do if they receive a 'suspicious' item of mail. This is particularly important if you work for an organisation involved in sensitive areas of work – such as defence, nuclear fuel or government security. These establishments usually have expensive screening equipment in their mailrooms (similar to the type you see in airports) which scans all mail before it is opened.

However, all staff should be aware of security procedures as any firm can be an unexpected target – for instance, if someone has a vendetta against the firm for some reason.

The police Crime Prevention Department gives guidance on how to recognise a typical letter or parcel bomb. They warn that staff should be vigilant if they receive unexpected deliveries by hand – whether in the mailroom or at the reception desk – and to encourage regular correspondents to mark all envelopes and parcels with their name as sender. A firm's franking label or stamp, with the company name, is the most obvious way of doing this.

Consider a parcel or letter as suspicious if:

- the address is 'odd', does not contain the name of a known individual, or the handwriting, spelling or typing are poor

- there is no return address

- the postmark is unusual and/or there are too many stamps for the weight of the package
- there is any discoloration on the packaging which could be caused by a leak or grease marks
- the package is wrapped by special string or tape which is the only way of gaining access
- there is visible wiring or tin foil on a package or envelope which is damaged
- there is excessive wrapping
- there is a slight odour of almonds or marzipan.

If you think you have detected a suspicious item, *don't* be worried about telling someone in case you will be considered foolish or alarmist. Better safe than sorry!

A damaged item is one where the wrapping or envelope has become torn. If the damage is caused by the Royal Mail the item is delivered in a special plastic bag, which gives information on the damage. Note that in this case some items may be missing – so notify the recipient that the item was damaged on arrival – then steps can be taken to follow up any possible omissions.

 KEY NOTES ON HANDLING SUSPICIOUS ITEMS

Don't

- Mess about with the parcel
- Cover it
- Put it in water or a bucket of sand
- Throw it out of a window!
- Use a telephone in the room to give a warning – some devices can be activated by telephone signals.

Do

- Put it on a table in the middle of the room (away from windows and doors)
- Ask people to leave the room and lock the door
- Tell your supervisor – who may want to evacuate the building
- Notify the police by dialling 999 from another phone – be ready to give your name, company name, location and your reason for calling.

Directing mail to the right person

Mailroom staff can help people to be more productive, or they can cause irritation and delays by wrongly delivering items to people. This is annoying both for the person who receives items for other people and for those who don't receive items when they expected them! In some organisations it is amazing how much mail is wrongly delivered. With an urgent or important item, this can cause a considerable amount of inconvenience.

 ## KEY NOTES ON DELIVERING MAIL

- Be aware of any 'duplicate names' in the organisation. Hopefully these people will try to ensure that, wherever possible, their initials are included on the envelope.

- Use the contents to give you a clue if no recipient is named. With a basic knowledge of your organisation, you should know which department would deal with the matter.

- If an item is urgent or important, but you cannot tell who it is for, *don't* just put it in the nearest mail basket to get rid of it! Using the contents and the sender's name as your information, telephone likely recipients to see if anyone is expecting such a delivery. If you have e-mail, you could e-mail all staff if you are absolutely desperate.

- If you deliver mail to desks, make sure you put it on the right ones. Carry small piles and check where each person's mail ends and the next begins.

- If a desk is empty or it looks as though an office is deserted, check with someone if you should be leaving today's mail there or if someone else is dealing with it.

- If someone complains that they have received the wrong mail, or an item they wanted urgently was sent to the wrong department, *don't* become defensive and annoyed because you have been criticised. Apologise, if it was your fault, and try to find out what went wrong.

Reporting delays

Delays in sorting and delivering internal mail can occur for many reasons. The mailroom may be short-staffed, there may be much more mail than usual, the mail itself may have been delivered late. However, your team members won't know this – unless you tell them. There may be several people waiting for their mail who have no idea there is a problem.

If the mail will be ready within 5 or 15 minutes of its normal time, then this is not usually problematic. If, however, there will be a longer delay then people need to know, so that they can make alternative plans if necessary.

The first person to whom you may be expected to report a delay is your own supervisor. The *earlier* you warn that there *might* be a delay, the better. This helps that person to consider the problem and decide what should be done. If you then confirm there *will* be a delay, action can be taken immediately. Don't tell someone at the last minute that there's a backlog which will take at least an hour to clear.

Finally, always explain why the delay has occurred and when the mail is likely to be available. Then people can make their own plans accordingly.

EVIDENCE COLLECTION

You will need to prove to your assessor that you receive, sort and distribute *all* of the following types of mail: internal, external, parcels, letters. You must also be able to show that you can deal with confidential and urgent mail correctly.

You can supply evidence from witness testimony provided by your mailroom supervisor or your own supervisor – and can supplement this with witness testimony from colleagues to whom you regularly deliver mail.

Be prepared to answer questions from your assessor as to how you would identify damaged or suspicious items – and the action you would take – and how you would cope with delays in mail distribution. However, if either of these situations actually occur, write a brief account of what took place – clearly identifying your own role – and ask your supervisor to countersign this for authenticity.

Key facts on dispatching mail

Checking for missing items

It is very easy for people to send items for mailing and forget to include an attachment or enclosure. This irritates the recipient (who has to go to the trouble of contacting your organisation to tell you) and makes extra work for your team. In addition, your firm's postage costs will increase.

The easiest way to check for missing items is to:

* encourage letter writers to indicate an enclosure or attachment by the letters 'Enc' at the bottom
* remember that compliment slips are normally only sent attached to something else

- scan each document quickly to see whether an attachment or enclosure is mentioned
- if more than one attachment is listed, check they are all present.

If an enclosure is missing, a useful tip is to check that it hasn't become 'hooked' to another item, before you contact the person concerned. This is apt to happen when many documents are in a pile and some are fastened with paperclips.

Ensuring mail is securely sealed

Dispatching mail which is not securely sealed is likely to result in someone receiving a damaged item. Or it may not arrive at all if it drops to pieces inside a Royal Mail distribution centre. If it jams one of their conveyor belts and slows down the delivery across an entire area, you may find your mailroom supervisor receives a rather sharp letter! If items are missing on delivery, then someone will also have the inconvenience of trying to replace them. If you were the one who sealed the parcel, you are unlikely to be very popular.

 KEY NOTES ON PACKING ITEMS

Do

- Pack items properly using the correct materials. These include a wide range of envelopes (included card-backed envelopes for items such as photographs), padded bags, bubble plastic and polystyrene chips or foam. You can also use the contents of your shredder.
- Use a box which is both large enough for the contents and strong enough for their weight.
- Make sure fragile items are individually wrapped and can't knock against each other.
- Use plastic or reinforced carton sealing tape – either 38 mm or 50 mm wide – preferable in an 'H' seal, top and bottom.
- make sure that, as sender, your name and address is clearly shown on the outer carton or wrapper.
- Put a 'fragile – handle with care' sticker on fragile goods – or write this clearly on the outside.

Don't

- Try to squeeze too much into too small an envelope.
- Wrap items with ordinary paper.
- Use ordinary sticky tape to fasten parcels or boxes.

- Use staples to close a padded bag, without covering them with adhesive tape to avoid injury to handlers.
- Re-use fragile boxes or cartons.
- Leave space between separate items in a box – fill any gaps with packaging material.

Addressing mail correctly

Your organisation will want to conform to the postal service requirements for addressing mail correctly, to minimise delays with delivery. If you use a courier or Special Delivery, you also need to check whether they have any special requirements. Check, too, how internal items should be packed and addressed.

 KEY NOTES ON ADDRESSING MAIL

Do

- Type (or print) the envelope or label. If you must handwrite it, use a black pen.
- Start half-way down an envelope. On a label, use the space appropriately for the length of the address and stick it where the address would be written on the package.
- Write special instructions for the addressee, e.g. Personal or Private & Confidential, first. Then leave a space before the addressee's name.
- Otherwise start with the name of the addressee and his/her title (e.g. Mr, Mrs, Ms, Miss, Dr).
- Start a new line for every line of the address.
- Put the town or city (and country, for overseas mail) in CAPITALS.
- Put the postcode on the last line. If this is impossible, leave about 10 spaces after the last word before writing it and *never* insert any punctuation in the postcode.
- Write any mailing instructions on the top left, e.g. URGENT or BY HAND. Some mailrooms like instructions such as First Class or Airmail written on as well – even though they may cover the latter with an airmail sticker.

Don't

- Write on envelopes with a roller ball or felt tip pen where the ink will run on a rainy day!
- Expect overseas addresses to follow the same conventions as in the UK. For instance, in some cases the number of the property

is put at the end of the line, rather than the beginning, or the town goes before the street.

- Panic if you have no postcode – either telephone the Royal Mail postcode enquiry line on 0345 111222 or use the Internet (www.royalmail.co.uk).
- End a written address with a fancy underline or underscore the postcode on a printed address.

EVIDENCE COLLECTION

Prepare a brief account of the procedures you follow when dispatching mail. In particular, identify the checks you make to ensure that mail includes all the relevant items and how you pack or seal mail to prevent accidental damage.

Attach examples of labels or envelopes you have produced to prove you can address these correctly and in accordance with postal and organisational requirements.

Ask your supervisor to countersign your account when you have completed this.

Choosing an appropriate postal service

The most appropriate service will depend upon:

- the item you are sending (letter or parcel, small or large, light or heavy)
- whether it is routine, urgent, valuable or important
- whether the destination is in the UK or overseas.

Routine items

Envelopes are used to enclose most routine mail items, such as letters, invoices or brochures. They are available in a wide range of types and sizes, such as those with a cardboard backing for photographs, or with side pleats so that they expand easily. Many firms use window envelopes for standard items but it is important you check that every line of the address is clearly visible. Never select an envelope that is too small for the items being inserted.

Internal mail for branch offices or representatives is often put into large envelopes which are left open all day – and then sealed and mailed. This is done to minimise postage charges.

External routine mail is usually sent by Royal Mail. Many organisations routinely send everything second class unless an envelope is specifically marked to be sent first class.

If proof of posting is required, you can obtain a **certificate of posting** from the post office, but this is no guarantee of delivery. There is no charge for this service.

Most routine items are sent abroad by airmail. Either attach an airmail sticker or write AIRMAIL on the envelope clearly by hand. The cost of postage will depend upon the country. Note that you don't need an airmail sticker for European countries, nor a customs declaration sticker in most cases.

Parcels may be sent via the Royal Mail or by Parcelforce – or your organisation may prefer to use a private delivery company if the parcel is urgent (see page 418).

Airmail parcels are more expensive to dispatch than those sent by surface mail, and heavy parcels are dearer than lightweight ones. The service chosen by your organisation is likely to be that which meets the needs of the company most economically.

Special items within the UK

Urgent letters and parcels (up to 10 kg) are usually sent by the Royal Mail's Special Delivery service. Delivery is guaranteed by 12 noon the next working day or the additional cost of the service is refunded. Royal Mail also operates a Track & Trace service, so you can ring them (0845 7001200) to find out the current status of your item at any time. You can also get confirmation of delivery on the website www.royalmail.com.

Heavier parcels (up to 30 kg) can be sent by Parcelforce. If your company has a Parcelforce contract, very urgent items can be sent by Parcelforce ServiceMaster for overnight distribution – though the item must be collected after 8 am from a local depot. Other urgent services include Parcelforce by 9 am, Parcelforce by 10 am, Parcelforce by Noon and Parcelforce 24. All guarantee next working day delivery to most UK destinations.

Confidential items need to be clearly indentified on the envelope or label (see page 413). If you are including a confidential document in an internal mail envelope that will contain various other items, then make sure the document is put into a separate, marked envelope first.

Important documents are usually sent by Royal Mail's Recorded Delivery. Recorded delivery items can be sent by first- or second-class post and a signature is requested on delivery. If no one is available to sign for the item a 'while you were out' card is left instead and the item is held for collection at a local delivery office. If the item is lost or damaged, a small compensation fee is payable – currently up to £27. The service is not, therefore, appropriate for sending valuables through the post but is useful for original documents, such as birth or examination certificates, passports, legal documents – where proof of delivery is desirable. Note that you cannot send heavy items (over 750 g) using second-class post.

Valuable items are those which have a monetary value, such as cash. In this case you want a guarantee that you would get your money back if the package were lost. You would again use the Special Delivery service because, for the fee, you also can obtain compensation up to £250. If you pay more, you can enhance this limit to up to £2500. Parcels can also be sent by Parcelforce with enhanced compensation for an additional fee.

Special items for overseas

Urgent overseas items can be sent by Swiftair – and arrive more quickly than by airmail. Additionally Swiftair plus Recorded is available for urgent and important items. Valuable items can be registered to enable compensation to be paid.

Valuable items which are not urgent can be sent by airmail, but in addition you can opt for International Recorded or International Registered. The first is used for important documents and the second for valuables. Delivery is usually within three days for Europe and up to eight working days outside Europe.

If there is no rush for a valuable item to be received, you can save money by sending it by surface mail – you can still send it by Recorded or Registered post. However, you would now have to allow between 2 and 12 weeks for it to arrive, depending on its destination.

Calculating postal charges

Today most organisations use electronic scales, rather than the traditional scale platform type, on which letters and parcels were placed and weighed. Electronic scales use a chip which has been pre-programmed with the current postal rates. The scale therefore weighs and calculates the postage at the same time. You simply select either first or second class, overseas rates, and any special fee services such as Recorded or Special Delivery. In a mechanised mailroom both the scales and franking machine will be linked, so that the franking machine is set by the scales, not by the operator. Providers argue that electronic scales rapidly pay for themselves because they are so accurate, whereas manual weighing is apt to lead to the practice of over-stamping 'just to be on the safe side'.

When postage rates change, electronic scales must be re-programmed with the new tariffs. This means inserting a new chip – which these days is often provided in a plug-in pack. Suppliers send these out to their customers in advance of the change.

If you are still having to cope with the old type of manual scales, you could try to persuade your supervisor that investment in a new set of electronic scales would pay for itself very quickly. However, all mailroom staff should be able to use a basic system in case of an emergency.

KEY NOTES FOR CALCULATING POSTAGE (without electronic scales)

- Weigh the letter or parcel by placing it on the platform of the scales.
- Read off the weight and note it – in pencil – on the envelope or package (in case you forget it half-way through).
- Read off the standard charge against a postal rate charge chart (supplied by Royal Mail). Note that weights are always 'up to' so that each weight band is the maximum that is allowed at that price.
- Add on any charges for special services.
- Use stamps or frank the item for the total value.

Using a franking machine

Today most organisations use franking machines. These process outgoing mail quickly. The franking impression or label can include an advertisement for the organisation (which also operates as a return address if the item is undeliverable), and exact postage can always be put on the item. The problem with stamps is that there may not be quite the right denominations for large packages so you have to put on excess postage on a 'just in case' basis.

Franking machines vary from the very basic to the highly sophisticated. On a basic machine you may need to change the date manually. More expensive machines not only change the date themselves but have a 'smart date' facility – so that they know which date it is (for instance, to cope with leap years). Most machines use an ink cartridge which also needs to be replaced regularly, or the franking impression will become too faint to read. Before you use your franking machine you should also find out:

- its maximum speed of operation – which can range from 2400 envelopes per hour to 15,000!
- the maximum thickness of the envelopes it can process
- whether it can cope with envelopes inserted in a portrait orientation (most are landscape only)
- what type of labels you need – pre-cut, on a roll, or either – and how you replenish these
- how to print a label
- how to stop the machine quickly in an emergency.
- what to do if you make a mistake (see below).

Franking machines are loaded with postage units which decrease every time an item is franked. Eventually the machine would run out of units and be unusable. Most machines today can be re-credited by modem – you simply telephone the supplier who transmits the units down the line and then bills the company. This takes about a minute, so there is never any reason to have insufficient units for a mailing.

Unless you have a completely automated system, it is easy to lose concentration and frank an item with the wrong amount. Don't be tempted to hide the mistake! It is a common error and one which is easy to resolve:

If you *under-frank* an item, then – if there is space – you could frank a label for the amount of the shortfall and stick this on as well.

If you *over-frank* an item (or have an under-franked envelope in your possession which is of no use and won't take an additional label) then *keep* this safely. You can normally obtain a refund for items franked in error, but will need to check how this system works with your particular franking machine manufacturer.

 INFORMATION UPDATE

Two developments are currently in the pipeline for franking machines. The first are the new Royal Mail approval standards under which, by 2002, all franking machines which rely on the traditional method of replenishing units manually (by taking them to the post office) will be phased out. So if you have an older model, your company will have to make plans to replace it shortly.

The second is a development of interest to small businesses who often argue they cannot afford a franking machine. A new PC-based system is being developed which can be used instead. The postage credit is loaded into the PC and a small, dedicated printer is attached which produces franked labels. These systems already operate in the United States and are currently awaiting Royal Mail approval before they can be introduced in the UK.

Services available for urgent mail, and mail containing valuable or important items

You have already seen that the Royal Mail and Parcelforce offer specific services for urgent mail – both within the UK and to overseas destinations. However, private options are also available – as you will see in *Yellow Pages*. Courier firms will transport items by van and motorcycle quickly around the country, but the charges tend to be high. However, if your boss is stranded at the airport having forgotten his passport, such firms are a godsend!

National express delivery firms, such as DHL, transport packages and parcels all around the world rapidly and safely – and you may have seen advertisements for such services yourself on television. Another development has been firms which rival the Royal Mail – such as TNT Mail Services which, for instance, transports over 60,000 packages for the Department of

Social Security every night. They guarantee to deliver within a specific half-hour period so that staff have their mail at the start of the working day.

If you have a crisis with an urgent item, therefore, there are many options available – but you should note that most of these are at a price. The faster you want an item delivered and the greater the distance, the more it is likely to cost!

The various services for mail containing valuable and important items were described on pages 415–416.

Reporting problems with outgoing mail

If there is a problem sending the outgoing mail, then, depending upon the reason, you may have to notify several people.

If there is a serious difficulty which means most of the mail will be delayed, do make sure your internal colleagues know. At least they will then be aware that important or urgent items are delayed and can take alternative action. In most cases it is both sensible and courteous to notify your line manager, team leader or supervisor first.

If you have problems meeting dispatch deadlines for a particular item, you may need to contact the post office (to check the latest posting times) or the courier who is calling to collect the item (and see if the collection time can be changed). This is better than expecting a courier to wait around your office whilst you rush to pack something important. Again, notify the sender too, and explain the reason for the delay.

EVIDENCE COLLECTION

You need to prove that you can dispatch three of the following types of mail, and to state how you would deal with the remaining items: envelopes, parcels, routine, urgent, confidential, mail containing valuable items. You must also prove that you send mail to *both* internal and external destinations.

The easiest way to do this is to keep a log of the mail you handle over a period of two or three weeks. Then check off, from the list above, which items you have dealt with and be prepared to answer questions on the others. Ask your supervisor to sign your log for authenticity.

If you have had to cope with any problems, such as making an error when you were franking mail or trying to meet a tight deadline and 'missing' the post, make a note of the difficulty, what action you took and who you notified. Ask your supervisor to countersign your statement for authenticity.

Option Unit 211 Contribute to the arrangement of events

FOCUS OF THE UNIT

To obtain this unit you must be able to:

- **help to provide** equipment and materials for events
- **provide** invitations and additional information.

EVIDENCE COLLECTION

It will make evidence collection easier if you can obtain the following information.

a Start by listing the events you have helped with in the past – as well as those scheduled over the next few months. These may be in-house *or* external and include staff training events, seminars, conferences, exhibitions or large-scale meetings. They may include only your internal staff *or* may include people from outside the organisation. So your in-house annual sales conference or a training day for staff would count, as would a seminar in a hotel to which you have invited customers. However, you must need to arrange relevant equipment and materials – so you can't count the company's Christmas party or summer barbecue!

b You may have evidence already which you can get together quite easily – as most event organisers keep a special file for each event. However, *your* role in helping to make the arrangements must be clear. Don't use paperwork containing other people's names unless you can write add a note clearly stating how you were involved and then ask your supervisor to verify this.

c Finally, if you help someone to organise an event, ask them in advance if they will be prepared to provide you with witness testimony to confirm what you did.

Key facts on helping to provide equipment and materials for events

The importance of obtaining clear instructions

Many organisations hold a number of events every year. Some of these are just for staff, others involve outside visitors, customers or members, or prospective customers. Every *type* of event is different – although event planners who organise the *same* event each year will usually keep paperwork from the previous year's file to use as a guide for the next. They should also have made notes about anything which went wrong last year, or could be improved – so that each year the job becomes easier than before. It is always the 'first time' that is worse – because everyone is learning by experience!

If you are asked to help, expect to get involved in an activity which becomes more frenetic as the day of the event approaches. Few events are planned which do not have minor hitches and some have major problems that must be solved quickly. You will therefore be worth your weight in gold if:

a   you attend all the planning meetings and *listen* to all the discussions, so that you have a good appreciation of what you can do to assist

b   you make clear notes of *everything* you are asked to do and then put these into a logical order – so that you know exactly what to do and when to do it

c   you *check* anything you are not sure about

d   you *remember* what you are told – so that you don't have to keep asking people for information you have already received

e   you use your own initiative where you can – but operate within company rules and regulations.

If the event has been held before, your instructions may, if you are lucky, be precise and detailed. If this is a 'first time' event then your instructions may be rather more hazy and include a number of queries, such as: 'Jim Brown wanted to do a demonstration – find out what he needs for it, will you?' If you are collecting information like this, start a file and put into it absolutely everything that is relevant, so that everything is safe and in one place.

At the end of this process you will be able to draw up a list of what you think is required. Before you do anything further, however, you need to agree this with the organiser.

Usually the type of equipment and materials required are determined by:

* the type of event
* when it is being held (summer or winter, for instance)
* what is happening at the event
* the number of people attending
* what activities they will be involved in

- the budget – how much money can be spent.

If the budget is low, then you are likely to have to use equipment and materials you already possess. If the budget is more generous, you may be able to buy or hire items you do not possess, arrange for specialist materials to be printed and so on.

Before you commit your company to spending any money, you need to make absolutely certain that the item is required and that you don't already have it! This is why you need the organiser's approval before you take any action.

 KEY NOTES ON INSTRUCTIONS

Check you have instructions related to:

- the quality of materials or equipment required
- the quantity required
- the approximate cost of each item
- the dates (and/or times) when the materials and equipment are required.

KEY NOTES ON THE REASONS FOR OBTAINING CLEAR INSTRUCTIONS

- To help the organiser keep within budget
- To save duplication of items or jobs
- To ensure deadlines are met
- To make sure essential items are identified
- To make sure company procedures are followed
- To make sure all the required items are available at the right time, of the right quality, in the right quantity and in the right place
- To save the embarrassment or problems that would occur if important items were forgotten or items were below the standard required.

EVIDENCE COLLECTION

You have to show you can obtain *two* of the following types of equipment and materials: audiovisual equipment, documents prepared for the event, stationery, refreshments. You also have to explain how you would obtain the others.

Begin by identifying which types you regularly provide and start a file relating to these for your portfolio. Then read the section below to identify the main considerations you need to bear in mind. The next evidence collection will guide you on how to produce your evidence.

Types of equipment and materials

Audiovisual equipment is a common feature at any event where there is to be a presentation or talk by a speaker. However, it ranges from relatively low-tech to high-tech. Few companies possess very expensive high-tech equipment, but some conference venues specialise in supplying this on request. Hotels often have a reasonable range. Examples of audiovisual equipment you may be asked to obtain are listed in the table opposite. Check how many you know and ask your tutor or supervisor for further details of the remaining items, if you are unsure what they are.

Documents prepared for the event will depend upon the type of event being held. For a meeting, there will be an agenda and minutes of the last meeting, plus any documents to be given out and discussed. At a seminar or conference, there will be a programme and copies or summaries of the talks being given, and advertising material if the event is being sponsored. At a training event there will be a programme and documents related to the sessions being undertaken. These may be prepared in-house (photocopied, for instance) or specially printed if the event is high-profile.

Stationery is likely to include pencils and/or pens plus paper for those attending. You will also need to think about stationery linked to any AVA equipment being supplied (e.g. non-permanent pens for whiteboards, new flipchart pads and overhead transparencies). You may also be asked to provide folders or plastic wallets in which prepared documents will be placed. Sometimes the folders, too, are specially printed. Finally, many events also require the preparation of badges for visitors – which again can range from plastic holders with a printed card inserted or specially printed badges.

Refreshments can range from tea/coffee and biscuits on arrival and soft drinks during the day, to sandwiches at lunchtime or a buffet lunch. Any food should be easy to eat – bearing in mind people may be standing up with a plate in one hand and a glass or cup in the other! Expecting them to use a knife and fork at the same time is not usually wise. Even if alcohol is being served, a range of soft drinks should always be on offer. Remember to cater for the needs of any guests with special requirements (see below).

Coping with special needs

All organisations have to comply with the requirements of the **Disability Discrimination Act**. This means, for instance, that an event must not be held in circumstances where some people cannot attend because they are disabled and cannot gain access. You need to be aware of staff or visitors who may have special needs so that you can provide for them appropriately. Most event booking forms ask people to specify any special needs so that requirements can be borne in mind at the planning stage. If the event is going to be held at a hotel, it is sensible to check the facilities with this in

AUDIOVISUAL EQUIPMENT

Low-tech

Blackboard	The most simple type of equipment, but the chalk dust has made these unpopular.
Whiteboard	The modern version of the blackboard. The presenter writes on a large white screen using non-permanent colour pens.
Overhead projector (OHP)	A device which illuminates and transmits the images on overhead transparencies (OHTs) via a glass screen and a lens to a projector screen. To work properly, the glass and the lens must be scrupulously clean.
Flipchart	A large (A1) pad of paper that stands on an easel and is fixed by screws at the top.
PA system	A public address system used to transmit messages over a large area.
Microphones	The best type are the roving, halter or radio microphones which enable the user to walk around.
Slide projector	A projector which projects 35 mm slides.

High-tech

PC presentation	A presentation devised on computer through the use of special software (such as PowerPoint) and transmitted through a linked computer and projector, or computer, LCD panel and OHP.
Video projector	A projector that shows video recordings on a large screen.
Copyboard	Combines a whiteboard with a projection screen so that information can be written on the board, downloaded on computer, printed out and even transmitted to a distant location.
LCD panel	A panel placed on an OHP and linked to a computer. The computer images are transmitted to the panel and projected on to the screen by a high-intensity OHP.
LCD projector	A portable projector that uses liquid crystal display technology and can be linked to audio speakers to give stereo sound.
Multimedia	Presentations that combine different types of media; e.g. text, clipart, graphics, photographs, sound and video.

mind. The types of special needs you may meet – and how to cope – are considered below.

Special dietary requirements are quite common today. Many people are vegetarians, for instance. Others have special requirements for medical or religious reasons. Buffet meals are one way of coping with a mixture of requests relatively easily – even vegans can be accommodated if you receive prior warning.

Physical disabilities can be relatively minor, but visitors who use a walking aid or are in a wheelchair need access to the building and any rooms being used, and enough space once they are inside. Today, ramps are common and some buildings have special lifts installed next to steps for wheelchair users. Remember that if you need a lift to transport someone to an upper floor, you need a contingency plan if there is an emergency, such as a fire alarm. Discuss this with your event organiser.

Visual impairments have to be catered for. Some people may be partially sighted, others may be blind. Materials should be available in large print for the partially sighted and speakers should be informed about the presence of any blind visitors and discouraged from making visual references, such as 'As you will see from this slide'.

Hearing impairments can vary from the partial to the profound. Profoundly deaf people find it useful if additional written information is available. Check, too, if a *signer* should be present. If you have to contact a deaf person to confirm arrangements then use the Typetalk service – which enables them to communicate with you over the telephone.

 KEY NOTES ON OBTAINING EQUIPMENT AND MATERIALS

If you wish to obtain equipment you have five possible sources:

- you can search the cupboards to see if you already have it
- you can borrow it
- you can buy it
- you can hire it
- you can hold the event at a venue which will supply it for you.

If you want to obtain materials, your options are:

- find out what you have already that you can use
- find out what additional materials you could obtain from elsewhere in the organisation
- buy additional materials
- arrange for external printing where required. The budget for the event will be the main determining factor. Check with the organiser *first*.

Procedures for hiring or purchasing equipment and materials

Your organisation may have specific suppliers you must use if you are purchasing equipment or materials, hiring equipment or having materials printed. Or the organiser may have a list of 'approved' suppliers who have been reliable in the past. Even when you have this list, it is unlikely you can just pick up the phone and place an order! You may have certain organisational procedures to follow first.

EVIDENCE COLLECTION

Obtain a copy of all the organisational procedures you have to follow when you are obtaining equipment or materials. Where you have to complete specific forms, try to include copies of some you have written or printed yourself, rather than blank ones. If you also have to make any transportation arrangements for equipment or materials, attach copies of these forms or confirmations as well.

Then prepare a summary of each event with which you are involved.

a   Put the event title, the date and the organiser's name at the top.

b   Then summarise the instructions you were given (attach these if they were in writing). Add any notes relating to queries you had or items on which you needed clarification.

c   List the equipment and materials you provided and clearly state the quality, quantity and deadline date in each case. If you were told to keep within a certain cost, enter the figure alongside the appropriate item. Make sure you cover at least two types of the required equipment and materials and can discuss the others.

d   List your sources – if possible state why you made these choices. Remember your sources and the place where you organised availability can be *either* internal *or* external – but be prepared to answer questions on the other.

e   Now attach copies of any order forms, requisitions or faxes you made out to make the arrangements.

If there is no list, you may be asked to phone a number of suppliers and ask for quotations. Do be clear about what you want and when you want it for, and check that all the quotations are exclusive of VAT – this can make a considerable difference when comparing quotes. (Your organisation will almost certainly be able to reclaim the VAT element of the charge.)

If you are asking about hiring an item, check whether a deposit is required and find out if the firm is prepared to invoice your company for payment –

as some will not and you would have to arrange to pay on collection. Find out, too, what would happen if the item is lost, stolen or damaged – particularly if you are transporting it to another venue – and whether the item would be covered by the hirer's insurance or must be covered by your company's insurance. Your organiser will require all this information to make a decision.

Because every event normally has a budget, there will be specific forms – or purchase orders – to complete to ensure that:

- the item is purchased or hired in the approved way
- authorisation is given by the event organiser
- the cost is set against the event budget.

There are likely to be several copies – one of which will be sent to the supplier, one retained by the organiser and one sent to your accounts or finance department.

It is important that you check the exact procedures in your organisation and never order anything without authorisation.

Checking deliveries and coping with problems

When items are delivered they need to be checked against the order to ensure first that they are complete. If an item is missing, check the delivery note and see whether the item has been omitted in error or is marked 'to follow'. Are the items sent the same as the ones ordered? If anything has been substituted by the supplier, is it acceptable? Finally, check that nothing is damaged and everthing is in working order.

Problems can include:

- missing items – in which case notify the supplier immediately
- items which will arrive too late for the event – in which case you need an alternative supplier
- damaged items – notify the supplier immediately and arrange for a substitute to be sent
- incorrect items – again notify the supplier and arrange for these to be collected (the same applies to substitute items you cannot use)
- malfunctioning equipment – notify the supplier and ask for a replacement.

There can be **even worse problems**!

- You discover you ordered the wrong things in the first place! The supplier is under no obligation to take them back but may do so if you are persuasive or if your organisation does a lot of business with them.
- With a hire firm, you might find that the item you booked is the wrong one – or doesn't function – and a substitute is no longer available for that date. If you are dealing with a national hire company, they will have

a better chance of obtaining it for you – otherwise it means ringing around the area yourself and, at the same time, trying to work out how you will cope without it.

- You discover that 'out of stock' items cannot be delivered in time. Again you need to ring around if your usual supplier can't help.
- A supplier makes promises and lets you down. In this case, even if you find someone else who can help you, remember to ask your event organiser to cross the first firm off the approved list!

If you are faced with a difficult problem, let the organiser know immediately. Don't worry and fret for two days until it is too late for anyone to rescue the situation. Often simply talking over the problem helps everyone to decide on a solution.

Completing documentation

The type of documentation to be completed when goods are delivered varies from one organisation to another, but many use goods received notes (GRNs). An example is shown below. If your organisation operates a fully computerised system then you may find the expected items are pre-printed on it; otherwise you write them in yourself. You then indicate whether there are any problems. The top copy of the GRN goes to the finance office which checks your notes against the invoice. This helps to ensure that missing or

GOODS RECEIVED NOTE			**Max Stratton Associates**	
Supplier:			**GRN no:** 8030	
Statline Ltd 14 Baxton Road HIGHTOWN HG4 3MP			**GRN date:** 10 May 200–	
			Delivery note: 3048	
Supplier a/c no: 156			**Delivery note date:** 8 May 200–	
Carrier: Statline van			**Checker:** JL	
Order no	**Quantity ordered**	**Quantity delivered**	**Description**	**Tick box or enter details if goods damaged or discrepancy identified**
49078	10	10	Flipchart marker pens	✓
"	5 boxes	5 boxes	Laser printer OHP film	✓
"	10	10	Flipchart pads (A1)	*One bent so unusable*
White copy: Accounts		Pink copy: Purchases file		

damaged equipment and materials are not paid for until the matter has been sorted out.

Always check whether there is any special paperwork needed for the event files as well. There is likely to be extra paperwork to complete if you have hired some items.

Finally, you may be expected to keep a list of all the items you have purchased and a second list of all the items you have hired. Against each item should be recorded the name of the supplier and the cost. Against hire equipment you also need to note the date by which it must be returned (or you will incur an additional charge). Tick off each item as it is received and checked. On your hire list, enter the date when it is returned.

Storage requirements for equipment and materials

Ideally you will have a separate, lockable area for the equipment and materials to be stored. This needs to be clean and dry, with a good air flow, so that printed materials are not spoiled. If you have to make do with existing storage areas, then follow this guidance:

a   Store stationery items away from sunlight and radiators and anywhere that is damp. A corner of your stationery store is probably ideal. Label these items clearly so they are not used for something else by mistake.

b   If there are any 'freebies' to be given out at the event, lock these away in a cupboard or in your filing cabinet – or you may find there are very few left when you want them!

c   Make sure valuable items are in a secure cupboard and there is a limited number of keyholders. If your organisation employs security staff, then tell them – so that they can take appropriate action if they see anything suspicious.

d   Always make a note of the serial numbers of items you have hired or will be transporting. If they are lost or stolen, this is the first question you will be asked.

Arrangements for the return of hired equipment

Don't put off this job! It is very tempting, at the end of an exhausting event, to forget all about the 'clearing up' that has to be done afterwards. If you delay returning the goods, there is likely to be an additional charge – and there is a greater chance of the items being lost or damaged.

If items are heavy, ask for help in returning them. Depending upon your organisation and its resources, you may be able to arrange for the item to be returned by a caretaker or a member of the security staff, or you may have to ask a colleague with a car to help you out (but note that some motor insurance does not cover this).

Before you return any equipment, check that it is still functioning and no bits are missing. If it has been damaged in any way whilst in your possession, be honest when you return it. Don't wait for the hire shop to ring you later. You also need to be prepared for the hire shop to inspect the items thoroughly on their return and refuse to refund the deposit for any item which has been damaged. Report this situation to the event organiser immediately you return to work.

If the equipment gave you problems or malfunctioned you must inform the supplier – as it will need to be repaired. A more difficult problem is trying to negotiate a refund because the equipment didn't work at all. Hopefully you had the foresight to ring the hire shop the moment you found out there was a problem – but it is sensible to leave any serious or difficult negotiations to your event organiser.

EVIDENCE COLLECTION

You have to prove to your assessor that you can deal with problems in a sensible way – either by providing evidence of problems you have dealt with or by answering questions. You will also have to show that you know how to return hired equipment, even if this does not occur at the time you are taking the award.

Finally, make sure you have copies of any documentation you completed when the goods arrived, and ask for witness testimony from your event organiser to prove that you are capable of storing equipment and materials securely under the right conditions.

Key facts on providing invitations and additional information

The importance of providing invitations

Invitations may be formal or informal, included in a letter or sent as a printed card. They should always be sent in writing, so that there is a record of who has been invited.

One of the first jobs is to list all the people who should be invited and check the total against the size of the venue. If there are too many people, then, depending on the event, either the list may have to be reduced or the venue changed. The correct number of invitations must then be printed and *methodically* sent off to everyone on the list (on a 'tick off as you go' basis). Ideally, all are marked RSVP – so that people have to reply.

KEY NOTES ON PROVIDING INVITATIONS

Invitations *must* include the title of the event, day and date, time, venue and the address to which replies must be sent. Failure to send clear written invitations and to dispatch these in good time can result in:

- important people being missed out – and offended
- many people receiving their invitation too late to attend
- fewer people attending than expected
- too many people attending (if invitations have been issued verbally without any checks or controls)
- people getting confused about the date and time
- people going to the wrong place
- people not realising what the event really is.

Providing directions and information on travel options

Most organisations have a 'how to find us' map which they send to visitors. Ideally this provides information for people travelling by car or public transport. If the event is being held at a hotel, the manager will normally supply you with their map and directions which you can send out to people.

Directions can range from being excellent to totally misleading! They also go out of date if road systems change – so check that any you are given are up to date. Key information should include:

- links to motorways or main roads (with road and junction numbers)
- positions of train and bus stations, and the nearest airport if appropriate
- approximate distances
- one-way road systems
- helpful landmarks nearby
- car parking facilities nearby.

It is often better to have two maps – one showing the links to main roads and another 'close up' to help to find an actual building. This is particularly important in a city area.

If you have to draw a map or write directions yourself, ask someone else to 'test it' – and be prepared to change any part that is confusing. Otherwise, expect some visitors to get lost, others to arrive late or not at all, and most to arrive in a state of considerable stress!

It is useful if you can provide information on appropriate travel options to your venue. For instance, if the location is in a city centre with limited parking but 5 minutes away from a railway station, this may tempt several people to travel by rail. If the venue is in the countryside with easy parking but difficult to reach by rail, then this will probably mean most people would prefer to arrive by car.

For your own college or workplace, prepare a useful map giving clear directions, and attach to it a note giving the most appropriate travel options in your opinion. Then check your work with your tutor or supervisor.

Providing supporting papers

Supporting papers are the documents people are sent before they attend the event. The organiser will have listed all the documents which need printing or preparing, and these must be assembled and sent to people in good time. If the event includes external participants (such as a conference) then papers should be sent out about 3–4 weeks beforehand. If the event is internal, such as a staff training day, then two weeks will usually suffice.

Again a methodical system should be used for dispatching the documents (such as ticking off names on the list of people attending) to make sure no one is missed. Failure to send out the papers to someone – or sending them out late – is likely to result in numerous telephone enquiries which will delay you even more. It may even mean some people don't receive them in time, particularly if they are travelling a considerable distance to attend.

Dealing with individual requirements

Dealing with people with special needs was described on page 423. However, you may find that you receive further queries after the invitations have been issued, such as:

- when the event will end
- what accommodation in the area you would recommend
- whether it would be acceptable if someone can arrive only at a later time.

Remember, the more details you provide at the time you issue the invitations, the less likely it is that you will be besieged with questions afterwards! Also, the more you know about the event, the easier it is to answer enquiries.

If you have done your job properly in the first place, you are likely to receive enquiries only from a few people who have a specific question. Finally, if there is any question you cannot answer, don't panic. Simply explain that you will find out the answer and ring back – then do so.

EVIDENCE COLLECTION

Keep copies of invitations you have issued, together with a copy of the invitation list. Don't worry if you have ticked off people's names or amended addresses – this is better as it shows you used it properly! If you issued maps or directions of any type, then keep a copy. However, do remember that standard maps or directions produced by someone else are not your own personal evidence – so you may prefer to use the travel directions you prepared in the 'Check it out' activity on page 432.

Your assessor may ask you how you would deal with giving directions to your venue over the telephone, for instance, and what information you would give to visitors (either from your own organisation or outside it) who had a special query or requirement.

Finally, keep copies of any supporting papers you have produced. On them, write a note of what you actually did – whether you prepared them on computer and/or photocopied them, for instance.

Assisting people on arrival

This is a critical task as, especially for a large event, a number of people will be arriving over a very short period of time. You need to be organised so that you can prevent queues, give people the information and the paperwork they need, record their attendance, and keep calm and unflustered yourself!

 KEY NOTES FOR ASSISTING PEOPLE ON ARRIVAL

- Set up a reception point near the entrance and make sure this is clearly signposted. Be there early yourself.
- Prepare name badges and/or a list of people expected to attend. Face the badges outwards on the reception table so guests can select their own.
- Unless there is lots of room, keep packs of information material in boxes behind you, with just a few on the table.
- Greet people with a smile and welcome them. Ask them to select their badge and tick them off your attendance list.
- Give each person a pack of information material. It is also sensible to have spare sets of supporting papers that were sent out early, in case some people have forgotten them.
- Give brief directions to the room(s) in which the event will be held and tell people where they can find the cloakroom and/or toilets and where refreshments are being served (such as coffee on arrival).

- It helps if you have made a note in advance of anyone who has a special need – then you can give them specific information on arrival.
- Know where your organiser is to be found – or someone else who can answer difficult queries that you cannot.
- Don't leave the desk unattended unless you are desperate to find help for some reason.
- Don't panic if a queue forms – visitors are like buses, none arrive for a while and then several at once. Stay calm and deal with everyone politely and efficiently – otherwise you will give people the wrong impression from the outset!

Recording arrivals

There are various ways of doing this.

If you have prepared name badges for everyone this can operate as a check system in itself. Simply, the ones you are left with are your non-arrivals.

As a safeguard, people are often asked to 'sign in' on a printed list.

At a meeting or a small workshop, the event organiser may ask each person to introduce him/herself at the outset, and record the names of those present.

The reason for recording arrivals accurately is to enable the event organiser to:

- write and thank attendees and/or send additional material to them afterwards
- send non-attendees papers from the event, if this was agreed beforehand
- know who to invite if a 'repeat' session is held in the future
- keep a complete list so that the mailing list or database can be updated.

In the case of an internal event, where staff are expected to attend during working hours, a line manager may also want to check attendance and may expect only those with a good reason to have been absent!

EVIDENCE COLLECTION

Ask your organiser to provide witness testimony so that you can prove to your assessor that you can deal competently with visitors at an event and deal with them appropriately. Attach copies of any documentation you completed or gave out at the time and, if you can obtain a photograph of yourself dealing with people, so much the better.

Remember that your assessor will need to know that you can deal with people both inside and outside your organisation, and that you can cope at venues inside and outside your organisation.

Option Unit 212 Receive and assist visitors

FOCUS OF THE UNIT

To obtain this unit you must be able to:

- **receive** visitors
- **assist** visitors.

EVIDENCE COLLECTION

It will make your evidence collection easier if you can obtain copies of the following:

a organisational procedures which must be followed by reception staff (such as recording visitors or appointments and issuing identification badges)

b appointment books or visitor books you have used (or electronic recording systems)

c other reception records you have completed

d directional information or company information you have provided to visitors.

Key facts on providing reception services

Many administrators also undertake reception duties, either on a full-time basis or on a relief basis during specific times of the day. Whereas a very large organisation may have a specialist reception desk, smaller firms are likely to expect a receptionist to undertake a variety of administration or telephone duties at the same time. Whichever function you undertake, you will need the same skills:

- a thorough knowledge of your organisation, its structure and the names and job roles of people who work there
- the ability to project a positive image to all visitors and help them with their needs and problems
- an excellent understanding of your company's procedures which specify how visitors must be dealt with.

Organisations, structure and responsibilities

All visitors who arrive at reception do so for a reason. They may be attending or making an appointment, leaving a parcel, making an enquiry or asking for information. The receptionist's duty is to make sure they are dealt with promptly and efficiently. You can do this only if you have:

a   a good knowledge of your organisation's departments, and the work carried out in each

b   a list of staff, with job titles and extension numbers, so that you can contact people quickly

c   general information about your organisation at your fingertips:
   - details of your products or services and prices
   - information about the site, where people are located and which areas are off-limits for visitors
   - knowing how to respond in an emergency
   - knowing your company's policies for dealing with casual callers or salespeople.

In addition, you need to know who is expected to visit that day, and whom they are seeing. Some organisations have pegboards or computer screens upon which names of important visitors are placed with a greeting – so that they know they are expected and are welcome. You are less likely to find this facility if you work for a dentist or solicitor!

Keeping records

Visitors may be 'logged' by security, when they enter a large industrial site, or by reception in a small organisation. If visitors mainly attend by appointment, such as in a health centre, then their arrival is noted in an **appointment book**. If a number of casual visitors or callers may arrive during the course of the day, then a **visitor's log** or **caller's register** is usually completed. Either of these systems may be manual or computerised.

Recording visitor details

In some cases, collecting visitor information automatically results in the production of a visitor pass – either from a copy of the paper entry which is folded and placed in a transparent wallet, or by the production of a printed pass by the computer system.

The type of information usually collected includes:

- visitor's name
- name of visitor's organisation and/or purpose of visit
- person being visited (and department, if relevant)
- date and time of arrival

- estimated time of departure (ETD)
- car registration number.

Most of these are fairly obvious but you should know *why* visitors may be asked for their ETD and car registration number. Both are for security reasons.

Firstly, although many organisations ask all visitors to return their pass or visitor badge on departure, not all do so. Unless your reception area is designed so that it is impossible for visitors to leave reception without passing your desk, someone will always 'escape' and take their badge with them. This can be checked at the end of each day – and outstanding badges cancelled.

However, in an emergency evacuation, your visitor list and reception records should match. If they do not, you may find yourself having to answer some awkward questions from the fire marshal or fire brigade! Having an ETD helps. If this was three hours ago, and the person whom the visitor was seeing confirms their departure, this will prevent a building search for a missing person.

Car registrations are important for three reasons. A visitor might park a car in an inappropriate location (unless you have reserved them a special place) and the car may have to be moved. This may also happen if emergency vehicles need access to your car park. Finally, a car alarm might sound.

Dealing with hostile visitors

A key skill of reception staff is the ability to cope with people who are hostile. This may be because they are angry or annoyed – but not always. Some visitors who have little experience of dealing with organisations or are nervous may display hostility as a form of defence. So don't jump to conclusions!

Try the techniques below and, if you feel you are losing control, don't hesitate to refer the matter to a more experienced colleague or to your supervisor and ask them to deal with the person. Listen to what they do and how they do it – then you will be better able to deal with the situation yourself next time.

Someone seems to be very hostile

- There may be several reasons for this. In particular, remember that they are not annoyed at you, personally.
- Stay calm, and take a few deep breaths if necessary.
- Look sympathetic and interested.
- Suggest a face-to-face conversation is continued away from any main public areas.
- Find out what they want and *really* listen. Make notes if the situation is complex.

- *Never* interrupt, say the visitor 'must be mistaken', or do anything to make the situation worse.
- Use your questioning skills to find out what the visitor wants to achieve.
- Check with your supervisor before you make any promises.
- Make sure whatever is agreed is done. Quickly.

Someone seems impossible to please

- Use listening and questioning skills to find out what they want (you can read about these in Unit 207 on pages 368 and 376).
- Suggest only solutions and actions that are in accordance with your company policy and procedures.
- Explain carefully why you cannot comply with their request.
- If they still won't accept this, ask your supervisor or a colleague to speak with them.

Remember that the most awkward people do not necessarily have the most cause to be so! Some visitors may have a valid complaint or problem and have to pluck up courage to talk to you about it. They should not get worse treatment just because they are polite or do not shout – in fact, it is arguable they should get *better* treatment! Listen to the facts, rather than the 'tone' and respond fairly to everyone.

Finally, you should never have to deal with a visitor who is threatening, intimidating or of whom you are afraid. If you are ever in this type of situation, get help immediately.

EVIDENCE COLLECTION

Obtain a copy of your organisational chart, showing the main departments or sections. Attach a staff list which includes extension numbers (if you use a computerised version, print a hard copy for your portfolio). Then write a brief explanation as to how you would contact different departments and what you would do if a person were not available. Do your senior staff carry pagers, for instance, or would you contact a deputy or administrator?

Obtain examples of your organisation's system for recording visitors – preferably with entries you have made yourself. Explain why each of the items of information is required.

Find out the procedures you should follow if you had to deal with a particularly awkward or aggressive visitor, or one who made you very nervous. If you ever have to deal with a difficult visitor whilst you are doing this award, obtain witness testimony from your supervisor to confirm what you did.

Key facts on receiving visitors

Virtually all organisations have reception procedures. These are likely to cover:

a   how visitors should be greeted

b   how the arrival of visitors should be recorded

c   what information should be given to visitors on arrival (such as what to do when the fire alarm sounds)

d   what information should be obtained from visitors on arrival

e   whether visitor badges should be issued and, if so, whether these should be collected on departure

f   whether visitors can walk freely around the building or must be accompanied (or are banned from certain areas)

g   what information can, and cannot, be given to visitors.

If you work for a large organisation, particularly one involved in any type of 'sensitive' work (such as the defence industry), there are likely to be rigorous procedures. If you work in a smaller organisation – such as for an accountant or solicitor – then there may be general procedures but they are less likely to be so prescriptive.

In either case, you must know them by heart and follow them!

Specialist equipment and materials

Some organisations spend a considerable amount of money on their reception area, to impress visitors. You need only to think of the reception area of a 5-star hotel! In a smaller organisation there may be a desk and computer behind a glass screen – or open window – to which visitors report on arrival. A compromise is an open area with a reception desk and several chairs, tables and magazines. Some companies also have today's newspapers on hand and a percolator with fresh coffee constantly available.

The receptionist's specialist equipment and materials are likely to include:

*   an appointments or visitors book – this may be paper-based or appointments will be logged on computer

*   reference materials and reference books – including an internal telephone list

*   a telephone (often two) – and sometimes a switchboard as well

*   a cash register or safe if money is handled at reception

*   a computer terminal

*   relevant security items, such as visitor badges, car park passes and keys or ID permits for specific access points

- various stationery items – including pens (that work!) for visitor use if they have to 'sign in'.

Needless to say, it is impossible to create a good image if the area is generally untidy and stationery is spread all over the desk! In reception, there must be a place for everything and everything in its place. This includes having immaculately tidy desk drawers if they will be visible to visitors!

Finally, if you are in charge of a reception area, you may also be responsible for ensuring that flowers are watered (and thrown away the minute they wilt), newspapers and magazines are tidy, chairs are kept orderly and used coffee cups are removed. The whole area should give the impression of quiet efficiency, not disordered chaos!

Projecting a positive image

If the area is immaculate, what about you? Do you continue the theme or are there days when you feel you are operating at less than your best? If you are fortunate, you may have a specific uniform to wear – otherwise your choice of clothes is important. This will depend upon the organisation you work for – the correct outfit for a receptionist in a local authority is not usually the same as the most appropriate attire for the receptionist at the local radio station! Reflect the 'culture' and image of your organisation, if you want visitors to identify with you the second they arrive.

Appropriate clothes and careful grooming, however, are of no use at all if you don't appear friendly and welcoming – even on your worst days. All visitors should be greeted with a smile and a welcome, no matter whether they are expected or not, or important or not. Don't mistakenly assume that the best-dressed visitors are the most important – many a receptionist has made this mistake and, in some cases, annoyed some very key people! Treat everyone with the same courtesy, and make everyone feel you have time for them. This is obviously easier to do when life is calm than on a frantic day, when it is raining outside, ten people arrive simultaneously and all the phones keep ringing. This is a test of your professionalism – so think of it as a challenge. *Anyone* can do well on a good day, but it takes a professional to do well on a bad one!

 KEY NOTES ON PROJECTING A POSITIVE IMAGE

- Dress appropriately for your organisation and its image.
- Be well groomed.
- Look pleasant, cheerful and welcoming.
- Smile when you greet people and make eye contact.
- Have time for people.
- Be polite and courteous – even when you're busy.
- Treat everyone the same – regardless of their appearance.

Dealing with visitors on arrival

There is a sequence of activities to be carried out when visitors arrive. Although this may vary slightly from one organisation to another, the main points are usually very similar.

1 Greet each visitor *promptly*. If you are on the telephone or talking to another visitor, acknowledge their presence with a smile so they know they're not invisible!

2 As soon as possible ask if you can help them. This usually triggers a response which tells you why they are visiting.

3 Find out the visitor's name. Do this tactfully. 'Could you give me your name, please?' is far more courteous than 'What are you called?'

4 Find out if the visitor is expected and, if so, whom they have come to see.

   • If the visitor is expected, check with your appointments book or log.

   • If the visitor is not expected, find out more about whom they were hoping to see or what the enquiry is about. Much will depend upon the reason for the call and your organisation's policies on unexpected visitors (see below).

5 If the visitor is expected and your organisation issues badges or asks visitors to record the visit in a book, now is the time to complete this process. Make sure you provide the visitor with any specific instructions regarding emergency evacuations, car parking and so on. Inform the visitor if the badge or pass has to be returned on departure.

6 Ask an expected visitor to be seated whilst you contact the appropriate member of staff. If there is a slight delay, it is courteous to warn the visitor – e.g. 'Mrs Turner will be with you in five minutes.' If the delay is likely to be longer than five minutes you may be able to offer a cup of coffee or today's newspaper to help to alleviate the wait.

7 Depending on your organisation's security procedures, you may have to arrange for visitors to be collected from reception or for someone to take them to their location. Never leave reception yourself to do this, unless someone else is also on duty. If your visitor can find his or her way unaccompanied, then give *clear* directions – or a location map if the site is large.

8 Be aware that occasionally executives forget that someone is waiting to see them. After a while, if the visitor is still waiting, re-contact the person he or she has come to see. Keep the visitor informed if the delay is going to be longer than expected and, if necessary, point out where the cloakrooms are!

Dealing with unexpected visitors

These may range from people collecting money for charity, workpeople no one told you about, casual callers hoping to see someone 'on the off-chance', or sales representatives. Much will depend upon the type of organisation you work for and the business it undertakes.

You need to know how to deal with *each type* of unexpected visitor according to your organisation's procedures. In some organisations, certain types of unexpected visitor are seen wherever possible – your school or college, for instance, would try to find time for someone to talk to a pupil's or student's parents wherever possible, and solicitors try to see callers rather than lose their potential business to a rival. In other types of organisation, casual visits are discouraged (see below).

If you are in doubt, make the visitor welcome and then find out what to do. Try to do this where the visitor cannot hear you, so neither of you is embarrassed by a negative response. There will be no problem if someone will see the visitor. If this is not possible you may have to:

- arrange for the person to make an appointment for a future date

- explain that your organisation cannot see casual visitors and ask the visitor to ring in or write in to make an appointment.

The visitor will probably accept your explanation. However, if he or she is hostile or disagrees with your suggestion then calmly explain that you have been asked to pass on this information. Be polite but firm. If the visitor still won't accept your explanation, it is sensible to ask someone more senior to have a word with the person.

Complying with security procedures

Security in an organisation may:

- allow for unrestricted visitor access

- restrict visitor access to certain areas

- allow restricted visitor access to certain areas only if accompanied, and then only after have visitors have fulfilled certain 'screening' procedures (this would be the case, for instance, in an organisation concerned with military or defence work).

It is extremely important that you know the security procedures in force and that you *always* comply with these – otherwise you will be breaching security regulations yourself by allowing someone else to do so. If you are ever in any doubt, err on the side of caution and then check with your supervisor or line manager.

EVIDENCE COLLECTION

For both elements of this unit you have to prove you can deal with three of the following types of visitor: internal, external, expected, unexpected, hostile. You also have to explain how you would cope with the other two.

1 Make out a list (similar to the one on page 441) of the sequence of activities you regularly follow when dealing with:
   • expected visitors • unexpected visitors.
   State whether this sequence varies if you are dealing with internal visitors, rather than external visitors.

2 Keep a log (or photocopy your visitors or appointments book) to identify the visitors you have dealt with over the past few days or weeks (depending upon how often you deal with visitors). Identify which visitors were internal and external and which were expected and unexpected.

3 Write a brief account of the organisational and security procedures you have to follow in relation to visitor entry and access to the buildings or offices. Make sure you include details of:
   • which areas are restricted, if any
   • what type of visitor identification system you use
   • what information you must obtain from visitors on arrival – and why
   • how you try to ensure visitors return identification on departure.

4 Obtain witness testimony from one or two of your colleagues who regularly expect visitors, to confirm that you contact them promptly when visitors arrive and can cope effectively if there is a slight delay. You could also ask any internal visitors for witness testimony that you dealt with them pleasantly and effectively. Do *not* ask external visitors for witness testimony without the specific agreement of your supervisor.

Key notes on assisting visitors

You already know that visitors need basic assistance on arrival. They need more attention if there is likely to be a delay, such as being directed to comfortable seating and having refreshments offered.

However, you also need to be able to answer a range of visitor queries and cope with a host of possible problems before you can confidently claim to be able to do your job professionally. This section looks at the type of queries you may have to handle and the sort of problems which can occur – and gives you advice and guidance on how to cope.

Visitor queries

These are likely to include:

- queries about location – 'Where is the meeting?', 'Where's the personnel office?', or 'Where's the nearest ladies' room?'
- queries about your products or services
- queries about additional services and facilities, such as personal consultations, delivery services, days/times of opening, facilities available
- queries about a specific transaction – from a visitor who is also a customer
- queries about local facilities and amenities – if your organisation has visitors from overseas or other parts of the UK who are staying overnight (anything from the nearest express laundry or florist to health club or restaurant!).

The first thing to know is what type of information you are allowed to give, and what type you are not allowed to divulge. Sensitive issues are likely to include information about:

- the location of top management or special departments involved in 'sensitive work' – especially if these should be of no interest to the visitor
- other firms with which your organisation does business (including its suppliers)
- your organisation's financial affairs
- personnel employed by the company
- your organisation's computer system
- the future plans of the organisation.

It helps if you develop a 'sixth sense' which warns you when a question seems strange or out of place. Then, rather than say you cannot supply the information, simply say you 'don't know' the answer. Suggest to the visitor that he or she asks the person being visited, or writes to the personnel office with the query. If the visitor responds, 'Oh no, it's not important, I was just wondering', then you can be certain that you have done the right thing.

If the question is entirely legitimate, but you genuinely don't know the answer, then it is your job to find out! You should have a range of reference sources in reception to help you. These can include:

- catalogues and price lists
- leaflets and advertising material
- local directories and *Yellow Pages*
- internal telephone listings
- local maps and a list of recommended hotels/restaurants, taxi firms and car hire agencies
- your own files and folders containing information you often need to supply to visitors.

If the query is unusual and your reference sources are of no help, you can either refer the visitor to someone else who will know the answer, or contact that person yourself whilst the visitor is waiting. In that way you have added to your own store of knowledge in case anyone else asks you the same thing.

TEST YOUR KNOWLEDGE AND UNDERSTANDING

How well can you give directions? Are you clear, unambiguous and precise? Or do most people get lost if they try to follow what you are saying? Test yourself by working with a team member (or fellow student) and:

a describing clearly how to get to your house, or place of work, on foot from the nearest train or bus station

b describing clearly how to get to your house, or place of work, by car from the nearest motorway

c describing clearly how to get to a completely different part of the building (or site or campus) from where you are now sitting.

 ## KEY NOTES ON GIVING DIRECTIONS

- Start from a point you both know.
- Use road and junction numbers for clarity.
- Give approximate distances.
- Draw a small sketch map with arrows, to help.
- Identify landmarks or major points of reference (e.g. behind the church or next to the blue door).
- Make sure you know the difference between left and right!
- Don't use the word 'right?' to check understanding – you'll confuse everyone!

Problems, problems!

There are two aspects to handling problems on reception. The first is being able to solve them. The second is dealing with the visitor in such a way that you continue to give a positive image, no matter what the outcome.

An experienced receptionist would probably need a book in which to describe the range of problems that can occur. However, most of these can be divided into specific categories:

Problems relating to the appointment can include: a mistake about the time or date, no record of the appointment, or the person to be seen is unexpectedly unavailable.

Problems relating to the visitor's experience can include: an extended delay (especially if the visitor is in a rush), problems finding a car parking space, no one to accompany the visitor to a specific location, staff unwilling (or unable) to answer the visitor's queries, or an emergency situation occurring whilst the visitor is on the premises.

Problems relating to the visitor him/herself can include: confusion over the time or date of the appointment, an unexpected delay so that the visitor is late arriving, or a health emergency.

In some cases, a problem may mean the visitor becomes frustrated or angry and takes it out on *you*. Coping in this type of situation is not easy – so the more you can prove how good you are at solving problems, the less likely you are to find yourself in this situation!

 ## KEY NOTES ON DEALING WITH PROBLEMS

- **First** check your organisational procedures to see what help and guidance they provide.
- **Second**, always apologise on behalf of your organisation for any inconvenience caused.

Problems with appointments

These are often the fault of you or your colleagues! Find someone else to help (ring from an inner office and explain the situation). Perhaps offer refreshments. If a different person will see the visitor from the one expected, assure the visitor that the person is capable of dealing with the matter. **Key point** – *someone* must see them, or expect an argument as the visitor's time has been completely wasted.

Problems with the experience

Offer refreshments if there is a delay and keep the visitor informed. Offer to make an alternative appointment if the delay is prolonged. Do all you can to solve the problem – don't hesitate to contact a supervisor for advice if necessary. Use creative thinking. Could a member of staff move his/her car? Who else would know the answer to a query? Can you ask someone to talk to the visitor for a while as a distraction?

Problems with the visitor

If the visitor has made a mistake don't expect an admission of guilt! Be polite and courteous but remember also your assertiveness skills (see page 68). Know your company's procedures for health emergencies (i.e. who is your nearest first-aider, what is the emergency number).

When you have a spare five minutes, list all the emergencies you can think of and check you could cope with them all! If not, ask your tutor or supervisor for advice on what to do in that situation.

Retaining your positive image

If you solve a visitor's problem begrudgingly, you won't make much of an impression. If you accept the visitor's problem as a challenge and tackle it willingly and positively, then you are likely to make a considerable impression on the visitor – whether you actually manage to solve the problem or not.

The key to this is **empathy** – whereby you actually identify with the visitor's situation by considering how you would feel in that same situation. Then you start to appreciate how important the problem is for the visitor. You could find this making you more persistent! If you genuinely feel sorry for someone who is delayed because of an administrative mistake, you are far more likely to make every effort than if you shrug and think 'it's not my problem'. At the end of the day, the visitor will remember your efforts – and that is what your job is about. Reception work is not just filling in forms, issuing badges and giving directions; it is also about relating to other human beings. If you can do that well and find it interesting and challenging, then you will not only be a positive asset to your organisation, but you will be remembered by all the visitors you help in the course of an average day.

EVIDENCE COLLECTION

Keep a record or diary of difficult situations you encounter on reception and how you have dealt with them. This may include:

a   information you were asked for but could not supply

b   visitors who could not be seen by the expected person or at the expected time

c   visitors who arrived very late (or early!) for an appointment

d   visitors without an appointment who insisted they saw someone

e   hostile visitors who were annoyed for some reason

f   emergency situations (such as a health emergency in reception).

State clearly what the problems were and say how you solved them. Describe how you felt about the inconvenience caused for the visitor, and explain why you think sympathetic handling of a visitor is important. Make sure that you can provide evidence that you have dealt with three of the following types of visitor and that you can discuss the other two types:

a   internal

b   external

c   expected

d   unexpected

e   hostile.

Option Unit 213 Support the use of information technology

FOCUS OF THE UNIT

To obtain this unit you must be able to:

- **start up** your computer equipment
- **maintain** file structures
- **close down** your computer equipment.

Important note

The major difference between this unit and the compulsory Unit 204 is that this unit can be used to relate to *any* type of computer software – whether you deal with text, graphics or numeric data. You should therefore apply the tasks to the software and hardware you use regularly. Basic information on starting up and closing down computer equipment is provided in Unit 204, but in this section you will find more detail on related operations you need to know. It would be quite possible – and sensible – to obtain evidence for this unit and Unit 204 simultaneously and to maximise the opportunities for cross-referencing your evidence. Your tutor or supervisor will give you further guidance on this.

The main difference between this section and Unit 204 is that you need slightly more technical understanding and appreciation of how your computer system operates to complete this unit successfully.

EVIDENCE COLLECTION

It will make evidence collection easier if you can obtain the following:

a   a list of the hardware and software you regularly use, and the operations you routinely carry out on it

b   a description of the procedures you have to follow when powering up your equipment and closing it down

c   examples of the type of storage media you use, with a description of how you label and store this to ensure it is easily located, and how you keep it to ensure it is not damaged

d   a printout (or summary list) of the files and folders you have created over time, showing the system you use.

Key facts on supporting the use of information technology

You need to know and understand:

- the importance of following organisational procedures and manufacturer's instructions and the consequence of not doing so
- data protection legislation – but only to a basic level – and health and safety and other relevant legal requirements.

No matter what computer system you use or what software you have, there will be certain constraints on the operations you can undertake. These may be:

- defined by the organisation – for instance, you may be allowed access only to certain 'levels' of information and may have to follow specific instructions to log in or out of the system or contact specialist personnel if you have a problem
- specified by the manufacturer – this will include installation instructions and trouble-shooting advice.

Ignoring instructions can have two effects:

1 Valuable information may be lost (forever, in some cases!), causing yourself and others considerable inconvenience and extra work.
2 Problems may arise with the system and need expert assistance to remedy. It is unlikely, unless you are particularly silly, that you will actually damage your equipment or software. The only action that is likely to cause such a problem is the use of unauthorised disks or software which may contain viruses or if you inadvertently download a virus from the Internet (see also page 227, Unit 204).

For basic information on data protection legislation, see Unit 205 (pages 286–288). For information on health and safety and computers, see Unit 102 (pages 12–13) and Unit 204 (page 224). Finally, for information relating to copyright and defamation see Unit 205 (pages 286–287) and this unit.

 INFORMATION UPDATE

Under the Computer Misuse Act 1990, anyone obtaining unauthorised access to computer material, or accessing a computer to modify data held on it without permission, is committing a criminal offence. People who do this are more commonly known as 'hackers', but note that under the Act, merely accessing the data is a crime – even if none of it is damaged or changed.

A more recent Act, which relates to computer users, is the Regulation of Investigatory Powers Act. This came into effect in October 2000 and gives the managers of an organisation the right to read any communications without consent – the most obvious result, of course, being e-mail monitoring.

Key notes on starting up your computer equipment

This was covered in Unit 204, page 215. In addition, for this unit, you need to be aware of each of the following areas.

Knowing your equipment and software

Understanding your computer equipment is obviously important for this unit. You have already learned about some types of hardware on pages 211–212. For this unit, you need to know more about the different types of storage and other devices and what they do, so that you can identify those which are most appropriate for the tasks you routinely undertake in your team. The following are examples.

- A **tape streamer** is used to back up large quantities of data sequentially.

- A **Zip program** is used to compress data so that it takes up less room on a disk or drive.

- A **CD writer** stores data on a compact disk.

- A **high-definition monitor** is invaluable if you undertake graphics work.

- A computer with a **fast processing speed** or **large memory** is required to store and retrieve graphics files (which take up more memory than text).

- A **scanner** is needed if you input large numbers of documents which have already been typed.

- A **laser printer** will produce large quantities of high-quality hard copies.

- A **colour printer** (laser or inkjet) is needed to produce coloured slides or coloured hard copies.

- A **laptop computer** is useful if you are regularly expected to work from home or if a member of staff needs to access organisational data when travelling.

- A **high-speed modem** (and/or access to an ISDN line) is required if you regularly transmit information electronically.

The specification of your computer system is important if you are buying or installing software. In Unit 204 you learned that to run Windows 2000 you need a minimum of 32 megabytes (MB) of memory and a fast processing speed. What is meant by these terms and how do they relate to your system?

 KEY NOTES ON PROCESSING SPEED AND MEMORY

Processing speed

This determines the length of time it takes your computer to perform an instruction. Fast computers are usually required for graphics work. For text-based work – such as word-processing, databases and spreadsheets – speed is less critical. Processing speed is measured in MHz (megahertz). Regard this as the 'thinking time' of your PC. The higher the number, the quicker your PC can 'think'!

Memory

There are different types of memory you need to understand.

Main memory – commonly known as **RAM** (random access memory) – determines the amount of data that can be processed by a computer at one time. It is measured in bytes. Your PC's memory will be in *megabytes* (MB) and a megabyte equals 1,048,576 bytes. Most PCs are sold with a minimum of 64 MB of main memory but this can be increased by the addition of extra memory chips.

You use RAM when you work on your computer. RAM is fast – because data is accessed randomly the computer can go direct to any information it needs. But RAM is also *volatile* – data in RAM is lost if the power is turned off. For that reason you need additional memory in which you can store files for later use.

ROM (read-only memory) keeps instructions for starting up the computer. You cannot change this without using special techniques, and this information is not lost if the power is disconnected – otherwise the computer would forget how to start up again!

Backing store memory is where you store documents for later retrieval. The capacity available will depend upon the hardware you have (see below).

Backing store memory and hardware devices

Much will depend upon the exact type and model of equipment you have but you can compare your hardware against the following list.

a   On a new computer the hard disk (C: drive) may hold up to about 30 gigabytes (GB) of data. A gigabyte equals *one million million* bytes – or roughly four times the size of the *Encyclopaedia Britannica*. On a 30 GB disk you could hold this 120 times!

b   **Floppy disks** were first described in Unit 204 (page 219). The most usual type holds 1.4 MB of data – which is fine if you are saving word-processed documents or spreadsheets, but insufficient if you are saving graphics files.

c   **Zip disks** allow much more information to be stored than do floppies (currently up to 250 MB). They are used in a Zip drive which is a piece of hardware connected to the PC. Zip drives compress data as it is stored, so are sold with their own software, which is used to compress (or 'shrink' the data). A 250 MB Zip disk is the equivalent of approximately 170 floppy disks.

d   **CD-ROMs** are another method of storing data. Today most software is supplied on compact disks. This is much more appropriate for large programs which may take up dozens of floppy disks. A CD holds about 650 MB – roughly the equivalent of 460 floppies. To record information on a CD you need an additional piece of hardware – a CD writer (commonly known as a burner).

e   **DVD disks** are likely to replace CDs in the future, simply because they have even greater storage capacity – up to 5.2 GB.

f   Another method of storage is magnetic tape, used in a **tape streamer**. This is a hardware device used for backing up large quantities of data. The space available will depend upon whether the data is compressed or

---

CHECK IT OUT!

You can find out all about the system you are using by double-clicking on the My Computer icon on your desktop. You will see a dialogue box which identifies all your disk drives – and their identification letters.

Right-click on the C: drive icon and select the last option on the drop-down menu – Properties. You will now see how much capacity you have on this drive, how much space has been used, and how much is still free. Put a floppy disk into drive A: and select that option instead. You will now see how much space is remaining on the disk you have inserted. You can repeat this exercise for Zip disks or CDs if you have a Zip drive or CD-ROM drive installed.

Finally, double-click on the Control Panel icon and double-click the System icon. This will display a dialogue box showing all the properties of your system, including the type of operating system installed, your processor type and amount of RAM available on your computer.

not and the capacity of the cartridge. Compression roughly doubles the space available and data cartridges can currently be purchased with a capacity up to about 20 GB. The disadvantage with this method is that the information is stored *sequentially* and cannot be 'randomly accessed'. Instead, the computer has to read all the information through from start to finish before it finds a particular item.

Powering up and logging on

In addition to knowing how to power up your system and how to log on, (see Unit 204, page 215), you should also know how to connect additional input and output devices (such as Zip drives, scanners and printers) so that they operate effectively.

Many devices operate only if the correct software has been installed. Printers, for instance, operate only with the correct **printer driver** so that your computer can recognise the make and type of printer you are using. If you buy a new monitor, it may have a floppy disk or CD enclosed with the driver software to operate the hardware.

The device also needs to be physically connected to your computer. Zip drives, for instance, are often connected to the parallel port at the back of your computer with a connection which allows for the simultaneous connection of a printer – so that you can save data and use your printer at the same time.

CHECK IT OUT!

Check the various devices attached to your computer and ask someone to point out the difference between the parallel and serial ports and the main uses of each.

Either through My Computer, or by clicking on the Start button and then selecting Settings and Control Panel, discover the 'wizards' you have for installing new hardware or software. Alternatively, you will receive an instruction manual with new hardware, saying exactly how to install it (the manual may be contained on the installation CD).

Click on other options on Control Panel to discover what else you can do. For instance, you can change the screen saver and the period before it comes into operation, or change the date or time if this is set incorrectly.

Finally, when you select System, choose the Device Manager option. This shows all the drivers and other programs installed which are controlling the system at the moment. There is probably far more involved than you ever thought!

Removable storage media

Removable storage media are items on which to store data that is not an integral part of your system. The hard drive forms part of your system, but floppy disks, CDs and Zip disks are not. All these are useful for backing up data and for transporting it to be used on another machine or system. However, the storage media has to be handled carefully to prevent damage or data corruption.

• For all types of disk, keep it in its box until you need to use it.

• Write the paper label *before* you stick it on the disk.

• If possible, label the disk 'electronically' as well. You will see that option on your screen (and you can name the disk or check the label when you view the disk contents from My Computer as explained on page 453).

• Store disks in a proper disk box, away from direct heat and sunlight.

• Never overfill a disk box so the disks rub against each other, otherwise they will be damaged and the data may be corrupted.

Most floppy disks today are purchased pre-formatted, so you can use one immediately. Otherwise, follow the instructions on your computer screen to format the disk ready for use (you can easily do this in Windows Explorer – just check in Help). Formatting can also be used to 'clean' all the data from a disk you want to reuse for new data or to prepare a disk for use on a different type of system (e.g. from an IBM machine to an Apple Macintosh).

If you use Zip disks or data cartridges, you can usually select whether to buy these pre-formatted or unformatted. The latter may be cheaper.

INFORMATION UPDATE

When you format a disk the computer deletes any information already there, tests the disk and identifies any 'bad sectors' (scratched or damaged areas). It also creates address tables which it needs to locate information you will put on the disk. If you then re-format a disk, these address tables are erased – but the data is not. Therefore, if you re-format a disk in error, it is possible to recover the data by using a special program. However, do note this is a job for a specialist!

Selecting the correct software

All software is designed to be used for a particular purpose. However, some general packages may be used in a limited way for tasks that can be undertaken better on a specific package. For instance, you can produce a page with columns using word-processing software, but if you want to produce a sophisticated newsletter it is better to use desktop publishing software. The table on page 456 identifies the most common applications of the main types of software you are likely to use.

Type of software	Main use	Examples
Word-processing	Creation and editing of documents.	Word for Windows WordPerfect
Database	Electronic filing system for creating records containing specific details on customers, products, etc. Records can be sorted rapidly and by a range of criteria.	Paradox Access Filemaker Dataease
Spreadsheet	Financial analysis and projections, statistics, the production of charts and graphs and any other operations based on financial or numerical data.	Excel Lotus 1-2-3 Quattro Pro
Presentation packages	The creation of slide shows and overhead transparencies combining graphics and text.	PowerPoint Presentations Freelance
Desktop publishing	The creation of newsletters, notices and adverts which incorporate graphics and text and look like a professional publication.	Pagemaker Publisher 2000 QuarkXPress
Web page design	The creation of web pages for posting on a company website.	FrontPage 2000 Web Designer 2
Graphics	Enables graphics and animation to be incorporated into presentations or web pages.	PhotoShop Illustrator GoLive
E-mail software	Enables users to organise, find and view electronic mail messages and store addresses.	Outlook 2000 Lotus Groupware
Communications	Enables computers to connect to remote locations for electronic messaging.	PCAnywhere FaxServe
Accounting/ payroll/stock control	Enable financial and other data to be stored and manipulated for a specific purpose, such as the creation of accounts and book-keeping records, the calculation of wages and the monitoring of stock usage.	Sage Instant Accounting Sterling Sovereign

Accessing stored files

You read about files and folders in Unit 204 – and about the importance of keeping an 'orderly' electronic filing system. For this unit, you must be able to access the most appropriate file for a particular job. For this reason – as well as being a requirement of the unit – it helps if you keep a record of where you have stored your files.

My Computer can be used to display all your folders and files in different ways. Click on the My Computer icon and then double-click on the C: drive icon. All your files and folders on the hard drive will then be listed. Click on View to see the options available.

- **Large Icons** displays folders and files using quite large graphic representations.
- **Small Icons** reduces the size of the graphics. Your folders and files are listed in columns. Folders are listed first in each column with files underneath.
- **List** displays folders and files in columns, but all the folders are shown first, and then the files.
- **Details** provides the most information. You can check, at a glance:
  - the title or name of the file or folder
  - the size (storage space) it needs
  - the date when the file or folder was last modified.

  As you click on each file, its size is displayed on the taskbar below.

You can **sort** information in a variety of ways. Normally, folders and files are listed by name, alphabetically.

- Click on **name** (in the bar at the top) to list them in *reverse* alphabetical order.
- Click on **size** to see them in order of decreasing size or, if you click again, increasing size.
- Click on **modified** to see them in the order in which they were most recently created or, with another click, view the oldest files first.

KEY NOTES ON FILE EXTENSIONS

The type of icon shown and the file extension can be used to find particular types of files. In Unit 204, you learned that file extensions vary depending upon the software package – so that '.doc' is used for Microsoft Word files but '.wpd' for WordPerfect files, for instance. Other suffixes which are useful to know include:

.xls   Microsoft Excel spreadsheet
.wb3 – Corel Quattro spreadsheet
.mdb – Microsoft Access database
.ppt – Microsoft PowerPoint presentation

.wpg – Corel Presentation
.htm – Web page file
.pdf – Adobe Acrobat file
.zip – WinZip file (see page 464)
.txt – plain text file

Never try to erase or move files with extensions you don't understand. Some will be systems and applications programs your computer needs in order to operate!

CHECK IT OUT!

1 Finding a file or folder using Windows' Find option was explained in Unit 204. Refresh your memory now on how to use the facility by turning back to pages 246–247.

2 Check the contents of two or three of your floppy disks by using My Computer – especially one or two buried at the back of your desk drawer! If you are *certain* you won't need them again, reformat them for reuse.

3 Vow to keep a record of where you store files from now on. A useful tip is to learn how to put a footer at the bottom of your documents saying where the document file is located (e.g. c:\myfiles\reportsjan.doc).

Coping with common problems

Every user occasionally has a problem when starting up his or her equipment. You should know the basic checks to carry out before asking for assistance. Telling a busy computer services person that you did not bother to check that the computer was plugged in before calling for help won't make you very popular! Problems usually occur in one of four areas:

- with the monitor or another output device
- with an input device
- with the processing unit
- with the software.

Monitor problems can include: no display at all, faint display, too bright display, incorrect colours on display, or a 'blue' screen. Assuming the base unit is switched on, check all the obvious connections and plugs. You can easily trace the connections from the monitor to the mains and/or from the monitor to the computer. Next check the brightness and contrast to make sure the settings are correct. If you use a network, it is worth checking with another user if there is a general fault with the network. If all these checks don't help, then you need expert assistance. A 'blue' screen, incidentally, occurs when you have a hardware problem which you cannot possibly put right yourself.

Input and output devices include your keyboard, mouse, Zip drive, printer and scanner. If any of these don't function, check first that they are connected properly. Sometimes switching a device on and off again can help and so can closing down and rebooting your system – particularly after checking and making good any loose connections. Watch for any error messages appearing on your screen and report these to your help desk or expert. Let an expert check your device drivers to ensure they are still installed correctly – unless you have specific permission to do this yourself.

The **processing unit** will fail to boot up if there is no power. You need to check the plug is in, the power is on and the mains lead is properly connected. If you are doubtful about the power, test another piece of equipment in the socket. The fuse in the plug might have 'blown' because of a power surge or other problem.

If you have a **software problem**, you are likely to find the equipment powers up but you cannot access or use a particular program properly. If you are using a network, check whether other users are having problems. If not, then close down and reboot your machine before you report the matter. Sometimes computers can be slightly unpredictable – and just need a fresh start to get it right! On your own PC ask an expert to check – just in case you have deleted an important file in error.

TEST YOUR KNOWLEDGE AND UNDERSTANDING

Below is a list of problems you may encounter when starting up your equipment.

1   Identify those for which you should make some basic checks yourself as a first step – and say what you would do. Then say to whom you would refer the problem.

2   Identify those which you would refer to someone else immediately – and say why.

   a   The system does not respond at all when you try to power it up.
   b   The hard disk light flickers but your VDU remains blank.
   c   Shortly after powering up, there is a 'popping' noise from the plug and everything goes off.
   d   You try to load a file from your floppy disk but receive a 'disk unreadable' message.
   e   Your printer doesn't respond when you try to make a hard copy of a document.
   f   The screen display is very dim.
   g   The colours on the screen are different from normal.
   h   When you try to access a software program you receive the message 'File not found'.

Key facts on maintaining file structures

For this element, think of 'structures' as the way in which your files are organised. In Unit 204 you read that files should be in folders, should be stored in a logical manner and labelled clearly. If you think of your computer as an electronic filing cabinet, then the way you structure the files will show whether you are neat and tidy worker or messy and chaotic!

The danger with having files in a mess is that you will 'lose' them – probably because they will have the wrong name or be in the wrong location. You may also lose work you have carefully prepared – either by deleting the wrong files by accident or by not copying them properly.

If your system is more messy than you would like, use this unit as a very good opportunity to have a clear out and a tidy up.

File structure operations

For this unit, you have to prove that you can undertake *all* the following operations:

- save a file
- copy a file
- create a new file
- delete a file
- locate a file
- move a file
- name a file
- rename a file
- select a file.

You may like to note that if you can undertake these operations on files, it is often very simple to undertake them on folders as well – as you will see below.

Storage capacity

Before starting any operation, it is important to check that there is enough storage capacity for your new files – and to know what to do if there is not. Otherwise you may try to copy a large file on to a floppy disk with insufficient free space. Although your system will warn you, if the job is urgent and you have no more spare disks, you could have a problem! You can check the space available on any disk by using My Computer (see page 452). You can also check the size of a file already saved (see page 258). Use these techniques to check the space available *first* if the job is important – rather than just using the first disk you find and crossing your fingers!

CHECK IT OUT!

Saving files was covered in Unit 204 (page 243). This option is found under the File option on the menu bar. **Save** enables you to name and save a new document, whereas **Save as** enables you to rename an existing document (but you will then have two versions). Alternatively you can **Rename** a document by clicking on your right mouse button. Check out these options now on your system.

 KEY NOTES ON USING WINDOWS EXPLORER FOR FILE STRUCTURE OPERATIONS

Start by opening Windows Explorer. You can do this by:

- clicking on Start, then Programs and then selecting Windows Explorer, *or*
- right-clicking on the Start button and selecting Explore.

Points to note

- In Explorer you will see a **split screen**. This is because Explorer is divided into two *panes*. The left pane lists drives or folders, the right pane shows folders and files in the drive or folder you select in the left pane. This pane displays information similar to My Computer and, again, View and Details will always give you the most information. (See also the screen shot on page 220.)
- Click on a file or folder and check its size in the status bar at the bottom – plus the remaining free space on the disk.
- A plus sign (+) in front of a folder indicates that it contains at least one subfolder.
- A minus sign (-) in front of a folder indicates that it is open – and the subfolders and files are showing in the right pane.
- No plus or minus sign means the folder has only files in it, no subfolders.

Operations

- **Create a new folder** in Explorer. In the left pane, click on the

C: drive. Then, from the menu bar, select File, New, and Folder. Enter a name for your folder and press Enter.

- **Create a new subfolder** by clicking on an existing folder and then selecting File, New, and Folder.

- **Rename a folder** by right-clicking on an existing folder and then selecting Rename.

- **Delete a folder** by right-clicking on it and then selecting Delete, *or* click on the folder and then select Delete on the Explorer toolbar (or press the Delete key). Confirm that you want to remove the folder by clicking on 'Yes'. This will move both the folder *and* any subfolder and files it contains to the Recycle Bin.

INFORMATION UPDATE

When you delete an empty folder, then the folder is permanently deleted. However, when you delete a folder that contains files, Windows moves these to the Recycle Bin. You can tell if your Recycle Bin is empty or full by looking at its icon. One containing files looks as though papers are stuffed into it! If you 'empty' the Recycle Bin, you will lose those files forever – but you will free up space on the hard disk. However, as long as the files remain in the Bin you can retrieve them again. Using Windows Explorer, scroll down the left pane until you see the icon for the Recycle Bin and click on it. The contents are now shown in the right pane. You can select Edit and then Undo Delete to restore any files or folders you deleted in error.

CHECK IT OUT!

All stand-alone systems utilise the Recycle Bin, but not all networks! If you operate on a network, check what happens when you delete files and folders and, if you have no Recycle Bin, find out whether there is any way of 'rescuing' files deleted in error.

Managing your files

You create a new file each time you save a document using a particular software package. This may be a letter produced in Word or a spreadsheet produced in Excel. As you saw in Unit 204, files are created by selecting File and Save and then identifying the drive and folder in which you want to save your document. You must then give your document a name. If you have forgotten how to do this, refresh your memory by turning back to page 221.

KEY NOTES ON FURTHER OPERATIONS IN WINDOWS EXPLORER

Copy a file from one folder to another by:

- identifying the folder in which it is located
- opening the folder so that the files are displayed in the right-hand pane
- clicking on the file you want to copy and selecting Edit, Copy (or click on the Copy icon)
- opening the folder in which you want to place a copy of the file
- selecting Edit, Paste (or click on the Paste icon).

Alternatively, select the file, and then drag it to the second folder whilst holding down the Control key.

Move a file from one folder to another by doing the same as above, but using Edit and Cut, rather than Edit and Paste. *Alternatively*, select the file and then drag it to the new location, without holding down the Control key.

Copy a file from the C: drive to the A: drive (a floppy disk) by:

- identifying the folder on the C: drive in which it is located
- opening the folder so that the files are displayed in the right pane
- putting a floppy disk in the A: drive
- clicking on the file you want to copy and dragging this to the A: drive icon in the left pane.

Delete a file by right-clicking on the file name in the right pane and then selecting Delete and Yes (or click on it and then press the Delete key).

Rename a file by right-clicking on the file name in the right pane and then selecting Rename.

Select several files simultaneously (useful for backing up, moving or deleting several files) in one of two ways:

- When the files are grouped together, click on the first one, hold down the Shift key and click on the last file. All the files in between will also be highlighted. You can now copy or move them all together.
- If the files are separated, click on the top file, hold down the Control key, and go down the remaining files, clicking each one you want to select. Again, the selected files are highlighted. If you make a mistake, simply click again to 'unselect' a file.

Special note on deleting files

Do be *very* careful when you are selecting files or folders to delete, and never do this without prior authorisation from your supervisor. If you are in any doubt, *don't*! Even with the back-up of the Recycle Bin, you can give yourself a nasty shock if you suddenly realise you have deleted several important files!

Archiving files

Copying files means, of course, that you are going to be taking up additional space on a particular disk or drive. If you are copying very large files (particularly graphics files), you need to check that you have adequate space available before you start (see page 248).

Another system used to reduce the space required for files is to **zip** or **compress** them. This is often done for files which are **archived** – i.e. put into longer-term storage because they are less frequently used. This is often done using WinZip® software. This is a package which will compress files and then unzip (or decompress) them when they are required. If you have WinZip installed you can compress and save data by using the WinZip Wizard. Ask someone to show you how to do this, as different versions of WinZip exist and the operation can vary. Alternately, practise with an old file you are going to delete and use the Help screens for guidance.

 INFORMATION UPDATE

Many people 'zip' files before sending them by e-mail to reduce the amount of time it takes to transmit them. If you have WinZip installed, you simply use this package to 'unzip' any zipped files you receive by e-mail.

Dealing with problems

If you are interrupted when manipulating files and folders it is easy to forget where you were up to and 'lose' a file! Choose a quiet time to make any complex changes and, if necessary, list the steps you will take on a piece of paper and tick them off as you go. You are unlikely to have any major difficulties if you remember the following.

- Until you empty the Recycle Bin, deleted files can be restored.

- If you can use the Find facility properly, and if your files and folders are labelled fairly logically, you will be able to locate most files and folders without too much difficulty.

- If you try to save a file on a disk with insufficient space you will see an error message on screen. If you are using a floppy disk, then simply insert a new one. If the file is too big to fit on one disk you need to either compress the data first or split the file into subsections and store each on a separate disk. If your C: drive has no free space, ask for assistance before you try either defragmenting it (see Unit 204, page 248) to make more room, or deleting items on it. Finally, if you use a networked system, you will have a limited amount of space in your Home area. Find out how much you have, and try to keep sufficient space free by copying old files and folders regularly on to (clearly labelled) floppy disks, and routinely deleting documents you will never need again. Then remember to update your records to show where your files are stored.

EVIDENCE COLLECTION

Keep a log of your file structure operations. This should show all the occasions when you have created, deleted, copied, moved or renamed files or folders – and why you have done so.

It is possible to print out a copy of your Explorer screen by taking a 'screen dump'. This can show the files and folders on which you are working both before and after you have made changes. Ask your IT staff or tutor to show you how to do this. It will provide proof to your assessor about the files and folders which exist on your computer – but not that you, personally, undertook these operations! Therefore, be prepared to back up these documents with an explanation of the operations you carried out – or write a brief explanation on each one.

Key facts on closing down your computer equipment

The main issues when closing down your system – or 'logging off' – were covered in Unit 204 (page 217). You should develop methodical working practices so that, whenever you finish working, you remember the following.

a   Routinely save the data you are working on in the correct folders and on the correct drives.

b   Close down all the applications in a systematic manner.

c   Follow the established procedures for closing down your equipment.

d   Unload removable storage media only when the device has finished working and the operating light has gone off.

e   Label all storage media correctly and put it away in the right place.

f   Switch off all the equipment and associated peripherals you are allowed to close down before you turn off the main power.

It may be irritating to sit and wait whilst your computer closes itself down, particularly when you are in a hurry. But if you simply press the 'Off' switch you might be storing up problems for yourself the following day. At the very least your computer will take longer to boot up, as it checks why it was not closed down properly and scans your hard drive for potential errors. If you are a network user, you may find yourself having to respond to a sharp message from your Network Administrator!

CHECK IT OUT!

A most irritating problem is a computer which 'hangs' when you are trying to close down; i.e. the system doesn't respond to your request. This was discussed in Unit 204 (page 218). Turn back now and refresh your memory on the correct action to take if this happens to you.

EVIDENCE COLLECTION

Make a note of any problems encountered when you have been closing down your equipment and state how you dealt with these. In addition, state what would happen in your organisation and with your own computer if you failed to close down the system correctly.

Obtain witness testimony from your supervisor or line manager that you regularly undertake file structure operations as part of your job and that you follow procedures when powering up your equipment, closing it down and dealing with any problems.

Option Unit 214 Communicate information electronically

FOCUS OF THE UNIT

To obtain this unit you must be able to:

- **transmit** messages electronically
- **receive** messages electronically
- **access and retrieve** information stored electronically.

Note that this unit covers the use of the following electronic communications facilities:

- e-mails
- computer-generated fax messages
- computer-based information services, such as the Internet, your company intranet, an organisational database or bulletin board.

You have to use two of these facilities for elements 214.1 and 214.2, but *must* have access to the Internet or a company intranet to achieve element 214.3.

EVIDENCE COLLECTION

It will make evidence collection easier if you can obtain the following:

a   a copy of any organisational procedures relating to the use of e-mails, computer-generated faxes or computer-based information services (this should include, if possible, any guidance notes for users and any restrictions on use or policies about use which warn users about their legal responsibilities – see below)

b   a copy of any manufacturer's instructions or guidance notes you use

c   witness testimony from your supervisor that you regularly use electronic communications systems as part of your job, and are authorised to do so

d   hard copies of various types of electronic communications you have produced and received over a period of several weeks.

Key facts on electronic communication facilities

The growth of electronic communication facilities has presented many benefits – and a few problems – for business organisations. The benefits are fairly obvious.

- Communications are sent easily and rapidly around the world. These can include simple e-mails, fax messages and documents, graphics or film clips attached to e-mails.
- Business transactions can be carried out 'on-line' from the sending and completion of forms to the buying and selling of goods.
- There is a wealth of information available over the Internet or from company intranets. Most people are familiar with the Internet. A company intranet is the internal information system. This may be partially accessible by those outside the organisation or not accessible at all by them.
- Organisational databases are today used for the collection and sorting of internal data and are also often a key aspect of a company's website. If you access a company which lists its products or services on-line, you are effectively searching through their database when you are finding an item.
- Finally, bulletin boards can be available for internal staff use, for the exchange of opinions and the buying and selling of items internally. Remote bulletin boards are gaining in popularity for the exchange of information or opinions on common interests.

However, several problems have emerged as information and communication systems have grown.

- Staff may be tempted to surf the Internet for personal interest during working hours or access chat rooms.
- Staff may access some sites containing undesirable material, such as racist comments, pornography or extreme political views.
- E-mails may be sent on inappropriate occasions – or contain inappropriate language which offends other staff.
- Staff may send personal e-mails to friends.
- Computer viruses can inadvertently be downloaded from the Internet and cause havoc to an organisation's computer system.
- Staff may spend some of their time shopping 'on-line' on the company computer system.

To get round these problems, most organisations have certain controls over electronic information use by employees. Many use 'monitoring software' which checks the content of e-mails both transmitted and received by the organisation and automatically rejects incoming messages with an inappropriate content. Similar software can monitor the websites accessed by each employee and the time spent on the Internet each day. The use of this software is perfectly legal – see pages 450 and 469.

Organisations are concerned because there are also legal implications inherent in the use of electronic communications.

If you send an e-mail message containing false or malicious information about someone, then you could be prosecuted and found guilty of **libel**.

If someone accesses pornographic material he or she could be disciplined for causing serious offence to other staff.

Some information on the Internet is restricted by **copyright** – and you would need the author's permission to reproduce it for general use.

For all these reasons, employees are given **authorisation** to use electronic communication facilities and must abide by their organisation's procedures or face disciplinary action. It is therefore important that you access electronic communication facilities only if you have permission to do so and *never* breach your company's policies when doing so.

 INFORMATION UPDATE

Newspapers have reported many cases of employees being disciplined or sacked because they have abused their e-mail facilities or sent libellous messages. The largest e-mail-related libel action in the UK involved Norwich Union, a large insurance company, paying a rival, Western Provident Association, £450,000 in damages and costs for circulating untrue rumours about WPA's financial situation on its internal e-mail system. Companies can also scan employee e-mails automatically and examine incoming and outgoing e-mails and take disciplinary action if they disapprove of their subject, content or attachments. So beware!

Key facts on transmitting information electronically

When you have permission to use electronic communication facilities it is important to understand that you have a very powerful tool at your fingertips! For instance, one of the problems with e-mail, according to many people, is that it is so easy for messages to be sent quickly, without any thought of the recipient's reaction. E-mails sent externally are impossible to retrieve once you have pressed the send button! What is more, your message is in writing and is a permanent record. So be careful and *think* before you write.

For all electronic communications you need to check the facilities available to the other receiver. You can't send an e-mail to someone who hasn't a computer, or a fax via e-mail to someone without Internet access. Neither is there any point in attaching files unless your recipient has the software to open and read the file (see Unit 204, page 244).

You also need to check:

- the recipient's exact e-mail address (with all the punctuation correct) and/or fax number and/or website address
- what you are allowed to send (or say) in response to a customer's electronic enquiry

- the enquiries you are allowed to make on your organisation's behalf
- what you are allowed to order, on your organisation's behalf, electronically – and how payment will be confirmed

You need to think about how your electronic enquiry or response should be phrased and the degree of formality required. Whilst electronic communications are usually relatively informal, it would still raise a few eyebrows if you sent an e-mail to a senior director of another company and started it 'Dear Sam'!

Therefore, before you start, establish exactly what you are supposed to be doing, to whom you are communicating (one person or several), and the type of relationship that exists already. If you have any doubts, draft out a message first and get approval before you actually send the message.

Communication skills

Any e-mail or fax messages you send must be professional documents, even if they are expressed informally. This means they should be grammatical, properly punctuated, accurately spelt and clearly worded.

You can reduce the number of errors by using automated checking facilities – such as a spell-checker. If you use e-mail you can use Help to find this facility and how to turn it on. Refer to the Communications section in this book (see Appendix, pages 495–502) if you are concerned about your ability to use punctuation or grammar.

CHECK IT OUT!

Learn the 12 golden rules about sending e-mail which are shown on the next page. Then you are unlikely to go far wrong!

 INFORMATION UPDATE

The main benefit of all types of electronic communications is speed. If you e-mail a company, complete an electronic order form or request information electronically, you expect your enquiry to be dealt with promptly. Companies which have set up websites and which welcome customer enquiries must therefore have the back-up systems in place to deal with these quickly.

If you are responsible for responding to customer enquiries or if you handle e-mails, you must regularly check your electronic mailbox and process queries promptly. Otherwise you defeat the whole purpose of electronic messaging and give your organisation a poor reputation for customer responsiveness.

TWELVE GOLDEN RULES OF E-MAILING

1 Take your time! Think before you write.

2 Check your organisation's policy (if there is one) as to whether you should start your e-mail 'Dear (name)' or not. Many users consider the most appropriate ending for an informal, external e-mail is 'Best wishes'.

3 Check your e-mail address carefully and keep your address book up to date. Many packages will automatically save the addresses of people you reply to. Remember that an undelivered e-mail may take several days before it comes back to you, and in the meantime your recipient is still waiting.

4 Keep your message brief and to the point, and avoid long sentences.

5 Always put a heading in the subject box. That way it is obvious what it is about and this helps someone with a large number of incoming messages to prioritise their mail.

6 Never use capital letters. This is known as SHOUTING and is considered impolite.

7 Proof-read your message carefully before you press Send. Or store it in your Draft folder and ask someone else to check it for you.

8 *Always* check whether you should be including any attachments and that the recipient has the right to see these.

9 Mark important messages 'high priority'. This can be done on most packages. Access the Help screen for information on how to do this.

10 Check carefully whether you should have copied the e-mail to anyone, and whether your list is both correct and complete.

11 Take a hard (paper) copy of important e-mails, particularly those where you will have to take further action if a response isn't received promptly.

12 Don't use an e-mail for confidential information or when personal contact would be better. Use the telephone instead.

Know your system!

If you work on a computer system which is constantly on-line, you will be able to check and respond to electronic communications very quickly indeed. For instance, simply accessing your e-mail in-box will enable you to glance through all new messages, whether they are internal or external. As you create each message and click on the send button, the messages will be transmitted. Similarly, you will be able to access any Internet site simply by clicking on the Internet Explorer icon. You will immediately access a particular site. This may be your organisation's intranet site or it may be the home page of your ISP (Internet Service Provider).

If you operate on a dedicated system, you will have to dial up the ISP and enter a password before you can access the Internet or send messages. In this case, you must learn how to work 'off-line' to save money. If you select this option you can create enquiries or write replies and store these in your 'out box' until you make a connection. Then all your transmissions will be sent at once.

Understanding e-mail copies

There are several 'copy' options when sending an e-mail.

- You can enter the name of several recipients (or groups) in the To: box. Put a comma after each one (or semi-colon) and add a space for clarity. In this case, the message goes to each person for action.
- You can enter the name of a recipient and then send a copy to someone else for information. Do this by entering the e-mail address of the person receiving the copy in the CC: box. In this case, the recipient will receive the e-mail *and* know to whom the e-mail has been copied.
- You can enter the name of a recipient and any person authorised to receive a copy and then *blind* copy someone else by entering their e-mail address in the BCC: box. In this case, neither the recipient nor the other persons will know that you have sent the other copies. Neither will each 'blind' recipient know about the other! Do be careful not to abuse this facility, however. It should be used only when your line manager has particularly asked for a blind copy to be sent on a particular topic.

Understanding e-mail attachments

You can attach any type of file to your e-mail simply by typing the message in the usual way and then clicking on the Attach button (or selecting Insert and File attachment). Then locate the drive and folder in which your attachment is situated and click Attach. On your e-mail, the title will be added as an attachment and, if you want to double-check you have selected the correct file, you can click on it to 'open' it and read it. A few words of warning:

- A common mistake is to send a message and forget to add the attachment!
- Don't send an attachment which your recipient can't read because the format is incorrect – see Unit 204 (page 244).
- Compress (zip) a large file (e.g. a graphics or sound file) before transmission otherwise it will take a long, long time to transmit and download – see page 464.

Successful transmission

There will be occasions when you are unable to connect with a remote location. On the Internet, you will receive an error message if you enter the wrong website address, if the server which controls the website is not operating, or if the site is 'down' for some other technical reason. Check that the address is correct and, if so, try later when the location may be back on line.

An e-mail which is undeliverable is said to 'bounce' – that is, it comes back to you, usually with a message to that effect. However, occasionally messages are lost in cyberspace for no obvious reason, so don't assume that just because a message doesn't bounce back to you the recipient has received and read it.

On an internal system you can tell which messages have been read by accessing your 'sent' box and looking at the envelopes to see whether they are closed or open. If you send an external e-mail you cannot do this. However, on some e-mail packages you can request a receipt! On later versions of Outlook Express, for instance, you can select Tools and Request Read Receipt. When you send the e-mail the recipient is told that you have requested confirmation and can click 'Yes' to acknowledge receipt. You will then receive a brief message of confirmation.

If this facility is not available on your equipment, you may have to resort to low-tech devices such as the telephone, to check whether your message has been received!

Saving messages

You can save any message received electronically by creating a folder for types of messages and labelling this properly. You can then usually move all the appropriate messages into this folder. On all e-mail systems, for instance, there is the option to create folders in much the same way as you would in a word-processing or other software package.

In most Windows-based software packages (such as Outlook Express for e-mail) you will find the folder option under the File option on the menu bar. Click on New and you have the ability to create a new folder. This can be a subfolder of your Inbox, or you can create it at the same level as your Inbox and Outbox.

To transfer an e-mail you have sent to your folder, simply click on the folder, click on the e-mail and drag it to the folder.

CHECK IT OUT!

Score yourself on a rating of 1 to 5 for each of the following e-mail operations, where 1 is poor and 5 is good. Then talk to your tutor or supervisor about how to improve your score on your weak areas – as this will depend on the particular system you are using.

E-mail self-assessment

I can undertake each of the following operations:

a   access my 'out' mailbox to see the messages I have sent recently and select a particular message

b   print out a selected message

c   send e-mails to one person

d   send e-mails to several people

e   check the spelling in an e-mail

f   send an e-mail externally and send copies to internal recipients

g   send a blind copy of an e-mail to a colleague

h   access my address book, find a particular name and insert this on a new message

i   attach a file to an e-mail

j   delete messages from my Inbox and 'sent' box

k   use the program Help facility to undertake an operation I am unsure about.

Key facts on receiving messages electronically

Checking received messages

Whether you use a system that is constantly on-line, or have to dial up the ISP to receive messages and information, it is important to do this regularly. You already know that electronic communications are used for urgent and important items and the benefits are defeated if you check only once or twice a week!

It is very rare for an e-mail message to be corrupted, but it can happen. The sender might have forgotten to include the promised attachment! Another occasion is when you can't read an attachment for some reason. Then either e-mail the person immediately and ask for the information to be re-sent, possibly in a different format, or telephone and explain the problem.

Occasionally you may receive an e-mail which really isn't meant for you. Many senders complete their e-mails with a 'signature' and most companies have a clause printed at the foot of their e-mails to cover this eventuality. The most polite response is to respond to them, saying you have received the message in error.

If you regularly receive messages which are unwanted, inappropriate or not for you, report the matter to your supervisor or another relevant person.

Processing messages

Incoming messages can be categorised as
- A – those needing immediate action
- B – those providing important information
- C – those providing routine information
- D – those providing no useful information but which are just fun to read!

In reverse order:
- Delete the category 'D' messages after you've read them, so they don't clutter up your Inbox.
- Either print out or save category C messages in an appropriate folder (see page 473).
- Print out and/or forward category B messages to the people who need the information.
- Respond to any category A messages you can as quickly as possible. Otherwise print out and/or forward these messages to someone who can help you *and follow these up* until you can reply with a response.

 INFORMATION UPDATE

On most e-mail packages, when you reply to a message the message you received is printed below that. If you receive a reply, all three messages are connected – and so on.

It is considered impolite to let this stack of messages 'grow' unchecked – as the size of your printouts will eventually become unmanageable and it will be difficult to make out the last message. The time taken for transmission will also increase slightly. You can usually solve this problem by highlighting and deleting any former parts of the message which are no longer relevant to the communication.

EVIDENCE COLLECTION

As evidence for your portfolio, collect as many of the following as you can:
- a examples of e-mails you have sent to single addressees and multiple addressees on different dates
- b details of any e-mails you have received in error, and the action you took
- c examples of e-mails you have received over a period of time, preferably with a copy of your response above or attached
- d a note of any problems you encountered when using e-mail, and the action you took
- e a copy of the folders and files you have created when you have saved e-mails
- f copies of faxes you have sent or received from your computer.

Key facts on accessing and retrieving electronically stored information

To obtain evidence for this element, you must be accessing remote information systems – that is, the Internet or information held on an organisation's intranet. As you saw on page 468, organisations normally operate some controls over access to remote systems – otherwise there is a danger employees will spend a large part of their day surfing the Net to find their next holiday destinations, or using 'chat' rooms!

Whether you are allowed permanent access to the Internet or have to ask for specific permission to go on-line, you should be aware of your company's regulations and follow these.

Meeting requirements when using electronic information systems

If we assume that the person who has asked you to obtain information is your 'customer', then it helps you to search for, and retrieve, the correct type of information more quickly if you know what it is they require – and where to find it. Simple checks to make include:

- clear details about the type of information required
- the URL (website address), if known (or some useful suggestions)
- alternative types of information which may be suitable, if the original choice is not available
- the depth of search you are supposed to undertake.

The depth of search will depend on the importance of the information. You may be told to 'keep looking' if something is very important, but to 'have a quick look' if something is not.

You are then likely to find your information *either*:

- by accessing a site direct
- by searching for sites via a search engine (see page 479).

Locating and retrieving information by directly accessing a site

Your search will always start at a particular page – this is the home page which has been decided by your network administrator or your ISP (Internet Service Provider). From this page you can either link to other pages or you can type the name of a site you know in the Open dialogue box at the top of your screen, under the toolbar. You can bring this on screen either by choosing File and then Open *or* by holding down the Control key and depressing the letter 'o' key. If you have accessed similar addresses before, Windows Explorer will try to suggest entries you want. You may find this useful – or not – as the case may be!

Alternatively, you can double-click on the current address showing in the address bar under the toolbar, delete the entry and replace it with another of your choice. Another option is to click on the down arrow at the right of the address bar. This shows all the sites you have accessed recently (or since you last logged on, if you are on a network system) and you can reselect one quickly and easily.

Moving around on the Internet

There are several ways you can move around on the Net.

- All sites contain **hyperlinks** – these are graphics and text which turn your cursor into a 'hand' when you move over them. Clicking on them moves you to another page within the site or to another site.
- Clicking on the Back button at the top left of your toolbar takes you back through previous pages or sites you have viewed.
- Clicking on the Forward button, to the right of the Back button, takes you forwards again.

Processing retrieved information by printing

You can print any Web page for future reference by selecting File and then the Print option. It is sensible to check Page Setup before you do this, and note that:

- you can choose A4 paper or a different size, and landscape or portrait orientation
- you may be able to select a range of pages and the number of copies you require
- you can decide the most appropriate margins
- you can include or exclude specific information in the header and footer areas of your pages – page title, Web page address, the page number in the printout and total pages and the date of printing (these are all 'coded' in the header and footer dialogue boxes as &P and &d).

Also check whether it is possible to change the printer's setup (usually by clicking the Properties button in the Print dialogue box). If you can do this, printing will be speeded up if you select 'grey scale' (rather than 'colour') and 'draft' or 'econofast' rather than 'normal' or 'best'.

CHECK IT OUT!

A useful facility in on-line Help is the question-mark. Click on this and you 'collect' the question-mark. You can then drag it to any item, release it, and receive an instant description of the item. Try this now by selecting Page Setup again and moving the question-mark to the header and footer codes.

Processing retrieved information by saving text and images

To save time – and money if you are logged on specifically for your search – it is more sensible to save Web pages and images so that you can read them later.

KEY NOTES ON SAVING FROM THE WEB

- Save a page by first going to File and then Save As. Select the Web Page Complete option. Next, decide where you want to save this on your computer. The options will be shown in the main part of the dialogue box. You can select the drive or folder to suit yourself. A useful technique is to have a folder especially for all your Web pages which you then sort through and empty regularly.

- If you want to save only the text but not the images, then do as before, but after selecting File and Save As choose the Text File (.txt.) option, rather than the Web Page Complete option.

- You can highlight specific text you want and then copy this to your Clipboard and paste it into any file you wish (as you would do if you were word-processing)

- You can save an image by right-clicking on it and selecting the Save Picture As command which now appears in a pop-up menu. Don't worry if you see an unusual file extension – image files on the Web are normally suffixed either '.gif' or '.jpg'.

- In any of these cases, of course, you can select whether to include the information in an existing file folder.

INFORMATION UPDATE

The World Wide Web is growing so quickly that new Web address suffixes are being decided, both to extend the total number of addresses available and to help surfers to locate different types of organisations more easily.

At present, the suffix shows the type of organisation and – apart from the United States – the country. So, an address ending with **.com** or **.gov** is a website based in the USA. If it were based in the UK it would end with **.co.uk** or **.gov.uk**.

A British address ends with **.co.uk** if it is a commercial organisation, **.ac** if it is an educational establishment (this is **.edu** in the USA) and **.gov** if it is a government office.

You can use this knowledge to help to refine some of your searches. For instance, Ask Jeeves is a popular search engine and can be accessed either at www.ask.com (the American site) or www.ask.co.uk (the British site). Use the former if you are looking for detailed information on USA topics, e.g. NASA space launches, but the latter if you want to find information relating to Britain.

Locating and retrieving information by using a search engine

This is an option if you have a question you want to answer. The Ask Jeeves site is useful because it understands questions written in plain English, such as 'How old is Bill Gates?' It will then search other websites and give you numerous choices.

Alternatively you may develop a liking for a 'favourite' search engine, such as Yahoo!, Altavista, Google or Excite. Searches on these sites are improved by using some special techniques:

Exact phrases should be put inside quotes (e.g. 'Bill Gates').

Put a plus sign to indicate additional criteria for your search (e.g. 'Bill Gates' + Microsoft). You will now receive information both on Bill Gates *and* on Microsoft.

Put a minus sign to reduce criteria on which you *don't* want information (e.g. 'Bill Gates' − Microsoft).

CHECK IT OUT!

To reduce work trying to note down or remember websites you find useful, use the Favorites facility (American spelling!). Click this option on the menu bar. A pop-up menu then enables you to save the address for the site you are currently viewing. Do change the suggestion given in the pop-up menu, if necessary, so that you will recognise the name immediately. To view your list of favourite sites, simply click the button labelled Favorites.

However, if you are not careful you will end up with a huge list of addresses in no useful sequence or order! You can sort these out by selecting Favorites and then clicking Organise. This option suggests folders you can use (or you can create your own) so that you can store search engine addresses and other related websites in appropriate and clearly labelled folders.

Select Favorites and Organise and see what options there are. Remember, when you are exploring your choices, that you have a right as well as a left mouse button! Try creating a few folders and then you will be ready to store favourite addresses in an orderly manner!

INFORMATION UPDATE

Many organisations now post **interactive forms** on their websites. These may be in place to enable:

- enquirers to receive specific information quickly and easily
- customers to complete order forms for items they wish to purchase
- customers to pay for items on-line
- new customers to request information to be sent to them by mail
- customers to be added to a mailing list or regular e-mail service
- customers to send detailed enquiries to the organisation.

If the form is designed properly, it should be easy to complete. All the questions should be straightforward and unambiguous. It should be impossible for the form to be electronically transmitted unless all the key questions have been answered.

Checking retrieved information

To be of any value, information you retrieve must be up to date and what your 'customer' wanted. As an obvious example, retrieving train timetable information when Railtrack was replacing miles of track during the autumn of 2000 would not have provided reliable information (although enquirers were warned to double-check information they downloaded).

It is easy to make a mistake when you are searching for this type of information, by not searching for the correct day or for the correct time, or by mistaking a station name or forgetting to reduce the number of 'changes' a person wishes to make.

Even with less detailed information, it is always worth checking the date it was posted on the website. Finding key information which was posted in 1995 is obviously less valuable than finding information posted in 2000.

The costs of accessing remote information systems

Accessing the Internet incurs a charge for the telephone call from the receiving computer to the Internet Service Provider, or for the service provided by the ISP, or both. This is more noticeable if you have to log on specially. If you have continuous Internet access you may be less aware of it, but that is only likely if you work for a very large organisation.

Your employer will want to keep these costs as low as possible. One way of doing this is to save Web pages and print them out later, rather than spend a long time printing them out while on-line. Another option is to disable the graphics on your screen, as these take longer to load and slow you down. That is annoying if you are trying to get information quickly and find yourself held up by banner adverts and company logos in which you have no interest. You can switch off graphics in Internet Explorer by selecting Tools and then Internet Options. Select the Advanced tab and scroll down until you find the option Show Pictures under the Multimedia heading. Deselect this by clicking on the box. When you access websites you will now see a marker where the images should be – but won't view them. You can, however, see an individual one by right-clicking on the icon and selecting Show Picture. And, of course, you can re-select your Show Pictures option at any time you want.

CHECK IT OUT! contd.

Internet self-assessment

I can undertake each of the following operations:

a access a company intranet or website

b use a search engine (such as www.yahoo.com) to find the website address of an organisation and a structured search engine which links to other sites (e.g. www.ask.co.uk)

c save important website addresses under Favorites

d view my favourites and select a required website

e use the address bar to connect quickly to a site accessed recently

f enter a website address correctly in the address line

g use the Help facility to undertake an operation I am unsure about

h disable graphics to view a site more quickly

i navigate around a site using the site map, search facilities and appropriate buttons

j use hyperlinks to connect quickly to related sites

k complete an interactive form correctly and completely to search for information

l check that information is relevant, correct and up to date

m print out information

n save information and include it in an existing folder

o save information in a new folder

EVIDENCE COLLECTION

For this element you need to prove you comply with relevant regulations in relation to current legislation, the requirements of your ISP, your manufacturer's instructions and your organisation's procedures. You also need to prove you can process retrieved information and save this in existing and new folders and well as printing it. You will therefore find the following helpful.

1 Obtain any regulations or procedures you have to comply with when using your computer system and accessing electronically stored information, or obtain witness testimony from your supervisor that you know and routinely follow all the required procedures.

2 Keep a log of all the occasions on which you are asked to access the Internet to obtain information. Record the date, the site accessed and the information obtained and why it was required.

3 Save Internet information on a floppy disk and be prepared to submit this (or a printout of its contents) as evidence that you can save information from the Internet or an intranet.

4 Obtain witness testimony from people for whom you access information that you have checked their requirements properly, can search for information effectively and provide them with up-to-date information as requested.

Option Unit 218 Photocopy, present and distribute complex documents

FOCUS OF THE UNIT

To obtain this unit you must be able to:

- photocopy complex documents
- present and distribute those documents.

EVIDENCE COLLECTION

It will make evidence collection easier if you can obtain the following information:

a   a copy of any organisational procedures issued to staff who undertake photocopying on (e.g. who can ask for photocopying, whether there is a limit on copies, types of forms used to request jobs, etc.)

b   a copy of any information in your organisation regarding copyright – saying what you can and cannot copy legally (as an example, there is often a notice in your college library to this effect)

c   access to the manufacturer's instructions for the photocopier you use regularly – a quick read through this to refresh your memory is a good idea!

d   a copy of any instructions for staff on remedying photocopier problems – with information on those which must be referred to someone senior or reported to the supplier

e   a copy of any routine photocopier records *you* have completed.

Key facts on photocopying

The importance of obtaining instructions

It is essential to obtain clear instructions before you start photocopying. Many organisations have a form on which staff request photocopying work. The form will cover the options available, such as single- or double-sided, enlarged or reduced, number of copies required, whether the document should be stapled or bound, etc. Often the form needs to be authorised by someone in authority – but not always.

If the form has been carefully designed, this should provide evidence that you obtain clear information in the format required. If there is no form, perhaps you could think about designing one yourself. In the meantime, keep a record of the instructions you receive for photocopying jobs and queries you make to check specific details.

If a request form also covers binding, the options to check are whether a ring, comb or slide binder should be used (assuming all three are available) and what type of cover is preferred. Covers are available in a range of colours, or with transparent fronts, or with a blank or transparent panel. In this case the title of the document must be aligned to show in the panel. Some organisations have their covers specially printed with their name, but use these only for important, external documents. They may also use **thermal** binding which uses heat to fasten the pages and cover. Check with your assessor if this can count as a 'variation' on slide binding.

KEY NOTES ON OBTAINING INFORMATION

The consequences of not having clear information include:

- time is wasted – and the job has to be redone because the format is wrong
- a deadline may be missed because of delays
- copies are sent to too many/too few people
- copies are sent to the wrong people
- materials are wasted
- confidential information may be circulated but not placed in sealed envelopes
- confidential information may be circulated to those not allowed to receive it.

Copyright legislation

Copyright is covered by the **Copyright Designs and Patents Act 1988**. Under this Act, apart from single copies for personal research or private study, you cannot copy printed material from a book, magazine, newspaper or other printed source unless you have special permission. There are some exceptions, such as for educational establishments and libraries, but these do not apply to commercial organisations.

If your organisation wants to make copies from a printed source regularly, then it must obtain a **licence**. For instance, the Newspaper Licensing Agency can give permission for newspapers to be copied legally.

You do not need to worry about copyright if you are copying a document that has been produced within the organisation, because then it is an 'original work'. But if you are asked to make 50 copies of a magazine article you should know that you are being asked to break the law, unless your firm has negotiated a licence to do so.

CHECK IT OUT!

Copyright legislation was dealt with in Option Unit 205, too. Turn back to page 287 and check the additional information which was given there.

 KEY NOTES FOR DEALING WITH CONFIDENTIAL AND SENSITIVE INFORMATION

- Don't talk about what you read.
- Don't leave the document(s) lying around on your desk.
- Even worse – don't leave a copy on the glass of the photocopier.
- Don't take 'spare' copies on a 'just-in-case' basis.
- Distribute the finished documents in sealed envelopes, clearly marked 'confidential'.
- Return the original to the person who gave you the work to do.
- Shred any spoiled copies.

EVIDENCE COLLECTION

Collect together copies of forms, memos or e-mails you have received asking you to undertake photocopying work. If your organisation uses a form, comment on this, identifying whether it regularly meets your requirements or whether you think improvements could be made.

If no form is used, but you think one would be useful, draft a design and submit it to your supervisor as a suggestion, together with a list of the benefits you think it would achieve. Then include a copy in your portfolio.

Key facts on photocopying complex documents

Checking materials and obtaining authorisation

Before you start any job you need to make sure that:

- you have sufficient materials
- you have authorisation to do the job.

Materials

There should be a proper system for re-ordering materials such as photocopier paper, card, toner, covers for bound copies, comb or slide binders and any other materials you use regularly. Check what these are and make sure you understand the ordering system used in your organisation. If you are asked to do a large job, which will use a lot of supplies, you must notify the person in charge of the stock. Otherwise you may find out that although you need 500 slide binders, only 100 are normally kept in stock, so you miss the deadline date for a job. Or you empty the stock cupboard so that no one else can bind anything until the next delivery has arrived.

Authorisation

The best procedures include some necessary controls – to prevent **unauthorised** photocopying, for example – but still retain flexibility for urgent jobs.

CHECK IT OUT!

In your own organisation (or college) find out:

a what, if any, 'controls' exist for photocopying – for instance, authorisation by a senior member of staff for 'large' jobs

b what would happen in an emergency if no senior member of staff was available to give authorisation

c whether strict controls exist which have to be followed carefully *or* whether controls are lax and/or everyone ignores them so they may as well not exist.

Discuss with your tutor or supervisor the benefits of strict controls – and their limitations.

Manufacturer's instructions

Photocopiers are apt to be regarded rather like video recorders. Everyone can do the basics (but very little besides) and the only time anyone reads the instruction book is the day the machine is installed! If you were trained how to use the machine *properly,* you should have been trained to use it in accordance with the manufacturer's instructions. If you acquired your knowledge just by watching someone else for a few minutes it may be useful – and quite enlightening – to check your working methods against the manufacturer's guidance!

To be awarded this unit you need to be adept at:

a producing single or multi-page copies (easily!)

b enlarging or reducing (and selecting the correct ratio)

c   changing from single- to double-sided – and back again

d   refilling the paper tray(s)

e   changing the toner cartridge

f   remedying a simple paper jam.

It is also sensible to learn the other main features available and which you may be asked to do (e.g. stapling, copying on to A3 paper, using the interrupt feature so that you can break into a long job to do an urgent one).

TEST YOUR KNOWLEDGE AND UNDERSTANDING

Test your own knowledge by doing the brief quiz below, and then check your answers against those on page 493. It is a good idea to repeat the quiz when you have finished reading this unit – hopefully your score will have improved!

Answer 'True' or 'False' to each of the following questions:

1 A photocopier should be switched off immediately after use.

2 The fusing unit should not be handled.

3 If copies appear dirty, this can be because the image density level is too dark.

4 Damp paper is more likely than dry paper to jam in the machine.

5 Toner cartridges should never be incinerated after use.

6 Torn scraps of paper, left after a paper jam, do not need removing from the machine.

7 The document glass should be washed regularly.

8 Toner should be stored in a cool, dark place.

9 In a serious emergency, switch off the machine and unplug it at the mains.

10 Delicate originals are safe to put into the document feeder.

Keeping waste to a minimum

The better you know your job, and the more care and attention you take, the more you will reduce waste!

 KEY NOTES ON MINIMISING WASTE – AND CARING FOR THE ENVIRONMENT

- Get clear instructions before you start.
- Use the correct paper for the machine.
- Repair any torn originals.

- 'Clean up' an original with dirty marks on (using the special correcting fluid for the job) or retype these if they are very poor quality.
- Make sure the glass is kept clean.
- Make sure the original is the right way up and in the correct position on the glass.
- Check a multi-page document is in the right order, with all the pages the correct way up, before you select 'collate'.
- Double-check your settings before you start.
- Take a 'trial' copy before starting a long run.
- Check the density setting is not too dark (this wastes toner).
- Have the photocopier serviced regularly.
- Print only the number of copies requested.
- Use recycled paper when you can.
- Routinely make double-sided copies to save paper.
- Reduce waste using the tips above, *and* put any sheets of paper you do spoil in a recycling container rather than a rubbish bin.
- Dispose of used toner cartridges properly.

Problems, problems!

You will have to prove you can deal with various problems, including being out of paper or toner, a straightforward paper jam, a wrongly positioned original and a damaged original. The information you have just read and the quiz above should check your abilities on these points!

Occasionally you may meet a really difficult problem – such as a serious misfeed or a fault developing on the machine. Check the action you should take in your organisation. Normally one person in the office has received special training and the first step is to tell that person about the incident. He or she may be the only one allowed to contact a mechanic. If you are in any doubt, have a word with the person who gave you the work to copy, or your line manager, team leader or supervisor. A clear notice must be put on the machine so that other users know there is a problem which either limits operations (e.g. only single copies can be made) or means the machine is inoperable until it has been repaired.

Records of photocopying

Many types of modern photocopier automatically create their own records and provide a readout. In this case, each user, or group of users, will have their own identification code against which their individual usage is logged. On such machines a limit can be pre-set to prevent overuse by any individual or group.

In other cases, a more general record is kept by identifying how many copies have been taken over a particular period. This is often checked against the invoice from the supplier or rental company. The factors which influence the type of records kept include:

- whether your organisation wants to monitor and/or restrict individual use
- whether your organisation needs to know the overall usage to check against the rental bill.

The latter will not be the case if the organisation has an agreement which allows unlimited usage, but that is rare. In most cases, the invoice will be based on usage, even if a certain number of copies each month is free.

The organisation might keep a record to help it identify when the machine should be replaced. The 'life' of a photocopier is dependent upon how often it is used. Large, heavy-duty machines can do far more copies than smaller ones before they have to be replaced.

EVIDENCE COLLECTION

Keep two logs over the next few weeks. The first should record your photocopying jobs and the second should record problems you rectify. Suggested headings are given below.

LOG 1			
Date	Description of task	Special instructions	Wastage and reason

LOG 2		
Date	Description of problem or fault	Action taken

In addition, retain one copy of different types of photocopying jobs you have undertaken, to prove you can undertake various operations, such as enlarging, reducing, printing on one or both sides of the paper, collating multi-page documents, etc. Check, however, with the originator that the document is not confidential before you include it in your portfolio.

Ask your supervisor or a responsible colleague for witness testimony that you can reliably carry out photocopying jobs without wasting paper or toner and can be trusted to deal with routine problems sensibly and promptly.

Finally, check that your list of problems includes being out of paper, out of toner, rectifying a paper jam, remedying an incorrectly positioned original and a damaged original. Your evidence must cover at least *three* of these problems. If the others do not occur whilst you are collecting your evidence, be prepared to discuss with your assessor what you would do in these situations.

Key facts on presenting and distributing documents

Checking how documents should be presented

On page 484 you saw how useful an official form can be which states the format required for a documents and how it should be presented. For this element, this means checking whether it should be collated or not, stapled or bound. The types of bindings you may be asked to provide are discussed on page 491.

The importance of checking collated documents

All large, modern photocopiers automatically collate documents. However, the collation will be correct only if the original was also in the right order! The whole job will be wrecked if you muddle up the pages at any stage, such as by dropping them, by putting them down in batches – and picking them up in the wrong order or with some upside down – by 'facing' them (so some pages are the other way round), or by not keeping your individual sets stacked separately.

 KEY NOTES ON CHECKING COLLATED DOCUMENTS

- Double-check the original before you start.

- *Carefully* remove the completed sets.

- Stack the sets 'side on' (i.e. at 90 degrees) to each other, so that they are easy to separate.

- Don't carry more than you can easily manage.

- Use a machine which automatically 'picks up' from where it left off if there is a paper jam or if you need to refill the paper tray.

- If you can't use such a machine, and a problem occurs in the middle, make a note of where you were, remove the sets done so far, *carefully* remedy the fault and don't lose concentration. Then, at the end, double-check the 'set' that was interrupted.

If you have to collate a large document by hand, try to obtain help. Use a large space and spread everything out. Work methodically and check each finished set before you staple or bind it.

Finally, a good quality check is to flick through some finished sets chosen at random. Often, if there has been a problem, it will have occurred throughout the whole job and you can easily spot it. If you find something wrong, 'count to ten' – and then check the whole lot!

Choosing an appropriate cover and checking requirements

Before you can choose you need to know:

a what types of cover you have available as regular items of stock

b what types of cover you can buy if you want (check in a supplier's catalogue)

c your company's policies on using covers.

Generally, the quality and type will depend upon the importance of the document and whether it is required externally or internally. You are always wise, even if you think you have found a suitable cover, to check that it is appropriate with the person who asked you to do the job.

In some cases the cover may be a simple piece of card, one of which has been prepared as a title page to go at the front with a plain piece of card for the back. If you are using a sophisticated photocopier you may be able to instruct the machine to insert these automatically. Again, knowing what options are available is often the key to success!

If the author of the document was undecided about the best type of cover, it is sensible to make up one completed document and ask for approval – before binding dozens and then having to re-do your work because it doesn't meet the requirements.

Binding documents

The best way to learn how to use a binder properly is to ask someone who is skilled at the job to show you – and then practice.

 KEY NOTES ON BINDING DOCUMENTS

- Bound documents need wide margins – otherwise the text will be partly obscured. If the pages are single-sided you need a wide margin only on the left. If the pages are double-sided you need a wide margin on both sides.

- Documents to be ring-bound must be punched. See if your machine punches as well as inserts the binder – otherwise you start by punching holes into the document yourself. The pages must be aligned correctly at the outset. The punch must be capable of coping with the amount of paper in the document – otherwise punch in batches. The number of holes needs to match the number of rings if it is to look professional! All the holes must be in exactly the same place, otherwise the document will be higgledy-piggledy at the top and bottom!

- Comb binders are available in different depths – thick documents need a deeper comb than one which is only a few pages. A comb which is too small won't fit, one which is too big will look out of proportion. Cut the length of a comb binder to fit a document which is less than A4 using a sharp pair of scissors – after you have finished binding. Comb binding is quite economical because, if you get it wrong, you can open the comb and start again.
- Slide binders also come in different depths. They literally slide over the left-hand edge of the document but must be large enough to cope with the thickness. They can be difficult to use and there is a 'trick' to opening these, and keeping the paper level, without losing your fingernails or your temper! Their disadvantage is that you cannot easily make changes to the document, such as by inserting additional pages. Nor can the document be opened flat.
- Another variation is a thermal binder, which binds the pages and spine by heat. This looks very professional as the spine is less bulky than with other methods.

Dealing with originals when you have finished the job

An essential basic tip is to check, with the person who gives you the job, whether the originals should be returned. It is too late to find out, after you have shredded them, that you were supposed to give them back! Normally originals are retained – and carefully stored – in case additional copies are required. They are usually always 'cleaner' than even the best photocopy. Remember that if the document is confidential the originals should be returned in a sealed envelope.

If you can destroy the originals, then either put them in a recycling bin or shred them. The shredded 'bits' make useful packaging material.

EVIDENCE COLLECTION

Ask colleagues who want you to prepare a bound document if they will put their request in writing (a short note will suffice) – or you write out the request and ask them to sign it to confirm you understand it correctly. Also check if you can make a spare copy for your portfolio. Attach their note to your finished work and write a short account of when and how you carried out the job, the equipment and materials you used, how you checked requirements, who you distributed the document to, and what you were asked to do with the original.

If the document is confidential, ask for witness testimony as you will be unable to keep a copy of the final document.

Key to quiz on page 487

True: 2, 3, 4, 5, 8 and 9. *False*: 1 – Turn the machine on/off only at the beginning and end of every working day. 6 – No, they can burn or cause another misfeed. 7 – No, use a damp cloth or methylated spirits to remove stubborn marks. 10 – Not unless you have a special setting on the machine – otherwise they will tear.

Appendix

Improve your written English

Spelling

People's ability to spell varies greatly. Usually, the more you read and *use* words, the better at spelling you become. Words start to 'look wrong' if you misspell them. Today, of course, you also have certain 'helpers'. All word-processing packages contain an autocorrect or spell-check facility – although these have their limitations (see Unit 204, page 237). Many e-mail packages also contain spell-checkers. Whilst these may stop you making some of the more horrendous errors, they cannot help if you are drafting out information in writing or if you neglect to use them!

A useful strategy is to concentrate on improving your spelling on the 'key words' you are expected to use regularly as an administrator – especially those which frequently cause problems. Slowly, you can increase your list of known words until only the most unusual words or technical terms cause you problems – and these you can look up in a dictionary.

TEST YOUR KNOWLEDGE AND UNDERSTANDING

1 Below are 51 words commonly written by administrators. Twenty are wrongly spelled. Can you identify and correct them?

receipt	plausible	assessment
liase	payed	achieved
criteria	acceptible	competant
embarassed	concise	convenient
priviledge	comparable	indispensable
threshold	budgetted	undoubtedly
wierd	genuine	appropriate
alcohol	colleegue	succesful
desparate	permanent	prestigious

Punctuation

Full stops and capital letters

Few people have problems with full stops and capital letters, but even in these areas fashions change. The modern trend is towards open punctuation in letters and formal documents and the minimum of capital letters. However, if you are employed by a boss who prefers you to use a more traditional style, don't argue!

'Open punctuation' means that full stops and commas are omitted from addresses and other key parts of documents, such as dates, salutations (e.g. Dear Mr Brown) and complimentary closes (e.g. Yours sincerely). Full stops are also omitted from capital-letter abbreviations (e.g. BBC/ITV). Another modern trend is the use of a capital in the middle of a word, especially for a trade name (e.g. WordPerfect or InterLink).

Traditionally, initial capitals were used frequently (e.g. 'The Research Assistant is employed in the Production Department.'). Today, these are often left as lower-case letters ('The research assistant is employed in the production department.'). However, you should still use an initial capital at the start of a sentence and for proper nouns (names of people and places). Incidentally, seasons *don't* take an initial capital, whereas months do.

Question marks

A question mark replaces a full stop at the end of the sentence when you are asking a direct question (e.g. 'Are you going to the meeting?'). However, do be careful. You should continue to use a full stop if the question is indirect ('Can you please let me know whether you will be attending the meeting.').

Commas and dashes

Commas are used in the middle of a sentence to denote a pause. They enable the reader to draw breath! However, where you put a comma can be critical to the sense of the sentence. Compare:

'Molly, James and I went to the station.'

'Molly James and I went to the station.'

Read the sentence for sense when you are testing for commas. If you would pause if you were speaking, it is likely a comma is required.

If you want to denote a longer pause, then you can put a dash, as in 'Molly, James and I went to the station – but not until it was dark.'

Both commas and dashes can be used to separate a clause in the middle of a sentence. You can 'test' for a clause as the sentence would make sense without it. In this case you want a comma (or a dash, depending upon the length of the pause) both before *and* after the clause. Compare:

'We will return the repaired item, as agreed over the telephone, immediately we receive payment.'

'We will return the repaired item – as agreed over the telephone – immediately we receive payment.'

In both cases, if you removed the clause 'as agreed over the telephone' the sentence would still make sense.

Finally, commas are also used:

- to separate a list of words (e.g. 'paper, envelopes, pens')
- to separate words such as 'therefore', 'however', 'unfortunately', 'interestingly' and 'consequently' from the rest of the sentence.

Semi-colons, colons and brackets

Semi-colons are used when you want to link two closely connected phrases or sentences without using a conjunction such as 'and', 'but', 'as' or 'because'. An example is: 'Robert was thinking of going back to live in the sun; he felt strange now in a cold climate.' If you can't get used to semi-colons, use a conjunction or write two sentences instead.

Colons are most commonly used to separate a clause which introduces a list, as in: 'We have several items of summer stock on sale at present: barbecues, picnic chairs, garden umbrellas and loungers.'

Brackets are rarely used in formal business documents – you are safer to use a dash instead. However, they can be useful at times to add relevant additional information. If you start to write something in brackets, do remember to close them afterwards!

Apostrophes

The punctuation mark which causes people the greatest headache – by far – is the apostrophe. Yet the rules are not too difficult if you take your time to learn them. If you skim through them you are likely to get completely muddled or to scatter apostrophes everywhere! Below are some simple rules to follow.

Use 1 – missing letters. This is the easiest of all. Apostrophes are used to denote a letter or some letters missing from a word or phrase. The apostrophe is positioned in the exact place the letters are missing. Examples include can't (cannot), didn't (did not), won't (will not), haven't (have not). However, contracted words such as these are used only in *informal* business communications, such as e-mails, and not formal ones, such as letters.

Use 2 – possession or ownership. The following are the golden rules you should learn:

- One owner = add an apostrophe + an *s*. Examples are: the manager's office, a week's holiday, John's wedding. (Tip: turn these round for a 'double check' – the office of the manager, the holiday of a week, the wedding of John.)

- Several owners = just add an apostrophe. Examples are: the ants' nest, three weeks' holiday, the shopworkers' union. (Tip: again turn these round to check – the nest of the ants, the holiday of three weeks, the union of the shopworkers.)

The final point to remember is that if you use a noun which changes its form or spelling in the plural (e.g. child/children, woman/women, company/companies) then you still need an apostrophe. This time you add apostrophe + an *s* if the plural doesn't end in *s*, and just an apostrophe if it does. Examples are: the children's toys, the women's changing room, the companies' representatives.

Don't, however, be tempted to put apostrophes in ordinary plurals – they don't need them! Greengrocers' signs proclaiming potato's and cauliflower's for sale are simply wrong!

Finally, one **exception** you need to remember is the difference between it's/its. Spelt with an apostrophe it means 'it is'. For possession, there is no apostrophe (e.g. '*It's* a long time since the dog wore *its* collar.').

TEST YOUR KNOWLEDGE AND UNDERSTANDING

Punctuate the following sentences and correct any misspellings.

1 Please report to the personal office therefore at 9 am on Monday 25 October bringing with you this letter the enclosed visitors pass and your examination certificates.

2 Toms train which he caught every morning was invariabley late and today its arrival surprised everyone when it sped into the station ten minutes early.

3 We need a draught copy of the report ready for Tuesday three copies of each of the new leaflets and fourty sets of application forms the latter to be sent to the managers office immediatly.

4 She is visiting several countries in europe on next months trip including france belgum holland and italy but she still aims to get back before the book fair in may.

5 They expect to leave wolverampton about six oclock although this depends upon there meeting finishing on time which is rather optimistic in my opinion.

Grammar

In this case, start by testing your own ability to write grammatical sentences – then look up the questions that caused you difficulty.

CHECK IT OUT!

Each of the sentences below contains a grammatical error. Identify the error and rewrite each sentence correctly:

1 Me and Paula wrote the report.
2 I am sorry we didn't contact you sooner.
3 Is this who you saw yesterday?
4 I know it was Tom that dealt with the customer.
5 He never gives her nothing but problems.
6 It's absolutely vital he attends the meeting.
7 British Telecom are a large company.
8 The football team has been playing their best this season.
9 Each member of staff have to sign the form.
10 One of the documents which were sent to the accountants was wrong.

Pronoun problems

Four pitfalls exist with pronouns.

- The first is when to use 'I' and when to say 'me'.
- The second is mixing singular and plural pronouns.
- The third is when to say 'who' and when to say 'whom'.
- The fourth concerns wrongly used pronouns.

1 Say 'I' when – if there were two of you – you would use the word 'we'. Say 'me' when – if there were two of you – you would use the word 'us'. Alternatively, leave out the other person and see which pronoun makes sense. For example:

> 'Can you help Mary and I/me with this job?'
> Test 1 = 'Can you help us (= me) with this job?'
> Test 2 = 'Can you help me with this job?

> 'Do you think Tim or I/me should attend?'
> Test 1 = 'Do you think we (= I) should attend?
> Test 2 = Do you think I should attend?

Finally, remember it is polite *always* to mention yourself last!

2 Stick to the singular or plural. Therefore write:

> *either* 'We would like to assure you the matter will receive our immediate attention'
> *or* 'I would like to assure you the matter will receive my immediate attention'
> *but not* 'I would like to assure you the matter will receive our immediate attention.'

3 Use 'who' when the person is the subject of the sentence – i.e. the main focus of the sentence or the person carrying out the action. Use 'whom' if the person is the object of the sentence – i.e. the person that is being acted upon. For example:

> 'Martin (*subject*), who works as an engineer, will be qualified next year.'
> 'When you (*subject*) tried to ring Kelly (*object*), to whom did you speak?'

If you don't like using 'whom', change the sentence around so that the object becomes the subject. In the second example you would simply say: 'Who spoke to you when you tried to ring Kelly?'

4 The main pronouns which are wrongly used are:

- 'which' or 'that' when you are referring to people – always use 'who' or 'whom'
  (e.g. 'It was Brian who forgot the date' *not* 'It was Brian what forgot the date')

- 'what' instead of 'that' or 'which'
  (e.g. 'This is the car that I want to buy' *not* 'This is the car what I want to buy').

Finally, beware of **sexist** problems with pronouns! It is incorrect to write a sentence such as 'Each visitor must state his name on arrival.' It assumes all visitors are male! Neither should you say 'Each visitor must state their name on arrival', as that confuses singular and plural. Instead make everything plural: 'All visitors must state their names on arrival' – which gets rid of the problem.

Double negatives and redundancy

Double negatives cancel each other out. You shouldn't say 'I haven't done nothing' as this means you *have* done something!

Redundancy is when you use words unnecessarily. Examples are: 'He never goes there *at all*' or 'Thank you for *replying so promptly and* letting me know so quickly that the parcel had arrived.' You can cross out the words in italics in these sentences and they mean the same – and read much better!

Verb agreement

You already know what is meant by the 'subject' of a sentence. Now you need to remember that any verbs you use must 'agree' with the subject. If the subject is singular, the verb must also be singular ('The bus is delayed'). If the subject is plural, the verb must be plural (The buses are delayed'). Various traps for the unwary are listed below.

Organisations are all one thing – so they take a singular verb (e.g. 'Marks & Spencer *is* having problems at present.').

A singular pronoun should be treated as a singular noun (e.g. each, every, everybody, somebody, neither, nobody). For example: 'Each of the staff *has* been given a bonus.' This often makes more sense if you think of 'each one', 'every one', etc.

A collective noun can be either singular or plural – so long as you are consistent. For example: 'The group *is* meeting to discuss its membership next week' is correct, as is 'The group *are* meeting to discuss their membership next week'. But 'The group is meeting to discuss their membership next week' is incorrect.

The main danger is when you insert a phrase in the middle of a sentence. If you identify the subject of the sentence you can't go wrong. For example, both the following are correct: 'The vases (*subject, plural*), one of which was very valuable, were on sale yesterday' *or* 'One of the vases (*subject, singular*), which was very valuable, was on sale yesterday.'

TEST YOUR KNOWLEDGE AND UNDERSTANDING

1   Go back to the sentences on page 500 and try them again. This time, the errors (and the way to correct them) should be obvious!

2   Other common traps are given in the sentences below. See if you can rewrite each one correctly and check your answers with your tutor or supervisor.

   a   I lent her pen this morning because I forgot my own.
   b   Whose coming with me tomorrow?
   c   I could of had it ready yesterday, if only someone had told me it was urgent.
   d   Neither Susan or James have had a pay rise.
   e   Thankyou for your letter.
   f   I think I'll be alright after a short break.
   g   Jim is the tallest of the two brothers.
   h   If you will let me know by Monday, I should be grateful.
   i   Hoping to hear from you.
   j   I am pleased you learned me how to do this.

3   There is a distinct difference between the abbreviations 'e.g.' and 'i.e.'. The first means 'for example'. It is non-specific and indicates a general list. For instance – 'There are many types of footwear in the sale, e.g. sandals, boots and trainers.'

   The second means 'that is'. This is specific and indicates a particular item. For instance – 'His favourite haunt is the pub down the road, i.e. the Duck and Drake.'

   a   Look back over this Appendix and find at least *three* examples of when each abbreviation is used. Check that you understand why each one has been selected in each case.

   b   Test your own understanding by writing two sentences yourself, one with 'e.g.' and one with 'i.e.', and check with your tutor or supervisor that you have used the abbreviations correctly.

Index

Visitors *see* Reception services
Voicemail 154

W

Waste
  minimising 120, 487
Web addresses 478
Web sites 480
Windows Explorer 213, 220–222, 248,
      454, 461
Windows glossary 277
Windows software 205, 211, 213, 216
WinZip 464
Word processing 205
  and document layout 259
  and tables 257
  checking and correcting 236–237
  clarifying instructions 208
  confidential documents 226
  creating professional documents 207
  editing text 240
  file management 219
  finding files 246
  folders and files (creating) 220

formatting text 253
functions 215
house styles 223
importing text 251
printing documents
problems 252
saving text 243
software 214
Working habits 118
Working relationships 72, 77
Working with Others Key Skills 50
Workplace (Health, Safety and Welfare)
      Regulations 8, 10, 28
Workplace policies
  and health and safety 26–27, 34–35,
      38–39, 46
Workstation 11–14, 45, 234
World Wide Web 478
Written communications 64, 167
Written English skills 495

Z

Zip disks 450, 452–454
Zipping files 464